144 YEARS
THE HARD FACTS AND STRANGE REALITIES OF FOOTBALL IN ENGLAND BEFORE THE PREMIER LEAGUE

BRIAN MATTHEWS

Grosvenor House
Publishing Limited

All rights reserved
Copyright © Brian Matthews, 2025

The right of Brian Matthews to be identified as the author of this
work has been asserted in accordance with Section 78
of the Copyright, Designs and Patents Act 1988

The book cover is copyright to Brian Matthews

This book is published by
Grosvenor House Publishing Ltd
Link House
140 The Broadway, Tolworth, Surrey, KT6 7HT.
www.grosvenorhousepublishing.co.uk

This book is sold subject to the conditions that it shall not, by way of
trade or otherwise, be lent, resold, hired out or otherwise circulated
without the author's or publisher's prior consent in any form of
binding or cover other than that in which it is published and
without a similar condition including this condition being
imposed on the subsequent purchaser.

A CIP record for this book
is available from the British Library

ISBN 978-1-83615-188-3

Introduction

England has the longest footballing history of any nation, and yet today it's common to talk as if we have the shortest. The phrases "... in Premier League history" and "... a Premier League record" are trotted out as if nothing of any real significance happened in English football before 1992 when the Premier League was created. It's as if 1992 was 'year zero' as far as English football is concerned. Do a Google search on any English football record, and all you're likely to get is a list of webpages that give the post-1992 record rather than the all-time one.

It is true that today's Premier League is a lot different to how the top-flight of English football was in the 1970s and '80s, but football, like everything else in life, has always evolved. Football in the '70s and '80s was very different to football in the '50s, and football in the '50s was very different to football before the First World War. Tactical revolutions have been happening throughout the game's history, as has the growth in the guile and skills of players, with the most gifted players of every era bringing something new to the game which then influenced the way those who came after them played. The improvements made to boots, balls and pitches, also played a part in changing the game, and even using different materials for the kits did as well, since once they ceased being made of cotton in the 1950s then they no longer got heavier when wet.

The big change that came with the Premier League was merely a change to the game's financial rules, a way of ensuring the richer clubs got richer and it initially made no difference to football as a spectacle. The first Premier League season of 1992-93, featured the same players playing the same tactics inside the same scruffy grounds with terraces as in 1991-92. The number of teams in the top-flight was the same as well, as were the rules on relegation and promotion and the Premier League was top of the same League structure as the First Division had been, and so was, in every sense, the same level of football and a part of the same competition. And yet, right from the very beginning, it was treated as if it were a higher level of football and a different competition, as if England had never before had a division that contained all the best teams and all the best players, when it had had one for over a century. Sky Sports called the Premier League "a whole new ball game" to promote their coverage of it, and the rest of the English media gladly went along with the falsehood and still do.

This book kind of does the reverse of what people do today. Rather than treating 1992 as the year English football history began in earnest, it treats it as the year it ended. It's an attempt to show how rich and fascinating England's football history was before the Premier League and how, unlike the well-ordered and pretty predictable game we have now, just how crazy and chaotic it could be. For the first 144 years of football in England so much happened that would defy belief today, and not just in team performances, but in the way we watched and absorbed the game as well. This book attempts to pick through much of it, in roughly chronological order and at very high speed.

It is basically a book of facts spanning football's birth in Victorian times through to 1992 when the game's first 144 years seemed to get virtually written off. As well as tracing most of the important and muddled changes the game went through during those years, I've also attempted to record many of the obscure or largely forgotten achievements of teams and players and the times when other teams and players failed in ways that few would believe possible. Plenty of the game's quirks and bizarre happenings are recorded as well, and I've also touched on some of the sad and tragic stories too.

Obviously, one person cannot know the entire universe of interesting football facts that are out there, let alone include them in one book. Because of this there are probably plenty of people who could come up with some corkers that I've missed out and/or top some of the ones that I've included. All I can say is that I read extensively and went through countless lists of scores, scorers and team line-ups to find out what I did so I'm fairly confident most of the stuff within these pages will be previously unknown to anyone who hasn't done the same.

Notes on the text

Readers may notice that all numbers from one to eleven that appear in the text of this book are spelt out, whereas numbers over eleven are written in digits. This isn't sloppiness. I just felt that the lower numbers work better in a text if they're written in words, whereas the higher numbers work better when written in digits. The only time I have written the lower numbers in digits is if using them in giving scorelines, dates, prices or percentages, and times of day that aren't on the hour.

Before 1979, the Football League was the only national league in England, and it is all of national level football that I'm referring to when I use the term 'the Football League'. Since 1979, there has also been a national league below the Football League and so when using the term 'the Football League' in reference to football during or after the 1979-80 season, I'm referring to the top four tiers of national level football only. The Football League's rebranding as the EFL didn't come until 2016 and so isn't used here, especially as the name is synonymous with football below the Premier League, which the Football League wasn't for most of the years it operated under its original name.

The Euros were not called 'the Euros' until 1996. Before then they were called the 'European Championships' which is how I have referred to them.

In the Beginning

The first unified rules of football were drawn up at Cambridge University in 1848, although this was probably done more out of practical necessity than anything else. During the first half of the 19th century, the rules of football had differed wildly across the various English public schools that played it, which was a problem when organising matches at university as students were only familiar with the version of the game practiced at the school they had come from. These unified rules, therefore, were drawn up to end all disagreements on the form football should take.

After being revised twice, it was these Cambridge rules that were largely adopted by the FA following its formation in 1863, although six years prior to this, Sheffield Football Club had drawn up its own rules of the game and between 1863 and 1877 football was played mainly by the FA's rules in the south of England and by the Sheffield rules in the north. Both sets of rules allowed various forms of handling until the FA outlawed all handling in 1870, before reintroducing it for goalkeepers only the following year. Although the Sheffield rules lost out in the end, corner-kicks, the halfway line kick-off, having a crossbar between the posts and 90-minute matches all come from the Sheffield rules game. It was also players playing the Sheffield game who originated the practice of heading the ball as the FA's game was, essentially, a dribbling contest where the ball rarely left the ground.

The first football club

Sheffield Football Club was founded on 24 October 1857. Some claim it was the world's first football club, while others that it's merely the oldest football club still in existence, although neither is strictly true, as Cambridge University's University Foot Ball Club was founded in 1856 and still exists today as Cambridge University AFC. There was also a football club (called simply the

Foot-Ball Club) that existed in Edinburgh between 1824 and 1841 but, unlike Sheffield and the Cambridge club, it appears to have had no direct influence on the development of the game. It should also be noted that neither Sheffield nor the Cambridge club were initially association football clubs as there was no such thing as association football in the 1850s. The original association football clubs – that's to say, the clubs (rather than the schools) that became founding members of the Football Association – were Barnes, The Civil Service, The Crusaders, The Wanderers, The N.N. Club, Blackheath, Surbiton and the original Crystal Palace (who disbanded 30 years before the current Crystal Palace were formed).

The first match

On Boxing Day 1860, the world's first ever football match between clubs took place when Hallam hosted Sheffield at their Sandygate ground. Not that the game would have looked exactly like football as we know it now, since, as well as being 16-a-side, it was also played under Sheffield rules, one of which stated that if a player caught the ball with his hands then it would be his own side that got the free-kick. Knocking the ball on with the hands was also allowed under Sheffield rules, as was pushing opponents off of the ball. Sheffield won 2-0. Hallam still play on the same ground today.

Blackheath and the end of (legal) hacking

Six weeks after they became founder members of the Football Association, Blackheath resigned from it, partly over the Association's decision to outlaw hacking (kicking opponents in the shins) from the game. Blackheath subsequently became a rugby union club.

The first association football match

The first football match played under FA Rules was Barnes v Richmond at Limes Field, Barnes on 19 December 1863. Just as in the Sheffield game, if a player caught the ball with his hands then his own team would get a free-kick. The match finished 0-0.

Football forever

"Let us hope that by the football season of 1864-65 all disputes [over the rules] will be settled satisfactorily and football be enthroned for ever as the winter pastime of England". This was written in *The Sporting Gazette* in January 1864. The anonymous writer certainly got his wish.

The crossbar

It was not until around 1865 that the first football matches were played with crossbars between the goalposts, although even then they were only used in the Sheffield-rules game where the goals were over twice as high as they were wide. In the FA's game, an effort on goal could not 'go over' and a goal was given no matter how high above the posts it went. The FA didn't set a height to the goal until 1875 and didn't make crossbars compulsory until seven years after that.

A game with no forward passing

Until the offside law was introduced into the FA's version of football in 1866, the only passes that were allowed were backwards or sideways ones. As already mentioned, football was seen as a dribbling contest in the south, so a player had to take the ball forward himself and could not run onto a ball kicked forward by a teammate. Instead, the dribbler's teammates were expected to run behind him and pick up the ball in order to begin a dribble of their own if the dribbler couldn't go any further.

Scoring a rouge

In the 1860s it was possible to score a 'rouge' in a football match as well as a goal. If a player from the attacking team put his hand on the ball after it had crossed the byline then that was a rouge to the attacking team, and it was followed by a free-kick to the attacking team to be taken from the same byline, thus giving the team a chance to turn their rouge into a goal. It's now claimed that the number of rouges scored in a match was used to decide the winner if the two teams drew on goals, but in many match reports of the time the number of rouges scored were given in the scoreline even if one of the teams had scored more goals than the other. For example, in November 1867, *The Sportsman* carried a report of a match between Fir Vale and Broomhall that concluded: "at five o'clock time was called, leaving the Fir Vale team victors by one goal and two rouges to their opponents' nothing". Then, the following month, a report on a match between Mackenzie and Garrick in *Bell's Life in London* read "when time was called the Mackenzieites were declared the winners by one goal and two rouges to their opponents one rouge".

The FA eventually removed the rouge from the game in 1872 which was when goal-kicks and corner-kicks were introduced to restart the match after the ball had gone out over the byline.

The Youdan Cup

The Youdan Cup was a Sheffield rules cup competition contested between 12 teams from the Sheffield area over an 18-day period in early 1867. Although there had been a cup awarded for the winners of a football match played between members of Cheltenham College the previous year, it's the Youdan Cup that stands as the game's first ever knock-out cup competition, as well as the first cup competition contested between clubs. Hallam won it, beating Norfolk by two rouges in the final which took place at Bramall Lane cricket ground (as it was then) on 5 March. In doing so, Hallam became the first ever football club to win a trophy. Price of admission for the final was three pence ('thruppence' as they used to say) for men and free for women.

The first international that wasn't

The first England v Scotland game was staged at Kennington Oval on 5 March 1870 but, although it could be cited as the first ever football international, it's not officially recognised as such since the Scotland team was assembled in England and included only one Scottish-born player. The scorer of the game's opening goal was Scotland's Robert Crawford who in later life would be jailed for having one of his African servants flogged to death.

The FA Cup begins (although it wasn't called that)

11 November 1871 was the day that the first ever matches were contested in the FA Cup, which was the world's first ever national football competition. Except that it wasn't really national at first, nor was it called 'the FA Cup' either. It wasn't national because it was only open to clubs that belonged to the FA and played by the FA's rules which, in 1871, excluded almost all clubs outside of London and the Home Counties, and it wasn't called 'the FA Cup' because it was called 'the English Cup'. In fact, it was officially called 'the English Cup' (or 'the English Challenge Cup') for the first 40-odd years that it was running, and some journalists would still be calling it by that name in the 1930s.

The arrival of the match officials

It was the launch of the FA Cup in 1871 that saw the first use of match officials to ensure all the rules of the game were being obeyed during matches. Initially these officials were peculiar to the FA Cup and wouldn't be incorporated into the laws of the game until 1874, which was the first year that free-kicks could be awarded for fouls and players could be booked or dismissed. At this time, the officials consisted of two umpires appointed by each club and an independent referee who watched from the sidelines and who would only be called upon if an umpire's decision was disputed.

On 4 October 1890, an FA Cup tie between Gainsborough Trinity and Lincoln City became the first ever to have the referee on the pitch making all the decisions and two linesmen running the touchlines to alert him to infringements (mainly offsides). It was only an experiment, but it seemed a big improvement on the old method of officiating matches and from the start of the following season all matches would be officiated in this way.

Getting to the semi-finals without playing

Queen's Park were semi-finalists in the first FA Cup of 1871-72, despite only playing one match in the competition and not scoring any goals. They were drawn against Donnington School in the first round, but as neither club could decide on a venue, both were allowed to progress to the second round without playing. This, however, only meant that their first-round tie became a second-round tie instead, and again it wasn't played as Donnington School scratched so giving Queen's Park a walk-over to the third round, which was the quarter-final. They were then given a bye to the semi-finals where they drew 0-0 with the Wanderers before withdrawing from the competition rather than take part in a replay.

Charles Alcock

Charles Alcock was both the man who came up with idea for the FA Cup and the first man to captain a Cup-winning side. He managed this by being the Secretary of the FA whilst still playing and playing for the first FA Cup winners, The Wanderers, who he also help found. Alcock was also the first player known to have had a goal disallowed for offside following the introduction of the offside law in 1866.

The uncertainty surrounding an historic goal

Nobody's really sure who scored the only goal in the first ever FA Cup Final of 1872. It's officially recorded as being by Morton Betts (who played under the assumed name A.H. Chequer) but some contemporary reports gave it to Thomas Hooman and, obviously, there's no film footage that can be used to settle the issue.

W.G. Grace

The most famous Victorian cricketer, W.G. Grace, played in two matches for The Wanderers in the season they became the first ever FA Cup Winners (although neither of them were Cup ties).

The first passing team

The Royal Engineers, who reached three of the first four FA Cup Finals, were the first English club whose players passed the ball to each other. Their style of play subsequently became known as 'the combination game' as it combined passing with dribbling instead of just consisting of dribbling as was originally the case with all the other clubs who played under the FA rules.

Queen's Park v England

Officially, the first ever football international was played between Scotland and England at Hamilton Crescent, Partick on 30 November 1872. This match, however, was really between Queen's Park and England because Scotland didn't have an FA at the time and so was represented by its biggest club. England were expected to win but couldn't do any better than a 0-0 draw, largely because the Scottish players passed the ball to each other, something the England players hadn't thought of. In the second England v Scotland match the following year, Scotland were again represented by Queen's Park, which makes the first match between two nations with their own football associations, the Scotland v England game at Hamilton Cresent on 7 March 1874.

Charles Clegg

Charles Clegg was the only player in the first ever official England team of 1872 who never went to public school. He was consequently ignored by the other players.

The Wanderers and their semi-final bypasses

The Wanderers won the first two FA Cup Finals but didn't win a semi-final in either season. In 1872, they drew their semi-final with Queen's Park who then decided to withdraw from the competition after refusing to play extra-time or take part in a replay. Then in 1873, being the holders, the Wanderers were awarded their place in the final without having to compete in the earlier rounds. They also received a bye in the semi-final when they won the FA Cup for the fifth time in 1878.

Gotta see the Boat Race

The 1873 FA Cup Final between The Wanderers and Oxford University kicked-off at 11.30 in the morning so that the players could attend the Boat Race in the afternoon. For the remainder of the 19th century, both the Boat Race and the Derby would remain bigger sporting events than the Cup Final.

Alfred Goodwyn

When Alfred Goodwyn died the day after his 24th birthday in March 1874, he became both the first England international to die and the first player to die who had played in an FA Cup Final. Goodwyn was a lieutenant in the Royal Engineers and his death resulted from injuries he sustained after falling from a horse whilst on military service in India. A year earlier he had played in only the second ever England international (against Scotland) and a year before that had represented the Royal Engineers in the first ever FA Cup Final.

The half-time break

The half-time break was first introduced to football matches in 1875, although initially it was taken on the field rather than in the dressing rooms, which would remain the case for many years. The rules stated that the length of the break "shall not exceed five minutes except by consent of the referee", although eventually referees began regularly extending it to ten minutes and the ten-minute half-time break soon became the standard. Proposals to extend it to 15 minutes were rejected by the majority of clubs in both 1972 and 1980 before the 15-minute half-time break finally arrived for the start of the 1992-93 season. This extension was probably made so as more TV commercials could be shown at half-time when games were televised live and it wasn't widely welcomed by fans who now had to wait around for longer, often in bad weather, for the second half to start (this being a time before going for a beer at the interval was common practice amongst football supporters).

The only photograph from 21 years of England internationals

Although the first England international was in 1872, there's only one photograph of an England team from before 1893 – and it wasn't discovered until 2008. The photo shows the team that took on Scotland (who were the only team they ever played in those days) at Hamilton Crescent on 4 March 1876.

The match with three final scores to choose from

In December 1876, The Wanderers beat Southall in the second round of the FA Cup, although by what score has always remained something of a mystery. Some contemporary reports gave it as 5-0, others as 6-0 and others as 6-1.

The scoreline that got changed (and then changed back again)

After The Wanderers beat Oxford University 2-1 in the 1877 FA Cup Final, the Wanderers goalkeeper Arthur Kinnaird, unhappy that he was down as the own-goalscorer of Oxford's goal, protested that the ball hadn't crossed the line and successfully got the goal struck from the records. For the next 104 years, the score of the game was officially given as 2-0, until, in 1981, the original score was discovered and reinstated. By giving the score as 2-0 for over a century, the FA was making two separate errors, since if Oxford University's goal was annulled then The Wanderers' second goal should also have been annulled as it was scored during an extra-time period that shouldn't have been played.

The outright winners of the FA Cup

When the FA Cup was launched, the FA declared a rule that if ever a club won it three times in a row, then that club would get to keep the trophy for life. The Wanderers, therefore, won the trophy outright following their third consecutive FA Cup Final victory of 1878, but decided to return it on the condition that it could never be won outright.

Fergie Suter

Between 1876 and 1878, the Scotsmen James Lang, Peter Andrews, Jimmy Love, Fergie Suter and Archie Hunter all came south to join English clubs, with Lang and Andrews joining Sheffield Wednesday, Love and Suter joining Darwen and Hunter joining Aston Villa. It's believed that some, if not all, of these players were getting paid to play and were the first players ever to do so. Of the five, Lang and Andrews came south first, but it's Suter who most would come to see as the first ever professional footballer.

At a time when football was supposed to be an amateur sport, Suter's professionalism was never official, but since he was a stonemason who gave up his trade after joining Darwen and had no other source of income, it was widely assumed that Darwen must have been paying him for playing. It was also believed that when Suter left Darwen for Blackburn Rovers in 1880 it was for more money, which would also make him the first ever player to move clubs for financial gain.

It was probably the perception of Suter as a professional that triggered the spread of professionalism in the north of England, which in turn led to the formation of the Football League in 1888. The League, therefore, may not have come about when it did had it not been for Suter, and yet Suter's record in it would be ridiculously insignificant. In his 1916 obituary in the *Sheffield Independent*,

Suter was said to have been "one of the most capable full-backs in the country" and it was as a full-back that he won three FA Cup-winners medals, but his one and only appearance in the Football League (for Blackburn at West Bromwich Albion in December 1888) was as a stand-in goalkeeper.

The first football publications

The first weekly football publication was *The Goal: The Chronicle of Football* which was launched in 1878 – a decade before there was any league football to write about. Other sporting publications covered football to some degree in the 1870s and '80s, but after the Football League was founded in 1888, it was in *The Athletic News* where the most extensive football coverage of each weekend's matches could be found, and this would remain the case for the next 40 years, as in those days the national Sunday papers only carried small sports sections. It should be noted, however, that the 'extensive coverage' *The Athletic News* gave was only extensive by the standards of the time and would seem pretty inadequate today. In its early years it didn't always name the goalscorers in its match reports and it wasn't until the 1920s that it began publishing a results section that provided the names of all the goalscorers in each match.

The first FA Cup shock

Arguably the first major FA Cup shock occurred in 1879, when Darwen came from 5-1 down to draw 5-5 with Old Etonians at Kennington Oval. At the time, the FA Cup was dominated by southern teams of former public schoolboys or serving military officers, and Old Etonians were one of the elite clubs. By contrast, Darwen were a team of cotton mill workers from a poor northern community. At the end of the match, Old Etonians, knowing the momentum was with their opponents, refused to play extra-time and insisted on a replay which would again be played at the Oval as, in those days, all FA Cup ties from the fourth round onwards were. This meant Darwen having to make a second 240-mile journey south, and they then had to make a third after the replay finished 2-2 and Old Etonians refused Darwen's request to play the second replay at home. At the time of the first two matches, Darwen's cotton mills weren't running at full capacity, but they were by the time of the third which meant the Darwen players having to travel overnight following a full day's work. Old Etonians won 6-2 and went on to win the FA Cup that year, but their attacking play, whereby all the forwards followed the ball and stayed close together, looked antiquated against Darwen. Darwen's forwards, by contrast, kept their positions across the width of the pitch, a tactic which all teams would adopt eventually.

The rapid demise of football's first dominant club

The Wanderers won the FA Cup five times in the competition's first seven years, but just three seasons after their fifth triumph of 1878, they withdrew from the competition as they were unable to get a team together for their first round tie against Rangers F.C., London. By this time, it was expected that all good footballers should play for the club of their old public school, which made it difficult for The Wanderers to find players. As a result, they went from playing 32 matches in the 1877-78 season to just nine in '80-81, and then only one in '81-82. They eventually folded at the end of 1883, just five years and nine months after winning the FA Cup for the fifth time. Their final match was at the Oval on 18 December of that year and saw them go out in style with a 6-1 win over Harrow School. 99 years later they had still won the FA Cup more times than Manchester United and Liverpool.

The greatest team we've never seen (in a photograph)

There's a photograph that exists of The Royal Engineers line-up that were runners-up in the first FA Cup Final of 1872, but there's no photo of The Wanderers team that beat them. In fact, even though The Wanderers won the FA Cup five times between 1872 and 1878, the only photograph that exists of them is from 1863 when they were called Forest FC and only Charles Alcock from any of the Cup-winning sides played for them. This is especially strange considering there are quite a few 1870s photos of lesser teams, including an 1878 one of Grimsby who wouldn't even compete in the FA Cup until 1882.

Of course, this doesn't necessarily mean that a photograph of The Wanderers was never taken. Newspapers didn't carry photographs until the 1890s, so any photographs that were taken of football teams before then would have been taken merely for framing and hanging on a wall. It's therefore possible that such a photograph of The Wanderers did once exist but was then either lost or thrown away long before anyone cared about football history.

Taking the game to the world

As well as inventing the game, the English, along with the Scots, also played a big part in kick-starting football in many other countries. It was an Englishman, James Richardson Spensley, who both organised the first official football match in Italy and founded the first Italian football club (Genoa), while another Englishman, Herbert Kiplin, founded AC Milan. The first football clubs in France, Spain, Belgium, Switzerland, Uruguay and Mexico were also founded by Britons and it was Britons who organised the first ever football matches in both Brazil and Argentina. The first Argentinian League championship was then created by the Scotsman Alec Lamont before another Scotsman, Alexander Walter Hutton, founded the Argentinian FA. The Englishman William Poole, meanwhile, was instrumental in the founding of the Uruguayan FA.

Although Britain had a large empire at this time, the British showed no interest in spreading the game to the native populations of its colonies as it had done to the peoples of Europe and South America, and because of this the growth of football would be slow in Africa (no African country would progress beyond the first round of the World Cup until 1990) and would barely happen at all in south Asia.

Howard Vaughton and Arthur Brown

In February 1882, Aston Villa's Howard Vaughton and Arthur Brown scored nine goals between them on their England debuts against Ireland in Belfast. Vaughton became the first ever player to score five in a match for England but would only go on to score one more goal for his country after that, while Brown's four would prove to be the only goals of his international career.

Money for grassing on your local team

After Nottingham Forest lost a third round FA Cup replay to Sheffield Wednesday in 1883, they became suspicious that their opponents had fielded two ineligible players and offered a cash reward to anyone in Sheffield who came forward with information that could help them prove it. This they did through notices placed in local newspapers and placards they put up in the city. The good people of Sheffield, however, either didn't know anything or weren't prepared to be bought and so Wednesday's 3-2 victory stood.

Arthur Kinnaird

Arthur Kinnaird played in nine FA Cup Finals out of eleven between 1873 and 1883, appearing as an outfield player in eight of them and as a goalkeeper in the other. Kinnaird was the most famous footballer of his day and also, reputedly, one of the dirtiest. In 1890, he became President of the FA and remained in the post until his death 33 years later. In honour of his services to football, he was given the FA Cup to keep in 1911 (after which a new cup was made for the competition).

Harry Cursham

Notts County's Harry Cursham scored 32 recorded goals in 19 games in the 1881-82 season, and there may have been some unrecorded ones as well since no record was made of County's scorers in the 13-0 win against Grantham. The following season Cursham scored 37 in 21 games, thus giving him a record of 69 goals (at least) in 30 appearances over two seasons. Unfortunately, this was before any league existed, so aside from the 18 he scored in the FA Cup over these two seasons, all of these goals were in, what we would now call, 'friendlies' and so don't officially count. Cursham did play in the Football League when it was launched in 1888, but only nine times and mainly as a defender. The only two League goals of his career came against West Bromwich Albion and Wolves in consecutive matches in January 1889 (when he was playing up-front).

The workers seize power

Blackburn Olympic's 2-1 victory over Old Etonians in the 1883 FA Cup Final was a watershed moment in the English game as it ended the dominance of the sport by the former public schoolboys who had invented it. Blackburn Olympic were a team of working-class players from a working-class community and they were the first club of this kind to win the Cup. Only around 300 of their fans made the trip south for the game and their cloth caps amongst the thousands of top hat-wearing Old Etonian supporters said everything about the difference between the two clubs. With Blackburn's victory, football had completed its transition from being a 'gentlemen's' game' to primarily the game of the workers and no public school-connected club would ever reach an FA Cup Final again. Somewhat fittingly, this was also the first FA

Cup Final where the Cup was presented straight after the match in front of the spectators, rather than at a presentation dinner as had previously been the case.

When the FA Cup Final was the biggest match but not always the biggest crowd-puller

Despite the great prestige the FA Cup Final enjoyed during its early, pre-Football League years, it was a match played in the south at a time when football was more popular in the north and so was not always the best attended fixture of each season. The 1880 Lancashire Cup Final between Blackburn Rovers and Darwen drew a bigger crowd than that year's FA Cup Final and only 4,000 watched the 1884 FA Cup Final which took place the same month that 12,000 attended a friendly between Burnley and Padiham.

Soccer

It was after the Football Association was formed in 1863 that the game played under its rules became known as 'association football', with the 'soc' in 'association' subsequently expanded into the word 'soccer'. In recent times 'soccer' has come to be thought of as the American (or Australian) word for football, but its first appearance in print came in a journal for former pupils of a Shropshire prep school in 1885. It's usually claimed that the 19th century England player Charles Wreford-Brown first coined the term, although to have done so before 1885 would have meant he was a teenager when he did.

Before the 1990s, the word 'soccer' was commonly used by British journalists (if not by fans) and tended to be seen as the educated person's word for football. Britain's first football magazine, *Charles Buchan's Football Monthly*, carried the words "the world's greatest soccer magazine" on its front cover, while the country's only football weekly for most of the 1950s and '60s was called *Soccer Star*. These magazines usually referred to football as 'soccer', as did the popular 1970s football mag *Shoot!* Looking through a random issue of *Shoot!* from November 1974, we find the word 'soccer' cropping-up 16 times over its 47 pages. *The Sun* newspaper also published *The Sun Soccer Annual* every year from 1972 to 1984 and Matt Busby called his 1974 autobiography *Soccer at the Top*. As For the BBC, during the 1970s and '80s, it regularly broadcast live coverage of midweek football matches on Radio 2 and did so as part of programmes called *Soccer Special*, *European Soccer Special* and *International Soccer Special*.

Football seasons before there were football seasons

Today we tend to think that there were no such things as football seasons before the Football League was launched in 1888, when, in fact, references to 'the football season' in the English press go back to the 1860s.

To give one example: "To secretaries of the football clubs, colleges, schools. As the football season is now commencing, we shall be glad to receive from the various secretaries lists of their fixtures for the season as well as accounts of the matches when played". This appeared in an edition of *The Sporting Life* in October 1868 — 20 years before there was any league football in England.

Football was, of course, an amateur game back then, but by the early-1880s many clubs were paying their players and by the time professionalism was eventually legalised in 1885, the football season had grown immeasurably from its amateur-only days. A Derby County fixture card from the 1884-85 season shows that they had 23 matches scheduled between September and March excluding the ones in the FA Cup and the Derbyshire Cup, and the same season Notts County played 27 excluding the ones in the FA Cup and Nottinghamshire Cup. In the first Football League season teams only played 22 matches.

Most would, of course, now dismiss these pre-League matches as 'friendlies' but they were no doubt seen as competitive at the time, a time when there had never been any League games and so there was nothing to compare them unfavourably to. In fact, it was one of these pre-League 'friendlies' between Burnley and Bolton at Turf Moor in 1886 that was the first ever football match to be attended by Royalty, as Queen Victoria's son, Prince Albert, was amongst the spectators.

The biggest win

In October 1887, Preston beat Hyde United 26-0 in the first round of the FA Cup with Jimmy Ross grabbing eight goals, Jack Gordon and Sam Thomson scoring five each and Geordie Drummond also getting a hat-trick. The hapless Hyde goalkeeper that day, Charles Bunyan, eventually went on to become something of a hero outside of football as, 28 years later, he would lie about his age (claiming he was 38 when he was really 46) so as he could go and fight on the Western Front in the First World War.

Preston's 26-0 victory remains the biggest ever by a professional English football club. The second biggest is also by Preston – 18-0 against Reading in 1893.

The match that was literally one-sided

Before Accrington and Preston were due to play each other in the 1888 Lancashire Cup Final, Preston requested the venue be moved from the scheduled venue of Blackburn due to the hostility that city's football fans had towards them. When the Lancashire FA refused, Preston boycotted the match, and so the Lancashire FA simply allowed it to go ahead without them. Accrington kicked-off with no opposition on the field, scored straight away into the undefended goal and were immediately declared 1-0 winners and presented with the trophy. This non-match must have only lasted seconds but was watched by 2,000 people. Preston won the League and FA Cup double less than a year later.

Local heroes

West Bromwich Albion's victory in the 1888 FA Cup Final was achieved with a team comprised entirely of players born in the West Midlands, eight of whom were born in West Bromwich itself.

League football arrives

The Football League was created in 1888 as a way of providing regular fixtures between England's top professional clubs which needed to draw the crowds in order to pay their players. Ostensibly, it was a national league but, as professionalism was still yet to be adopted in the south of the country, it was far from national in reality, with all of its members coming from the professional hotbeds of the Midlands and Lancashire (Liverpool was within Lancashire at the time).

The first season's opening day was 8 September 1888, with all the matches kicking-off at 3.30, except Bolton v Derby and Preston v Burnley which were delayed by 15 and 20 minutes respectively owing to the late arrivals of the away teams. The first ever League goal was scored by Bolton's Kenny Davenport at 3.47 that afternoon. The second also came from Davenport a minute later, thus making Davenport the scorer of both the first ever goal and the first ever brace in the Football League. On the same day, Aston Villa's Gersham Cox scored the League's first ever own goal at Wolves, which would prove to be the only League goal of his career.

Initially, there were no points awarded for results in the League, with positions in the table being determined by the number of wins only. It wouldn't be until 21 November that it was decided to award two points for a win and one for a draw and to have goal average used to separate teams that were level on points, a system that would eventually be adopted throughout the world.

The Football Combination

The Football League was not, as is always claimed, the first league of its kind in world football, as there was a rival English league called the Football Combination, and some of its fixtures were played on the same day that the Football League kicked-off. In fact, at least one of its matches – Grimsby v Long Eaton Rangers – took place a week before the Football League's opening day, so it could be argued that the Combination actually predates the Football League (although it would be a pretty slim argument).

With 20 clubs, the Combination was bigger than the Football League, but it was very poorly organised. Some of its clubs were made members without being consulted, clubs were expected to arrange their own fixtures and there weren't enough weekends in the season for all of the clubs to play each other home and away. Consequently, the Combination ended up being dissolved before the completion of its first season. After playing Long Eaton Rangers on 1 September, Grimsby then went another three months before playing their next combination match, while Blackburn Olympic only played five Combination matches in the seven months that they were members of it.

3-0 is never enough (apparently)

Bolton lost each of their first two matches in the Football League (against Derby and Burnley in September 1888), despite leading 3-0 in both of them. In the first, against Derby, they went 3-0 up in the first five minutes before conceding four in the next 25. They eventually lost 6-3, making this a rare instance of a team losing by a three-goal margin having earlier led by three goals. Against Burnley a week later, they led 3-0 after 25 minutes before going on to lose 4-3.

Bill Tait

Bill Tait only ever made five appearances in the Football League, but he may have been the scorer of the first ever League hat-trick. The debatable hat-trick came for Burnley at Bolton on 15 September 1888, and the reason it's 'debatable' is that not all sources identified him as the scorer of the second of the three. In fact, even the 1991 book *Burnley: A Complete Record* only credits him with two.

Archie Goodall

Archie Goodall was the first player ever to be transferred between League clubs when he moved from Preston to Aston Villa in October 1888.

Jimmy Ross

According to current sources, Preston's Jimmy Ross scored four times in Preston's 7-0 League victory over Stoke in October 1888, but for around a hundred years he was widely believed to have scored all seven of his side's goals that day. In the 1970s, the *News of the World Football Annual* was Britain's biggest-selling football reference book and in its section entitled 'Chief Records', it listed Ross scoring seven against Stoke in 1888 as one of only two occasions when a player had scored seven in a match at the highest level of English football. Britain's biggest-selling football magazine, meanwhile, was *Shoot!*, and that too informed its readers that Ross had scored seven against Stoke in an article it published in 1974.

In the 1880s, the recording of goalscorers didn't have the importance that it does today, and it wasn't unusual for goalscorers to be misidentified by inexperienced reporters or not even given at all. Also, the scorers in most games were named only in local, rather than national, newspapers, which made discovering the facts of who got the goals even more difficult. Still, Ross's distinction of being believed to have scored three more in a match than he really did does seem to be unique. It's unknown whether the claim that Ross had scored seven against Stoke came from an unreliable match report of the time or whether it was made years later and then widely accepted because it was so difficult to prove that it hadn't happened.

Ross himself died in 1902 at the age of 36 and so had been dead for around 80 years when he got three goals that had been credited to him chalked off.

? Harboard

When Derby visited Everton for a League match in October 1888 with only ten players, the home side obligingly lent them one of their reserves to play at right-half. The player's surname was Harboard but there's no record of his first name and this game in which he played against the club to which he belonged would prove to be his only ever appearance in the Football League.

E. Siddons

E. Siddons (first name unknown) only ever made one appearance in the Football League, for Bolton at West Bromwich Albion in November 1888, and it's notable for two reasons. Firstly, because Siddons was a ringer who was playing under the name of Bolton's regular left-back, Peter Bullough. And secondly, because he caused the match to be ended early by starting a fight with a West Brom player which sparked a pitch invasion by angry home fans.

OK Jimmy, we believe you

In a League match in December 1888, Notts County's Jimmy Brown hit a shot against Blackburn which, according to reports, went two foot over the bar but a goal was given as Brown claimed it went under the bar and the officials couldn't see in the fog and so took his word for it (this being the days before there were goal nets to catch the ball if it went in).

Screamer

The word 'screamer' to describe a powerful long-range shot was used in match reports in the very first Football League season of 1888-89.

The Invincibles

The Preston side which won the first League title of 1888-89 were the original 'Invincibles'. They won 18 of their 22 League games and drew the other four and also won the FA Cup without conceding a goal in the entire competition. Over half of their League victories were by a three-goal margin or more, and the leading football journalist of the time, J.A.H. Catton, was still describing them as "the finest football team I ever saw" in a book he had published in 1926. Catton went on to say, "It has been my privilege to enjoy the best matches for more than forty years, and so far as I am capable of judging, as one who lives in the present, I hold that Preston, given the same players in the same condition, would be as powerful as ever [today]". Unlike Arsenal's 'Invincibles' of 2003-04, who weren't given the moniker until they completed their unbeaten season, Preston appear to have been known as 'The Invincibles' before their unbeaten season had even started.

The closest they ever came to losing was at Blackburn when, what would have been the home side's winning goal, was controversially disallowed after Preston's appeal that the ball had gone out of play was upheld by the referee (these being the days when goals could only be disallowed if the conceding team appealed against them). They were also 2-0 down at Derby before coming back to win 3-2.

Of the players who played for Preston in the invincible season, Fred Dewhurst died just six years later, while Jack Edwards lived until 1960.

The staggered finish

The first ever Football League season of 1888-89 had an incredibly staggered finish. The last game was played on 20 April, which was over two months after the champions, Preston, had completed their fixtures, and over three months after they had clinched the title.

No outsiders

Between 1885 and 1889, there was an FA rule that required all professional players to have been born within a six-mile radius of their club's ground or to have lived within that six-mile radius for at least two years.

Francis Marindin

Francis Marindin played in two of the first three FA Cup finals before going on to referee eight of the finals played between 1880 and 1890, which included seven in a row.

The popularity grew

The average attendance for the first Football League season of 1888-89 was 4,639. Ten years later, the First Division average (the League was too small to have divisions in the first season) was 10,058. It then rose to 16,444 over the following ten years.

Goals, goals, goals

Over the first two Football League seasons there were 264 matches played and only three finished goalless.

Bouncing back

In the 1890-91 season, Derby lost 8-0 away and won 9-0 at home in consecutive games.

The first southern professionals

When the FA was founded in 1863, it was an unspoken agreement that football was a game for gentlemen amateurs, played out of dedication and never for money. It was only, however, after it was discovered that some northern clubs had been harming the 'respectability' of the game by paying their players that professionalism was officially banned in 1882. The ban was subsequently lifted three years later, but professionalism continued to be frowned upon in the south and when, in 1891, Royal Arsenal became the first southern club to turn professional, they were effectively blacklisted and struggled to get games. This forced Arsenal into joining the northern professionals in the Football League, becoming the League's first southern club in 1893.

Goal nets

Goal nets were the invention of the civil engineer John Alexander Brodie and were first introduced into football in 1891. The idea behind them being to provide proof that a goal had been scored, since before there were nets, a ball that passed just inside the post would end up in roughly the same place as one that passed just outside, which could sometimes cause confusion as to whether a goal attempt had gone in or gone wide. By having nets, there would be no such confusion as the ball would only end up in the net if it went inside the post. The fact that the ball hitting the back of the net would also enhance the dramatic effect of a goal happened purely by accident and presumably had not been envisaged by Brodie.

Goal nets were first used in a North v South trial match in Nottingham on 12 January 1891 when Everton's Fred Geary became the first ever player to hit one when scoring. A month later, however, the FA Cup semi-finals were played without them and saw what everyone thought was a late winner by Sunderland's Johnny Campbell against Notts County ruled out because the officials adjudged his effort to have gone wide. The game subsequently went to a replay and Sunderland lost. It was largely this incident that prompted the FA to use nets in the final for the first time that year and then recommend that clubs should use them wherever possible from the start of the following season.

For the first hundred years or so of their existence, the top corners of nets were held in place by back stanchions, with the ones in England causing the back of the net to come down at an obtuse angle to the top of the net, which often led to the ball nestling in the back of the net after a goal was scored. Since the late-90s, however, the top corners of the nets have been held in place with cords attached to poles, causing the net to come down at a right-angle to the top of the net and the ball to usually bounce out after a goal is scored.

Trouncings galore in the FA Cup

The biggest away win in senior football in England is Nottingham Forest's 14-0 FA Cup first round victory at Clapton in January 1891. Sandy Higgins scored five of Forest's goals despite being unwell and Tinsley Lindley scored four while wearing walking shoes (which he always preferred over football boots). On the same day, Aston Villa beat Casuals 13-1, Sheffield Wednesday beat Halliwell 12-0 and Notts County won 9-1 at Sheffield United.

England at the double

On 7 March 1891, England were beating Wales 4-1 in Sunderland at the same time that they were beating Ireland 6-1 in Wolverhampton.

This was the second of three consecutive seasons that England played Wales and Ireland simultaneously with different line-ups, although it was the only time that the two matches were both home ones.

The arrival of penalties

The penalty area was first introduced into football in 1891, with penalty kicks being awarded for fouls inside them from the start of the 1891-92 season. Back then, however, the penalty area was not a box, but an area that spanned the full width of the pitch. The first player to score from one was Rotherham Town's Albert Rodgers, away to Darlington St Augustine's on 5 September 1891, with John Heath of Wolves being the first to do so in the Football League when he converted at home to Accrington on the 14th of the same month. Not that these penalties would have looked much like the penalties we see today, as during that first season there was no requirement for a penalty to be a single kick and, as there was no penalty spot, the first kick could be from anywhere along the 12-yard line. It wasn't until the following season that the requirement for a penalty to be a single kick was introduced and not until 1902 that the 18 and 12-yard lines were replaced with a penalty box with a penalty spot inside.

The Football Alliance

The Football Alliance was founded in 1889 as an alternative to the Football League and existed for three seasons before all of its clubs, with the exception of Birmingham St. George, were absorbed into the Football League when the latter was expanded into two divisions. Sheffield Wednesday won the title in the first Football Alliance season, and then finished bottom in the second. Stoke won the title in the second season which was the only season that they were members of the Alliance and, in the final season, Nottingham Forest won it, also in the only season they competed in it.

Geordie Drummond

When Notts County entertained Preston in 1891, Preston's Geordie Drummond was sent-off for fighting but was later allowed back on again and went on to score four times in a 6-0 Preston win. By the end, Notts County were down to five men as six of their players had left the field in protest.

Liverpool – the club made for Anfield

Liverpool FC were formed in 1892 to make use of the Anfield ground after Everton – its previous occupants – left it. Just a year later, Liverpool were elected into the Football League and won the Second Division title in their first season.

The birth of the English football ground

Everton's Goodison Park was the first fully developed football ground in England when it was opened in 1892, since all the others were still in a fairly primitive state at that time. Goodison had a stand on three sides at a time when all other grounds only had them on one, and it was also the first ground in the country to have a high man-made bank behind one of the goals.

The ultimate early kick-off

The FA Cup preliminary round match between Burton Swifts (who were then a Football League club) and Singers in September 1892 kicked-off at eight o'clock in the morning. Although the minutes of the goals aren't recorded, it was reported that Arthur

Worrall put Burton 1-0 up early on, and so is probably the scorer of the earliest ever FA Cup goal in terms of the time of day when it arrived.

Geordie Drummond (Again)

The 2-3-5 formation of two full-backs, three half-backs, two wingers, two inside-forwards and a centre-forward only came into being in the 1880s, which meant that, before the 20th century, footballers were not really moulded into playing in only one position within it as they would be in later years. Those who played in Victorian times usually had their favoured positions, but most could easily change position if so required and many did. None, however, took versality to such an extreme as Preston's Geordie Drummond did in the 1892-93 season. That season saw Drummond play as a goalkeeper, a left-back, a right-half, a left-half, an outside-right, an inside-right, an outside-left, an inside-left and a centre-forward. The only position he didn't play was right-back.

The League's best ever goalscorers

The Football League was given a Second Division for the 1892–93 season and, although the teams only played 22 matches each, the winners of the title, Small Heath, managed to score a total of 90 goals. This remains the only time a team has averaged over four goals per game in a Football League season. 51 of their goals came in the last nine games. Small Heath changed their name to Birmingham City in 1905.

The club with the shortest League history

The 22 Second Division matches Bootle played in the 1892-93 season were the only matches they ever played in the Football

League. The club were one of 12 that were made inaugural members of Division Two for the start of that season, and went on to finish above Lincoln, Crewe, Walsall and Port Vale, but they chose to resign from the League at the end of the season and then folded in the summer that followed.

C. McLafferty (first name unknown) was an ever-present for Bootle that season and finished as their joint-top scorer in the League (along with three other players) but would never make any other League appearances for any other club during his career. This was also true of A. Montgomery (first name also unknown) who was one of their other joint-top scorers. Montgomery scored a hat-trick in the 5-3 win over Ardwick, while McLafferty hit three in the 7-1 demolition of Walsall.

Test matches

The creating of the Second Division of the Football League in 1892-93, meant that this was the first season to have promotions and relegations, with these being decided through three test matches that pitted the Second Division champions against the team that finished bottom of Division One, the Second Division runners-up against the team that finished second from bottom in Division One and the third-placed team in the Second Division against the team that finished third from bottom in Division One. These matches were all played on neutral grounds with the First Division club in each game needing to win to avoid relegation and their Second Division opponents needing to win to be promoted. Technically, the promotion wasn't automatic as the victors then needed to be elected to the First Division, but this was really only a formality as their application for election would never be refused. In the first season, these test matches produced a never-to-be-repeated outcome when the second and third-placed teams in Division two (Sheffield United and Darwen) both won promotion, while the Second Division champions (Small Heath) didn't. This also meant that the team that finished bottom of Division One (Newton Heath) stayed up, while the two teams that finished above them (Notts County and Accrington) went down.

After three seasons, the test match format was changed to one that involved each of the top two Second Division sides playing each of the bottom two teams in Division One home and away in a mini-league, although it was a pretty odd mini-league as not everyone played everyone else. The two teams that gained the most points would be the two that played in the First Division the following season, with goal average being used to separate teams that were level on points as in the main League season.

Test matches were eventually done away with in 1898 and their abolition appeared to be almost entirely due to the controversy surrounding the final test match of that year between Burnley and Stoke. A draw in this game would see Stoke avoid relegation and Burnley win promotion at the expense of Newcastle who would be promoted on goal average if either team won. The game finished 0-0 and, according to reports, was played largely around the centre-circle and produced only one goal attempt on target which was easily saved. It seemed obvious to those who watched it that the teams had decided on playing out a 0-0 beforehand, thus making this probably the first stitch-up match in football history. The Football League's drastic response was to effectively make all of that season's test matches null and void by expanding the First Division from 16 to 18 clubs from the following season and giving a place in it to all four teams that took part in the 1897-98 test matches. Ironically, this meant that Stoke and Burnley's nefarious attempts to deny Newcastle promotion ultimately resulted in Newcastle getting their promotion.

From the 1898-99 season, therefore, there would be no more test matches as it was decided that, from here on, the top two teams in Division Two would replace the bottom two in Division One automatically. It now seems incredible that it took the Football League five years to come up with this simple and obvious method for deciding promotion and relegation. It perhaps seems equally incredible that almost 90 years later they would complicate it again by introducing the play-offs.

Sorry, that victory doesn't count (and nor does that one)

Prior to the 1893-94 season, it wasn't unusual for FA Cup ties to be replayed because the losing side lodged a protest, which could sometimes be over the condition of the pitch or the behaviour of the crowd but was more usually over the eligibility of opposition players. The last case of this happening during this era was when Sheffield Wednesday played Derby in the first round in 1893 and the farce it descended into was what ultimately forced the FA to change the rules on protests. Wednesday originally won at home with a goal in the last minute of extra-time, but the two teams had to go again after Derby complained that their opponents had used an ineligible player. The replayed game was at Derby who won 1-0 only for this result to also be annulled after Wednesday complained that a Derby player had been ineligible. It was, therefore, back to Wednesday's Olive Grove ground for another match which, this time, Wednesday won 4-2. Even after this, Derby lodged another protest, which wasn't upheld, although if it were, Wednesday had a counter protest of their own ready. After this, the FA decided enough was enough and from the following season all clubs had to submit their squad details two weeks before the tie and protests over the ineligibility of players could only be made before the game, and not after a defeat.

Jack Southworth

Jack Southworth was the subject of the first ever big-money transfer between top-flight clubs when he moved from Blackburn to Everton for £400 in August 1893, which was just 14 months before his career was ended through injury. Southworth was the League's top scorer in his only full season at Everton. He subsequently became a professional violinist.

Possibly the worst end to a great start

Port Vale won all of their first seven Second Division matches of the 1893-94 season, scoring 30 goals in the process. They then lost their eighth game 8-1 to Ardwick who had only scored once in their previous five matches, all of which had been defeats.

Joe Lofthouse

After playing his last game for Darwen in October 1892, former England international Joe Lofthouse never made another appearance in senior football until he made his debut (and scored on it) for Walsall in December 1893. During the 14 months that he was out of the game several newspapers wrongly reported that he had died.

The crazy battle of the Swifts

The 1890s was the only decade in which there were two teams in the Football League with the word 'swifts' in their name, and in February 1894 they played each other in one of the League's craziest ever matches. Burton Swifts were the home team and Walsall Town Swifts the visitors and Burton came from 4-1 down to level the scores at 4-4 before even half-time had arrived. Five more goals then followed in the second half, with Burton ending up winning by the ludicrous score of 8-5. This is the only time in Football League history that a team's scored five goals in a match and still lost by a three-goal margin. Sandy Rowan and Joe Dewey both scored hat-tricks for Burton.

The Southern League

In 1894, the Southern League was formed as a southern equivalent of the Football League which, at that time, had no southern clubs aside from Woolwich Arsenal. Although technically non-League, such became the stature of many of its clubs, that the early Southern League wasn't really 'non-League' at all by the modern definition of the term. Some Southern League matches attracted crowds of more than 20,000, there were Southern League players who represented England, and between 1899 and the beginning of the First World War, top-flight League clubs were beaten by Southern League sides in the FA Cup on no fewer than 43 occasions.

Eventually, in 1920, the entire First Division of the Southern League became members of the new Third Division of the Football League, apart from Cardiff who were given a place in the Second Division even though they had only finished fourth in the Southern League the previous season. Most of these clubs initially remained members of the Southern League as well, playing their reserves in the Southern League, while their first-teams competed in the Football League. Exeter City reserves would still be playing in the Southern League in the late-1950s but, by then, all the giants of the early Southern League were long gone, replaced by small semi-professional outfits like Bedford Town, Chelmsford City and Dartford. By this time the Southern League was very much 'non-League' and has been ever since.

The doomed club that thrashed the giants

The 1894-95 season was Burton Wanderers first in the Football League and during the course of it they beat Newcastle 9-0 which, to this day, remains Newcastle's all-time record defeat, and Manchester City 8-0, which is still one of only three occasions in Man City's history that they've lost by an eight-goal margin. Burton were voted out of the Football League after just two more seasons and in 1901 were merged with Burton Swifts to form Burton United, a club which only existed for nine years before folding.

Johnny Campbell (both of them)

Sunderland's top scorer when they won the League title in 1894-95 was Johnny Campbell with 21 goals, and when Aston Villa won it the following season their top scorer was a different Johnny Campbell with 26.

Jimmy Logan

Jimmy Logan died from pneumonia at the age of 25 and was buried in an unmarked pauper's grave just two years after he had scored a hat-trick for Notts County in the 1894 FA Cup Final. Logan was a Loughborough player by the time of his death, and it's been said that his pneumonia was caused by him playing for Loughborough against Newton Heath in torrential rain and then having to make the long journey home in the same wet clothes that he had played in. It should be noted, however, that he did play against Burslem Port Vale a week after the Newton Heath game and then against Crewe the week after that, and that his death didn't come until more than a month after the season had ended.

Eleven versus eight

Walsall were only able to field eight players when they visited Darwen for a Second Division match on Boxing Day 1896. Darwen took full advantage and beat them 12-0.

Victorian hooligans

Between 1895 and 1897 there were 32 instances of the FA ordering football grounds to be closed due to cases of spectator disorder, the worst of which probably occurred in January 1895, when Woolwich Arsenal supporters beat the referee unconscious during their side's

1-1 draw with Burton Wanderers. It resulted in Arsenal's ground being closed for five weeks.

The shortest lived top six club

Accrington were a club that existed for less than 18 years but spent five of them in the Football League, during which time they finished above future League Champions Everton, Derby and Aston Villa. At the end of the 1889-90 season, they were the sixth best professional team in the country but were relegated from the top-flight three years later and, rather than join the Second Division, decided to resign from the League altogether and become members of the Lancashire League instead. This decision was based on the calculation that playing in Division Two would prove too costly as it would mean them having to lower their admission prices as well having to pay for the long trips to away games. Joining the Lancashire League, however, proved to be disastrous for the club. After just two seasons in it, they dropped down to the Lancashire Combination which they then resigned from four games into the 1895-96 season. They eventually folded at the beginning of 1896 after briefly resurfacing to play one final game in the Lancashire Senior Cup (which they lost 12-0). At the time of their demise, their smaller neighbours, Accrington Stanley, were playing in the North East Lancashire League, but Stanley would go on to flourish in Accrington's absence, eventually becoming a Football League club themselves in 1922.

Arsenal's record defeat (part one)

Arsenal's record defeat is 8-0 away to Loughborough in a Second Division fixture on 12 December 1896. This is especially remarkable considering Loughborough were a club that only existed for 14 years, were only in the Football League for the last five of them and during that time never finished any higher than fifth from bottom in Division two when the Second Division was the lowest tier of League football. What's more their 8-0 win over Arsenal – or Woolwich Arsenal as they were then known – came just three and a half years before they folded.

Arsenal's record defeat (part two)

Arsenal's aforementioned record 8-0 defeat to Loughborough in the League came on the same day (12 December 1896) that they also beat Leyton 5-0 at home in the FA Cup. Only 500 spectators were at the Loughborough game, while 3,000 attended the Leyton game and, although the scorelines would suggest otherwise, it was actually a second-string side that beat Leyton and the first-team that lost to Loughborough.

George Allan

George Allan was Liverpool's top scorer in the 1895-96 season with 29 goals from just 26 appearances and topped their scoring lists again the following season with 19 from 35 games. He was still only 21 when the latter season ended but lived for only another two and a half years after that. He died of tuberculosis in October 1899 by which time he was in his second spell at Liverpool following a brief stint at Celtic.

John Fisher

John Fisher was a member of the Workington team that beat Carlisle City in the 1897 Cumbrian County Cup Final and may well be the only English footballer to have been killed by an opposition fan. At the end of the game, he was struck on the head by a stone thrown by a Carlisle supporter, suffered severe brain damage as a result and died 19 days later.

The match that took four months to complete

In March 1898, Sheffield Wednesday and Aston Villa were brought together to play each other for ten and a half minutes in order to complete a League match that had been abandoned four months earlier. The only goal scored during this ten and a half minutes came from Wednesday's Fred Richards which would prove to be the only goal of his League career.

The end of all-amateur England line-ups

1898 was the first year that the England selectors were able to name a team of professional players for every game as, prior to this, it was standard practice to field an entirely amateur England line-up in one international out of every three.

Football on film

The film camera wasn't invented when the FA Cup was launched in 1871, but early experiments in filming were underway by the time the Football League arrived 17 years later. It's believed some filming was done at the 1898 FA Cup Final, although the earliest professional football match in England for which film footage still exists is the First Division clash between Blackburn and West Bromwich Albion on 24 September of that year. The footage was discovered in 2014, lasts for just 42 seconds and doesn't show any of the game's five goals, although this is hardly surprising considering there was probably only one camera and one film reel at the game and the reel would have been too short to capture anything more than a few minutes of action.

During Edwardian times, the films of football matches would continue to be short and primitive, with the goals from the match rarely featuring in them, but things began to change after the First World War. In the 1920s, matches often had more than one camera present and it had become possible to film for longer, although, that said, goals continued to be missed. The cinema newsreel of the 1928 FA Cup semi-final between Huddersfield and Sheffield United, for example, only showed one of the game's four goals, while the newsreel for that year's final didn't feature either of the two goals scored in the second half. This problem then continued into the '30s as the newsreel for England's 3-0 win over Germany at White Hart Lane in 1935 didn't show any goals at all.

It was only once television arrived in the late-30s that it became possible to screen an entire football match without cuts, although it wouldn't be until the late-50s that the majority of households in Britain had a TV set and matches would continue to be filmed for cinema newsreels until 1970.

Southampton's ground of the future

In 1898, Southampton's new ground, the Dell, became the first in English football to have a stand with seating on both sides of the pitch. The first game played on this ground-of-the-future was Southampton v Brighton in the Southern League on 3 September of that year.

C. Bibby

The five games C. Bibby (first name unknown) made for Second Division Darwen in the 1898-99 season were his only ever appearances in the Football League even though he scored a hat-trick in one of them. That hat-trick came in Darwen's 4-1 win at home to Luton on 11April 1899, and they were the only three League goals of Bibby's career.

Low-scoring Loughborough

When Loughborough lost 4-2 at Lincoln on 4 March 1899, it was the first time they had scored more than once in a League match for eleven months. Of the 27 Division Two matches they played over that period, they failed to score in 17 of them and scored one and only one in each of the other ten. Ironically, after finally hitting two in a match against Lincoln, they then went on to beat Luton 4-1, Darwen 10-0 and New Brighton Tower 6-0 during the final seven weeks of the season.

The team that couldn't defend (seemingly at all)

During the second half of the 1898-99 season, Second Division Darwen suffered three 10-0 defeats in seven weeks, with one of them being to Loughborough who eventually finished second from bottom. As well as the three 10-0s, they also lost 9-0, 9-2, 8-0 and 8-1 in the League that season, and the 141 goals they conceded in total is still a League record despite the fact that they only played 34 games. Loughborough's Dick Pegg, Manchester City's Fred Williams, New Brighton Tower's Harry Hammond and Small Heath's Walter Abbott all scored five-in-a-match against Darwen that season.

The dirtiest Victorian match

The 1899-1900 FA Cup second round replay between Sheffield United and Sheffield Wednesday at Bramall Lane was one hell of a rough derby match that put three Wednesday players out injured for the second replay two days later. It was, however, this second replay that became the more notorious of the two matches, being described in one local newspaper as a match that "tarnished the image of Sheffield football". This was a time when dismissals were rare in the game, and yet Wednesday's Jack Price and Ambrose Langley were both sent-off in United's 2-0 win. In the Football League, it wouldn't be until 1967 that two players were first sent-off from the same team in the same game, which says everything about how extreme Price and Langley's offences must have been. Price went for kicking George Hedley and Langley for charging into Walter Bennett, and both Hedley and Bennett had to go off injured as a result of the assaults on them (although Hedley returned five minutes later). As well as these injuries, Wednesday's stand-in centre-forward, Lee (first name unknown), was carried off with a broken leg and United's Harry Johnson and Wednesday's Jocky Wright both spent the latter stages of the match as hobbling passengers due to brutal fouls on them. The toll the match took on the United players is thought to have ultimately cost them the League title that season.

In 2020, an article on the BBC website described the 1970 FA Final replay between Chelsea and Leeds United as "the most brutal game in English football history", and two years later, Jon Spurling's book on 1970s football, *Get It On*, described the same game as "arguably English football's most violent match". There are many others who share this opinion, but maybe they wouldn't had television been around in 1900. For the record, the 1970 Cup Final replay produced no sending-offs or serious injuries and was nothing more than "a great game" according to BBC commentator Ken Wolstenholme at the time.

The top-flight's smallest ever club

Glossop remains the smallest populated town ever to have had its football club play at the highest level of English football. Glossop FC's one and only season in the top-flight was 1899-1900 when the population of the town was just 25,000. This was less than some other First Division clubs were getting at their best attended home games. Indeed, the crowd at the Aston Villa v Sheffield United game of that season was double the population of Glossop. Glossop's own ground, North Road, held just over 7,000 and their average attendance for the 1899-1900 season was 4,000.

The arrival of diving goalkeepers

Although the position of goalkeeper was created in 1871, there is no mention in match reports of keepers diving to make saves until the beginning of the 20th century.

Steve Bloomer

Steve Bloomer, who spent 17 full seasons at Derby and four at Middlesbrough, was the only player to score 300 goals under the original offside law that required there to be three defending players between the furthest forward attacker and the goal rather than just two. Bloomer retired before the start of the First World War but his 314 goals in the top-flight of English football has only been bettered by two players since.

Albert Smith

Albert Smith possibly had the most unsuccessful Football League career ever. His one and only League appearance was for Loughborough on a day they lost 12-0 to Woolwich Arsenal in March 1900.

A club on its last legs

In March 1900, Loughborough travelled to Barnsley for a Second Division match with only nine players and no kit. The nine men were subsequently beaten 7-0 in a borrowed strip. Loughborough folded three months later.

The largest pitch

When West Bromwich Albion's ground The Hawthorns opened in 1900, it had a pitch that was 127 yards long by 87 yards wide. This remains the largest pitch ever to have had Football League matches played on it. It was 12 yards longer and 13 yards wider than the present Wembley pitch.

Jack Jones

Bristol Rovers' Jack Jones scored six goals against Weymouth in the third qualifying round of the FA Cup in November 1900, and then got five against the same club in the first qualifying round of the competition a year later.

G.O. Smith

Because his only clubs were Corinthian and Casuals, G.O. Smith never played in any league during his career, but in 1901 he became the first player to win 20 caps for England and was still being proclaimed by journalists as the "the greatest centre-forward of all-time" when he died 42 years later. J.A.H. Catton was one journalist who saw Smith play many times and wrote that "anyone could knock Smith off the ball if he could get into contact with him. But he was difficult to find, so elusive was he. His value consisted chiefly of wonderfully accurate passes to either wing; either to the inside or outside man". Playing in such a way made Smith the first ever deep-lying, or roving centre-forward. Although his first name was Gilbert, he was always known by his initials in the same way the cricketer W.G. Grace was.

110,820

110,820 attended the 1901 FA Cup Final between Tottenham and Sheffield United at Crystal Palace. This remains the third highest attendance in the history of English football, with the big crowd possibly having something to do with the fact that Tottenham were the first ever London club with a working-class fanbase to reach the final. The match finished 2-2, with the London side winning the replay 3-1. Tottenham were in the Southern League at the time and remain the only club from a regional league ever to have won the FA Cup.

New Brighton Tower – English football's most commercially driven club

New Brighton Tower FC were formed in 1897 by the owners of the New Brighton Tower complex on the Wirral Peninsula, and remain probably unique amongst newly formed clubs in that they instantly had ambitions to play at the highest level, only wanted to do so for the money and attempted to fast-track their success by immediately signing players from some of the biggest clubs in the country. Everton's Alf Milward and Smart Arridge, Sunderland's Donald Gow and Derby's Jack Robinson had all played regularly in the First Division in 1896-97, but all dropped down to the Lancashire League to play for New Brighton Tower from the start of the following season, with Robinson doing so even though he was England's first-choice goalkeeper at the time.

Unsurprisingly, New Brighton Tower won the Lancashire League in 1897-98 and were then elected to the Football League the following month. In their first season as a League club they finished fifth in the Second Division, followed by tenth the season after and then fourth the next season. Considering there were only 18 clubs in the top-flight at the time, New Brighton Tower certainly hadn't done bad in becoming the 22nd best side in the Football League just four years after forming. But their owners were more interested in gate-money than results and the club's support was poor. Consequently, just three days before their scheduled opening fixture of the 1901-02 season, they decided New Brighton Tower just wasn't worth the bother and closed them down. What proved to be the club's final game had been a 1-0 win at home to Woolwich Arsenal on 27 April 1901.

Because they were so new and founded for purely commercial reasons, few seemed to care about their demise and probably the saddest thing about it was the loss of their visually unique ground to the footballing world. The New Brighton Tower itself was the tallest structure in Britain at the time, and it stood imposingly over the club's ground, providing, what was by Victorian standards, an awe-inspiring sight to spectators at the matches. After the Second World War, a different New Brighton club moved into the same ground but by then the tower had been dismantled.

The twice-abandoned Cup tie

When Bristol Rovers and Bristol City met in the second qualifying round of the FA Cup in 1901, the first attempt to play the game was abandoned with ten minutes left and so was the second. First time round it was the fog that caused the game to be stopped and second time it was bad light as the first 90 minutes were completed but the match went to extra-time. This meant that the second attempt to play the game lasted 110 minutes before it was abandoned. Three days later, the two teams had another go at completing the tie and this time succeeded, the final whistle eventually blowing after four hours and 40 minutes of football. City won 3-1, which was harsh on Rovers who had been 2-0 up when the original game had been stopped.

Tommy Brown

Chesterfield's top scorer in the 1901-02 season was Tommy Brown with ten goals. These came from just ten appearances which were the only ten appearances he ever made for the club.

Matthew Ferguson

Matthew Ferguson died of pleuropneumonia in June 1902 just under seven weeks after winning the League title with Sunderland, for whom he was club captain. The top footballers in those days, however, didn't enjoy the celebrity status they would in later years, and Britain's biggest sports paper of the time, *The Athletic News*, reported Ferguson's death in just one small paragraph at the bottom of a column headlined 'Notes from the North'. The heading to the paragraph read simply "M. Ferguson Dead".

When international football ceased to be exclusive to the British Isles

The first football international played in mainland Europe was Austria v Hungary on 2 October 1902. By this time England had been playing the other home nations for 26 years and there were no fewer than 25 former England internationals who were no longer alive.

Fred Harrison

In March 1903, Southampton's Fred Harrison scored five goals in each of two consecutive home games in the Southern League.

A team truly on fire

In the 1902-03 season, Manchester City won 6-0, 7-1, 4-0, 9-0 and 5-0 in consecutive Second Division matches.

Sheffield Wednesday's strange title triumph of 1902-03

Sheffield Wednesday won the League title in 1902-03 despite losing eleven matches in what was only a 34-game season. This meant that

32.4 per cent of their games ended in defeat, which is still a record proportion for a League title-winning side. Seven of those defeats came in their last ten away games, which included a 4-0 reverse at lowly Bury in their third from last game of the season. This was then followed by a 1-0 defeat at Derby five days later, which left their title chances looking incredibly slim. For although they were still top, they only had one game left to play while Sunderland were just one point behind with three games left. Sunderland, however, lost two of those last three games which meant that Wednesday's 3-1 win over West Brom in their final match was enough to land them the title, even though they weren't crowned until Sunderland lost at Newcastle a week later. By then, Wednesday were down in Devon playing Notts County in the Plymouth Bowl. Wednesday won that game and so had the strange distinction of lifting the Plymouth Bowl on the day they won the League title.

One other odd aspect of Wednesday's title success was that, with just one game left, they were nine points ahead of Aston Villa (the equivalent of 13 under three points for a win), but Villa blitzed through their games in hand and would have been champions themselves had Wednesday dropped just one more point. In fact, in the eight games leading up to their final game, Wednesday scored three penalties but only managed two other goals. Had they not been awarded just one of those penalties (or missed one of them) then the title would have gone to Villa on goal average.

The following season, Wednesday won the title again and again it was a bit of a strange one, since they scored fewer goals than Liverpool who finished second from bottom.

Who are ya?

Bradford City were founded at the end of the 1902-03 season and then elected to the Football League for the start of the following season. Their election was achieved before they had played a match or even put a team together, and yet, despite having literally no history, 11,000 attended their first home League game against Gainsborough Trinity.

Chelsea – the club made for Stamford Bridge

In 1904, Stamford Bridge athletics ground in Fulham was developed into a football ground and offered to Fulham FC. Fulham, however, declined the offer so a new club was formed to play there instead. As the name 'Fulham' had already been taken it was decided to name the new club after the neighbouring district of Chelsea.

Alf Common

Alf Common became the world's most expensive footballer twice in the space of eight months at the start of the 20th century. In June 1904, he moved from Sheffield United to Sunderland for, what was then, a record fee of £520, and then, in February 1905, he became the first footballer to command a four-figure fee when Middlesbrough brought him for £1,000. Despite the money clubs were prepared to pay for him, however, Common only ever won three caps for England, and only one as the world's first thousand-pound footballer.

Robbed by the fog

Everton missed out on the League title by one point at the end of the 1904-05 season, and it was probably the London fog that cost them. They had been leading 3-1 at Woolwich Arsenal with 12 minutes left when the fog rolled in and caused the game to be abandoned. When it was replayed Arsenal won 2-1.

An assault which led to a scandal which led to another scandal

Newcastle and Manchester City were both level on points at the top of the First Division as they went into their final matches of the 1904-05 season. Newcastle took the title with a 3-0 win at Middlesbrough, as City went down 3-2 at Aston Villa, but the drama of that final Saturday was nothing compared with its repercussions for City.

It all began when City's Sandy Turnbull began throwing punches at Villa's Alex Leake during the game that City lost, an assault which led to Turnbull being bundled into the Villa dressing room after the final whistle and getting assaulted himself by the other Villa players. The incident led to an FA inquiry, and it was during the inquiry that it was alleged that Leake had turned down a bribe to throw the game from the Manchester City captain Billy Meredith. As a result, Meredith – who was City's best player – was suspended for the whole of the following season. During that season, however, he often turned up at the club asking for money, a habit City weren't happy about and so they decided to report him to the FA. This naturally angered Meredith who already believed he was carrying the can for a corrupt club and so he took revenge by blowing the whistle on the club's over-payment of players. At the time there was a pay cap on players' wages and, according to Meredith, City had been breaking it for years. This led to another FA inquiry in 1906 which resulted in an indefinite ban from football for City's manager, Tom Maley, and a seven-month ban for 17 City players, all of whom were also given a lifetime ban from playing for Man City. This meant that all but two of their first-team regulars who had nearly won the title in 1905 were out of the club by the start of the 1906-07 season. And all because Sandy Turnbull threw a couple of punches on the day City missed out on the title.

Colin Veitch

When Newcastle won the League title in the 1904-05 season, their captain, Colin Veitch, appeared for the club at left-half, centre-half, inside-right, inside-left, outside-right and centre-forward. Veitch also captained Newcastle in five FA Cup Finals, playing at inside-left in the first, centre-forward in the second, left-half in the third and right-half in the fourth and fifth. Veitch was certainly one of the most versatile footballers ever, but his versatility didn't end with football, as he was also a playwright, an actor, a theatre producer, a composer and a conductor, as well as serving as an artilleryman on the Western Front in the First World War.

The loneliest London club

For 12 years between 1893 and 1905, Woolwich Arsenal were the Football League's only London club. It was in 1905 that Chelsea joined them, although Chelsea were initially in Division Two, while Arsenal were in the First Division. Chelsea eventually won promotion in 1907 and on the 9th of November of that year they beat Arsenal 2-1 at Stamford Bridge in the League's first ever London derby.

Steve Bloomer (Again)

Steve Bloomer finished as Derby's top scorer in each of 13 consecutive seasons between 1893-94 and 1905-06. He was also their top scorer in the 1910-11 and 1911-12 seasons when in his second spell with the club, even though he was in his late-30s by then.

The big club that came out of nowhere

In the 1905-06 season, Chelsea finished third in Division Two of the Football League and had an average home attendance of more than 13,000 despite having only been formed six months before the season started and having only played one match ever prior to their opening fixture. Two years later they were in the First Division and were the best supported club in the country.

Walter Bennett

Walter Bennett was an outside-right who finished top scorer for Sheffield United in their League title-winning season of 1897-98 and then became an FA Cup-winner with them the following season when he scored in both the semi-final and the final. In all he made 238 appearances and scored 70 goals for United in major competitions before moving to Second Division Bristol City in 1905. He went on to score 20 times from the right-wing as City won the Second Division title in 1905-06, but at the end of that season he quit professional football and returned to Yorkshire to become a coal miner. He was killed in a mining accident at the Denaby Main Colliery just over a year later at the age of 33.

George Hilsdon

George Hilsdon is the only ever player to have scored five goals on his League debut, which he achieved for Chelsea in a 9-2 win over Worksop on 1 September 1906. Hilsdon had previously played in the Southern League and went back there six years later, although in between he did become the first player to score 100 goals for Chelsea. When he died in 1941, only four people attended his funeral, and he was buried in an unmarked grave.

Beaten by the heat

When Woolwich Arsenal beat Manchester City 4-1 on the opening day of the 1906-07 season, City finished the game with only six players on the field as five had had to go off with heat exhaustion. The temperature in London that day reached 33 degrees.

Corinthian FC

Corinthian were one the greatest and most significant English football clubs of the late-19th and early-20th centuries, but because of their refusal to join any league or enter the FA Cup they are barely mentioned in the record books. They were a club dedicated to playing the game for the love of it rather than for silverware or money and so, aside from their games in the Sheriff of London Shield, all of the matches they played during their heyday were friendlies.

At that time, in order to play for Corinthian you had to be an amateur, had to have gone to public school or university and (as well as not getting paid) had to pay a subscription fee for the privilege of representing them. Most Corinthian players played for other clubs as well so playing for Corinthian was seen as a special duty akin to playing for your country. When you played for Corinthian you were supposedly representing the elite in every respect since Corinthians saw themselves as elite in terms of their playing ability, elite in terms of the fact that they were all educated gentlemen and also elite in their conduct, as they always sought to embrace the highest standards of sportsmanship and fair play, so much so, in fact, that it wasn't unknown for their players to dispute incorrect decisions that had gone in their favour.

As a team, Corinthian were far from invincible and took a fair few pastings in their time, but on their day they could beat anyone. Indeed between 1889 and 1907 they won a total of 57 matches against top-flight professional sides, with seven of those victories coming against clubs that went on to win the League title in the same season. This included Preston's League and FA Cup double-winning side of 1888-89 whose only defeat of that season came against Corinthian. Other notable victories for Corinthian during their heyday were an 8-1 victory away to FA Cup holders Blackburn in 1884, a 5-0 win over Preston in the latter's second title-winning season of 1889-90, a 7-3 win away to Sheffield United in 1894 (United finished sixth in the League that season), a 4-2 win away to Derby in 1896 (Derby finished runners-up in the League that season), an 8-4 win at Wolves in 1900, an 8-2 win at Sunderland in 1902 (Sunderland finished third in the League that season), an 11-3 win against Manchester United in 1904, a 10-3 win against FA Cup-holders Bury the same year, a 7-5 win away to reigning champions Newcastle in 1906, a 7-1 win against Aston Villa that was also in 1906 and two 5-2 wins against Liverpool in 1895 and 1898.

As well as their domestic exploits, Corinthian also toured 14 different countries between 1903 and 1911, playing in continental Europe five years before the England national side first did and outside of Europe 47 years before England first did. Their players also figured heavily in England line-ups between 1883 and 1896, a period in which there were eleven England sides that contained six or more Corinthians, including two that were made up entirely of Corinthians.

In 1909, one journalist wrote that Corinthian were "the greatest and most attractive team that football has ever known", but by then their heyday was already over, brought to an abrupt end two years earlier when they committed an irreparable act of self-harm by resigning from the FA. After this they could no longer get games against professional clubs and their fixtures dried-up. By the time they entered the FA Cup for the first time in 1923 (following a reconciliation with the FA) they were a shadow of the club they had once been and lost to Third Division Brighton in their first ever FA Cup tie. The following season they knocked-out First Division Blackburn which stands as the only time an amateur side has knocked a top-flight club out of the FA Cup. It was a remarkable achievement considering Corinthian's decline but it was never to be repeated. Between 1925-26 and 1932-33, Corinthian were the only non-League club to enjoy the privilege of being exempted from the FA Cup until the third round, but never once got beyond the fourth round.

Eventually, in 1939, they merged with their sister club, Casuals, and joined the Isthmian League. Corinthian-Casuals are still active in the lower levels of the game today although few are aware of their history.

Palace pulling off the impossible

When Newcastle won the League title in 1906-07 their only home defeat of the season was to non-League Crystal Palace in the FA Cup. This result is all the more remarkable for the fact that Palace didn't win a single away game in the Southern League that season.

When a Scotland v England game changed the offside law

The rule that a player cannot be offside in his own half of the field was first introduced into football in 1907, and was largely in response to a farcical Scotland v England game the previous year when England played the offside trap so far forward that Scotland players were getting caught in it just outside their own penalty area.

Herbert Chapman

Northampton's player-manager, Herbert Chapman, scored a hat-trick of disallowed goals against Sutton in an FA Cup fifth qualifying round tie in December 1907. He also scored two that counted as Northampton ran out 10-0 winners.

In a League where they didn't belong

Bradford Park Avenue spent the 1907-08 season playing in the Southern League which made their nearest away game 140 miles away. During the same season their reserves played at the other end of the country in the North-Eastern League.

Nothing to choose between the sides

In the 1907-08 season, Arsenal and Blackburn finished joint 14th in Division One with identical records. Both teams won 12, drew 12 and lost 14, and both scored 51 goals and conceded 63.

England finally go abroad

England played their first matches outside of Britain when they toured the Austro-Hungarian Empire in June 1908 to play two games against Austria and one each against Hungary and Bohemia. These matches came nearly 36 years after England's first recognised international against Scotland and it was testament to how further advanced British football was at the time compared with the game in mainland Europe that England won the four matches 6-1, 11-1, 7-0 and 4-0.

Albert Shepherd

Prior to the Newcastle v Notts County First Division match of January 1909, Newcastle's Albert Shepherd asked his club if he could leave the game ten minutes early as he had a train to catch. In those days there were no substitutes so if Shepherd went off it would reduce the team to ten men, but the club nonetheless agreed on the condition he had scored a hat-trick by the 80th minute. With 80 minutes of the game gone, Newcastle were 4-0 up, Shepherd had scored all four and so off he went to catch his train.

Harry Swift and Spen Whittaker

Harry Swift made his debut for Burnley in April 1910, eight days after the death of the manager who signed him. Spen Whittaker was the recently deceased Burnley boss, and it was the signing of Swift from Accrington that had ultimately led to his death. Whittaker had fallen from a moving train whilst travelling to London to register the signing and died in hospital a few days later.

The mother of all blips

Newcastle won the League title in the 1908-09 season despite losing one of their home games 9-1 to Sunderland. This would remain the record top-flight home defeat for the next 111 years. Five of Sunderland's goals came in the last eight minutes and the score was still 1-1 with just over half-an-hour left.

Promotion guaranteed (supposedly)

In 1909, Aberdare Town were invited into the Southern League Division Two and promised that, provided they remained there for two consecutive seasons, they would be promoted to Division One regardless of where they finished. This promise, however, was clearly not kept as they ended up spending five seasons in the league's second division before eventually folding in 1914.

Undercover goalkeepers

Before the 1909-10 season, goalkeepers wore the same colour tops as the outfield players. As there was no shirt numbering in those days either, all keepers were required to wear a cap to indicate their playing position.

Millwall uprooting

Millwall's last game in Millwall was a 3-1 win against Portsmouth on 8 October 1910. After this they went from being an east London club to a south London one but retained the name of the district they no longer played in. Although they only finished 16th in the Southern League the previous season, their new ground, the Den in New Cross, was officially opened by the President of the FA, Lord Kinnaird.

The Reverend Kenneth Hunt

There were several England players during football's early years who subsequently went on to become ordained ministers, but the

Reverend Kenneth Hunt was the only player to play for England after he had been ordained. Hunt won two caps in 1911 whilst with Southern League Leyton, a club he had four spells with altogether. He also had six spells with Wolves and three with Crystal Palace as he was an amateur player who just gave his services to clubs as and when he could. In 1908, he won the FA Cup with Wolves, scoring the opening goal against Newcastle in the final, although this was before he was ordained.

Robert Evans

Robert Evans played for England against Wales in March 1911 having played for Wales against England a year earlier. Evans had, in fact, played in ten of Wales's 15 matches between March 1906 and April 1910, but at the beginning of 1911 the FA discovered that he was born in Chester and so was ineligible to play for Wales. They then informed the Welsh FA of this, as well as the England selectors who subsequently wasted no time in picking Evans for England's next match. Although born in Chester, Evans had Welsh parents, only lived the first three weeks of his life in Chester before his family moved back to Wales and always regarded himself as a Welshman even when he was playing for England. He remains the only player called 'Evans' ever to have played for England.

It only took eight years

Bradford City won the FA Cup in 1911, which was just eight years after they were founded.

Vivian Woodward

Vivian Woodward was an amateur footballer who earnt his living as an architect, and yet for 45 years between 1911 and 1956 he stood as England's joint all-time top goalscorer. Woodward was the first

England player to score a hat-trick in mainland Europe when he got four in the 11-1 win in Austria in 1908, and the following year scored hat-tricks away to both Austria and Hungary on consecutive days. As well as scoring 28 times for the full England side, Woodward also scored a record 53 in official internationals for the England Amateur team who he captained to Gold at both the 1908 and 1912 Olympics when they competed as Great Britain.

It was a long time coming

The rule that goalkeepers are not allowed to handle the ball outside their own penalty areas was not introduced until the start of the 1912-13 season, which was the 23rd season of League football in England.

The fall and rise of Arsenal

Woolwich Arsenal failed to win any of their first 15 League home games of the 1912-13 season and failed to score more than a single goal in any of the first 16. In fact, they only scored more than once in two of their 38 First Division matches that season, with one of those occasions coming in a 5-2 defeat.

This was Arsenal's last season playing at the Manor Ground in Plumstead, and they finished bottom of Division One and were the worst supported team in the top-flight. Their final game at the Manor Ground was a 1-1 draw with Middlesbrough that attracted a crowd of just 3,000 two weeks after 50,000 had watched Chelsea play Tottenham.

After moving to Highbury, they dropped the 'Woolwich' from their name (although not immediately) and finished third in Division Two in 1913-14 and then fifth the following season, which was the last before League football was suspended due to the First World War. After the War, the size of the First Division was expanded and Arsenal were given back their top-flight place, which didn't seem right as they had finished below Barnsley and Wolves in the last season before the War, and both of those clubs had been left in the

Second Division, while Tottenham had been relegated into the Second Division to make way for Arsenal.

Arsenal had been rubbish before the First World War, then got lucky straight after the War, but between the Wars they went from strength-to-strength. Just over ten years after being given back their place in the top-flight, they would be League champions and the best supported team in the country.

Massive crowd – shame about the game

The 1913 FA Cup Final between Aston Villa and Sunderland at Crystal Palace was watched by a crowd of 120,081. This remains the second highest attendance in the history of English football, although the match itself was an ugly affair of aimless hoofing, violent conduct and so many stoppages that 17 minutes of time was added on at the end. The fight between Sunderland's Charlie Thomson and Villa's Harry Hampton led to both players receiving one-month suspensions from the start of the following season (incorporating six games for Thomson and five for Hampton), while referee Arthur Adams was also suspended for his poor handling of the match.

The game's only goal was scored by Villa's Tommy Barber who would be shot in the leg at the Battle of Guillemont three years later.

Bob Crompton

Bob Crompton was England's most capped player of all-time for 53 years and had been dead for eleven years by the time his record was eventually broken. He played in 41 of England's 46 games between 1902 and 1914 (he broke the record in 1909) and won his 41st cap at a time when no other player had won more than 23. As well as being a footballer, Crompton also had his own plumbing business and patented his own inventions of plumbing equipment.

A seriously tough league

Luton Town won all but six of their 30 matches in the Southern League Second Division in 1913-14 and scored 92 goals, but still only finished runners-up, while Stoke won 12 of their first 15 games and only finished fifth. The title was won by the soon-to-be-defunct Croydon Common.

Crystal Palace – the 'picturesque' Cup Final venue

Every FA Cup Final between 1895 and 1914 was played at Crystal Palace which according to J.A.H. Catton "Provided a picturesque setting that has never been equalled on any ground". Catton probably attended every final at the venue and wrote of it in the 1920s, "the sea of grass, the border of trees, the old switchback railway, and the rising ground behind one of the goals... the great charm of the Crystal Palace was that it was so utterly unlike any other place where football was ordinarily played". "Wembley is a wonder", Catton continued, "but it is a big building – man's work. The sports arena at the Palace was not a building. It was just space – sylvan, verdant, luscious – God's work". No doubt its aesthetic appeal was also enhanced by the fact that The Crystal Palace itself – the grand iron and glass structure that housed the Great Exhibition of 1851 – stood just yards away from the football ground in those days.

After Crystal Palace FC were formed in 1905, they had the privilege of using the venue for their home games until 1915, as did Corinthian after Palace moved out.

The Royal presentation

In 1914, Burnley's Tommy Boyle became the first FA Cup winning captain to have the trophy presented to him by the reigning British monarch (George V). For the next 45 years after this, the FA Cup would mostly be presented by the monarch, but the practice became rarer in the '60s and stopped altogether in the '70s. In 1976, Southampton's Peter Rodrigues became the last captain to receive the Cup from Queen Elizabeth II whose reign would last another 46 years.

Brazil v Exeter

The Brazilian national side's first ever match was against Exeter City during Exeter's 1914 tour of South America. According to Wikipedia, a 2004 article in *The Guardian* and a 2014 article on the BBC website, Brazil won the game 2-0, but the 1990 book *Exeter City: A Complete Record 1904-1990* claims it was a 3-3 draw.

You don't get anything like that in the Southern League

Exeter City's 1914 tour of South America included a match against the Argentinian champions Racing Club in which play was suspended when the Racing Club secretary threatened the referee with a gun after Exeter scored. Despite the firearms-brandishing intimidation, Exeter went on to win the match 2-0, thus showing that Argentina's skills-based game was not yet a match for the rugged English brand of football.

The heroes of Croydon Common

Croydon Common FC existed for just 20 years between 1897 and 1917 and never finished any higher than second from bottom in the Southern League Division One, but no club's players had a greater sense of duty to their country when the First World War broke out in 1914. 13 of their players immediately volunteered for military service which was the most from a single professional football club in England at that time. A further six then volunteered for the Footballer's Battalion (more of which later) the following year.

The fans have gone to war

The First World War broke out in the summer of 1914, but the 1914-15 football season still went ahead and was completed. Needless to say, playing the season when so many football fans were away on the Western Front severely affected attendances. The League average for 1914-15 was 9,980, down from 16,359 the previous season.

Unreported football

In November 1914, the Council for Newspaper Proprietors took the decision that newspapers should not carry reports of football matches in protest at the number of footballers and supporters who had not volunteered for military service since the outbreak of the First World War.

The Footballers' Battalion

The Footballers' Battalion was the nickname given to the British Army's 17th Middlesex Battalion during World War One as it was set up specifically to recruit footballers, football club staff and football fans following criticism at the way football had carried on as normal following the outbreak of war and that too many men of fighting age were still playing and watching football when they should have been fighting for their country. During the War 3,570 men served in the Battalion with some of those being professional footballers from the Football League, although most of the players who enlisted were either amateurs or Southern League professionals.

The rigged match

Manchester United's 2-0 victory over Liverpool on Good Friday 1915 is the only professional English football match known to have been rigged by players from both sides as part of a betting scam. An unusually high number of bets had been placed on the 2-0 United win and further suspicions were raised by the strangely uncompetitive nature of the game and the fact that United's Patrick O'Connell appeared to deliberately miss a penalty and then laughed after doing so. Also, some of the Liverpool players had gestured angrily to their teammate, Fred Pagnam, after he had shot against the crossbar.

Following an investigation, four United players and three from Liverpool received lifetime bans, although five of the bans were subsequently lifted in recognition of the players' service to their country during the First World War. Of the other two, Sandy Turnbull was killed in the War and Enoch West's ban was upheld.

Billy Cook

The Middlesbrough v Oldham First Division match of April 1915 was abandoned after 58 minutes due to Oldham's Billy Cook refusing to leave the field after being sent-off. Cook was subsequently given a 12-month ban by the FA, nearly all of which coincided with the four-year wartime suspension of League and FA Cup football. In fact, the only games Cook missed were the last three of this season, but it's thought his absence in those matches was enough to cost Oldham the League title. They lost two and drew one of those last three games and missed the title by two points.

Bob Thomson

Chelsea's top scorer in the 1914-15 season was centre-forward Bob Thomson who had been blind in one eye since childhood. Thomson scored 12 First Division goals that season, plus another six in Chelsea's run to the FA Cup Final. He would also finish top scorer for Charlton in 1923-24.

Wilf Nixon and Oscar Linkson

Queen's Park Rangers' goalkeeper Wilf Nixon and their right-back Oscar Linkson were both arrested for being absent without leave from the British army after taking part in their club's 0-0 draw at Tottenham in the London Combination in March 1916. It later transpired that the two players both had return railway tickets and so were intending to return to barracks after the game.

Richard McFadden and William Jonas

Clapton Orient's two top scorers of the 1914-15 season, Richard McFadden and William Jonas, were both killed on the Western Front in the First World War in 1916. The two had been friends since childhood and between them scored 33 of Orient's 51 League and Cup goals in 1914-15. Jonas was killed in action during the Battle of Delville Wood in the August of 1916 and McFadden was the last person he spoke to before going over the top. According to McFadden, Jonas was killed within seconds of the pair saying goodbye to each other. McFadden died himself two months later, although his death came in a military hospital. Their teammate George Scott also died from wounds the same year after being taken prisoner by the Germans.

Donald Simpson Bell

Donald Simpson Bell's Football League career consisted of just five appearances for Bradford Park Avenue during the 1912-13 and 1913-14 seasons, but he is notable for being the only professional footballer to win a Victoria Cross, which he was awarded for his bravery during the Battle of The Somme in 1916. He was killed in action shortly after receiving the honour. He was 25 years old.

Sandy Turnbull

During his career, Sandy Turnbull was the subject of an FA inquiry for assaulting an opponent, banned from football for seven months for receiving payments above the fixed limit at that time and eventually banned for life for his part in the rigged match between Manchester United and Liverpool in 1915. For all his misdemeanours, however, he does stand as the most successful footballer to have been killed in the First World War.

He was an FA Cup winner with Manchester City in 1904, scoring five goals in their Cup run and 21 altogether that season. He then scored 20 for City the following season and 28 for Manchester United when they won the League in 1907-08. He also scored the winning goal for United in the 1909 FA Cup Final, before going on to hit another 19 in all competitions for them when they won the League again in 1910-11. In all he made 330 League appearances and scored 143 goals. Both of these figures are the highest by any player who died in the War. His death came at the Battle of Arras in France in May 1917. His lifetime ban from football would have been rescinded for his military service had he lived.

Steve Bloomer (Yet Again)

Steve Bloomer, the Football League's record goalscorer at that time, spent almost all of the First World War interred in a civilian detention camp in Germany. He had been coaching in Berlin when war broke out and was arrested as he tried to leave the country. The Ruhleben camp, where he was held, was a disused racecourse just outside Berlin and it saw 4,400 prisoners crammed into eleven filthy stables where each prisoner had just ten square foot of space each. Many of these prisoners were British ex-pats, with quite a few being former footballers, and between them they founded the Ruhleben Football Association and spent their years in the camp arranging and playing football matches. Bloomer later said of this period in his life, "myself and many others couldn't have survived without football".

The big kick-off

Before the First World War, the first matches in a new football season were almost always played on either the 1st or 2nd of September, regardless of whether those dates fell at the weekend. The 1919-20 season was the first that began in August, and it was only from this season that it became the custom for all Football League clubs in all divisions of the League to begin their season at the same time on the same day and for that day to always be a Saturday. This custom would remain unchanged until the Premier League was launched 73 years later, although, initially, the Premier League did begin the same weekend as the Football League but just had two of its matches moved so as they could be shown live on Sky Sports (one on Sunday afternoon and the other on Monday evening). It wouldn't be until the 1998-99 season that the Premier League first kicked-off a week after the Football League.

A terrible beginning to a long League history

Coventry City were elected to the Football League in 1919 and began their first season with nine straight defeats before going on to complete eleven consecutive games without scoring, which is still a joint League record today. By Christmas they had played 19 games, lost 15 of them, drew the other four 0-0 and scored just four goals. 31 different players had played for them over those 19 matches but only two had scored.

Peter O'Rourke

In February 1920, Peter O'Rourke scored twice in the first six minutes of his League debut (for Bradford Park Avenue). These would prove to be the only League goals of his career.

Coventry buying their League survival

Lincoln City were voted out of the Football League at the end of the 1919-20 season and it was the consequence of two rigged matches in the space of three days between Coventry and Bury. Coventry needed to get three points from those two games to guarantee not having to apply for re-election, and they managed it by bribing Bury to throw the games, which finished 2-2 and 2-1 in Coventry's favour. This meant that Lincoln had to apply for re-election instead and when they did their application was rejected.

Rumours that the results of the two matches had been arranged began circulating almost immediately owing to the fact that Bury were a decent side and yet spent the two games constantly giving the ball away. It was, however, another three years before the Football League investigated and uncovered the truth. The two clubs were then both fined £100 each and six of the players involved in the matches plus five officials from the two clubs received lifetime bans from the game. Practically nothing was known about what actually happened, however, until Coventry's captain at the time, George Chaplin, told his story to the press in the 1940s. According to Chaplin, he and the Coventry chairman, David Cooke, had come up with the idea of bribing Bury between them, no one else at the club was aware of it and it was Chaplin himself who made the payments in two instalments. This could be true, but it was an uncorroborated story in which not everything added-up, so who knows?

Jimmy Sharp

When Fulham's Harry Crockford missed the team bus for a trip to Bury in April 1920, the club's 39-year-old trainer Jimmy Sharp stepped in to replace him in the side. Sharp had been a full-back in his playing days, but in this match he played up front and scored one of the Fulham goals in a 2-2 draw. It was his first goal in senior football for twelve and a half years.

As daft as it gets

Leeds City were expelled from the Football League eight games into the 1919-20 season after it was revealed they had made illegal payments to guest players during the First World War. This was actually common practice amongst all clubs during the War and the FA had turned a blind eye to it, but because Leeds were the only club officially reported for it, they were the only club the FA were obliged to punish. Following their expulsion, Leeds immediately disbanded, with their players being sold off in an auction, but the results of their eight matches were not expunged and instead were credited to Port Vale who were brought into the League to take over the remaining Leeds fixtures. If this all sounds slightly ridiculous, it was made even more so when, during the course of the season, Leeds City re-formed as Leeds United and then in the summer got elected to the same Division that Leeds City had been expelled from less than a year earlier.

The decline and double disappearance of South Shields

In the 1920-21 season, South Shields finished sixth in Division Two and had an average League gate of 16,450. This made them better supported than Leeds United. Within a decade, however, their average gate had fallen to just 3,300 and in the summer of 1930 they were relocated to Gateshead and had their name changed accordingly. In response, a new South Shields Football Club was founded to replace the original one, but when Gateshead (by now a non-League club) folded in 1973, the second South Shields were also moved to Gateshead and had their name changed. A third South Shields FC was then formed in 1974, which is the one that still exists today.

Women's football (yes, it was popular, but not *that* popular)

In December 1921, the FA banned its affiliated clubs from staging women's matches on their grounds, a ban which would remain in place for almost 50 years. This served to stifle the development of the women's game in Britain, which was growing in popularity, but was not, as many modern revisionists now claim, just as popular as the men's game. During the 1920-21 season, a number of men's First Division matches drew crowds of over 60,000 and there were 76,000 at Chelsea v Tottenham. There had also been 120,000 at the 1913 FA Cup Final and would be an estimated 200,000 at the 1923 Final (more of which later). The closest any women's game got to these attendances was 53,000 for a match between Dick, Kerr Ladies and St Helens Ladies at Goodison Park in 1920, but this was likely to have been unnaturally high due to it being played on a Boxing Day when there were no men's games.

Preston's Dick, Kerr Ladies were by far the biggest draw in women's football at the time, but the crowd sizes at their matches fluctuated wildly, suggesting they didn't inspire the same kind of devotion as the men's teams did. 25,000 watched them play St Helens again at Huddersfield's Leeds Road over Easter 1921, but their game against Atalantians on the same ground seven months later drew a mere 1,800, and only 5,000 were in attendance when they represented England against a visiting French side the same year. In 1921, Dick, Kerr Ladies 67 matches drew an average gate of just over 13,000, which wasn't bad for a touring team that didn't belong to any league, but it was still bettered by the average gate of five Third Division clubs over the 1920-21 season, a season when the average attendance in the First Division was 29,000 and the best supported club, Newcastle, averaged 41,265. That season's FA Cup Final drew a crowd of 72,805. The same month a photograph was published in the *Daily News* of 'the Women's Cup Final' and only trees are visible behind the players.

As for media coverage, women's matches were reported on in the local press, but there's little evidence they were seen as a big deal. When Dick, Kerr Ladies beat Staffordshire & Cheshire Ladies 12-0 in March 1921, *The Lancashire Evening Post* devoted fewer column inches to it than it did to a game between Breightmet United and Penwortham in the Lancashire Junior League. *The Athletic News*, meanwhile, never reported on women's matches despite being the publication that provided the most comprehensive coverage of football before the War. In 1923, it published an article entitled 'Women in Sport', which opined that "There are some sports which are obviously unsuited to women. Football under both codes is one of them". It then added dismissively, "although women have often played soccer". Equally dismissive was Nathan Barnett in a letter he wrote to the *Daily News* shortly after the ban on women's football was imposed in 1921. According to Barnett, "the ban of the council of the Football Association on women's participation in football will not be resented by any except the ultra-masculine type of girl". The fact that this letter was printed in a respected, Liberal-supporting publication illustrates that the opinion it expresses would have been seen as a perfectly valid one at the time.

Third Division North and South

When the Football League added a Third Division in 1920-21, it was comprised of the previous season's entire Southern League apart from Cardiff who replaced Grimsby in Division two, with Grimsby being relegated into the new Division Three. This made Grimsby the only northern club in the League's third tier, which prompted the Football League to rename it Division Three South for the following season and have it run alongside a newly created Division Three North made up of Grimsby, who were moved over, Stockport, who were relegated into it, and 18 former non-League clubs from the north. In theory Division Three North and Division Three South represented equivalent levels of football but, in reality, Division Three South was superior, containing as it did bigger clubs with greater potential. Of the 20 founder members of Division Three North, Grimsby remain the only one that have ever reached the top-flight of English football, whereas 14 of the 22 original Division Three South clubs have. Also, of the 12 clubs to lose their League status between the late-1920s and late-70s, ten were former Division Three North clubs.

Division Three North and South would exist for 37 seasons until a national Third Division and a national Fourth Division were created at the end of the 1950s.

The Old Trafford double-header

There were two League matches played at Old Trafford on 7 May 1921. Manchester United's First Division match against Derby was immediately followed by the Second Division match between Stockport and Leicester which was being played at Old Trafford due to Stockport's ground having been closed because of crowd trouble. 10,000 watched the first game, 2,000 watched both games and just 13 watched the second game only as most Stockport fans boycotted it.

No boys allowed

In 1921, Bradford Park Avenue banned all boys from their ground for five months after some had thrown stones at the referee during a game against Manchester City in April of that year.

Frank Richardson

During the 1921-22 season, Frank Richardson scored 20 out of 28 consecutive League goals for Plymouth.

The ultimate embarrassment

In January 1922, First Division Everton lost 6-0 at home to Second Division Crystal Palace in the first round of the FA Cup. This remains the heaviest ever defeat suffered by a top-flight club at the hands of a team from a lower division.

When Second Division players were the most expensive in the world

In March 1922, Sunderland broke the world transfer fee record twice in two days to sign two Second Division players. First came Michael Gilhooley from Hull for a fee of £5,250, followed by Warney Cresswell from South Shields for £5,500. Cresswell went on to spend several years as Sunderland's regular right-back but Gilhooley's time at the club would be blighted by injuries and he would make only 19 appearances in Sunderland colours before moving to Bradford City at the start of the 1925-26 season.

Jimmy Evans

Southend left-back Jimmy Evans scored over twice as many goals as any of his teammates in the 1921-22 season, even though he didn't score any goals that weren't penalties. He converted ten spot-kicks.

Johnny McIntyre

Johnny McIntyre scored four goals in five minutes when Blackburn beat Everton 5-1 in a First Division match in September 1922. Prior to this he had only scored twice in 21 appearances for the club.

Frank Osborne

When England played Ireland at home in October 1922, their centre-forward was Fulham's Frank Osborne who was being given a fairly unlikely international debut considering he was a Second Division player who had scored only four goals so far that season and got only eight the previous season.

Billy Minter and the craziest ever FA Cup match

In November 1922, St Albans City's Billy Minter scored seven times in an FA Cup fourth qualifying round replay at Dulwich Hamlet – and still finished on the losing side! Dulwich won 8-7 and had two hat-trick heroes themselves in Edgar Kail and William Davis, who scored four. Minter scored three in the first half to put his side 3-1 up, got another three after the break to turn a 5-3 deficit into a 6-5 lead and then scored an equaliser in extra-time to make it 7-7. Dulwich's late winner was highly controversial, being scored in fading light from a harshly awarded free-kick that St Albans felt came after the referee should have blown for time.

This Billy Minter, incidentally, should not be confused with the other Billy Minter who was a prolific goalscorer for Tottenham before the First World War.

David Ashworth

Liverpool were top of the First Division in December 1922 when their manager, David Ashworth, suddenly resigned to take the manager's job at bottom of the table Oldham. Ashworth never gave a reason for his decision.

The no-away-goals Saturday

On Saturday 28 April 1923 there were ten matches played in the First Division and they didn't produce a single away goal between them.

The goal shy champions

Notts County won the Second Division title in 1922-23 despite scoring more than once in only 12 of their 42 matches and more than twice in just two of them. Their 46 League goals that season remains the lowest by any of the Football League's divisional champions. 12 of their 23 victories were 1-0.

England's (and possibly the world's) biggest ever football crowd

The biggest crowd ever to watch a football match in England was the one that attended the first FA Cup Final at Wembley in 1923 between Bolton and West Ham. Unlike all subsequent FA Cup Finals, the match wasn't all-ticket which led to people descending on the ground in numbers that hadn't been anticipated. The official attendance when the turnstiles were closed at 1.45 was 126,047 which would be a record in itself, but the turnstiles were subsequently re-opened to stop people clambering over them, resulting in large numbers flooding through them without paying, while many others got in by scaling the walls. The FA originally claimed that nearly 25,000 entered the stadium without paying, but later estimates put it at around 70,000. We can, therefore, safely say that there was somewhere between 150,000 and 200,000 people in the ground that day.

At three o'clock, when the match was due to kick off, the pressure on the terraces had forced 10,000 supporters onto the pitch and when the game eventually got going 45 minutes later it did so with thousands watching from the touchlines and so many encroaching onto the playing area that the touchlines themselves weren't even visible. The two linesmen, therefore, ended up performing their roles more infield, while West Ham's usually dangerous wingers were unable to play their usual game since there was little in the way of wings for them to operate down. Bolton adapted better to the narrow playing area and won 2-0, although the crowd encroachment played a part in both of their goals. David Jack scored the first after his marker got stuck in the crowd after taking a throw-in, and John Smith got the second from a cross supplied by Ted Vizard after the latter had received a pass from one of the touchline spectators. West Ham also believed Smith's shot had hit the post, but the referee adjudged it to have come back off of a spectator who was standing by the post but behind the goal line. If this is true, then both goals came from shots that struck spectators as Jack's shot for the first hit a spectator who was squashed behind the back of the net and knocked him unconscious.

The club that chose to go down

Stalybridge Celtic were made founder members of Division Three North in 1921 but resigned from it two years later after their directors decided that the club was too small and poorly supported ever to succeed at League level. This despite the fact that they finished a respectable seventh in their first season as a League club and then eleventh in the second. Following their resignation, they joined the Cheshire County League for the start of the 1923-24 season, although they wouldn't enjoy much success in that either and would have to wait 57 years before first winning it.

The first English side to win away to Real Madrid

Nelson were the first English club to win away to Real Madrid. They achieved this on the Spanish tour they undertook just after winning the Division Three North title in 1923. The score of the match was 4-2, although they also played another match against Real on the same tour and lost it 4-1.

You could say they cancelled each other out

When Crystal Palace and Notts County met in the second round of the FA Cup in the 1923-24 season, the original match finished 0-0, the replay finished 0-0 and the second replay also finished 0-0. The third replay was finally won 2-1 by Palace.

Sam Wynne

In October 1923, Oldham beat Manchester United 3-2 with Sam Wynne scoring two of Oldham's goals and inadvertently scoring both of the Manchester United goals as well. This made Wynne, at the time, the only player to have scored twice for both sides in a Football League game, a record he still held three and a half years later when he became the first English professional footballer to die during a match he was taking part in. Wynne, by this time, was playing for Bury and collapsed as he was about to take a free-kick in a First Division match at Sheffield United. He was stretchered-off but died in the dressing room a few minutes later. The inquest gave the cause of death as pneumonia.

Tommy Ball

Tommy Ball was the first-choice centre-half for First Division Aston Villa when, in November 1923, he was shot dead by his neighbour and landlord the day after playing in Villa's 1-0 win at Notts County. Ball was 24 years-old at the time. His killer, George Stagg, went on to live for another 43 years, spending 40 of them in various mental institutions after being declared insane in 1926.

Arnold Birch

During the 1923-24 season, Chesterfield's regular penalty taker was their goalkeeper, Arnold Birch. He finished the season with five goals.

The unluckiest title miss

In 1923-24, Cardiff City missed out in the League title by 0.024 of a goal, which was the kind of bad luck peculiar to the days when goal average, rather than goal difference, was used to separate teams that were level on points. Cardiff would have won the title had they either put away the penalty they missed in the 70th minute of their final game, or had Huddersfield only won 2-0 instead of 3-0 on the same day, so this was really as close a miss as you could get.

The other three teams to be denied the title on goal average, were Wolves in 1949-50, Preston in 1952-53 and Leeds in 1964-65, although, unlike Cardiff, none of these would have won the League under today's rules. For anyone who doesn't know, goal average was calculated by dividing the number of goals scored by the number conceded.

The champions who only had five goalscorers

Huddersfield won the League title in 1923-24 despite the fact that only five of their players scored League goals over the course of the season. Their scorers were Tommy Wilson 18, Billy Smith 13, Clem Stephenson 11, George Cook 9 and George Brown 8, with one own goal also going in for them. There were six outfield players who played over 20 matches without scoring.

The only international worthy of Wembley

England's first ever match at Wembley was against Scotland in April 1924 and for the next 27 years England's matches against Scotland would be the only internationals played there.

Things ain't like they used to be

"I have been having a long look at the football of our own country, the country that invented the game. And I must confess I'm a disappointed man. All the old enthusiasm and energy are there, of course, plus a good deal more pace than there used to be, but I have no hesitation in saying that the finer points of the game, as we knew them in the '90s, are gradually disappearing". These words were spoken by the 19th century footballer Fred Spiksley in 1924. At the time Spiksley had just returned to Britain from a spell coaching abroad.

Fred Laycock

In March 1925, Fred Laycock was playing in a Third Division North match for Barrow against Rotherham when he left the field to sign for Nelson.

Hopeless from the spot

Northampton Town missed eight of the nine penalties they were awarded in the League during the 1924-25 season. They also missed the one they were awarded in the FA Cup.

The rise and fall of goals

It was in 1925 that the offside law was changed to make an attacking player offside if fewer than two defending players are between himself and the goal when the ball is played forward. Until then it had been fewer than three defending players, which meant there was no risk in playing the offside trap, as a team could leave a covering defender back deep behind the trap and he wouldn't be playing anyone onside.

This simple change in the law subsequently led to a big increase in the number of goals scored in matches with the average per game in the First Division shooting up from 2.58 in 1925-26 to 3.69 in 1925-26. The peak season for top-flight goals eventually came in 1930-31 when there was an average 3.95 per game. In this season more than one game in every eight at the highest level of English football produced seven goals or more and there were 17 that produced nine goals or more compared with only 12 that finished goalless.

The average number of goals in the top-flight remained over three per game until the late-60s, when, influenced by Alf Ramsey's 1966 World Cup winners, English teams dispensed with the attack-orientated WM and 4-2-4 formations and instead adopted the more cautious 4-3-3. Eventually, in 1970-71 the average number of First Division goals per game (2.36) fell below what it had been before the change in the offside law and that season remains the lowest-scoring top-flight season ever. In 1965-66 there had been 25 First Division matches that produced seven goals or more whereas in 1970-71 there were just six, and while there had only been 24 goalless draws in the First Division in 1965-66, the 70-71 season produced 47.

After the 1967-68 season, the average number of top-flight goals would never reach three again, although in 1981 the Football League tried to do something about teams playing for draws away from home by raising the amount of points awarded for a win from two to three. England was the first country to do this, although the rest of the world would soon follow. Ironically, however, the first English season under the three-points-for-a-win system, 1981-82, actually produced fewer top-flight goals than the previous season had, and even in the long run it wouldn't make a huge difference. As much as the media like to talk-up the entertainment value of the Premier League, it remains lower-scoring than the First Division was in the 1960s.

The worst away team ever

Over the eleven seasons they spent in the Football League from 1920–21, Merthyr Town won only 12 League away games out of a possible 231. Their worst years were the four seasons from 1922-23 to 1925-26 when they won only twice away from home, with the middle two seasons producing not a single away win between them. In fact, after winning 1-0 at Charlton in September 1922, they then went another three years before they next won away.

Dave Halliday

Dave Halliday scored ten goals in his first four games in English football. He joined Sunderland from Dundee for the start of the 1925-26 season and scored twice in his new club's 3-1 win at home to Birmingham on the opening day, which he then followed with another couple in their 6-2 win at home to Blackburn, before getting back-to-back hat-tricks in the 5-2 win at West Bromwich Albion and the 6-1 win at home to Sheffield United.

Bobby Gurney

Bobby Gurney scored nine goals on his debut for Sunderland Reserves in September 1925 but had to wait another seven months before being given his debut for the first-team. When that debut eventually came, so too did the first-team goals and he would go on to become Sunderland's all-time top scorer, an honour he still holds today.

Frank Osborne (Again)

Tottenham centre-forward Frank Osborne scored a hat-trick in each of three consecutive First Division matches in the autumn of 1925. The previous season Tottenham had only used Osborne as an outside-right and his record for that season had been 26 appearances and no goals.

Well, things started well enough

In a Third Division South match in January 1926, Bournemouth took a 2-0 lead at Swindon before going on to lose 8-2.

The highest scoring finalists

Northern Nomads beat Stockton 7-1 in the 1926 FA Amateur Cup Final. This remains the only time a team has scored seven in a national football final in England.

Tom Jennings

During the 1926-27 season, Leeds United's Tom Jennings scored hat-tricks in each of three consecutive games. He scored three in Leeds' 4-1 win at home to Arsenal on 25 September, then all four in their 4-2 win at Liverpool a week later, then all four again in the 4-1 win at home to Blackburn the week after that. Leeds then lost their next three matches 3-2, 3-1 and 4-1, with all the Leeds goals in those games being scored by Jennings as well and it was also Jennings who got the first of his side's goals in the following match at home to Sunderland, at which point he had scored 16 out of 17 consecutive Leeds goals. Jennings eventually finished the season with 35 goals in the League despite Leeds being relegated and only scoring 69 goals in total.

"Charlie Buchan has scored"

The Arsenal v Sheffield United match on 22 April 1927 was the first ever to be covered live on the radio, which makes Charlie Buchan's opening goal for Arsenal the first goal to be described in a live commentary.

George Camsell

In the 1926-27 season, the Middlesbrough centre-forward George Camsell scored 26 goals in a nine-match run. This included scoring four at home to Portsmouth on 8 November, four at home to

Fulham on 20 November, four at home to Swansea on 18 December and five away to Manchester City on Christmas Day. He went on to score 63 League and cup goals that season and hit ten hat-tricks, both of which are joint records for a national-level professional footballer. As well as his goalscoring exploits at club level, Camsell also has the best goalscoring record of any England player with 18 goals from just nine internationals.

The perennial nearly-men

Plymouth finished runners-up in Division Three South in each of six consecutive seasons between 1922 and 1927, at a time when only the champions went up.

Dixie Dean

In the 1926-27 season, Middlesbrough's George Camsell scored, what was then, a record 59 League goals. Everton's Dixie Dean then broke the record the following season – but only just. Dean got 60 but was only on 53 with two games remaining. He then scored four in the penultimate game at Burnley, before getting a hat-trick in the final game at home to Arsenal. Everton's biggest win of this season was 7-0 against West Ham, a game Dean didn't play in.

Taking a while to get going

In November 1927, Millwall beat Coventry 9-1 in a Division Three South match they were losing until the 43rd minute.

Supporting the boys

On 28 February 1928, a crowd of 10,275 attended Altrincham's Moss Lane ground to watch Altrincham Boys take on Sunderland

Boys in the English School's Shield. This was more than was at the First Division match between Bury and Notts County that was played on the same day.

Frank Womack

Full-back Frank Womack made 516 appearances for Birmingham in all competitions (a club record) but never scored a single goal for them. Add to this the 92 wartime games he played for Birmingham without scoring, and this gives him an overall record for the club of 608 appearances and no goals. He also failed to score in 20 appearances as player-manager for Torquay, but did bag a couple in the 43 he made as player-manager of Worcester City. These two Worcester goals save him from the distinction of having the worst goalscoring record of any English player who wasn't a goalkeeper, although the 510 appearances he made in the Football League still stands as the most by an outfield player who never scored.

When scoring goals was just fighting a losing battle

In March 1928, Aston Villa scored five times in a First Division match at Newcastle but were never in front and never equalised. Every goal they scored was a goal pulled back in a 7-5 defeat.

How many would they have got with a full team?

In the 1927-28 season, Abbey United (now Cambridge United) beat Godmanchester 14-1 in the Chatteris Engineering Works Cup, despite being down to ten men from the 15th minute.

Jimmy Cookson

Jimmy Cookson scored his 100th League goal in only his 89th League appearance. No player has ever reached a century of League goals quicker. Cookson scored 44 in 34 games for Chesterfield in 1925-26, 41 in 40 games for Chesterfield in 1926-27 and 38 in 38 games for West Bromwich Albion in 1927-28.

Huddersfield's depleted victors

On 31 March 1928, Huddersfield won a First Division match 3-2 at Bury despite having five of their first-team regulars missing as they were playing in the England v Scotland match that was taking place on the same day. Huddersfield's win was achieved with two goals from the second-string players brought in to replace the ones on international duty, with one of those scorers being George Wilson who had never played for the club before and never would again.

The tightest top-flight season

At the end of the 1927-28 season, all 22 clubs in the First Division were separated by just 16 points, and no fewer than eleven of them could still be relegated going into the season's final day. Such was the tightness of the division, that when Derby and Middlesbrough met on the penultimate Saturday, only five points separated them, and yet Derby ended up finishing fourth, while Middlesbrough finished bottom.

Argonauts

Argonauts are the only club ever to have had Wembley Stadium as a permanent home ground, although they never actually played there. The club formed in 1928 with the aim of becoming the new

Corinthian, in that they were to be comprised of the best amateur players in the country. The FA supported the idea and agreed to them using Wembley for their home games and, with this solid foundation, they immediately applied to join the Football League before they had even put a squad together. The application only just failed to gain the required number of votes and another application the following year also came close, but their third application in 1930 received no votes at all, after which the plan was knocked on the head, thus leaving Argonauts as probably the only football club never to have had a team or played a match.

Jimmy Shankly

Jimmy Shankly made his debut for Southend on the opening day of the 1928-29 season and went on to score 15 of the club's first 19 goals of the campaign. Shankly was the older brother of the future Liverpool manager Bill Shankly, and eventually ended up with 100 goals for Southend scored over five seasons, although he was apparently never popular with the fans.

Jim Barrett

West Ham's Jim Barrett reputedly only ever had one touch of the ball in international football. It came in (obviously) his only match for England, against Ireland at Goodison Park in October 1928, a match that saw Barrett stretchered off after eight minutes.

Ted Bowen

In the 1928-29 season, Northampton's Ted Bowen scored 34 goals in 39 League appearances without getting any hat-tricks. He scored twice in a match nine times.

Wembley Stadium – the home of Ealing Association FC

Ealing Association of the Southern Amateur League played eight home matches at Wembley Stadium between September and December 1928. The arrangement had come about simply because Ealing's club president had suggested it to the Wembley officials and they thought it was a good idea. Ealing would remain the club with the most Wembley appearances until Arsenal equalled it in 1969.

Frank Moss

Frank Moss made over 300 appearances for Aston Villa, Cardiff and England between the end of the First World War and the end of the 1920s, and reputedly wore the same pair of second-hand boots in all of them.

Jack Allen

Sheffield Wednesday's Jack Allen scored a brace in six out of seven consecutive games during the 1928-29 season. He then scored another two braces in the five games that followed.

Albert Whitehurst

In March 1929, Bradford City had back-to-back 8-0 wins in the space of three days, with Albert Whitehurst – who had only signed for the club a few weeks earlier – scoring seven in the first match and four in the second. Whitehurst would finish Bradford's top scorer that season with 24 goals, despite only playing in their final 15 games.

The biggest goal difference

The biggest goal difference ever achieved in the Football League was plus 85 by Bradford City in Division Three North in the 1928-29 season. This owed a lot to their phenomenal run-in that saw them score 46 times and concede just three in their last 12 games. Despite this, they didn't clinch the title until their final match.

Worst team – best defence

Cardiff had the best defensive record in the First Division in the 1928-29 season, but still finished bottom.

Edgar Kail

Edgar Kail was the last player to play for the senior England side but never for a professional club. Kail was an amateur player with Dulwich Hamlet in the Isthmian League when he appeared in all three of the matches England played on their European tour of May 1929. Before the First World War, it wasn't uncommon for non-League players to play for England, but Kail was one of only two such players to do so during the inter-war years (Corinthian's Jackie Hegan being the other).

England – kings of Europe

England won 21 of the first 22 matches they played in mainland Europe between 1908 and 1929, with half of the victories being by a four-goal margin or more. The only one of the 22 they didn't win was against Belgium in Antwerp in 1923 which finished 2-2.

Practice Matches

From the 19th century to the 1920s, teams often prepared for a new season by playing 'practice matches' that pitted one set of players from their squad against another set. These games were played at the club's home ground, were advertised to the public and often attracted thousands of spectators.

Centre-halves don't exist anymore... and nor do inside-forwards

Centre-halves disappeared from English football in the 1920s when they were replaced by centre-backs, which until then didn't exist in the game. Teams withdrew the centre-half into a defensive position between the two full-backs, and then filled the gap this left in midfield by having the inside-forwards drop deeper. This meant that, over the years, the term 'inside-forward' became a rather nebulous one that could apply to either an attacking midfielder or a striker, although many inside-forwards were a bit of both. We finally stopped calling midfielders and strikers 'inside-forwards' in the 1970s, although the term 'centre-half' never went away and centre-backs are still commonly referred to as 'centre-halves' today (and usually by people who have no idea what a real centre-half was).

Ralph Birkett

When Torquay beat Bournemouth 7-0 in March 1930, all seven goals were created by Torquay's left-winger Ralph Birkett who was a 17-year-old making his senior debut.

The most controversial FA Cup semi-final

The 1930 FA Cup semi-final between Huddersfield and Sheffield Wednesday perhaps stands as the most controversial ever. Huddersfield won 2-1 but Alex Jackson scored their equaliser after the ball had seemingly been punched to him by teammate Wilf Lewis. Jackson initially stopped believing Lewis had conceded a free-kick, before shooting and scoring once he realised the ref hadn't given it. If this was controversial enough, then it was nothing compared with what happened at the end. Wednesday's Jack Allen thought he had levelled it at 2-2 only for his effort to be disallowed because the ref had apparently blown for full-time between Allen unleashing the shot and the ball beating the keeper. What's more, according to Wednesday officials, this happened in the 88th minute so the ref shouldn't have been blowing for time anyway.

Alex Jackson

When Huddersfield reached the 1930 FA Cup Final, nine of the eleven goals they scored to get there came from their outside-right, Alex Jackson. Jackson scored all three in the 3-1 win over Bury in the third round, both goals in the 2-1 over Sheffield United in the fourth round, the winner in the 2-1 over Bradford City in the fifth round, the winner in the 2-1 win at Aston Villa in the sixth round and both goals in the 2-1 win over Sheffield Wednesday in the semi-final. Jackson only scored eight in 30 appearances in the League that season.

Two 7-5s in the same season

Blackburn had two 7-5 victories in the First Division in 1929-30. They beat Birmingham 7-5 at home in September, and then Sheffield United 7-5 away in March.

Brentford – the unstoppable (although only at home)

Brentford won all 21 of their home games in Division Three South in the 1929-30 season, but still missed out on promotion by seven points. This was a time when only the champions went up, and Plymouth won 18 of their home games, plus another 12 away. Brentford only won seven away, and so finished runners-up.

Dave Halliday (Again)

Arsenal's Dave Halliday scored four times away to Leicester in a First Division match in April 1930, but Arsenal dropped him for the FA Cup Final five days later and he never played for them again.

The Graf Zeppelin Final

Probably the biggest incident of the 1930 FA Cup Final between Arsenal and Huddersfield didn't happen on the pitch, but in the sky above it. For it was during the second half of the match that the giant German airship the Graf Zeppelin sailed low over the stadium on its way from Friedrichshafen to the airship site at Cardington. The Zeppelin was roughly seven times the length of the Wembley pitch and the film and photographs of it above the players and spectators still look pretty amazing today. The next morning a photograph of it above the stadium dominated the front page of *The Sunday Pictorial*.

The ultimate free-scoring champions

When Worcester City won the Birmingham League in 1929-30, they scored 153 goals in only 34 games. This gave them an average of 4.5

goals per game which may well be the highest by any club in senior football in a season of more than 30 matches. The club's high goal count came largely thanks to their storming home form which saw them win all of the 17 matches they played at their St George's Lane ground, with the 17 scorelines being as follows: 5-1, 5-1, 9-2, 4-1, 8-3, 6-1, 7-0, 13-1, 7-1, 9-0, 7-1, 3-1, 7-0, 2-0, 12-1, 2-0, 7-1.

The clubs four leading scorers on league goals alone this season (and remember only 34 games were played) were Billy Boswell with 41, John Russell with 34, Jack Byers (who was a winger) with 31 and Bobby Kerr with 22. Between them these four scored 16 hat-tricks in the league and 17 in all competitions. Sadly, Byers died the following year.

Pongo Waring

Aston Villa's Pongo Waring scored nine goals in the first three games of the 1930-31 season. He scored all four in a 4-0 win at Manchester United on the opening day, then scored the opener in a 2-0 win at home to Sheffield Wednesday two days later, before hitting another four in a 6-1 win at home to West Ham on the season's second Saturday.

Orient at Wembley

The Division Three South matches between Clapton Orient and Brentford on 22 November 1930 and Clapton Orient and Southend on 6 December 1930 were both played at Wembley due to Orient's Lea Bridge ground being closed for alterations. Fewer than 2,000 spectators turned-up for the Southend game.

Syd Dickenson

In January 1931, Bradford Park Avenue's Syd Dickenson scored twice direct from corners in a Second Division match against Burnley.

Manchester United's worst top-flight season

Manchester United lost all of their first 12 First Division matches of the 1930-31 season and didn't pick up their first away point until March. Their average home gate for the season was less than that of Third Division Crystal Palace, with fewer than 4,000 showing up to Old Trafford to watch their 4-4 draw with Middlesbrough on the season's final Saturday.

Jimmy Dunne

Sheffield United's Jimmy Dunne scored 41 top-flight goals in the 1930-31 season, despite United only finishing 15th in the table and scoring only 78 goals in total. Dunne scored in all but one of the club's 14 League victories that season and got a hat-trick in five of them. He also got a hat-trick in their only FA Cup win. Despite all this, he didn't finish the season as the First Division's top scorer as Aston Villa's Pongo Waring got 49.

1930-31's unique distinction

The highest number of goals scored by a team in a top-flight season in England is 128 by Aston Villa in 1930-31. The second highest is 127 by Arsenal the same season. When the two teams met each other that season, Arsenal won 5-2 at Highbury and Villa won 5-1 at Villa Park.

The title comes south at last

The Football League was founded in 1888, but it wasn't until 43 years later that it was first won by a southern club. Arsenal were the first southern champions in 1931, and they would win the title again 1933, '34, '35 and '38.

The unstoppable Arsenal trio

Jack Lambert and David Jack both scored over 30 League goals for Arsenal in the 1930-31 season, while the club's third highest scorer, Cliff Bastin, got 28 from the left-wing.

Ginger Richardson

West Bromwich Albion's Ginger Richardson scored in the fifth, seventh, eighth and ninth minutes of a First Division match at West Ham in November 1931, but never scored again after that.

The most boring match ever?

The First Division match between Newcastle and Portsmouth on 5 December 1931, not only didn't produce any goals, it didn't produce any corners either.

The magnificent seven

Ten players scored for Tranmere Rovers in the League in the 1931–32 season, and seven of them got into double-figures.

The worst team ever?

In the 1931-32 season, Rochdale lost 33 of their 40 matches in Division Three North, which included all of their last 13 home games and every single away game aside from the one at New Brighton in March which they drew 1-1. They also lost their only cup game.

The doomed Thames and their giant ground

During the 1930-31 and 1931-32 seasons, the worst supported club in the Football League was a club that played its home games at the largest sports stadium England has ever had. The club was Thames (originally called Thames Association), and their ground was the West Ham Stadium in east London which was also used for speedway and greyhound racing and had a capacity of 120,000.

It was shortly after the stadium was built in 1928 that Thames came into existence and they immediately joined the Southern League before being voted into the Football League two years later. In the summer leading up to their first season as a League club they made no fewer than 17 new signings but, with no history and all of London's football fans already supporting someone else, they had little chance of drawing the crowds to their massive home. Their average home gate in that first season was just 2,315, although they only got 469 for the game against Luton in December. By contrast, the speedway meetings at the ground were averaging 25,000.

Still, the new team did okay on their own patch, winning over half of their home games. The only trouble was they lost all but three of the away ones and so ended up finishing third from bottom. The following season the crowds were up slightly but the performances were down and they finished bottom and in dire straits financially. They initially applied for re-election to the Football League, but then withdrew the application and announced that they were folding. This was in June 1932, just four years after they were formed. Along with New Brighton Tower, they are the joint-shortest lived club ever to have played in the Football League. The West Ham Stadium carried on in their absence, with the speedway and dog racing continuing until the place was eventually demolished in 1972.

Sonny Gibbon and Syd Gibbons

Over the 1930-31 and 1931-32 season, Fulham fielded 61 line-ups that featured both Sonny Gibbon and Syd Gibbons in defence.

The longest scoring rolls

The player who holds the record for scoring in the most consecutive top-flight matches in England is Jimmy Dunne who scored in 12 in a row for Sheffield United during the 1931-32 season. This is also a joint record across all the top four divisions of professional football in England, along with Dixie Dean's 12 consecutive scoring games for Everton in the Second Division in 1930-31 and Bill Pendergast's 12 in a row for Chester in the Third Division North in 1938-39. It's Pendergast, however, who holds the record for most consecutive competitive games scored in by a Football League player as during his League run, he also scored in an FA Cup tie.

Many internet sources have claimed that Blackpool's Stan Mortenson scored in 15 consecutive matches in the 1950-51 season, but he didn't. It was only eleven. It was also claimed in the 1973-74 *Rothmans Football Yearbook* that Leicester's Arthur Chandler scored in each of 16 consecutive Division Two games in 1924-25, but this was also wrong, and wrong by some distance (the best he managed was seven in a row), but was probably accepted as a fact for years by everyone who read it, as in those days there was no way of double-checking such things.

Alex Jackson (again)

Scottish winger Alex Jackson won a League title with Huddersfield in 1926 when he was 21, scored a hat-trick against England at Wembley in 1928 when he was 23 and was the subject of a big-money move to Chelsea in 1930 when he was 25. Then, in 1932, when he was still only 27, Jackson signed for Ashton National in the Cheshire League.

Jackson had left Chelsea over a dispute with the club's directors, and despite Ashton's lowly status, he was actually the highest paid player in the country while he was with them, as there was a wage-cap for Football League players at the time but not for non-League ones. Ashton's reasoning was that, because Jackson was a talented crowd-puller, the crowds would flock to see him and so this would more than pay for his wages. But it didn't work out that way. Jackson's presence in the Ashton team did initially draw the crowds, but he was a largely ineffective player in the Cheshire League as he always had several players on him every time he got the ball. Consequently, the crowds soon dwindled as people quickly got bored with the sight of Jackson getting marked out of the game every week. He eventually left Ashton National by mutual consent in February 1933, but there was no way back into the Football League for him as he was still registered with Chelsea and so, under the rules of the time, couldn't sign for anyone else, and playing for Chelsea again wasn't an option either. He, therefore, remained in non-League football and joined Margate in the Kent League, although even there he was still on more money than any of the players at big clubs.

It's too cold to play football

When Workington played Whitehaven Athletic in the FA Cup in 1932, the weather was far too cold for the Whitehaven players to bear and one-by-one they began going off to get out of it. The match was eventually abandoned in the 70th minute by which time Whitehaven were 10-0 down and only had one player left on the field.

... And Too Wet

Chelsea finished with only six players on the field when they visited Blackpool for a First Division match in October 1932. One went off injured at half-time, and the other four walked off during the second half in protest at the game continuing on a pitch that they believed to be waterlogged. Blackpool won 4-0, although the first three goals were scored against eleven men.

Stewart Littlewood

Port Vale's Stewart Littlewood scored six goals in the first 57 minutes of a Second Division match against Chesterfield in September 1932, but then suffered an injury in the next game that kept him out for over four months.

Pat Glover

In October 1932, Grimsby's Pat Glover scored four times in the first 13 minutes of a Second Division match against Preston and still didn't finish on the winning side. The final score was 5-5.

Blitzing Through the Qualifying Rounds

Brighton won 12-0, 7-1, 9-0 and 4-0 in successive qualifying rounds of the FA Cup in the 1932-33 season.

Bet that wouldn't have happened at Halifax

In December 1932, Arsenal's newly built West Stand was officially opened by the Prince of Wales.

Syd King

Syd King was West Ham's manager (although he had the official title of 'secretary') for 30 years between 1902 and 1932 and became the first manager to take them into the First Division and to an FA Cup Final (the famous first Wembley final of 1923). He was eventually given shares in the club but had a falling out with the other board members who initially suspended him and then sacked him. He committed suicide six weeks after his dismissal.

Sort that defence out

Grimsby had a 6-5 win and two 5-5 draws in the space of nine months between April 1932 and January 1933.

Tommy Black

Tommy Black made his debut for Arsenal in an FA Cup tie at Third Division Walsall in January 1933 and it went so badly that Arsenal manager Herbert Chapman transferred him to Plymouth a few days later. Walsall won 2-0 and Black had needlessly given away the penalty for their second goal.

Perhaps they should have made it all-ticket

When Derby played an FA Cup replay at Sunderland in 1933, four train loads of Derby fans were around 130 miles into their journey to the match when the trains were stopped and turned around because the ground was already full.

Lost 4-1 again

Preston suffered four 4-1 defeats in a five-game run during the 1932-33 season.

Jack Bowers

Jack Bowers was the scorer of 12 consecutive Derby County goals during the second half of the 1932-33 season. He also scored 13 of Derby's first 16 goals of the following season.

Herbert Chapman (again)

Herbert Chapman was arguably the first football manager who was a tactician as well as a boss, and he remains the only manager of this kind to have won more than one League title at each of two different clubs.

His Northampton Town side that had won the Southern League by a 16-point margin in 1908-09 was the first ever to use the tactic of absorbing pressure before counter-attacking, while at Huddersfield in the 1920s, he became the first manager to have his wingers repeatedly pass inside rather just bomb down the flanks. Chapman's Huddersfield used to also be credited as the first team to use a centre-half as an extra central defender, but it's since been discovered he was only one of the first, although he may have come up with the idea independently. Huddersfield had never played in the top-flight before the 1920-21 season, but under Chapman they won the League title in both 1923-24 and 1924-25, and largely the same group of players won it again in 1925-26. By then, Chapman was no longer at the club as he had taken the Arsenal job in the summer of 1925, and it was Arsenal who finished runners-up behind Huddersfield that season. This meant that the team Chapman had built and the team he was now in charge of had finished in the top two positions of the Football League.

When Chapman arrived at Arsenal, the club had never won any major silverware, but by the time he died in office in January 1934, they had won the FA Cup and twice been League Champions. They were then on course for a third League title under Chapman in four years, when Chapman's life was suddenly ended by pneumonia with 19 games of the season remaining. He was 55 years old.

As well as the trophies he brought them, Chapman was also responsible for getting London Transport to change the name of their local tube station from 'Gillespie Road' to 'Arsenal' and changing the club's shirts from all red to red with white sleeves.

Cliff Bastin and Joe Hulme

The 33 goals scored by Arsenal's Cliff Bastin in the 1932-33 season remains the most ever scored by a winger in one season of national-level professional football in England. All of Bastin's 33 goals came in the League, as did the 20 Joe Hulme scored from the other wing in the same season. Hulme is also notable for scoring three hat-tricks from the wing that season (Bastin only scored one).

Who saw that coming?

When Newcastle hosted Liverpool on New Year's Day 1934, the score was 2-2 with half an hour left. It eventually finished 9-2 to Newcastle.

A crazy match in an obscure competition

The Football League Division Three South Cup was a short-lived cup competition that ran for just five seasons in the 1930s, but it did produce one of the craziest scorelines in football history when Exeter beat Crystal Palace 11-6 in the first round of the 1933-34 competition. 12 of the game's 17 goals came in the second half. Only 2,000 spectators were there to see it.

When Stockport couldn't stop scoring

In a Third Division North fixture in January 1934, Stockport County scored eight goals in a 16-minute spell against Halifax. They went on to win the game 13-0 which is the joint biggest ever win by one Football League side over another. The humiliated Halifax keeper, Stan Milton, was a 20-year-old making his senior debut.

Big wins for a poor side

In the 1933-34 season, Newcastle won 7-3 away to Everton on Boxing Day and 9-2 at home to Liverpool on New Year's Day, and yet still went on to be relegated at the end of the season.

Syd Gibbons

Fulham were trailing Southampton 3-0 at home in a Second Division match in November 1934, when, out of desperation, they moved central defender Syd Gibbons up into attack. This proved to be a highly effective ploy to say the least, as Fulham came back to get a 3-3 draw with all of their goals coming from Gibbons in a 20-minute spell.

Arsenal – world champions

Italy's first game after winning the 1934 World Cup was a 3-2 defeat to England at Highbury in November of that year. The Italian side that day featured nine of the players who had played in the World Cup Final, while the England team featured seven members of the Arsenal side that had drawn 2-2 at Grimsby four days earlier. England scored all of their goals and missed a penalty in the first

12 minutes, but the game became better remembered for the fact that Italy's tactics were dirtier than any seen in England at that time. It was said that most of the England players ended the game with some sort of injury, although the worst were suffered by Eddie Hapgood – who suffered a broken nose – Eric Brook, Ted Drake and Ray Bowden. It should be noted, however, that all four players were back in action for their clubs three days later and the only player who actually had to go off injured and then remained out injured for some time afterwards was Italy's Luis Monti.

After the match, Swedish referee Otto Olssen commented, "the Italians were very excitable. When they learn to control themselves, they will be a great side". A strange thing to say about World Champions.

Mirror-image victories

In March 1935, Nottingham Forest had back-to-back 5-0 wins in the Second Division with their scorers being Dent 3, Peacock 2 in both games.

Bob McGrory

Scottish full-back Bob McGrory made 514 League and cup appearances in English football between 1920 and 1935 but didn't score a single goal. This gives him the distinction of having the worst goalscoring record of any Football League player who wasn't a goalkeeper. All but three of his appearances were for Stoke.

Len Oliver

Len Oliver made 434 appearances in English professional football (all of them for Fulham) between 1924 and 1935 but only ever scored twice. This is probably the worst goalscoring record in the history of English professional football by a player who was neither a goalkeeper nor a defender. Oliver was a right-half.

The topsy-turvy Christmas of Oldham and Tranmere

On Christmas Day 1935, Oldham beat Tranmere 4-1 in a Division Three North match with Bill Walsh hitting a hat-trick. The two sides then met again the following day and again Oldham scored four with Walsh getting two of them, but this time it wasn't nearly enough as Tranmere beat them 13-4.

When no one bettered Southall in the FA Cup

The biggest win in the proper rounds of the 1935-36 FA Cup was by the Athenian League amateurs Southall, who beat Newport (Isle of Wight) 8-0 in the second round. They then lost to Watford in the third round and have never played in the proper rounds of the FA Cup since.

The season the scoring records tumbled

The 1935-36 Football League season was a unique one in that it saw most-goals-in-a-game-by-one-player records broken on three separate occasions. On 14 December, Arsenal's Ted Drake set a new record for most goals in a top-flight match when he got all seven in his side's 7-1 win at Aston Villa. Then, just 12 days later, Tranmere's Bunny Bell set a new Football League record by scoring nine in his side's aforementioned 13-4 Division Three North victory over Oldham. Bell, in fact, should have had ten that day as he also missed a penalty, and it was that penalty miss that ultimately led to his record being surpassed five months later when Luton's Joe Payne got ten in a 12-0 Second Division win against Bristol Rovers (see below).

Unsurprisingly, Drake's seven and Payne's ten are still records today, while Bell's nine is still the second highest in League history. Drake, incidentally, was unlucky not to get eight as he had another effort in the match at Villa that hit the underside of the bar.

Joe Payne

In April 1936, Joe Payne scored ten goals in Luton Town's 12-0 win over Bristol Rovers. These were the first ten goals of Payne's professional career in what was his first match playing up front, having previously only been used as a half-back. Payne would score a further 61 times in his next 47 matches, thus giving him a total of 71 goals from his first 48 appearances as a forward. As previously mentioned, the ten goals he got against Bristol Rovers are the most ever scored by a League player in England.

Payne's League career started relatively late – he was nearly 21 when he made his debut – and was then interrupted by the Second World War. As a result, he would only ever make 118 League appearances.

Mid-30s fatalities

Sunderland won the League title in 1935-36, despite their first-choice goalkeeper, Jimmy Thorpe, dying suddenly in the February of that season. This came two years after Arsenal had won the title a few months after the death of their manager, Herbert Chapman. Chapman had died from pneumonia brought on by watching too many games in bad weather when he wasn't well, while Thorpe's death was caused by a combination of his diabetes and the injuries he suffered in his final game against Chelsea when Chelsea players had kicked him after he had collected the ball. In between the deaths of Chapman and Thorpe, Gillingham's Simeon Raleigh had also died, suffering a fatal brain haemorrhage hours after sustaining a head injury in a Division Three South fixture against Brighton.

Louis Cardwell

Louis Cardwell scored five times in ten games for Blackpool in the 1935-36 season, but only scored one other goal in his 199 appearances in the Football League.

Bill Harvey

The 1935-36 season was Bill Harvey's only season at Chesterfield. While there he was playing under a manager who was also called Bill Harvey but was no relation.

Jack Bowers (again)

In September 1936, Manchester United were 4-1 up at Derby with 26 minutes left, but ended up losing 5-4 after Derby's Jack Bowers came to life and hit four goals in 15 minutes. This was a First Division match, and yet just two months later, Derby sold Bowers to Second Division Leicester.

Jimmy Harbot

Jimmy Harbot's only ever game for Stoke was in the club's record victory – 10-3 against West Bromwich Albion in February 1937.

Here we go again – and again

Scarborough v Peterborough was an opening day fixture in each of three consecutive seasons in the Midland League in the 1930s.

Something which happened twice in the 1930s but never before and never since

In 1937, Millwall beat Manchester City 2-1 in the sixth round of the FA Cup. Millwall went on to finish eighth in Division Three South that season, while Manchester City won the League title. This makes Millwall the lowest placed side ever to knock the eventual League champions out of the FA Cup. The only other instance of the champions-elect losing to a third-tier side in the competition occurred four years earlier when Walsall of Division Three North beat Arsenal 2-0 in the third round. This was especially impressive considering Arsenal were the dominant force in English football during that period, winning the League title in four out of five consecutive seasons and finishing runners-up in the other.

Ted Harston

Mansfield's Ted Harston scored five or more in a match three times in the 1936-37 season. He scored five in the 6-2 win at home to Rochdale, five in the 7-1 win at home to Port Vale and seven in the 8-2 win at home to Hartlepools. He also scored four in the 5-2 win at home to Hull and hit four other hat-tricks that season. He ended the season with 55 goals in Division Three North, which is all the more remarkable considering Mansfield only finished ninth in the table and the rest of the squad only managed 37 goals between them. In League and Cup Harston scored 20 more than all of his teammates combined.

No one could have guessed it at the time, but this would prove to be Harston's last full season as a Football League player. In the summer he signed for Liverpool and scored on his debut for them and then grabbed another couple in his second match but only made three more appearances for the club after that. After being released by Liverpool, he moved south and spent two months as player-manager of Ramsgate Town before becoming player-manager of Shorts FC in the Kent League, although he was only in charge of them for one month before war broke out.

Freddie Steele

Stoke City centre-forward Freddie Steele scored seven goals in England's three-match tour of northern Europe in May 1937, but was never picked for the national side again after that.

The strange top-flight season of 1937-38

So why was it strange? Here are the facts:

Manchester City went into it as the reigning champions but finished it in the bottom two despite being the division's highest scorers and recording the biggest away win of any League club that season (7-1 at Derby). The Division's second-highest scorers were Everton who finished 14th. Preston, meanwhile, finished third but won fewer games than Huddersfield who only avoided relegation by three points. On the last day of the season, there were still eight clubs fighting to survive the drop, and somehow Birmingham managed it despite losing four more games over the season than each of the bottom two. West Bromwich Albion finished bottom but would have finished mid-table had they won their last two matches.

At the top end of the table, Wolves only won four of their final 14 games but still would have been champions had they beaten Sunderland in the last one. Wolves' failure came despite their players receiving regular injections of supposedly performance enhancing monkey-gland extract. The title eventually ended up with Arsenal who had only been eleventh in mid-November and, with two games to go, were just one point ahead of Brentford who finished sixth. Eddie Carr scored five goals in the last three games to get them over the line, which is another strange fact considering he only played 12 times for Arsenal in his entire career. As in the 1927-28 season, the top team and the bottom team were separated by just 16 points.

The TV cameras arrive

The first football match to be televised in Britain was Arsenal v Arsenal Reserves in September 1937, although this game was only played so as the BBC could trial the broadcast of a football match and only 15 minutes of it were shown. The first competitive match to be televised was England v Scotland at Wembley in April 1938 when the BBC's cameras captured England failing to score at home for the first time in 12 years. Scotland won 1-0 with Heart of Midlothian's Tommy Walker scoring the first ever goal to be shown on British television.

John Hutcheson

In January 1938, Third Division Ipswich held First Division Aston Villa to a 1-1 draw in the third round of the FA Cup before losing the replay 2-1 at home in front of a crowd of 28,194, which was a club record at the time. John Hutcheson played right-half for Ipswich in both of these matches (and scored in the first one), but they were his only ever appearances for the club as he was unable to play in the League owing to a compensation payment he had received whilst at Chelsea. The Football League had paid him the compensation after an injury had seemingly ended his career and they only agreed to pay it on the condition that he would never make a comeback into League football.

England and Nazi Germany

England played two friendlies against Germany while it was under Nazi rule, at Tottenham's White Hart Lane in December 1935 and in Berlin's Olympic Stadium in May 1938. At the first match at White Hart Lane, the swastika flag was flown and both the German team and the German supporters in the ground did the Nazi salute during the German national anthem. At the time, the Jews were already having their civil liberties removed in Germany, and Tottenham's Jewish community, as well as the TUC and the

Communist Party of Great Britain objected to the game being staged, but the English media largely welcomed it and the attendance of 54,164 was one of the biggest ever for an England midweek game at that time.

At the game in Berlin two and a half years later, 105,000 attended with high-ranking Nazis Hermann Goering, Joseph Goebbels and Rudolf Hess amongst them. This game is the more infamous of the two because of the Nazi salute the England players did during the German national anthem. They were asked do so as an act of courtesy to their hosts, and as bad as it looks today, it doesn't seem to have been especially controversial at the time. *Pathe News* reported it in typically chirpy fashion, while *The Sunday Pictorial* – the Sunday edition of the *Daily Mirror* – displayed a picture of it next to an equally chirpy caption that read "Heil! The English football team give the Nazi salute before they beat Germany by 6 goals to 3 yesterday". This was the only mention of the salute in the paper. The match report began "England's soccer team brought a big rubber to the great Olympic Stadium here to-day and erased a great deal of the stain left on our prestige by continental blots in recent years". The salute, apparently, wasn't seen as important and taken in the context of the time, it isn't hard to understand why. Before the War, neither the Nazi salute nor fascism were associated with genocide (the word didn't even exist in the 1930s), and just eleven days before the match in Berlin, Hitler's Ambassador to Britain had been welcomed to Buckingham Palace. There was also a big demonstration in London that year calling for appeasement with Hitler and, after Prime Minister Neville Chamberlain helped secure that appeasement, he was treated as a national hero, standing alongside the King and Queen on the balcony of the Palace to greet the huge crowds of Londoners who had come out to celebrate his 'achievement'. These were clearly innocent times, and the England players' Nazi salute, and the country's failure to see any harm in it, were both products of that innocence. The previous year a group of Plymouth dignitaries had also given the Nazi salute during the playing of the German national anthem for a visiting German motorcycle team – and few had seen the harm in that either.

Dixie Dean (again)

Dixie Dean holds four scoring records for a national-level professional in England. Most League goals in a season (60 for Everton in 1927-28), most goals for one club (377 for Everton 1925-1937), most hat-tricks in a career (39 for Tranmere and Everton 1924-36) and the joint record along with Jimmy Dunne and Bill Pendergast of most consecutive League games scored in (12 for Everton in 1930-31).

When 105,000 watched a pointless match

In May 1938, Aston Villa played in front of 105,000 spectators in Berlin, despite the game only being a friendly against a German Select Eleven comprised almost entirely of Austrians. Villa won the match 3-2.

When the definition of amateurism meant more to England than winning the World Cup

The British nations did not compete in the 1930, 1934 and 1938 World Cups because they were not members of FIFA in the 1930s. They had all joined FIFA in 1905 but then withdrew just before the 1928 Olympics after FIFA refused to recognise the British definition of amateurism. The Olympic football competition was supposed to be for amateur teams, but it was only the British who defined an amateur player as one who was receiving no payment at all. Because of this they refused to enter a team for the Olympics and then withdrew from FIFA and would not rejoin until 1946.

Shirt-numbering

Although shirt-numbering had been experimented with before, it wasn't until 1939 that the Football League made it compulsory for all outfield players to wear numbers on their shirts. The initial purpose of shirt-numbering was to indicate each player's position on the pitch, with the two full-backs wearing two and three, the two wing-halves wearing four and six, the nominal centre-half (who was really a centre-back) wearing five, the two wingers wearing seven and eleven, the two inside-forwards wearing eight and ten, and the centre-forward wearing nine.

After changing ideas on team-formations rendered all of these playing positions obsolete around the mid-1960s, the numbering systems started to vary from team to team, but in the 4-4-2 formation that eventually became the norm, it was customary to have the two wide defenders wearing two and three, the two central defenders wearing five and six, one of the central midfielders wearing four, the two wide midfielders or wingers wearing seven and eleven and one of the forwards wearing nine. Eight could either be a central midfielder or a forward, as could ten. Much of the old terminology, however, survived the game's formation developments, so wide defenders continued to be called 'full-backs' even though there were no longer half-backs, central-defenders continued to be called 'centre-halves' even though there were no longer right-halves and left-halves and some forwards could still be called 'centre-forwards' if they resembled the old centre-forwards in their physical build and ability. A big forward who headed the ball a lot would therefore be referred to as a 'centre-forward', whereas a small forward who wasn't a threat in the air wouldn't be even though they both played in the same position.

Dave Mason

Dave Mason only ever made six appearances in the Football League but still managed to score all of Darlington's last five goals of the 1938-39 season.

Goals with no scorers

Before the Second World War, there were a total of 129 goals scored in the Football League for which no goalscorer was given. This was largely due to the game's early years containing 'scrimmages', with a scrimmage being a messy, scrum-like tussling for the ball by many players at the same time. Sometimes a scrimmage in front of goal would finish with the ball being forced over the line, and when this happened a goal would be given but no scorer would be named. The Royal Engineers' goal in the 1878 FA Cup Final was scored in this way and so had no credited goalscorer.

Cigarette cards

Footballer-themed cigarette cards were produced for 43 years between 1896 and 1939, and during those years provided the British public with more pictures of footballers than any newspapers or periodicals did, as well as being the best source of biographical information on footballers. Cigarette cards were collectable stiffening cards found inside cigarette packets that carried a picture on one side and text relating to the picture on the other, with each one being part of a set. Seeing as around two-thirds of British men smoked before the War, then a very large chunk of the population would have had them in their homes. They ceased being produced at the beginning of 1940 due to Wartime paper-saving measures and never reappeared after the War.

A new-look side that disappeared as quickly as it arrived

No fewer than seven players made their debuts for Darlington on the opening day of the 1939-40 season and all played their final game for the club just one week later due to the season being abandoned following the declaration of war.

Ray Bowden

Newcastle's Ray Bowden scored a hat-trick in his last ever appearance in professional football. It came in an 8-1 victory over Swansea on 2 September 1939, which was the last day of League football before the season was abandoned due to the outbreak of the Second World War and Bowden never resumed his career after the War.

Bolton at war

A few weeks after Germany's invasion of the Bohemia and Moravia regions of Czechoslovakia in March 1939, the Bolton Wanderers captain Harry Goslin took to the pitch before a home game against Sunderland and told the supporters that all the players would be enlisting for military service after the match. In fact, only six of the players on the field that day did, but they were joined by other members of the club's playing staff and the following year eleven of the players used by Bolton in the 1938-39 season, plus three of the club's reserves, were involved in the evacuation of Dunkirk. All then went on to serve together in North Africa and Italy and it was while in Italy that Harry Goslin was sadly killed in action.

When scoring bucket-loads of goals at the highest level didn't earn you many caps

During the 1920s and '30s, Blackburn's Ted Harper, Sunderland's Dave Halliday, West Ham's Vic Watson, Aston Villa's Pongo Waring and Arsenal's Ted Drake all achieved the rare feat of scoring over 40 top-flight goals in a season, and yet they finished their careers with only 16 caps between them. Watson, Waring and Drake won five each for England, Harper just the one for England despite his 43 goals in 1925-26 being a top-flight record at the time, while the Scotsman Halliday wasn't capped at all. Derby's Jack Bowers never scored 40 in a season, but he was the top-flight's top scorer two seasons running in the 1930s with 35 and 34, and yet he too won only five caps for England, while West Bromwich Albion's Ginger Richardson won only one despite topping the First Division scoring lists with an impressive 39 in 1935-36. As for Sheffield Wednesday's Jimmy Trotter, he finished as the top-flight's top scorer with 37 in 1926-27 but went on to finish his career without a single international appearance to his name.

The most capped centre-forward of the inter-War years was Everton's Dixie Dean who played 16 times for England, but all but three of those appearances came in consecutive games over a two-year period. Outside of that period he too was largely unwanted by his country despite scoring 60 top-flight goals in 1927-28 and 45 in 1931-32. The second most international appearances by an England centre-forward between the wars was nine by Middlesbrough's George Camsell, although it's hard to understand why he only made the nine when he scored in all of them, scored a hat-trick in two of them and got a brace in four others (one of which was against Nazi Germany).

Probably the reason so many big-scoring centre-forwards had such limited international careers between the wars was simply that there were too many of them and they ended up keeping each other out of the England side. Manchester City's Fred Tilson wasn't one of them – he only scored 18 in his best season for League goals – and yet had England played in the 1934 World Cup (the first one played in Europe and to be contested mainly between European teams) then they may well have done so with Tilson in the centre-forward position. Tilson had only scored 12 League goals in the 1933-34 season when he had played mainly as an inside-forward, but he had switched to centre-forward late in the campaign and had scored four goals in the FA Cup semi-final and then two in the final, leading to him being selected as centre-forward for England's away games in Hungary and Czechoslovakia in the May of that year. It would certainly have been ironic if, in an age of high-scoring centre-forwards, it had been the relatively low-scoring Tilson who had been the first ever player to wear the number nine shirt for England at a World Cup.

Gilbert Alsop

Walsall's Gilbert Alsop scored four hat-tricks in a run of five Division Three South matches over 17 days in April 1939. In two of those matches he scored four and in the only one in which he didn't score a hat-trick, he scored twice. He was, therefore, only one goal away from scoring a hat-trick in each of five consecutive matches.

Tommy Lawton

Tommy Lawton finished as the top-flight's top scorer in both the 1937-38 and 1938-39 seasons, despite being only 17 when the first of these seasons began. The 34 League goals he scored in '38-39 remains a top-flight record for a teenager. Lawton then scored four in the first three games of 1939-40 season, after which war broke out and he would not play another match in the Football League until he was nearly 27.

Wartime football

Football carried on during both the First and Second World Wars, but it was a huge deviation from the football of peacetime. During both wars, the clubs of the Football League were split into regional leagues and, with many players unavailable due to military service, it was common for clubs to field guest players from other clubs in order to make up the numbers. Military service also took away most supporters of fighting age as well, which made matches poorly attended, resulting in big-name players playing for big clubs in front of vast expanses of empty terracing. On 30 November 1940, Manchester United v Liverpool and Arsenal v Crystal Palace both drew crowds of less than 800, and the previous month only 500 had watched Charlton take on Tottenham.

As for the league tables during the War years, the ones from the First World War do make some sort of sense, but not so the ones from the second, which now look utterly alien and almost incomprehensible. In the 1940-41 season, the league positions in both the North Regional and South Regional were determined on goal average rather than points as it was thought separating teams on points was unfair when there was no way they could all play the same amount of games. This was actually reasonable enough considering the huge disparity in games played by the end of the season, with Stoke, for example, having played 36 matches in the South Regional, whilst Coventry played only ten. Leicester, meanwhile, played 33 and finished 14th with a goal average of 1.91, but if points had been awarded for wins and draws, then they would have finished top.

The Following season, 16 clubs from the South Regional broke away from the Football League to form the London League, while the North Regional had its name changed to the 'Football League Northern' and had its season divided into two. This meant that the league was concluded on Christmas Day and then restarted from scratch two days later. The Football League North – as it subsequently became known – would continue to be contested twice in the same season up to and including 1944-45 and would always contain more teams in the second half of the season as this was when it was joined by clubs from the West League. Looking at the strange table from 1942-43, we see that there were 54 teams in the Football League North (2nd) but that none played more than 20 games and Mansfield only played ten. Even stranger was the fact that, while Liverpool finished top and Manchester City, Aston Villa, Sheffield Wednesday and Manchester United finished third, fourth, fifth and sixth respectively, the team that finished second were Lovells Athletic, a small Welsh club named after the man who founded them. On the face of it, it appears an unbelievable achievement by Lovells, but all was far from how it seemed. For Lovells never actually played any of those big clubs they occupied the top end of the table with. In fact, they never played any clubs at all besides Bath City, Bristol City, Cardiff, Swansea and Aberaman. This was because, in order to avoid travelling long distances, the teams in the Football League North were divided into small groups and never played clubs from outside the group they belonged to. This was how the following season's Football League North (2nd) was won by Bath City who finished seven points ahead of Manchester

United and 22 points ahead of Wolves. The strangeness of that table is made stranger still by the fact that Bath is, of course, in Somerset and further south than the geographical locations of most of the clubs that played in the Football League South that season.

As well as the regional leagues, the War years also brought us the Football League War Cup North and the Football League War Cup South, which were played under very different formats from each other, even if their names suggest otherwise. The War Cup North was a straight knockout competition contested during the Football League North's second championship between the teams that had finished highest in the first championship, plus the six teams that had joined the second championship from the West League. The War Cup South, meanwhile, saw the teams from the Football League South split into four mini-leagues with the winner of each progressing to the semi-finals. Aside from its qualification criteria, the War Cup North was the more conventional cup competition of the two, but it did have one truly bizarre aspect to it in that the matches played in it also counted as league games, with results achieved or suffered in the cup being added to the clubs' league totals. This made the War years the only period in English football history when the same team could win a league game and a cup game with the same players in the same 90 minutes.

The War Cup North was eventually decided with a final played over two legs, but because nothing was straightforward in Wartime football, the South Final had an entirely different kind of climax, taking the form of a one-off showpiece final at Wembley. In 1944, the South Final drew a crowd of 85,000 – a record for a Wartime match – and concluded with Charlton captain Don Welsh being presented with the cup by the Supreme Commander of the Allied Forces, and future US President, Dwight D. Eisenhower.

The end of the War in Europe came before the end of the 1944-45 season, but it didn't bring about an end to bewildering football formats, as the Wartime leagues carried on into the following season. The 1945-46 season, however, did see the return of the FA Cup, although it wasn't like any FA Cup competition before or since, as all the ties from the first round to the sixth were two-legged. The sixth round, second-leg match between Bolton and Stoke that year attracted an official crowd of 65,419, but it's been estimated that around 85,000 were really in the ground that day and 33 were killed in the crush less than year after the VE Day celebrations.

Leslie Compton

In February 1941, Arsenal beat Clapton Orient 15-2 in the London War Cup with Leslie Compton scoring ten of their goals. This was twice as many as Compton scored in 253 League games for Arsenal as he played as a full-back before the War and then as a centre-half in the post-war years.

The (seemingly) eternal match

When Cardiff hosted Bristol City in the second round, second leg of the League War Cup North in April 1943, the aggregate score was 3-3 after 90 minutes and still 3-3 after the brief ten-minute extra-time period. In such a situation, the rule was that the next goal wins it and so the teams should play on until someone scores. This they did, but it took another hour and 42 minutes before the goal finally came, thus bringing the duration of the match up to a seriously endurance-testing three hours and 22 minutes. Cardiff's Billy Rees eventually hit the 202nd-minute winner. More than 23,000 spectators were late home for tea.

Jock Dodds

Jock Dodds scored 238 goals in just 176 appearances for Blackpool, but only 13 of those goals are officially recognised as the other 225 were scored in Wartime matches. Amongst Dodds' Wartime scoring feats are hitting seven in an 11-2 win against Oldham in 1940, eight in a 9-2 win against Stockport in 1941 and getting 12 in two games – seven in a 15-3 win against Tranmere, then five in a 13-0 win against Burnley – in 1942.

The friendly everyone wanted to see

In November 1945, Chelsea got a crowd of 74,496 for a friendly against Dynamo Moscow despite the game being played on a Tuesday afternoon. It remains officially the eighth highest attendance in Chelsea's history, although if you count all the people who got in illegally then it may be their best attended game ever.

Bernard Joy

Bernard Joy was never a professional footballer, but he did make 86 top-flight appearances for Arsenal on an amateur contract between 1935 and 1946, which included 28 during the Gunners' title-winning season of 1937-38. Joy was also the last amateur to play for the senior England side, making one appearance against Belgium in Brussels in 1936.

Bert Turner

In the 1946 FA Cup Final, Bert Turner equalised for Charlton just 30 seconds after giving Derby an 85th minute lead with an own goal. These were the first two goals of the game and, due to the break for War, also the first two goals in an FA Cup Final for seven years. Derby went on to win the match 4-1 after extra-time.

Dennis Westcott

No striker picked up from where he left off after the end of the Second World War as well as Wolves' Dennis Westcott did. Westcott scored 43 goals in the last season before the War and 39 in the first season after it.

A Cup win at last

Rochdale's 6-1 win against Bishop Auckland in the first round of the FA Cup in 1946 was their first FA Cup victory for 18 years. They had lost in the first round in each of the eleven seasons leading up to the Second World War, and then had lost in the first round again in the first year after the War. Ironically, their 6-1 first round win in 1946 was then followed by another 6-1 win in the next round.

Cyril Crawshaw

Cyril Crawshaw only ever made four appearances in the Football League. The first two being for Rochdale in Division Three North in December 1936, and the next two for Hull in the same division nearly ten years later. Crawshaw scored in both of his appearances for Hull which were the only two League goals of his career.

The Thomas brothers

Plymouth's top scorer in the 1946-47 season was Bob Thomas with 19 goals and their joint second-top scorer was Bob's brother, Dave, with 17.

Len Shackleton and Charlie Wayman

On 5 October 1946, Newcastle beat Newport 13-0 in a Second Division match in which Len Shackleton scored six times on his Newcastle debut and Charlie Wayman scored four and missed a penalty. Three of Shackleton's goals were reported to have come in the space of two minutes and 35 seconds.

The summer title decider

Due to the high number of postponements, the 1946-47 season dragged on for so long that the final First Division match between Sheffield United and Stoke wasn't played until 14 June. Stoke needed a win to take the League title on goal average and, with eight wins and a draw from their previous nine games, seemed unstoppable. This, however, was their first match in 19 days and the long wait had probably broken their momentum. They lost 2-1 and, according to reports, didn't play well. The result meant Liverpool were crowned League Champions two weeks after their season had finished. In 1934, Italy had won the World Cup earlier in the year than Liverpool won the League in '47.

Ron Turnbull

When Sunderland beat Portsmouth 4-1 in a First Division match in November 1947, all of their goals were scored by Ron Turnbull who was playing his first ever game in English football having just joined Sunderland from Dundee.

Tommy Lawton (again)

Tommy Lawton was England's first-choice centre-forward when he moved from First Division Chelsea to Notts County of the Third Division South in November 1947. Lawton had scored 30 goals for Chelsea the previous season and the £20,000 Notts County paid for him was a British record at the time. This remains the only occasion that the British transfer fee record has been broken by a club from the third tier of English football.

Jack Macartney

Jack Macartney scored 120 goals for Grantham Town in the first two seasons after the Second World War. He scored 56 in 1946-47 and 64 in '47-48.

The toughest Cup run

When Manchester United won the FA Cup in 1948, they beat a top-flight side in every round, which included four of the clubs that went on to finish in the top nine that season.

Stuffing the world (and Serie A) champions away

England's 4-0 win in Turin in May 1948 was the only home defeat Italy suffered between 1934 and 1953. It was also, therefore, their only home defeat during the 16 years that they were reigning world champions (they won the World Cup in 1934 and '38 and then there wasn't another one until 1950). The match was played at the home ground of Torino who had just won their fifth consecutive Serie A title and seven of the Italian team that day were Torino players. Tragically, all seven would lose their lives in the Superga air disaster a year later.

Ivor Broadis

In 1946, Carlisle appointed Ivor Broadis as player-manager even though he was only 23 and, not only had no managerial experience, but had no playing experience either at senior level. He remained in charge at Carlisle until early-1949 when he sold himself to Sunderland as a player only.

Fred Richardson

Fred Richardson finished as top scorer for Hartlepools United in the 1948-49 season despite leaving the club in October and only playing in 12 of their matches. He scored nine goals.

When the Sheffield County Cup mattered

Sheffield Wednesday's second-biggest home crowd of the 1948-49 season was 49,980 against Sheffield United in the Sheffield County Cup semi-final. There was also over 40,000 in attendance when the two clubs met again in the County Cup semi-final in 1951 and nearly 19,000 were there when they met in the final of the competition in 1974. All of these matches were played on FA Cup Saturdays.

Portsmouth – a title-winning side like none that had gone before

The Portsmouth side that won the League in 1948-49 remain the only champions of England to have had no full internationals on their books. As well as this distinction, they were also the first former Third Division club to win the League and the first former Southern League club to do so.

Crowd-pulling Hull

In the 1948-49 season, Hull City were a Third Division North club that had never played at the highest level of English football, and yet that season saw them draw a crowd of 54,852 for the visit of Rotherham, 46,725 for the visit of Doncaster, 43,801 for the visit of Darlington, 43,795 for the visit of Gateshead and 40,002 for the visit of York. Of their 16 other home games in the League that season, only two attracted crowds of less than 30,000. Their average home gate of 36,763, was more than Wolves averaged when they won the League title five years later, and more than the average of every single League title-winning side from 1982 to 1993.

George Brown

George Brown is probably the only player ever to have scored 500 goals in senior football in England and is certainly the only one to have scored 500 for one club. Brown got a total of 570 for Bromley between 1938 and 1961, with his best season being 1948-49 when he scored 48 in the Athenian League despite it only being a 26-game season and Brown missing the start of it through injury. He also scored another 52 in cup games and friendlies that season, thus bringing his overall total up to 100.

In the firing line

Between 1947 and 1950, there were 42 reports of missile throwing from spectators at English football matches, as well as one case – during a match between Preston and Burnley on Boxing Day 1947 – of a linesman being shot with an airgun fired from the crowd.

The Nigerian tour

When a Nigerian representative team toured England during August and September 1949, it was the first time a team of non-Europeans had played in Britain and also the only time a British colonial team would do so during the days of the British Empire. The history-making first match of the tour was against Marine on 31 August in front 4,000 spectators which is still Marine's record attendance. The Nigerians then took on Bishop Auckland, Leytonstone, an Isthmian League XI, a Corinthian League XI, Dulwich Hamlet, an Athenian

League XI, Bromley and South Liverpool, and finished with a record of won two, drawn two, lost five. Their best result was the 5-2 win against Marine and their worst the 8-0 defeat to the Athenian League XI, although the Nigerians were at a distinct disadvantage in every game owing to the fact that they didn't wear football boots and most didn't wear anything on their feet at all aside from strapping. The best attended match of the tour was the one at Dulwich Hamlet which attracted a crowd of 18,000.

Footballmania

On 27 December 1949, the Football League's 44 matches attracted 1,269,934 spectators. This remains the most amount of people that have ever attended matches in the top four tiers of English football on the same day. As well as those who got into the grounds, there were also reports of thousands being locked out at Aston Villa, Arsenal, Sheffield United and Liverpool, where many were injured in the crush. Eight of the eleven First Division matches drew crowds of over 40,000, there were more than 47,000 at three different Second Division matches and one of over 30,000 in the Third Division South. Even clubs like Chesterfield, Doncaster and Southend pulled in over 20,000 each. Millwall, who would finish the season bottom of Division Three South, got 27,012 against Walsall who would finish fourth from bottom.

Incredibly, the previous single-day aggregate attendance record for the Football League had been set just 24 hours earlier. The population of England and Wales at this time was 43.6 million.

Tommy Briggs

Tommy Briggs scored all of Grimsby's first nine goals of the 1949-50 season.

The biggest ever second-tier crowd

On 25 February 1950, a crowd of 70,302 attended a Second Division match between Tottenham and Southampton at White Hart Lane.

Tom Finney

The only hat-trick of Tom Finney's senior career came for England away to Portugal in May 1950 when he scored four. At club level, Finney hit 210 League and cup goals for Preston and scored twice in a match on 32 occasions, but never managed a hat-trick.

When the home nations never left Europe

England had never played a game outside of Europe before they travelled to Brazil for the 1950 World Cup. Scotland also qualified for the 1950 World Cup but refused to go and wouldn't play their first game outside of Europe until 1972 – a century after they played their first official match against England.

The greatest World Cup upset?

England's 1-0 defeat to the USA at the 1950 World Cup may well be the greatest World Cup shock ever and it's certainly the greatest World Cup shock for which no film footage exists. At the time, football (a word they never used for it) was a minor sport in the USA with league matches attracting crowds of only around 3,000 at most and a national side only occasionally being put together. In the nine months prior to the start of the tournament, England had played six games and won them all whereas the USA hadn't played at all and their World Cup squad had barely even trained together before the start of the tournament. Ed McIlvenny, who had been a fringe player for Wrexham in the Third Division before moving to America, was the USA's captain against England which perhaps says everything about his team's lack of quality.

Four days before the two sides met, England had beaten Chile 2-0 in their opening game of the tournament to make it seven straight wins with a goal difference of plus 20. They should have battered the USA, and they did in terms of possession and chances, but nothing went for them. They hit the frame of the goal at least twice (manager Walter Winterbottom claimed it was eleven times), had two goals disallowed and two good penalty shouts denied. In the end the USA's soft first-half goal proved to be the winner.

The bad luck and seemingly biased refereeing then continued for England in their next game against Spain as they again hit the frame of the goal, had another goal disallowed and had two more good shouts for a penalty turned down before falling to another 1-0 defeat which put them out of the World Cup. On the same day, the USA lost 5-2 to Chile and also went out. Their 1-0 win against England would prove to be their only win in the World Cup for the next 44 years.

Bill Eckersley

Bill Eckersley played for England at the 1950 World Cup despite having spent the 1949-50 season with Blackburn who only finished 16th in Division Two.

The World Cup doesn't count

The FA thought so little of the 1950 World Cup that they did not recognise the matches England played in it as full internationals and did not count them towards the international appearances of the players who appeared in them. This is stated clearly in the programme for the 1950 Charity Shield which listed the number of full international appearances of each of the players involved with the words "World Cup appearances do not count as full internationals" appearing at the top of the page. Billy Wright, for example, who had played 32 times for England by then (excluding Wartime appearances) was only listed as having played 29 times because his three appearances in the World Cup were discounted. In fact, the players who played in the 1950 World Cup were awarded one physical cap (as in a hat) for doing so, but only one regardless of how many games they played in.

Going to Colombia

In 1950, Everton's Billy Higgins and Jack Hedley, Stoke's Neil Franklin and George Mountford, Manchester United's Charlie Mitten and Swansea's Roy Paul, all walked out on their clubs to go and earn big money in the Colombian league – and most quickly came to regret it. Their signing on fees turned out to be not as big as promised, they had expensive rents to pay on apartments which were supposed to have been paid for by the clubs, and they were also prisoners in those apartments in the evenings owing to the 6.30 curfew imposed by the military. The football side of things also wasn't good with the matches being played at high altitude in grounds with poor facilities where barbed wire fences kept the fans back and armed police patrolled the perimeter of the pitch. It was all a world away from the homely English matchday experience they were used to. Managers and coaches were also useless by English standards, giving little in the way of instructions to the players, with the English ones ending up playing in matches without much idea what their role was supposed to be. Things were particularly bad for Higgins who was the only English-speaking player at Millionarios and was cold-shouldered by the other players who wouldn't pass to him during games. Higgins didn't last long in Colombia before returning home, nor did Neil Franklin, while Roy Paul and George Mountford both left Colombia before they had even played a game there. Charlie Mitten, a different kind of character to the others, was the only one to make a go of it and completed a full season with Santa Fe.

Upon their return to England, Higgins, Hedley, Franklin, Paul and Mountford were all banned for four months for breaking their contracts with their British clubs, while Mitten was banned for six months. None of the players, aside from Mountford, were re-employed by the British clubs they had left, and Franklin, the only England international of the six, never played for his country again.

Leslie Compton (Again)

Arsenal defender Leslie Compton won his first England cap against Wales in November 1950 when he was 38 years old.

Plucky Ashington

In December 1950, Rochdale won 2-1 at non-League Ashington in the second round of the FA Cup despite Ashington winning 14 corners in the last 15 minutes.

Joe Willetts

Joe Willetts' hat-trick for Hartlepools against Darlington in a Third Division North match in March 1951 was a rarity for three reasons. Firstly, because it was a hat-trick of penalties, secondly because it was a hat-trick of penalties by a player who never scored a goal from open play in his professional career and, thirdly, because it was a hat-trick by a full-back. In all Willetts scored 22 goals for Hartlepools between 1949 and 1954 and they were all penalties.

Pegasus

The 1951 FA Amateur Cup Final saw Pegasus beat Bishop Auckland 2-1 in front of 100,000 spectators at Wembley. This was some achievement for the victors considering they had only been formed three years earlier, didn't belong to any league and didn't have a ground suitable for staging the earlier ties. The club was jointly created at Oxford and Cambridge universities and all of their players were either Oxbridge students or former students. Two years later they won the cup again with a 6-0 victory over Harwich & Parkeston, which stood alone as the record victory in a Wembley final until Manchester City equalled it in 2019.

When New Brighton's best ever start to a season proved to be the beginning of the end

New Brighton won all of their first four League games of the 1950-51 season without conceding a goal but ended their campaign bottom of Division Three North and were voted out of the Football League in the summer that followed. In 1938, they had got a crowd of 13,000 for an FA Cup tie against Tottenham, but by the time they folded in 1983 they were playing in the Wirral League and splitting their home games between two unenclosed grounds in front of no paying spectators.

The goal machine that was Merthyr Tydfil

The three highest goals-in-a-season totals in Southern League history were all achieved by Merthyr Tydfil in consecutive seasons. They scored 133 in 1948-49, 143 in 1949-50 and 156 in 1950-51.

The pioneering thinkers of the 1950s

By pioneering the 'push and run' style of play, Tottenham manager Arthur Rowe became English football's first great innovator of the 1950s. 'Push and run' involved players playing short, quick passes and then running into space to receive the return at a time when no other team's players did this and it made Tottenham's game a uniquely fluid one by the standards of the time. Rowe was appointed Tottenham manager for the start of the 1949-50 season and led them to the Second Division title that season followed by the First Division title a year later. In doing so Tottenham became only the third team in League history to be crowned champions the season after winning promotion.

The antithesis of 'push and run' was the long-ball game which became known by the derogatory moniker 'kick and rush'. The idea of the long-ball game came originally from Charles Reep, an RAF officer and football analyst, who calculated that only two goals out of every nine came from moves of more than three passes and, therefore, stringing many passes together was counterproductive. Brentford were the first team to play the Reep-influenced long-ball game in 1950-51 and Wolves eventually won the title hitting it long three years later. The theory of Wolves' young manager Stan Cullis was that the more time you spent passing in non-scoring positions the less time you had to score and, therefore, it was more productive to launch the ball into the final third with one kick rather than pass your way there. This sounded logical enough except Charles Reep's calculations were fundamentally flawed and Wolves' success probably had more to do with their physicality than it did with the long-ball game. Because playing the long ball game required a lot of chasing and challenging, the players who played it needed to be fitter and stronger than their opponents for it to work and the Wolves side of 1953-54 was the most physical English football had ever seen at that time.

Runners-up to Wolves in that '53-54 season were West Bromwich Albion, whose manager Vic Buckingham had centre-forward Ronnie Allen constantly drop deep to provide passes from midfield as well as create space by drawing opposing centre-backs out of position. It's often said that the English had never seen a deep-lying centre-forward until the national side faced Hungary's Nandor Hidegkuti at Wembley in 1953, but Allen was employed in the same kind of role in the same season. The following season, Manchester City manager Les McDowall also went down the deep-lying centre-forward route with Don Revie operating in the role as part of a system fancifully dubbed 'The Revie Plan'. Revie performed so well that he was named the Football Writers' Association Footballer of the Year at the end of the season, although City only finished seventh.

It was also in the 1950s that managers first started getting players to work on their skills in training rather than simply build-up their fitness as had always been the case before. Jesse Carver, the West Bromwich Albion manager who preceded Vic Buckingham, was a notable pioneer of this, as was Ted Drake, the manager of the Chelsea side that won the League in 1954-55.

Meanwhile, at Manchester United, Matt Busby became the first manager to have the idea of developing youth and may also have been the first to get properly involved in training sessions. Busby believed that nurturing talent was all you needed and, unlike the other pioneering managers of the time, didn't think too much about tactics. As far as Busby was concerned success was best achieved by picking the best players and letting them play their own game and, according to those who played under him, his instructions before matches didn't amount to much more than, "make sure you pass to a red shirt". This worked like a dream for United whose young side won the League in 1955-56 and '56-57 and may well have won the European Cup in '57-58 had it not been for the Munich Air Disaster.

The first competitive floodlit game

A Football Combination match between Southampton Reserves and Tottenham Reserves in October 1951 was the first match in England played under floodlights that wasn't a specially arranged exhibition match. 13,654 people turned up to experience it.

They were giving them a game to begin with

In a Third Division North match in January 1952, Chester took the lead twice at Oldham and were still 2-1 up after half-an-hour but were trailing 5-2 by half-time and eventually lost 11-2. Eric Gemmell scored seven, which included all six of his side's second-half goals. Gemmell was a salesman when he wasn't playing football.

3-3 specialists

In the 1951-52 season, West Bromwich Albion had five 3-3 draws in the League.

2-2 specialists

In the 1951-52 season, Wolves had five 2-2 draws in a six-game run.

Joe Harvey

Newcastle United's Joe Harvey was the only FA Cup-winning captain to be presented with the trophy by Winston Churchill. This was in 1952, when Churchill took over presentation duties as the Royal Family were in mourning over the death of George VI. This final is also notable for being the first one ever played in May.

The reserves

In the 1951-52 season, Bedford Town Reserves had an average home attendance of 2,498 in the United Counties League, indicating that around half the people who attended the club's first-team games in the Southern League went to watch the reserves when the first-team were away. That same season Liverpool got an estimated 25,000 for a reserve team match (it's only an estimate because thousands broke in without paying), while the previous season had seen a Central League match between Newcastle Reserves and Leeds Reserves attract an incredible 60,000. This latter attendance was an anomaly caused by the fact that Newcastle were parading the FA Cup at the game, but in the 1940s and '50s, attendances at reserve team games were still high compared with later decades, with crowds of ten to fifteen thousand not uncommon for those involving the bigger clubs, and another anomalous one of 28,000 being recorded when Tommy Lawton played for Chelsea Reserves at Arsenal in 1949.

At that time, most men still worked on Saturday mornings which meant travelling to the first-team's away games wasn't possible unless the game was a local derby. Watching the reserves, therefore, was a handy way for fans to get their Saturday afternoon football fix when the first-team were away, hence the size of the crowds. By the 1960s, however, the five-day working week had gone from being a perk enjoyed by the few to the standard, resulting in a rise in away support and watching the reserves becoming much more of an eccentric activity. By the late-60s, Liverpool Reserves were only averaging around 2,000 for their home games, although this would seem big compared with the paltry average of 500 or so they would be getting for reserve team games in the late-80s. During the '60s, '70s and '80s, it was only exceptional circumstances that brought reserve team attendances up from the depths, such as, in March 1975, when Birmingham's Trevor Francis made his return from a long lay-off with a reserve team appearance and drew a crowd that was ten times the club's reserve team average for that season. The attendance at that game was still only 6,000, but Manchester United Reserves got a crowd of 16,000 against Everton Reserves in 1977 after they made it known that vouchers for the live screening of a European tie would be available at the game. Arsenal had also got a crowd of 13,000 for a reserve team game against Tottenham in 1970 due to the Tottenham side featuring several out-of-favour star names, including record goalscorer, Jimmy Greaves.

Throughout the hundred years (more or less) that all professional clubs had a reserve side, the two premier reserve leagues were the Football Combination and the Central League which, even when attendances were pitiful in the '70s and '80s, were still regarded as valid competitions within the game. Their results were printed in the national newspapers and the matches reported on in the local press, and we can also see the respect afforded to them when we look at old matchday programmes. The Chelsea programme for the 1964-65 season and the Arsenal programme for '72-73 were both slim publications consisting of only 16 pages each, but they still found room for plenty of reserve team stats and displayed them with the same prominence as those of the first-team. From the Arsenal programme we learn that Arsenal Reserves had a prolific goalscorer that season in John Ritchie who would never play for the club's first-team nor make it at any other League club, while Charlie George, who had an unremarkable goalscoring record for the first-team, was little short of a goal machine when he turned out for the reserves. On this evidence, reserve team football was like an alternative football reality, where little known or out-of-favour players appeared for the top sides in matches watched by a small devoted few in big grounds that were packed-out with tens of thousands when they hosted first-team games.

Eventually reserve team football died a quiet and practically unnoticed death during the second decade of the 21st century when it was replaced by academy football and the mass loaning-out of non-first-team players.

Derek Dooley

Sheffield Wednesday's Derek Dooley scored 21 goals in an eight-game run in the 1951-52 season and finished the campaign as the League's top scorer with 46 goals from just 30 appearances. Dooley was 22 at the time and this was his first full season in senior football, but the following season would prove to be his last. In a match at Preston in February 1953, Dooley ran onto a through ball which he poked wide of the on-rushing keeper but also wide of the goal. As he did so he was caught by the keeper's outstretched foot which broke Dooley's leg. This wouldn't have been enough to end Dooley's career, but at the hospital the plaster on his leg was put over an untreated cut and by the time the cut was discovered it had become badly infected, gangrene had set in, and it was spreading. Only amputating the leg would save Dooley's life, although even this wasn't guaranteed, and for days after the operation Dooley's condition was given as 'grave'. Eventually he pulled through, but less than a year after finishing as the League's top scorer, Dooley had a six-inch stump where his right leg had once been.

Fred Smith

Manchester City's signing of Fred Smith at the end of the 1951-52 season made so little sense that many came to believe they signed him by mistake. City were in the First Division at the time so why would they sign a Second Division centre-forward who had made only five League appearances and scored just one goal in the season just gone? At the time, Sheffield United had two Fred Smiths with other having had a good season, making 36 League appearances and scoring eleven goals, and the theory goes that it was this Fred Smith that City intended to sign but when their club secretary turned up to seal the deal he was presented with the other one.

Ironically Smith scored on his debut for City on the opening day of the following season but made only one further appearance for the club before being offloaded to Grimsby of the Third Division North the following month.

Billy Cairns

Billy Cairns scored 129 goals for Grimsby between 1946 and 1952, despite not making his debut for them until he was 34 years old. Cairns scored 35 goals in the 1951-52 season when he was 39.

Charles Buchan's Football Monthly

Charlie Buchan is Sunderland's all-time top League goalscorer with 209 goals despite losing four seasons due to the First World War. In the 1922-23 season, he was the First Division's leading scorer with 30 goals and he later played for Arsenal for whom he also scored over 100 League goals. After retiring, Buchan became a journalist and, at the start of the 1951-52 season, launched the seminal *Charles Buchan's Football Monthly*. This wasn't the first football periodical, but it was the first that looked more like a movie magazine than a sports paper and can, therefore, be cited as the first football publication that fitted the modern definition of a magazine. It's especially notably for featuring the first ever full-page photographs of players, photos which, of course, were perfect for pulling out and pinning on a bedroom wall. Arsenal's Joe Mercer, Leicester's Mel Griffiths, Aston Villa's Dave Walsh, Fulham's Jim Taylor and Third Lanark's Jimmy Mason were the ones who got the full-page photo honour in the very first issue and, although none of these five would rank amongst the biggest stars of 1950s football, they were all, by definition, the first ever footballing pin-ups. All of their photos were in black and white but before long *Charles Buchan's Football Monthly* would be including colour photos of players, as well as the first centre-page spreads of team photos. In this way Buchan's magazine brought the image of the footballer into British homes in a way it never had been before, as this was a time when most households still didn't own a TV set, and only low quality black and white photos appeared in newspapers and matchday programmes.

Charlie Buchan died in 1960, but the magazine continued to carry his name until 1971, when it became simply, *Football Monthly*. It eventually ceased publication in 1974, by which time *Shoot!* was dominating the market.

When over 61,000 had a wasted journey

In January 1953, 61,499 spectators attended an FA Cup third round tie between Newcastle and Swansea but only got to see eight minutes of football before the game was abandoned due to fog.

Tommy Taylor

In March 1953, Manchester United decided to pay £29,999 for Barnsley's Tommy Taylor because United's manager, Matt Busby, believed a £30,000 fee would have put too much pressure on him. Taylor went on to score 128 goals in 189 games for United before being killed in the Munich Air Disaster at the age of 26.

Jimmy Glazzard (and Vic Metcalfe)

When Huddersfield beat Everton 8-2 in a Second Division match in March 1953, Huddersfield's Jimmy Glazzard scored four headed goals with the cross for each one being supplied by left-winger Vic Metcalfe. This was just a couple of weeks before Glazzard's 30th birthday and it was the first hat-trick of his professional career. In the 1948-49 season he had scored just once in 30 League appearances, 24 of which were at centre-forward.

Stan Mortenson

The only player to score a hat-trick in an FA Cup Final at Wembley is Blackpool's Stan Mortenson against Bolton in 1953, although he was lucky to be credited with the first of the goals as it was Bolton's Harold Hassell who turned it into his own net after Mortenson shot across him. The TV footage clearly shows it as an own goal and the BBC commentator Ken Wolstenholme called it as such, although it does look like Mortenson's goal on the *Pathe News* footage which was filmed from a camera on the other side of the ground.

Stanley Matthews

Staney Matthews won the Football Writers' Association Footballer of the Year award for the first time in 1948 when he was 33 years old and won it for the second time 15 years later when he was 48. He was also named European Footballer of the Year in 1956 when he was 41.

During the 1953 FA Cup Final, BBC Commentator Ken Wolstenholme described Matthews as, "probably the greatest footballer of all time". A year later, he was "the world's greatest footballer" according to *Daily Mirror* journalist Bob Ferrier and when *Goal* magazine carried an editorial on Alfredo De Stefano in 1968, it opined that, "In world fame, adulation and stature he is the only player who has climbed to Sir Stanley Matthews' heights".

By then players such as Pele, Eusebio and Bobby Charlton were around and Ferenc Puskas and Garrincha had been and gone, but there still appeared to be nothing unusual in regarding Matthews as the greatest.

And yet, for all the praise heaped upon him and the awards he won, Matthews actually had the worst goalscoring record of any attacking player during his years at Blackpool for whom he managed just 18 goals in 440 senior appearances. Having scored twice in the first six games of the 1956-57 season, he then went on a 123-game goal drought that spanned six years.

It's also worth noting that, although Matthews' international career spanned an incredible 23 years (1934-1957), he was by no means a regular in the England side throughout those years, and won far fewer caps than his teammates Billy Wright and Tom Finney, the latter of whom often kept Matthews out of the side. Matthews' appearance for England against Spain at the 1950 World Cup was the first for his country in 14 months, and such was his apparent dispensability that he had been unavailable for England's first game of the tournament because he had been playing for an FA representative team in Canada at the time.

Len Shackleton and Trevor Ford

In February 1948, Sunderland broke the British transfer fee record when they bought Newcastle's inside-left Len Shackleton for £20,050. Then, 20 months later, they broke it again with the £29,500 purchase of Aston Villa centre-forward Trevor Ford. Despite being such a high-profile player, Ford also had a job as a car salesman (given to him by the club) which made him richer than his teammates and he made no secret of it. This was just one of the things Shackleton disliked about Ford and during the two years they played up front together the animosity between the two got so bad that Ford eventually refused to play with Shackleton and asked for a transfer which the club granted him. In all, Ford made 94 appearances with Shackleton and scored 59 times in those games, which is certainly impressive considering Shackleton had done his best to keep his teammate's goal tally down. This he did by not passing to Ford, putting too much spin on passes so Ford couldn't control them or slightly over-hitting them so Ford couldn't reach them. The fact that, in the 1951-52 season, the pair were way out in front as the club's two leading scorers with 22 each seems remarkable in the circumstances.

Despite being the biggest-spending club in the country during this period, Sunderland never finished any higher than ninth in the League and never beat another top-flight side in the FA Cup, which seems to suggest the animosity that existed between its two biggest stars had an adverse effect on team spirit.

England out of their depth for the first time

England's 6-3 Wembley defeat to Hungary in November 1953 was their first ever home defeat to a team from continental Europe and it could have been so much worse as Hungary had 35 attempts on goal to England's five. The visitors did most of the damage in the first 27 minutes when they scored four times (and had another effort disallowed), although anyone watching on TV wouldn't have seen it live as the match kicked-off at 2.15 but the BBC coverage didn't begin until three o'clock.

Before the game, England manager Walter Winterbottom had predicted it would be "a very close match". None of England's back three that day would ever play for their country again.

Jimmy Hogan

Hungary's 6-3 victory over England at Wembley in 1953 was something of a personal triumph for English coach Jimmy Hogan, since Hungary's superior play was based on the tactics Hogan had introduced into their country whilst coaching MTK Budapest during the First World War and in the 1920s. Hogan was the first coach to formulate a method of attacking that involved fluid passing moves rather than just dribbling and crossing and, as well as having a huge influence on Hungarian football, his ideas also became mainstream in Austria during the two spells he spent coaching the national team either side of the First World War, and in Germany where, in the 1920s, he was employed to tour the country teaching tactics. In the 1954 World Cup, West Germany beat Hungary in the final and Austria finished third.

Hogan had been appointed manager of Second Division Fulham in 1934, but English football was very stuck-in-its-ways at that time and neither the Fulham players nor the board approved of his unorthodox ideas, resulting in Hogan being sacked after only 31 League games in charge. He then took over at Aston Villa in 1936 and led them to the Second Division title and an FA Cup semi-final in the 1937-38 season. Villa subsequently finished 12th in the First Division in the last football season before the Second World War, which was the only season that arguably England's most influential coach was ever in charge of a club in the highest division of his own country.

John Charles

Leeds United's John Charles scored three hat-tricks against Rotherham in 1953. They were all in the League, coming in Leeds' 4-0 win in January, their 4-2 win in August and in another 4-2 win in December.

John Charles (again)

In the 1953-54 season, John Charles scored 43 goals as Leeds United's centre-forward – and then spent most of the following season playing as their centre-half. In truth, Charles was equally good in either position, with England centre-forward Nat Lofthouse apparently naming Charles as the best centre-half he had ever played against, and England centre-half Billy Wright naming him as the best centre-forward he ever faced.

When the Amateur Cup Final was massive

For each of four consecutive years from 1952, the FA Amateur Cup Final drew a crowd of 100,000 to Wembley. The four finals over these years were Pegasus v Bishop Auckland (1951), Walthamstow Avenue v Leyton (1952), Pegasus v Harwich & Parkeston (1953) and Crook Town v Bishop Auckland (1954). More people went to each of these matches than would attend any match at Wembley during the 1966 World Cup, and when Newcastle's St. James' Park hosted the replay between Crook Town and Bishop Auckland, the attendance of 56,008 was 10,000 higher than Newcastle's average home gate that season.

When a win for Wolves led to the creation of the European Cup

Six of the players who were in the Hungary side that beat England 7-1 in May 1954 were in the Honved team that lost 3-2 in a friendly at Wolves seven months later. The morning after Wolves' victory, the headline in the *Daily Mail* read "Hail Wolves, Champions of The World", a claim that didn't take into account the fact that the Yugoslavian side Crvena Zvezda had also beaten Honved a few days earlier. What's more, Wolves didn't exactly play fair either. Before the game they watered an already damp and muddy pitch in order to turn it into a quagmire that would be unplayable for the skilful Hungarians but would make little difference to Wolves who played a physical long-ball game.

The claim that this victory proved Wolves were the best team in the world was what led the French journalist Gabriel Hanot to suggest to UEFA that a club competition between the champions of all the European nations should be played to decide who was the best rather than have teams claiming to be the best on the basis of victories in friendly matches. UEFA agreed and the European Cup was launched at the start of the following season, although as Wolves only finished runners-up in the League in 1954-55 they didn't qualify for it. Instead, it was Chelsea who qualified but they didn't take part due to the Football League's disapproval of the competition.

Bugger!

Preston only committed two fouls in the first 70 minutes of the 1954 FA Cup Final against West Bromwich Albion, but the second one gave away a penalty.

Five-a-side football

The first *Evening Standard* London Five-a-Side Football Championships was contested between all of London's League sides at London's Earl's Court in the week after the 1954 FA Cup Final. It was probably this event that marked the birth of five-a-side football, as at this time there were still no purpose-built five-a-side pitches and five-a-side games had never been used in club training sessions. The London Five-a-Side Football Championships would go on to become a popular annual event that gave fans a chance to see many of the top London players in action at the same venue on the same night, and being forced to use close control all of the time as five-a-side football was a variant of the game that featured no heading or long balls and, because of the hard surface, no sliding tackles either. In 1956, the venue was switched to Harringay Arena where it was staged for three years until being moved to the Empire Pool Wembley (now Wembley Arena) for the 1959 championships. It was scrapped after 1960 but revived in 1967 and ran continuously until 1985, usually being played on either the Wednesday before or the Wednesday after the FA Cup Final.

These championships are notable for being the first football competition to carry the name of its sponsors, although from 1959 it became known as 'The London Five-A-Side Football Championships sponsored by the *Evening Standard*', which seemed to suggest it had grown in prestige, hence the FA no longer wanted it to be thought of as a competition being run simply to promote a newspaper.

In 1968, the *Daily Express* Five-A-Side National Football Championships were launched as a national equivalent of the London competition. Like the London championships, all the matches were played at the Empire Pool Wembley on a single evening, and although only a small selection of clubs took part, many of the day's top stars would feature in them. Whereas the London five-a-sides were broadcast by Thames Television and shown only in the London area, the national championships were broadcast to the whole nation on BBC1. In 1970, the event was described in the *Radio Times* as, "Midweek's most important sports night", which said a lot about the growth in popularity of this brand of the game back then, especially as on the same night Everton were playing Borussia Monchengladbach in the European Cup. Ultimately, however, five-a-side football on this level would prove to be a passing fad, and the Five-a-Side National Football Championships would eventually be scrapped in 1986, by which time it was no longer being televised.

Of course, five-a-side football never went away, but today is only used for training sessions or recreational games. The days when we would see someone like George Best scoring twice for Manchester United against Tottenham in a national five-a-side final – as happened in 1970 – are long gone.

The World Cup's on the telly – but don't expect to see much of England

The 1954 World Cup was the first to be televised, although only one of England's three matches (against Belgium) was shown live in its entirety. Of the other two, one (against Switzerland) wasn't televised at all, while the other (against Uruguay) only had the second half shown live even though it was the quarter-final.

England's worst World Cup quarter-final?

In the 1954 World Cup England somehow managed to lose 4-2 in the quarter-finals to a Uruguay side who only had eight fit men on the pitch from the 40th minute (no substitutions in those days).

Bedford Jezzard

Fulham won 28 home matches in the League between 17 September 1952 and 11 September 1954, and Bedford Jezzard scored in all of them.

England beating the World Champions – although not really

In December 1954, England beat West Germany 3-1 at Wembley five months after the Germans had won the World Cup. This result, however, is not as impressive as it seems on paper, since the team the Germans put out contained only three players from their World Cup squad.

Jack Froggatt and Stan Milburn

A First Division match between Chelsea and Leicester in December 1954 produced four goals but had five different scorers. This is because Chelsea's second in their 3-1 win went down as an own goal scored jointly by Jack Froggatt and Stan Milburn. Both players and the referee confirmed they had made contact with the ball together. In the results sections of the next day's newspapers the goal was officially credited as "Froggatt and Milburn shared o.g.".

All over as a contest after eight minutes

On New Year's Day 1955, Sheffield United led Newcastle 4-0 after only eight minutes of a First Division match at Bramall Lane. The final score was 6-2.

Tommy Briggs (Again)

When Blackburn beat Bristol Rovers 8-3 in February 1955, Tommy Briggs scored seven times, with five of his goals coming in the last 28 minutes, a period in which he also hit the post.

Harold Bell

Harold Bell played in every one of Tranmere Rovers' League and cup games over nine consecutive seasons from 1946-47 to 1954-55. In all he made 459 consecutive appearances for the club.

Birmingham coming from nowhere

Birmingham won the Second Division title in the 1954-55 season, despite only being 12th in the table at Christmas. Between 1 January and 2 March, they won five away games in a row – four in the League and one against a team from their own division in the FA Cup – having only won once on the road prior to that.

The arrival of floodlights

Until the 1955-56 season, floodlights were not allowed in either FA Cup matches nor Football League games, meaning all Cup replays and midweek League fixtures until then had to kick-off in the afternoon or – if played at the start or end of the season – very early evening between six o'clock and 6.30. Initially, the lifting of the ban didn't make a great deal of difference as only 36 of the 92 Football League grounds had floodlights at that time and many of those that did have them still sometimes opted for the traditional midweek afternoon kick-off and would continue to do so into the early-60s.

In 1955, the division between the clubs that had floodlights and those that didn't was incredibly random. For example, Aldershot, Torquay and Rochdale all had them, whereas Liverpool, Everton and Manchester United didn't. The first club to have permanent floodlights installed was Southampton in 1951, but it was in the seven years between 1953 and 1960 that most of them went up. Fulham were one of the clubs that lagged behind, not installing their ones until early in the 1962-63 season even though this was their fourth consecutive season in the top-flight. Chesterfield was the League club that held out the longest, with their Recreation Ground remaining without floodlights until October 1967.

One by-product of floodlights was that, from the late-1960s, Saturday afternoon matches were able to kick-off at three o'clock throughout the season, unlike before when they had to kick-off earlier between November and February so as they could be completed in daylight.

Giving your opponents a nice head start

Sunderland players scored two own goals in the first four minutes of a First Division match at home to Burnley in November 1955. The game eventually finished 4-4.

When the expected big win became an unexpected big defeat

The biggest ever win by a non-League club away to a League side in the FA Cup occurred in December 1955 when Boston United of the

Midland League won 6-1 at Derby County of Division Three North. It was one of only two home games Derby lost that season. The Boston team contained eight former Derby players.

How is that fair?

In February 1956, Chelsea beat Burnley 2-0 in an FA Cup fourth round fourth replay at Tottenham two days after the two sides had drawn 0-0 at Arsenal. These games were supposed to have been played on neutral grounds, which, technically speaking, they were, although it was hardly neutral territory. One wonders just how many Burnley fans were able to travel to London to watch two midweek afternoon games in the space of three days.

Ken Tucker

Ken Tucker scored a hat-trick on his West Ham debut in October 1947 but would only make 40 more League and cup appearances for the club over the next eight years, during which time he was a virtual mainstay in the West Ham reserves. Even scoring another hat-trick in a rare first-team outing in January 1952 only earned Tucker a four-game run in the first-team before he was back in the reserves again for the remainder of the season. It was in the 1955-56 season – his ninth at the club – that Tucker finally established himself in the West Ham first-team, by which time he was 30 years old. He played 42 games in all competitions that season and scored 14 goals which included yet another hat-trick from the left-wing.

The best home run by a poor side

Mansfield's last eleven home games of the 1955-56 season were a 3-1 win, a 5-1 win, a 4-0 win, a 6-1 win, a 3-0 win, a 6-0 win, another 6-0 win, a 3-2 win, a 2-0 defeat (to the eventual champions), a 5-0 win and a 3-1 win. Despite this they still only finished the season 18th in Division Three North, largely due to the fact that they only won one of their 23 away games.

The Wembley hoodoo (and the dirty Wembley forwards)

Manchester City's Jimmy Meadows slipped over in the 17th minute of the 1955 FA Cup Final and, in doing so, suffered an injury that ended his career. Meadows was 23 at the time and had made his international debut for England five weeks earlier.

This was the first and most extreme example of, what was dubbed, 'the Wembley hoodoo' which blighted a succession of FA Cup Finals between 1955 and 1960. The following year, Manchester City's goalkeeper Bert Trautmann broke his neck in the final, although didn't realise and carried on playing. Then the year after, Manchester United goalkeeper Ray Wood was stretchered off before returning as a labouring outfield player after having his cheekbone broken by Aston Villa's Peter McParland. McParland ran ten yards to clatter Wood after Wood had gathered the ball. He then completed his act of villainy by going on to score twice past United centre-half Jackie Blanchflower who was forced to deputise for Wood between the sticks.

In the 1958 Final, it was another United keeper, Harry Gregg, who took a clattering, this time from Bolton's Nat Lofthouse. Lofthouse brutally shoulder-charged Gregg in the back as Gregg attempted to catch a cross at the second attempt. Gregg recovered but the game was held up for four minutes while he received treatment, and he seemed very disorientated at one point. Gregg had been suffering from severe headaches since surviving the Munich Air Disaster three months earlier and it was later discovered that he already had a fractured skull when Lofthouse charged him. Because Gregg dropped the ball over the line as he fell, a goal was given and Lofthouse credited as the scorer even though he didn't make contact with anything other than Gregg's back.

The 1959 victim of the hoodoo was Nottingham Forest's Roy Dwight who scored in the first half against Luton but then broke his leg in the second, an injury that kept him out for almost all of the following season. Blackburn's Dave Whelan also suffered a broken leg in the 1960 Final and never played for Blackburn again, nor for any other club until Crewe signed him in January 1963.

The Inter-Cities Fairs Cup

As already mentioned, in 1955 Chelsea became the first English club to qualify for the European Cup but declined to take part in it due to pressure from the Football League. As a result, the first English club to play in a European competition was Birmingham City who were invited to take part in the inaugural Inter-Cities Fairs Cup which commenced at the end of the 1955-56 season. City's first game in the competition was a 0-0 draw away to Inter Milan on 15 May 1956, which was the first of four group matches for City that took almost a year to complete. City eventually finished top of the group and so qualified for the semi-finals but had to wait a further six months before they were played. No club cup competition had ever been so drawn out, but then no Cup competition had ever been quite so strange as the Inter-Cities Fairs Cup. While some of the teams that contested it were clubs, others were representative teams comprised of players from more than one club, and the only criteria for qualification was that each team had to represent a city that held international trade fairs, with the matches being staged to coincide with those fairs wherever possible.

The first final was eventually played in March 1958, almost four months after the semi-finals were completed and over two years after the first group games were played. Barcelona won it, beating London 8-2 on aggregate in the final and the fact that such big-name players as Danny Blanchflower, Jimmy Greaves and Johnny Haynes were all playing for a team called simply 'London' (they weren't called London XI as most internet sources now claim) added a further ingredient to the competition's strangeness. London's group game against Frankfurt (another representative team) was played at Wembley and is notable for being the first ever Wembley match to be played entirely under floodlights.

As the years progressed, the Fairs Cup became more normalized and pretty prestigious as well. When Newcastle won it in 1969, their home legs of the semi-final and final drew the biggest crowds seen at St James' Park since 1965, and when Leeds and Liverpool met in the semi-finals two years later, the two legs were better attended than the two League games between the sides that season even though Leeds were top of the table.

The Fairs Cup was eventually replaced by the UEFA Cup in 1971.

Symmetrical thrashings

Both the matches between Millwall and Torquay in the 1956-57 season finished 7-2. The first was a 7-2 home win for Torquay and the second a 7-2 home win for Millwall.

Neville Coleman

Stoke's outside-right Neville Coleman scored seven times in his side's 8-0 win against Lincoln in February 1957, which, unsurprisingly, is a League record for a winger. Somewhat more surprising is the fact that Coleman never scored again that season even though he played in every game.

Hughie Gallacher

Hughie Gallacher is arguably the greatest former British footballer ever to commit suicide. Gallacher, a small and skilful Scottish centre-forward, scored 143 goals in 174 games for Newcastle between 1925 and 1930, which included 36 in the League when Newcastle won the title in 1926-27. He subsequently moved to Chelsea and when Chelsea played away to Newcastle in September 1930, Gallacher's return to St James' Park was such a big event that the game attracted a record gate for the ground. 68,386 were packed inside an hour before kick-off with another 10,000 locked out, and they were all there to welcome back their former hero, Gallacher. This remains the only time an English ground's record attendance has been set due to the appearance of just one player.

Gallacher only scored a modest 14 goals for Chelsea that season, but hit 30 in the following one. After two-and-a-bit more seasons with the London club, he moved to Derby for whom he scored 24 goals in 30 appearances in 1934-35, which made him the first player ever to score 20-or-more goals in a season for three different top-flight clubs.

In 1957, at the age of 54, Gallacher had an argument with his 14-year-old son, Mattie, and angrily threw an ashtray at him which cut Mattie's head. The police were called and Gallacher was arrested and charged. It was claimed that when Gallacher spoke to Mattie – who he deeply regretted hurting – the week before he was due to go on trial, it came across as a final goodbye. He also spoke to a journalist friend on the Friday before the trial and reputedly said, "I don't think I'll be in court on Wednesday". According to the same journalist, he then said "My life is over now," when they met up three days later. The next day, which was the day before the trial was to begin, Gallacher threw himself in front of the York to Edinburgh express train at Dead Man's Crossing in Gateshead and was decapitated.

Malcolm Allison

After looking uncharacteristically slow and unfit during a match at Sheffield United in September 1957, and then developing a bad cough afterwards, West Ham defender Malcolm Allison was diagnosed with tuberculosis and had to have a lung removed. Unsurprisingly, he never played League football again but, after a few years spent as a professional gambler and nightclub owner, Allison eventually made a comeback with Southern League Romford and was a first-team regular at the club during the 1960-61 and 1961-62 seasons despite only having the one lung. As well as his appearances in the Southern League, he also played against Watford in the second round of the FA Cup in November 1961, the only time he ever took on League opposition with his disability.

Len Saward

In October 1957, Cambridge United forward Len Saward donated some of the money raised from his own testimonial fund towards the cost of Cambridge's new floodlights.

The greatest comeback

In December 1957, Charlton beat Huddersfield 7-6 in a Second Division match, having been 5-1 down and one player down with less than half an hour left. This makes Huddersfield the only team ever to have scored six goals in a League game that they lost. Charlton would draw 6-6 with Middlesbrough three years later.

Stuck in a rut

Queen's Park Rangers had six consecutive 1-1 draws in December 1957.

Never a dull moment

The Manchester City side of 1957-58 remain the only League team ever to have both scored and conceded 100 or more League goals in the same season. Their campaign included three 5-2 wins, a 5-1 win, a 5-4 win and a 5-1 defeat, two 4-3 wins and a 4-3 defeat, an 8-4 defeat and a 9-2 defeat, and a 6-2 win. Only two of their 42 matches produced fewer than three goals, and they lost their only FA Cup game 5-1.

Christmas fixtures used to be exactly that

Up to and including the 1957-58 season, all Football League clubs played League games on Christmas Day as well as Boxing Day every year, with the two matches usually being home and away to the same opponents.

Groundhog (third round) day

Leeds United lost 2-1 at home to Cardiff in the third round of the FA Cup in each of three consecutive seasons in the 1950s ('55-56, '56-57 and '57-58).

Arsenal's quickfire comeback

In February 1958, Arsenal were 3-0 down at home to Manchester United in a First Division match but came back to level the scores with goals in the 58th, 59th and 60th minutes. It was all to no avail, however, as United retook the lead five minutes later and eventually went on to win 5-4.

After Munich

In February 1958, Manchester United beat Sheffield Wednesday 3-0 in the fifth round of the FA Cup 13 days after seven of their players had been killed in the Munich Air Disaster. This was their first game following the disaster and their line-up included two of the players who survived it (Harry Gregg and Bill Foulkes) along with nine second-string players who were brought in to replace the injured and the dead. Two days after the match, another United player, Duncan Edwards, died in hospital, thus bringing the death toll amongst United players up to eight, seven of whom were first-team regulars, with four of those having been internationals. Incredibly, United then went on to reach the FA Cup Final the following month and then finished runners-up in the League the following season.

Frank Swift

The most capped – and arguably most famous player at the time – to die in the Munich Air Disaster, was not a Manchester United player, but the retired Manchester City goalkeeper Frank Swift who was on the plane as a journalist. Swift played 19 times for England in the late-1940s, was the first ever goalkeeper to captain England and was both a League title-winner and FA Cup-winner in the 1930s. He was also, it's said, one of the first goalkeepers to throw the ball out rather than just drop-kick it every time.

Alan O'Neill

Sunderland's top scorer in the 1957-58 season was Alan O'Neill who had gone under the name of Alan Hope the previous season. He had changed his surname by deed poll in September 1957 so as it could be the same as that of his stepfather.

England and the USSR getting sick of the sight of each other

England played the USSR three times in the space of three and a half weeks in 1958 and four times altogether that year. They first played them in a friendly in Moscow on 18 May, before playing them again in their opening game of the 1958 World Cup on 8 June.

The two countries then finished level on points in their World Cup group and so, under the rules of the time, were required to play each other again three days later to decide which one went through to the knock-out stages. The fourth meeting between the two nations that year was a friendly at Wembley in October. England won that one 5-0. The World Cup play-off had been a 1-0 defeat to largely the same Soviet line-up.

George Raynor

The first Englishman to lead a team to a World Cup Final was George Raynor who was in charge of the Sweden side that finished runners-up to Brazil in 1958 despite having a squad comprised largely of amateurs. Raynor had also led the Swedes to Olympic Gold in 1948 and the last four of the World Cup in 1950. In 1959, Raynor's Sweden beat England at Wembley with seven of their World Cup Final line-up absent.

Sam Pilkington

Sam Pilkington only ever made five appearances in the Football League (for Oldham in the 1910-11 season), but he was the man who originally proposed that four teams should be promoted from the fourth tier of English football when that tier was created in 1958.

Vic Groves

Arsenal's Vic Groves hit the crossbar three times in a First Division match at Everton in September 1958. Not that it mattered, as Arsenal still won 6-1.

Arthur Rowley

When Arthur Rowley was appointed player-manager of Shrewsbury Town in June 1958, he promised Shrewsbury would score 100 League goals in the coming season, which seemed more than a little optimistic considering they had only managed 49 in the season just gone. Unbelievably, however, Rowley's promise came good as Shrewsbury went on to score 101 in that 1958-59 season with Rowley weighing in with 38 of them (a club record) himself. This was the first of five consecutive seasons that Rowley was Shrewsbury's manager and also their top scorer and in every one of those seasons he scored 20-plus. When he eventually hung up his boots in 1965 he had scored 152 goals in 236 appearances for Shrewsbury. He remains the club's all-time top scorer and also stands as the only all-time top scorer for an English club who was also that club's manager when he scored all of his goals for them. If this isn't remarkable enough, there's also the fact that Rowley played for Shrewsbury between the ages of 32 and 39 in an era when most players retired in their early-30s.

When Liverpool came a cropper at Worcester

In January 1959, Liverpool were beaten 2-1 in the third round of the FA Cup by Worcester City. This wasn't quite as remarkable as it now sounds as Liverpool were in the Second Division at the time, but they did already have four League titles under their belt by then and had gone into the game on the back of six straight League wins. Having originally been postponed on a Saturday, the match was eventually played on a Thursday afternoon and eight of the Worcester players had been at work earlier in the day. An own goal by Liverpool's Dick White eight minutes from time proved to be the winner. Worcester went on to finish the season fifth in the Southern League North-Western Zone.

When a team produced a great fight-back and suffered a heavy defeat in the same game

In a Third Division match in March 1959, Mansfield came back from 3-0 down at Plymouth to make it 3-3, before eventually going on to lose 8-3.

Blackburn trying to sprint a marathon

The 1958-59 season was Blackburn's first in the top-flight for over a decade and they began it in emphatic fashion. They won 5-1 at Newcastle on the opening day, then beat Leicester 5-0 at home two days later, before getting another 5-0 win, this time at home to Tottenham, on the season's second Saturday. This was then followed by eight games without a win and they eventually only finished tenth.

Bill Lambton

Bill Lambton was appointed Scunthorpe manager on a verbal agreement in April 1959 and then dismissed by the club three days later. A 3-0 defeat at Liverpool was his only match in charge.

Man United's FA Cup humiliations of the 1950s

Matt Busby's Manchester United were a formidable League side in the 1950s, winning the title three times and only finishing outside of the top four twice, but in the FA Cup they suffered a surprisingly high number of humiliations at the hands of lower-level opposition.

In 1951, they finished runners-up in the League but failed to get past Second Division Birmingham in the Cup, and the following season they won the League but were knocked out of the Cup by Hull who were also in the Second Division but cruised to a comfortable 2-0 win at Old Trafford (both goals came in the first half). At the end of the season, Hull only avoided relegation to the Third Division by three points. In 1952-53, United lost to Everton in the fifth round of the Cup, but only after being held 1-1 at home by the amateurs of Walthamstow Avenue in the previous round, and three years later, a United side which went on to take the title by an eleven-point margin got thumped 4-0 by Second Division Bristol Rovers in the Cup. United then finished runners-up in the Cup in 1957 and '58 before being on the receiving end of another upset in '59. United won 16 of the 18 First Division matches they played between late-November '58 and late-March '59, but it was during this period that they were beaten 3-0 by Third Division Norwich in the Cup. United went on to finish runners-up in the League that season, and yet their defeat in this game could have been so much worse. Norwich also hit the bar and the post, had a goal disallowed and had another effort cleared off the line.

Jeff Hall

Jeff Hall died of polio in April 1959, just two weeks after playing his last game for Birmingham City.

Beating the best to win the Cup

Bolton only finished 15th in the League in 1957-58 but they won the FA Cup and beat both that season's eventual champions (Wolves) and eventual runners-up (Preston) en route to the final. They would also knock the eventual champions (Wolves again) out of the Cup the following season as well.

Billy Wright

No player has ever been such a permanent fixture in the England side as Wolves' Billy Wright. He was in every single England starting line-up from October 1951 to May 1959, and his unbroken run in the side only ended there because he retired. In fact, his final international appearance came a month after his final club game. In all, he played for England for 13 years and only missed three matches during that period. He was also the first player from any country to make 100 international appearances as well as the first to captain his country at three World Cups ('50, '54 and '58). He remained England's most capped player until 1970.

Wrapping the game up in the second minute

Wolves were 2-0 up after just 85 seconds of a First Division match against Newcastle in October 1959. The game produced no further goals.

John Bond

During the 1958-59 and 1959-60 seasons, West Ham's regular full-back, John Bond, played 12 times as a makeshift centre-forward and scored eight goals in those matches.

10-1 at half-time

Tottenham were 10-1 up at half-time when they played Crewe in an FA Cup fourth round replay in February 1960, with Bobby Smith and Les Allen both helping themselves to four goals before the break. The match eventually finished 13-2 which was probably a bit disappointing for Tottenham but perfect for trivia lovers as the Crewe players' train home that afternoon left Euston Station from platform 13 and arrived back at Crewe on platform two.

Tom Finney (again)

When Preston's Tom Finney retired from the game in 1960, he was England's most-capped attacking player of all-time despite the Second World War having delayed his senior debut in professional football until he was 24. Finney subsequently came to be thought of by many as the greatest English player of his generation, although during his playing days he was less highly regarded than Stanley Matthews, even though he often kept Matthews out of the England side. In terms of versatility, Finney was certainly beyond compare for an attacking player of the 1950s. Of the 473 League and cup appearances he made for Preston, 331 of the first 339 were as an outside-right, while 106 of the last 134 were at centre-forward. For England, he made 33 of his 76 appearances as an outside-left, a position he hardly ever played in at club level.

Preston converted Finney to centre-forward in 1956 when he was 34 and he scored 75 goals in the three full seasons he played in that position, being named the Football Writers' Association Footballer of the Year at the end of the first of them. He had also won the award three years earlier as an outside-right and remains the only player to have won it twice for performances in very different positions.

Finney spent his entire career with Preston and, since he was Preston born and bred, is probably the greatest footballer to have played only for his hometown club. As well as playing football, he also had his own plumbing business, and it wasn't unusual for him to play in home games on a Saturday afternoon having worked as a plumber in the morning. While Stanley Matthews was nicknamed 'The Wizard of Dribble' during his playing days, Finney was known less-flatteringly as 'The Preston Plumber'.

When money rarely bought success

When Burnley won the League title in 1959-60, the 18 players they fielded that season consisted of eight who had joined the club as juniors, seven who had been signed from non-League (and mostly amateur) clubs and three who had been brought over from Irish clubs. Not one of their players, therefore, had ever played for any League side other than Burnley.

Today it's hard to believe that such a cheaply assembled squad could become the best in the country, but it probably wouldn't have been so surprising at the time, since before the Premier League era of rich club owners, success in English football was rarely achieved by buying big. Wolves won the League title in 1953-54 using mainly players who had never played for anyone else, as did Manchester United in '55-56 and '56-57, Wolves again in '58-59, Leeds in '68-69, Everton in '69-70, Arsenal in '70-71 and Leeds again in '73-74. In 1958, Bolton won the FA Cup with a team that hadn't cost a penny in transfer fees and Portsmouth's League title winners of 1949-50 featured four first-team regulars who had been signed from non-League clubs. It was also in non-League football where Liverpool found Roger Hunt who scored 31 goals for them when they won the title in 1963-64 and another 30 when they won it again two years later.

Even success in Europe could once be achieved on a shoestring. Only two of the West Ham side that won the European Cup-Winners' Cup in 1965 had been signed from other clubs and one of those was Alan Sealey whose professional career prior to joining the Hammers amounted to just four appearances for Leyton Orient in the Second Division. Three years later Manchester United won the European Cup with a side containing seven players who had come up through the club's ranks plus one who had been bought from Maidstone United. After this, no English club would become champions of Europe again until Liverpool in 1977 and again it was with a cheaply assembled side. Of the eleven they fielded in that year's final, two had been signed from Third Division clubs (Ray Clemence and Joey Jones), two from Fourth Division clubs

(Phil Neal and Kevin Keegan), two from non-League clubs (Steve Heighway and Jimmy Case) and two had signed for the club as juniors (Tommy Smith and Ian Callaghan).

Although unfashionable and unlikely League champions, Nottingham Forest's 1977-78 side was the first to win the title mainly with players signed from top-flight clubs, although since it featured the likes of Colin Barrett, Kenny Burns, Peter Withe, Larry Lloyd and John McGovern, their squad was more a collection of top-flight journeymen than top-flight stars. It was probably Manchester United under Ron Atkinson that was the first club to attempt to buy the title with multiple big signings – but it didn't work. United never finished any higher than third under Atkinson despite buying ten players from other top-flight clubs between 1981 and 1986, as well as two Danish internationals (at a time when there were few continental players in England) and Aberdeen's Gordon Strachan who was one of the most highly rated players in Scotland at that time. Atkinson was eventually sacked early in the 1986-87 season, a season that saw Everton win the League using 13 players signed from lower divisions clubs and only five from top-flight sides, two of whom – Kevin Sheedy and Alan Harper – had only been reserve team players at Liverpool. The following season, Liverpool won the title with several big money signings including John Barnes, Peter Beardsley, John Aldridge and Ray Houghton and this could be cited as the earliest example of a team 'buying the title', although as Liverpool had finished runners-up the season before and had won the double the season before that, these signings merely served to strengthen an already good side, and the following season a kind of normality was restored when Arsenal won the League with five first-team regulars (Adams, Merson, O'Leary, Thomas and Rocastle) who had come out of the club's youth team.

The League Cup

The League Cup was launched in 1960 as a new domestic cup competition for the age of floodlit football. It was to be contested between all of the Football League clubs, with all of the games being played in midweek and under floodlights wherever possible at a time when floodlights were still a new thing. The original idea of calling the competition the Football League Floodlit Cup was probably ditched because not all League clubs had floodlights in 1960.

Initially, the League Cup was not embraced by everyone and several top sides refused to enter it at first and it wouldn't be until the 1969-70 season that all 92 League clubs took part.

As well as the floodlit aspect, the League Cup also had the novelty of both semi-finals and the final being played over two legs, although in 1967 the two-legged final was replaced by a Wembley one played on a Saturday afternoon during a full League programme, and this would remain the case until it was switched to a Sunday in 1984. Even after the introduction of the Wembley final, however, the competition still seemed to lack prestige, due mainly to its lack of history, the BBC's refusal to cover it which lasted for more than a decade (1969-1980) and the fact that, before 1984, only highlights of the final were shown on TV except in 1969 when ITV showed the whole match but not until the day after it was played.

Still, in the 1960s and '70s it was, if nothing else, a fascinatingly unpredictable competition. Seven of the first 12 winners were clubs that had never won major honours before, with Queen's Park Rangers and Swindon both being in the Third Division when they lifted the trophy. Queen's Park Rangers victory over West Bromwich Albion in 1967 and Swindon's turning over of Arsenal two years later remain to this day the only two occasions when third-tier sides have beaten top-flight ones in Wembley finals. Earlier in the decade Rochdale had finished League Cup runners-up and this remains the only time a club from the fourth tier of English football has ever reached the final of a national competition open to top-flight clubs.

Admittedly in the 1960s not all of the big clubs played in the League Cup every season, but they did in the '70s and success in the competition continued to defy logic even then. Nottingham Forest aside, none of the clubs that either won the League or reached an FA Cup Final between 1970 and 1980 managed to win the League Cup during that period, while Aston Villa and Wolves both won it twice during that period but never won anything else. The first of Villa's two victories was in 1975 when they were a Second Division club, they beat another Second Division club in the final and no top-flight side made it past the quarter-finals.

Eventually, in the 1980s, success in the League Cup did begin to fall in line with what was expected, with Liverpool winning it for the first time in 1981, Manchester United doing so in 1983 and Arsenal in 1987, but the trophy continued to elude Everton who won the League twice in the '80s, and the unfashionables briefly dominated again between '85 and '88 when Norwich, Oxford and Luton were all winners. Norwich had won it once before but had never won anything else, while for Oxford and Luton it was the first major trophy for both clubs.

A false start for live League football on TV

The first televised League match in England was Blackpool v Bolton in September 1960, which was shown on ITV's *The Big Game* from a camera positioned at the back of one of the ends, which, although unusual, would be done again for other televised matches later in the decade. *The Big Game* was supposed to have been a weekly show, but was scrapped after this one match because other clubs refused to let the cameras in. The second live screening of a League match in England wouldn't be until 1983.

4-2-4

In the 1960-61 season, Ron Greenwood's West Ham became the first English side to adopt the 4-2-4 formation pioneered by Brazil's 1958 World Cup winners. While this sounds like a positive advancement, it was actually a more defensive system than what had gone before as it meant dispensing with wing-halves in order to play with an extra central defender. Bobby Moore was the wing-half who was moved into defence, although he would continue to be referred to as a 'left-half' until the 1970s.

4-4 at half-time

In October 1960, a Second Division match between Charlton and Middlesbrough was 4-4 at half-time. That first half saw four equalisers scored and the lead change hands three times. In the second half Middlesbrough came from behind to lead for the third time before extending their lead to 6-4 through Brian Clough's third goal of the game. There were still 21 minutes left when Charlton's Dennis Edwards completed his hat-trick to pull it back to 6-5, but after this there would be no further goals until Charlton's Johnny Summers grabbed the fifth equaliser of the match in the last minute.

The same month Charlton also had a 7-4 win at home to Portsmouth and a 5-3 win at Brighton.

Jimmy Greaves

Jimmy Greaves scored five goals for Chelsea in a First Division match against Wolves in August 1958 when he was just 18 years old. He then scored five again for Chelsea against Preston in December 1959 when he was 19 and then hit five for Chelsea for the third time against West Bromwich Albion in December 1960 when he was 20.

It's always 6-4

Charlton 6 Plymouth 4 and Plymouth 6 Charlton 4 were Division Two scorelines on consecutive days over Christmas 1960. Charlton 4 Plymouth 6 had been a scoreline from the Second Division the previous season.

Footballers can now get rich

For 60 years between 1901 and 1961 the pay of Football League players was capped, and the cap was only lifted when players planned to go on strike over it. Until 1961, no player was allowed to earn more than a basic pay of £20 a week, which was higher than the national average but only by 30 per cent. Because of this it wasn't unknown for even some of the top players to do other jobs to supplement their income.

Following the lifting of the cap, Fulham immediately gave Johnny Haynes a 500 per cent pay rise to make him Britain's first £100-a-week player. Many other clubs, however, found it hard to meet the rise in wages now expected and in 1968 the Football League made a failed attempt to restore the cap.

Denis Law

In January 1961, Manchester City were 2-0 down in a fourth round FA Cup tie at Luton but came back to lead 6-2 with all six goals coming from Denis Law in a 48-minute spell either side of half-time. With 21 minutes left, however, the match was abandoned due to the deteriorating state of the pitch and so Law's six goals aren't in the record books and City didn't even progress to the next round either as Luton won the replay 3-1. Some sources at the time gave one of Law's goals to Joe Hayes, but, for the sake of a good story, it was credited to Law.

Taking the lead without touching the ball

Sheffield Wednesday took the lead before they had even had their first touch of the ball in a First Division match at Fulham in January 1961. Fulham kicked-off and immediately began 30 seconds of unbroken possession that ended with Alan Mullery beating his own keeper with an attempted back pass.

When one of the best attended matches of the weekend was in the fourth tier

On Good Friday 1961 a crowd of 37,774 attended a Fourth Division match between Crystal Palace and Millwall. This was more than attended seven of the nine top-flight games played on the same day and an incredible 13,000 more than would be at Manchester United's home game the following day. Neither Palace nor Millwall had ever played at the highest level of English football at the time and their only honours in the professional game were one Third Division South title each. Palace had also got a gate of 36,478 when they had played host to Peterborough six months earlier.

That's entertainment

In the space of four months in the 1960-61 season, Burnley had three 5-3 wins, a 5-2 win, a 6-2 win, two 4-4 draws and a 4-3 defeat.

The unstoppable newcomers

The 1960-61 season saw Peterborough United win the Fourth Division title in their first ever season as a Football League club, which was also their first ever season in a national league as in those days all non-League football was regional. Equally remarkable was the fact that they scored 134 goals in taking the title which is still a League record today. They won four of their matches by a six-goal margin and top scorer Terry Bly got 52.

The first all-seater stand

The first all-seater stand at a football ground in England was opened at Sheffield Wednesday's Hillsborough in 1961. Until then, all stands at English football grounds had a standing enclosure underneath the seats.

Halifax v Real Madrid

Actually this match never took place, but Halifax did audaciously try to set it up in 1961 to mark the switching-on of their new floodlights. In the end they had to make do with a friendly against Red Star Belgrade, which was still a bit of a coup considering Red Star were one of the biggest clubs in Yugoslavia at the time.

Alex Dawson

When Manchester United beat Chelsea 6-0 and Manchester City 5-1 in consecutive First Division matches in December 1960, their 20-year-old centre-forward Alex Dawson scored hat-tricks in both games. Dawson went on to get 20 goals from 34 appearances for United that season, and yet early the following season he was sold to Second Division Preston and would never play in the top-flight again.

The night a Third Division club played future World Cup finalists

In October 1961, Third Division Bradford Park Avenue played a friendly against Czechoslovakia to mark the first switching-on of their new floodlights. Seven of the Czech team that night would play in the World Cup Final eight months later.

Stanley Matthews (again)

On 28 October 1961, Stanley Matthews played his first game for Stoke City for over 14 years and his return to the club attracted a crowd of nearly 36,000 which was 22,000 higher than Stoke's previous biggest crowd of that season. Matthews was 46 years old at the time.

Arthur Rowley (again)

When Shrewsbury's Arthur Rowley scored his side's third goal in a 3-0 win over Notts County on 28 March 1962, he became the first

– and still the only – player to score 400 goals in national-level league football in England. Rowley eventually finished his career on 434 League goals which is an all-time record by a margin of 55 and also a record that no player, other than Jimmy Greaves, has come within 100 goals of since Rowley retired in 1965. This is all the more impressive for the fact that Rowley was an inside-forward in the era of the WM formation, when inside-forwards were as much attacking midfielders as they were strikers and didn't out-score the centre-forwards. The 44 League goals Rowley scored for Leicester in the 1956-57 season was the most ever by an inside-forward during the WM era which lasted for 40 years between the mid-20s and mid-60s.

The last of Rowley's 434 League goals came in his last ever League appearance, for Shrewsbury at home to Bournemouth on 24 April 1965 – when he was playing at centre-back.

Danny Blanchflower

Danny Blanchflower was the only footballer ever interviewed on BBC Television's *Face to Face*, which more usually interviewed people from politics or the arts. *Face to Face* ran from 1959 to 1962, with each edition being made up of a single, serious, half-hour long interview with a public figure whose face remained largely in close-up throughout (hence the programme's title). The Danny Blanchflower edition aired after the ten o'clock News on Sunday 18 March 1962, which was during the days when there was still only one BBC channel.

Real come to London – for Crystal Palace's floodlights

Real Madrid's first ever match in London was a friendly against Crystal Palace in April 1962 to mark the switching-on of Palace's new floodlights. Real won 4-3 in front of a crowd of nearly 25,000. The gate at Palace's previous home match had been just 8,000.

Keeping it clean

In April 1962, it was revealed that there were seven Football League clubs that hadn't had a player sent-off in the 16 League seasons since the end of the Second World War (the seven clubs being Fulham, Wolves, Brighton, Nottingham Forest, Tottenham, Brentford and Tranmere). The stat appeared in *Soccer Star* magazine and was actually reported in a negative way, as if 'only seven' was too few.

The unlikeliest of title winners

Ipswich Town are the only club ever to have won the League title in their first ever season of top-flight Football. They achieved this in 1961-62 without having any internationals amongst their first-team regulars until Ray Crawford was capped in November. Just three years earlier they had finished 16th in Division Two with largely the same squad and two years before that they were still in Division Three.

The season following their title success they only managed a 17th place finish, then the season after that they finished bottom. This meant that they had spent three seasons in the top-flight of English football and had finished top in one of them and bottom in another.

The unique medal hat-trick

John Elsworthy, Ted Phillips, Len Carberry, Roy Bailey and Jimmy Leadbetter all won Third, Second and First Division championship winners medals with Ipswich between 1957 and 1962.

Brian Clough

Brian Clough played just six full seasons in his professional career (1956-62) and scored over 30 League and cup goals in each of them.

In fact, he scored 40 or more in each of the first four. Clough didn't make his professional debut until he was 21 and retired through injury at 27, but still finished his career with 271 goals in all competitions, 250 of them in the League.

Thinking outside the box with squad and team selection

England's 1962 World Cup squad contained four Second Division players, but no player from the Ipswich side that had just won the League title. Of the players from Division Two who travelled to Chile, Huddersfield's Ray Wilson played at left-back in all four of England's matches at the tournament, while Middlesbrough's Alan Peacock played centre-forward in two of them, despite having had no previous experience of international football. Liverpool's Roger Hunt and Sunderland's Stan Anderson were the other two Second Division players in the squad, but neither of them got a game.

England qualifying for the knock-out stages as no other team had done before, nor would do again

England are the only team ever to have qualified for the knock-out stages of the World Cup on goal average. They did this in 1962, which was the first World Cup after it was decided to use goal average to separate teams that finished level on points in the group stages, rather than have them play-off against each other as had previously been the case. England finished level on points with Argentina in Group 4 but had a better goal average and so went through to the quarter-finals. No other second and third-placed teams in that World Cup's groups finished level on points, nor would they in the 1966 World Cup, and in 1970 it was decided to use goal difference instead.

Gerry Hitchens

Gerry Hitchens equalised for England against Brazil in the quarter-finals of the 1962 World Cup with what proved to be the final shot of his international career. Although the goal came in the first half, Hitchens barely had a sniff for the remainder of the game and was never picked for his country again.

Don't tell me the score

All of England's games at the 1962 World Cup were shown on BBC1, but not until two days after they were played. This was because the tournament was held in Chile and in 1962 it was not yet possible to beam a live TV broadcast from South America to Europe and so the tapes of the matches had to be flown over by plane.

The rise and fall and rise again of football on TV

Regular shows devoted entirely to Football League action first appeared on British television at the start of the 1962-63 season when the ITV regional companies Tyne Tees and Anglia launched *Shoot* and *Match of the Week* respectively. Tyne Tees, however, was only available in the north east of England and Anglia only in East Anglia, so it wasn't until the BBC launched *Match of the Day* at the beginning of the 1964-65 season that the whole of Britain had a regular TV show devoted entirely to football action. Except this wasn't quite true as throughout this season *Match of the Day* aired on the newly-launched BBC2 at a time when BBC2 wasn't available throughout the country and very few TV sets had a BBC2 button anyway. Consequently, the first ever match shown on *Match of the Day* – Liverpool v Arsenal on 22 August 1964 – was watched by just 20,000 viewers, which was less than half the number that attended the game. It, therefore, wasn't until *Match of the Day* was switched to BBC1 for the '65-66 season that the show became truly accessible to the whole nation and it was this season that it moved from being an early-evening show to a late-evening one in order to give supporters who had been to away games the chance to get home and watch it. Initially *Match of the Day* showed only one match per week, before eventually increasing it to two in 1970, although it never had complete freedom when choosing which games to screen owing to the rules imposed upon it by the Football League. These stated that the cameras could not visit the same ground more than three times in a season for League games and that a quota of five Second Division matches and two from the Third or Fourth Divisions had to be shown each season as well.

As for the ITV football highlights shows, Southern Television became the third regional company to launch one in 1966, with the remaining regions doing so in 1968. Not all of these shows were on every week, but London Weekend Television's *The Big Match* was and provided a regular Sunday afternoon diet of extended highlights of a match from the previous day involving a London club (usually one in which the London club was at home) plus shorter highlights from a couple of other games which it borrowed from other regional highlights shows. Other than on FA Cup weekends, *The Big Match* rarely deviated from this policy prior to the 1980-81 season, so that even if the London club's game was dull and low-scoring it would still take up more of the show than a high-scoring thriller played between two clubs from outside the Capital.

When League football games first began being shown live on TV early in the 1983-84 season, all of ITV's highlights shows were axed apart from *The Big Match*, although this became an occasional, rather than weekly, show. The BBC's *Match of the Day* continued as a weekly show during the 1983-84 and 1984-85 seasons, before itself becoming an occasional show. Due to a dispute between the TV companies and the Football League, there was no football on TV during the first half of the 1985-86 season, and although it returned in January, *Match of the Day* didn't resume regular broadcasts and aired only four shows devoted to League action over the season's final 17 weeks. Then, in 1986-87, it showed no League games at all as the BBC now saw it as a programme to be wheeled-out only on FA Cup days even though they still had the rights to show League action at that time. This was also the case in 1987-88 and, since live broadcasts of League matches during this period was limited to just 18 per season, the number of games shown on TV between 1985 and 1988 was absolutely paltry compared with a decade earlier.

This eventually changed when ITV got exclusive rights to show a First Division match live every week during the 1988-89 season. This live game was always on a Sunday with all the goals from the previous day's First Division matches being shown at half-time, which marked the first time ever that TV cameras were present at all top-flight matches. ITV continued to hold exclusive rights to First Division matches until the First Division became the Premier League in 1992, at which point *Match of the Day* began showing League highlights again having spent the previous six years showing FA Cup games only.

Arthur Wilkie

In August 1962, The Reading goalkeeper Arthur Wilkie injured his hand in a home match against Halifax and so, unable to continue in goal, took Dennis Allen's place on the left wing while Allen replaced Wilkie between the sticks. Reading then went on to win the match 4-2, with their third and fourth goals both being scored by Wilkie in what was his only ever senior appearance as an outfield player.

Ten bookings in an instant

All ten of Mansfield Town's outfield players were booked after the final whistle of an FA Cup tie at Crystal Palace in November 1962. They had sarcastically applauded the referee for awarding Palace a last-minute penalty.

The longest FA Cup third round

Because of the big freeze of early 1963, that year's FA Cup third round took over two months to complete, with the last matches of the round not being played until two days before what was originally the scheduled sixth round date of 9 March. Exactly half of the 32 ties were postponed ten times or more, with the Lincoln v Coventry tie being called-off a record 15 times.

Burnden Park – the winter ghost-ground

Due to the aforementioned bad weather of the 1962-63 season, Bolton never played a home game in any competition between 8 December and 9 March.

Colin Booth

Colin Booth scored 38 League and cup goals for Doncaster in the 1962-63 season, which was five more than the rest of the squad managed between them. Of Doncaster's final 22 goals of the campaign, 17 came from Booth.

The highest scoring mediocre side

In the 1962-63 season, Bristol City scored four or more in a League match nine times, had five of their players reach double-figures for League goals and hit 100 League goals in total – and yet still only finished 14th in Division Three. This remains the only instance of a League team finishing in the bottom half of the table in a season when they reached the hundred-goal mark.

Nick Sharkey

Nick Sharkey scored seven goals for Sunderland in the 1962-63 season, with five of them coming in the 7-1 win at home to Norwich in March.

Eddie Reynolds

Eddie Reynolds remains the only player to have scored four goals in a Wembley final. He achieved this for Wimbledon against Sutton United in the 1963 Amateur Cup Final. All of the goals were headers.

Roy Chapman and Ken Wagstaff

Roy Chapman scored 37 goals for Mansfield in the 1962-63 season but still only finished as the club's second-top scorer. His teammate Ken Wagstaff got 41.

The 1960s match-fixing scandal

When Bristol Rovers drew 2-2 at Bradford Park Avenue in April 1963, the Bradford keeper, Esmond Million, let in both the Bradford goals on purpose – something he later admitted to – as he would have got £300 from a betting syndicate had Rovers lost. Rovers' 16-goal top scorer Keith Williams had accepted the same bribe and, unsurprisingly, failed to score. The game was played on a Saturday and both players were in Rovers' side for the game at Bristol City three days later – a game Williams did score in – but after that the truth came out and neither ever played in the Football League again.

A year later, it was revealed that the same syndicate had tried to fix several other matches that season by bribing players, with one of those games being the First Division fixture between Ipswich and Sheffield Wednesday, with Wednesday's Peter Swan, David Layne and Tony Kay all having taken bribes. Layne was Wednesday's top scorer in 1963-64 with 28 goals, while Swan was their stalwart centre-back who had been a regular in the England side up to the 1962 World Cup, but the allegations against them led to both players being suspended with two matches of the season left and then banned for life following the trial in the summer. The same also happened to Tony Kay which was harsh on Everton who had bought him from Wednesday a few weeks after the Ipswich game and now had nothing to show for their money.

The lifetime bans on all the players involved was lifted in 1972 and Layne and Swan were both re-signed by Wednesday, with Swan playing 15 times for them in the 1972-73 season despite being 36 and having been out of the game for over eight years. Layne, however, couldn't get in their first-team and made no more appearances as a full-time professional aside from four appearances on loan to Fourth Division Hereford in December '72 and January '73 (he didn't score and was substituted in two of them). Kay was not re-signed by Everton and never returned to the game.

The mastermind of the match-fixing ring was former Everton player Jimmy Gauld who was jailed for four years a few months after selling his story to the press.

Short-sleeved shirts

Short-sleeved football shirts first appeared in the 1950s but fell out of fashion in the '60s when long-sleeved, round-necked jerseys became the only kind of tops worn by English footballers. The 1963 FA Cup Final was the first for a decade in which all of the players played in long-sleeves and after this a short-sleeved shirt wouldn't be seen in an FA Cup Final again until a short-sleeved Arsenal team beat a long-sleeved Liverpool in 1971. This remains the only FA Cup Final in which every player on one side wore long sleeves, while every outfield player on the other was in short sleeves, although there had been other famous finals in other competitions where this was the case. In the 1966 World Cup Final, England wore long sleeves, while the Germans played in short sleeves, and the 1968 European Cup Final saw a long-sleeved Manchester United take on a short-sleeved Benfica.

Arsenal's flirtation with short-sleeves in 1971 didn't usher in a new fashion and long-sleeved shirts continued to predominate in England throughout the early-70s, with even Arsenal themselves going back to the long sleeves for the 1972 FA Cup Final. It wasn't really until T-shirts became fashionable leisurewear in the mid-70s that short-sleeved football shirts became common. The 1977 FA

Cup Final was the first for 15 years in which all of the outfield players wore short-sleeves, and from the late-70s onwards many players wore short-sleeved shirts all-year round, whilst others wore them during the early and late parts of the season but switched to long sleeves during the winter months.

In the early-1990s, when loose-fitting clothes became fashionable amongst the young, football shirts followed suit, with the short-sleeved ones becoming almost a throwback to the original short-sleeved shirts of the 1950s – i.e. baggy with sleeves that came down to the elbow. It was also in the '90s that long-sleeved shirts came back into vogue, with some players, such as David Beckham, wearing them all year round, something which hadn't happened since the mid-70s.

Jimmy Adamson and Alf Ramsey

In 1962, Jimmy Adamson turned down the job of England manager which was offered to him even though he was only 33 years old and still playing for Burnley. Adamson had been a member of England's 1962 World Cup squad but also acted as manager Walter Winterbottom's assistant during the tournament, which was why, when Winterbottom announced he was stepping down, Adamson was seen as the best person to succeed him. Following Adamson's refusal, the job was given to Ipswich manager Alf Ramsey who spent the next seven months managing both Ipswich and England before finally resigning as Ipswich boss in September 1963. Unlike his predecessor, Ramsey was given full control of squad and team selections which, until then, had been the job of a selection committee.

When the TV companies showed little interest in the European Championships

The first two European Championships (which was then called the European Nations Cup), involved no qualifying groups or final tournament groups, but were instead knock-out competitions from start to finish, contested between all of the countries that entered. England were not one of the entrants of the first competition which ran from 1958 to 1960, but in the next one – contested between 1962 and '64 – they did compete, albeit briefly, as France beat them over two legs in the first round. The first leg was a 1-1 draw at Hillsborough, and the second a 5-2 win for the French in Paris in what was Alf Ramsey's first match in charge of the national side.

It says a lot about what the English thought of the competition at this time that the first leg wasn't staged at Wembley and neither leg was shown live on UK TV. The BBC did show highlights of both legs but deemed the second leg highlights so insignificant that they placed them below an England v Scotland under-23 international on the bill of a half-hour edition of their *Sportsview* show. On the evening the semi-finals were played, *Sportsview* showed athletics from Crystal Palace.

In the 1968 European Championships, England lost to Yugoslavia in the semi-finals, and this was the first ever European Championship match to be shown live in its entirety on British television. England had beaten Spain over two legs in the quarter-finals but the viewing public had only been able to watch half hour of highlights from each match. In 1972, England bowed out at the quarter-final stage and this time the first leg at home to West Germany was shown live, but as England lost 3-1 only highlights of the second leg were shown, although there couldn't have been much of them as it finished 0-0.

Like England's aforementioned first round matches against France in the early-60s, these quarter-finals are now referred to as 'qualifiers' but that's not how they were seen at the time – they were just the quarter-finals.

Jimmy Greaves (again)

Jimmy Greaves was not only the greatest striker of his generation, he was also the person who first coined the word 'striker' to refer to a goalscoring forward. Or, at least, the first time the word in its footballing sense appeared in print was in a handbook to the game that Greaves was commissioned to write. The book was called simply *Soccer* and was published in 1963. In it, Greaves initially uses the term 'goal-striker', before later abbreviating it to just 'striker'.

Transfers

Before 1964, English football's retain-and-transfer rule meant that, in theory, a player could be kept at the same club for his entire career whether he liked it or not. This is because the 'retain' part of the rule stated that once a player signed for a club, then that club held his registration, would never be forced to give it up and, while they had it, the player could never play for anyone else. At the end of every season a club produced a list of retained players (the retained list) and a list of players who were up for sale (the transfer list), and the players had no real say as to which list they appeared on. A player reaching the end of his contract did not mean his name being removed from the retained list, so if he wanted to carry on playing the next season he had no option but to sign a new contract with the same club again.

This first caused controversy at the end of the 1947-48 season when Middlesbrough's Wilf Mannion wanted a move to Oldham and so refused to sign a new contract with Boro, but because they held his registration, he was unable to sign for Oldham either. As a result, Mannion spent the first five months of the 1948-49 season out of the game having been England's first-choice inside-left up until that point. Eventually Boro slapped a price-tag on him that Oldham couldn't afford, leaving Mannion with little option but to re-sign for Boro. He then played there until the end of the 1953-54 season when he retired from the game at the age of 36, although, even after that, Boro continued to hold his registration, meaning that Hull had to pay a transfer fee for him when he came out of retirement to play for them seven months later.

The retain-and-transfer rule was eventually reformed following another high profile dispute that saw Newcastle's George Eastham go on strike for two months at the start of the 1960-61 season over the club's refusal to move him onto the transfer list. Newcastle eventually relented and sold him to Arsenal, but the PFA persuaded Eastham to take Newcastle to court to recover the earnings he had lost while on strike and to challenge the football authorities over the 'retain' part of retain-and-transfer. The case lasted from June to October 1963, with the court finding in Newcastle's favour over the loss of earnings but against the rule that allowed clubs to keep a player's registration after his contract had expired. Football League Secretary Alan Hardaker, however, was insistent that players should not become free agents at the end of their contracts as he believed this would harm the competitiveness of the League by making it more difficult for the smaller clubs to hang onto their biggest stars. Hardaker responded to the court's verdict by saying: "the retain-and-transfer system is fundamental to the League and must go on". And go on it did, only in an amended form that would not be deemed an 'undue restraint of trade'. From 1964, a club could no longer deny a player's request to be put on the transfer list, nor could they keep hold of a want-away player by pricing him out of the market.

Exactly how much difference this made is difficult to say, because it certainly didn't seem to lead to any great increase in the number of transfers. Of the 1,012 players who played on the opening day of the 1962-63 season, 128 had been transferred that summer, which was one fewer than the number of new signings who would play on the opening day of 1972-3 (when more players were involved in total because substitutions were allowed by then).

At end of the 1977-78 season, another big change in the rules came along in the shape of 'freedom of contract', which allowed players to offer themselves to other clubs and to conduct their own independent transfer talks. After losing Gary Collier through the 'freedom of contract' rule in 1979, Bristol City acted quickly to stop any more costly departures and handed all of their best players long, lucrative contracts that would ensure they stayed at the club until their best days were behind them, which in Clive Whitehead's case meant him getting a record-busting eleven-year one. It seemed like a good idea at the time, but the big wage bills became unsustainable following City's relegation in 1980, and only eight of the players agreeing to take redundancy saved the club from liquidation in 1982.

To say Bristol City overreacted to the rule change would be a colossal understatement since, just like the change in retain-and-transfer, 'Freedom of contract' did not appear to make a huge difference in the number of transfers. In the calendar year of 1977, 265 players were transferred between Football League clubs. In 1990 it was 302. Meaning that, on average, each League club signed 1.4 players from another League club in 1977, and 1.6 in 1990. And yet, that said, the 1977-78 saw 75 players play for clubs they had already made more than 300 League appearances for, where as in 1989-90 only 21 did (excluding a couple who did so over two spells), so something was obviously changing.

The biggest change of all, however, came with the Bosman ruling in 1995 which finally realised Alan Hardacker's worst nightmare and made all players free agents once their contracts had expired. With this rule a player was never likely to sign a new contract with his old club if he had a chance of getting more money and bigger games elsewhere, and clubs were less likely to offer a new contract to an average player when it would be so easy to replace him with a potentially better one for no transfer fee. Consequently, the movement of players since the Bosman ruling has been off-the-scale compared with earlier years. No fewer than 34 Football League clubs fielded no new signings on the opening day of the 1975-76 season. Today it would be highly unusual for just one club to do so.

Rodney Marsh

Rodney Marsh was left permanently deaf in one ear through a head injury he received while playing for Fulham at Leicester in September 1963.

The dart that changed Goodison Park

After Tottenham lost 1-0 at Everton in October 1963, Tottenham claimed that their goalkeeper, Bill Brown, had been hit by a dart thrown from the crowd during the second half of the match.

Everton responded by accusing Tottenham of lying and claiming the dart had been thrown in the first half when Brown was up the other end of the pitch. They also thought it was suspicious that Tottenham hadn't even mentioned the dart until after they returned to London. Nevertheless, the next game at Goodison Park saw the sections of terracing closest to each goal barricaded-off to keep the fans a safer distance from the goalkeepers, something that made Goodison the first football ground in England to have alterations made to it in order to combat hooliganism. The barricaded-off sections were then demolished altogether, giving the barriers behind the goal a peculiar curved shape which would remain until the front of the terraces were eventually rebuilt in the late-70s.

Two years after the dart-throwing incident, another dart was thrown from the crowd during a match at Birmingham and again it was aimed at Tottenham's Bill Brown. No one on the field saw it happen, but the dart was seen sticking out of the ground close to Brown's goal just before half-time and it hadn't been there at the start of the game.

Number One

No goalkeeper in England wore a number one on the back of his jersey until West Ham's Jim Standen started doing so in the 1963-64 season, and most keepers – even in the top-flight – were still wearing blank jerseys in the early-1970s. In fact, Chelsea were still fielding goalkeepers with no numbers on their backs as late as the 1978-79 season.

You wait forever for a 4-4 draw and then two come along at once

On 2 November 1963, Stoke City had their first ever home 4-4 draw. Their second came in their next home game two weeks later.

Mike Kear

When Trevor Hockey left First Division Nottingham Forest for Newcastle in November 1963, the man Forest signed to replace him on the right-wing was Mike Kear from Newport County, which could hardly have been a more bizarre choice since, not only were Newport a Fourth Division club, but Kear had only made six League appearances for them since moving there from Cinderford Town in the summer. After signing him, Forest put Kear straight into their starting line-up for the home game against Tottenham.

The top-flight's craziest day

The highest scoring day in the history of top-flight football in England was Boxing Day 1963 when the ten matches played produced a total of 66 goals. The scores were as follows:

>Blackpool 1 Chelsea 5
>Burnley 6 Manchester United 1
>Fulham 10 Ipswich Town 1
>Leicester City 2 Everton 0
>Liverpool 6 Stoke City 1
>Nottingham Forest 3 Sheffield United 3
>Sheffield Wednesday 3 Bolton Wanderers 0
>West Bromwich Albion 4 Tottenham Hotspur 4
>West Ham United 2 Blackburn Rovers 8
>Wolverhampton Wanderers 3 Aston Villa 3

Andy Lochhead (Burnley), Graham Leggat (Fulham), Bobby Howfield (Fulham), Roger Hunt (Liverpool), Fred Pickering (Blackburn) and Andy McEvoy (Blackburn) all scored hat-tricks. For some reason, Arsenal and Birmingham played what ought to have been their Boxing Day fixture on a Tuesday night in November. It finished 4-1 to Arsenal with Joe Baker getting a hat-trick.

Stanley Matthews (yet again)

Bob Kelly made his Football League debut for Burnley in 1913, and Alan Suddick made his final League appearance for Bury in 1978, and yet such was the length of Stanley Matthews' career that he played in League matches against both of them. Matthews' career spanned 33 years in all (1932 to 1965) and he never played at any level lower than the Second Division. His last League goal (in May 1963) came 30 years after his first (in March 1933) – and they were both scored for Stoke.

The greatest FA Cup upset by a rubbish Second Division side

Liverpool won the League title in the 1963-64 season but were beaten at home in the sixth round of the FA Cup by Second Division Swansea who only won once away from home in the League that season and would only avoid relegation to the third tier by one point.

Packing them in (somehow) at Sunderland

The Sunderland v Manchester United FA Cup sixth round replay of March 1964 had an official attendance of 46,727, but it was estimated that another 25,000 got into the ground without paying after the gates at the Roker End were forced open.

The worst five years ever

The 1963-64 season was the fifth in a row that Hartlepools finished in the bottom two of the Fourth Division. During those five seasons they also failed to win any cup games against League opposition.

John White

John White had been Tottenham's first choice inside-right for each of the four seasons leading up to the summer of 1964 when he was struck by lightning and killed while sheltering from a storm on a golf course. He probably stands as the most decorated player to have died in his 20s (he was 27), having been a League title winner and twice an FA Cup winner. He also won 22 caps for Scotland.

Derek Forster

Sunderland's goalkeeper for the first three games of the 1964-65 season was the 15-year-old Derek Forster. Forster conceded ten goals in those three games and would not play again until January 1968.

Dave Mackay

Tottenham's Dave Mackay missed the last four months of the 1963-64 season after breaking his leg in a European Cup-Winners' Cup match against Manchester United in the December. He eventually made his comeback for the reserves at the start of the following season but broke the same leg again in only his seventh reserve team appearance. This second leg-break in nine months would keep him out for a further eleven months. He eventually made his return to the Tottenham first-team on the opening day of the 1965-66 season and went on to play in all but two of the club's League games that season.

Peter Bonetti

Although it's pretty unthinkable that a player could play a full match without having a single kick of the ball, it may well have happened when Chelsea played Notts County in the League Cup in October 1964. That night, Chelsea keeper Peter Bonetti never kicked the ball out once, instead choosing to throw it out every time he had it. This was noticed by a Chelsea fan who wrote in to the club's programme with his observation, after which Bonetti himself confirmed it.

Terry Venables

Terry Venables only ever won two England caps – against Belgium and Holland in 1964 – but he does hold a unique record at international level as he's the only player ever to have been capped by England at both senior and amateur level as well as at three different age group levels (schoolboy, youth and under-23s).

Heads – you're in the semi-final

Liverpool reached the semi-finals of the 1964-65 European Cup on the toss of a coin. Before the away goals rule was introduced into European competitions for the 1965-66 season, all ties that were level on aggregate after two legs went to a third game and if the third game was also drawn then the winner would be decided by tossing a coin. Liverpool fought out two 0-0 draws and then a 2-2 draw with FC Cologne in the '64-65 quarter-final before winning the coin toss. This stands as the biggest club tie ever to be decided in this way, although Italy would win the European Championship semi-final on the toss of a coin in 1968.

Second Division strugglers to almost-double winners in three years

The 1961-62 season was Leeds United's first under Don Revie and it didn't go well. In the Second Division at the time, they finished below the likes of Leyton Orient, Scunthorpe, Rotherham, Plymouth,

Walsall and Bury in the table and only avoided relegation to Division Three on the season's final Saturday. And yet, just three seasons later, and still under Revie, Leeds were a First Division club going for a League and Cup double that was still in their sights five days before the FA Cup Final. They were top of the table going into their final League game of that 1964-65 season, and as it was at bottom-placed Birmingham all was looking very promising. Incredibly, however, Leeds found themselves 3-0 down after 55 minutes despite having had a man advantage for most of the game. They subsequently came back to make it 3-3, but their failure to find a late winner ultimately allowed Manchester United to pip them to the title on goal average. This disappointment was then compounded at the end of the week when they took on Liverpool in the FA Cup Final and went down 2-1 after extra-time. Had they managed to beat both Birmingham and Liverpool then they would still be the only team ever to have won the League and FA Cup double the season after winning promotion to the top-flight.

The BOAC Trophy

The BOAC Trophy was a competition arranged between the British state-owned airline BOAC and the New Zealand FA and contested between Sheffield United and Blackpool during May and June 1965. It involved BOAC flying the two teams to New Zealand where they played each other eleven times in four weeks and in nine different towns and cities. United won the trophy on account of winning six of the matches, and they would be its only ever winners as the competition was never staged again.

The day of the missiles

When Brentford took on Millwall in a Third Division match in November 1965, the Brentford keeper, Chic Brodie, had a full oil can thrown at him by the Millwall fans, as well as pieces of wood with protruding nails in them and even a hand grenade. In those days the British tended to take things in their stride a lot more than they do today, and Brodie's response to the bombardment was simply to toss the objects into the back of his goal net (yes, even the grenade) and carry on playing. At the other end of the field, meanwhile, the Millwall keeper, Alex Stepney, had a piece of iron hurled at him and several bottles, which would have been glass bottles as there were no plastic ones back then. Stepney was also attacked by a pitch invader at the end of the match. Commenting on the missile throwing, the Brentford chairman, Jack Dunnett, said simply, "you can't search everybody who comes into the ground".

Substitutions

The England national team made three substitutions in the 1950s (two of which were in the same game) and Liverpool brought Phil Chisnall on as a sub in the 1964 Charity Shield, but it wasn't until the 1965-66 season that substitutions were first allowed in League games in England, and then it was only one per team per game and for the replacement of injured players only. Charlton's Keith Peacock was the first sub to be used in a Football League match when he replaced injured keeper Mick Rose eleven minutes into his side's match at Bolton on 21 August 1965, an event which, because of its historic nature, doomed Peacock to forever be remembered as a substitute even though he went on to make more than 500 starts for Charlton and scored 107 goals for the club.

Although tactical substitutions were allowed from the start of the '67-68 season, managers initially still tended to use their substitutes sparingly and would continue to do so for many years. This is borne out by the fact that in the 1969-70 season, 32.4 per cent of matches played in the Football League were completed without a substitution being made by either side. Chesterfield's Jimmy McGuigan was one manager who appeared to be especially reluctant to use substitutes unless for the replacement of injured players. McGuigan made only four substitutions in Chesterfield's 46 League matches in the 1967-68 season and only five in their 53 League and cup games in 1971-72.

He also kept his substitute as a spectator in each of 19 consecutive League games in 1969-70. McGuigan wouldn't change much over the years either. He was still holding back on the substitutions when manager of Stockport in the early-80s.

Most managers, however, were not like McGuigan and, over time, more and more of them would come to see the usefulness of tactical substitutions. Consequently, in the 1986-87 season, which was the final season in which only one sub was allowed, the proportion of matches that started and finished with the same 22 players on the field had fallen to 13.9 per cent. Even so, Nottingham Forest still managed to go from 25 October to 7 March without bringing on a sub in a League game.

In fact, two substitutions per team were allowed in 1986-87, but only in the League Cup, and they had been allowed as early as the 1971-72 season in the Texaco Cup, but only providing one of the substitutions was a goalkeeper replacement. Two outfield substitutions were then allowed in the Watney Cup the following season, with Lincoln being the first English club to bring on two outfield subs in a domestic competition when John Ward and Colin Symm replaced Dave Smith and Percy Freeman at home to Burnley on 29 July 1972. We can probably, however, discard both the Texaco Cup and Watney Cup as they weren't major competitions, in which case the real starting point of the more-than-one-substitute era was the League Cup first round, first leg match between Gillingham and Northampton on 25 August 1986. This was played the evening before all the other ties in the round and so stands as the first match in a major competition in England in which more than one sub was allowed. Gillingham took full advantage of the new rule by bringing on Mel Eves and Paul Collins, but Northampton didn't use either of their subs even though they lost.

In 1987-88, two substitutes per team per game were allowed for the first time in both the League and the FA Cup, and this saw the proportion of Football League matches being completed without any substitutions being made falling to just 6.2 per cent. It was this season that Crewe became the first club to make at least one substitution in all of their League matches.

Bobby Knox

Bobby Knox had a fairly undistinguished 1965-66 season, starting only 12 League games for Fourth Division Barrow as well as making five further appearances for them as a substitute. He did, however, set two records from those five substitute appearances that season. At home to Wrexham on the opening day, he became the first substitute to come on and score in a Football League game, and then, at Christmas, after replacing the injured Barrow keeper, Lionel Duffin, he became the first ever substitute to save a penalty.

Peter Knowles

Peter Knowles was still a teenager at the start of the 1965-66 season but scored 12 goals for Wolves in that season's first eleven matches and finished the season with 21 goals in all competitions despite missing 12 games through injury. Knowles would remain a regular in the Wolves side for the next four seasons before, in September 1969, with Wolves riding high in the First Division, he announced his retirement from football for religious reasons, having recently become a Jehovah's Witness. Wolves, however, refused to accept his resignation and, although he never played professional football again, they continued to register him as one of their players until the end of the 1981-82 season, meaning that he was a professional footballer who went 12 full seasons without playing a single game.

Leaving the attacking to the kids

When Port Vale lost a Fourth Division match 2-0 to bottom-of-the-table Bradford City in January 1966, their ineffectual forward-line was made up entirely of teenagers. Outside left Paul Ogden was 19, inside-right Paul Bannister was 18 and outside-right Alex Donald, inside-left Mike Cullerton and centre-forward Rod Georgeson were all 17. Out of the five, only Bannister wasn't making his senior debut and only Georgeson wasn't dropped for the club's next game at home to Rochdale three days later.

Rodney Marsh (again)

In March 1966, Rodney Marsh dropped down two tiers of football when he joined Third Division QPR from First Division Fulham. This remains one of the most surprising transfers ever considering Marsh had scored 17 top-flight goals the previous season and was still only 21.

A mad first ten minutes

Birmingham City's Second Division home game against Derby in April 1966 was 3-2 to Birmingham after just ten minutes. It eventually finished 5-5.

The night there was a big game in London but everyone stayed in to watch the telly

When Arsenal entertained Manchester United early in the 1965-66 season they did so in front of a crowd of 56,757, and yet when Leeds visited Arsenal at the end of the season only 4,554 turned-up, which was 3,000 below the attendance of the Torquay versus Halifax Fourth Division match three days earlier. The fact that Leeds were third in the League at the time makes this strangely low attendance seem even stranger at first sight but, in fact, there was really no mystery to it at all. On the same night Liverpool were playing Borussia Dortmund in the final of the European Cup Winners' Cup and it was being shown live on BBC1. In those days live football on

TV was such a rarity that it was a must-see for anyone with an interest in the game, so few football fans would have been prepared to go out and miss it even if their own team were playing as well. It's also worth noting that, although Leeds were third, they couldn't mathematically win the title and Arsenal were in the bottom half, so why miss the Cup Winners' Cup Final in order to watch a meaningless end-of-season First Division match?

A very misleading away thrashing

York won 4-1 away to Hull in a Third Division match in September 1965 but went on to win only one more away game that season and eventually finished bottom, while Hull never lost another home game and went on to win the title.

The demise of Accrington Stanley

Accrington Stanley resigned from the Football League in March 1962 with 13 of their Division Four matches still remaining. Following their resignation, they joined the Second Division of the Lancashire Combination and were champions of it in 1963-64 but were relegated a year later and folded half-way through the 1965-66 season. When they played their last ever match at home to Glossop on 8 January 1966, they did so with only around 50 people in attendance. A far cry from the 15,454 that had watched their Division Three North Fixture against Rochdale on the same ground less than nine years earlier.

A new Accrington Stanley was eventually formed in 1968, although their ground was about five miles from where the original club had played. This second incarnation of Stanley was eventually elected to the Lancashire Combination in 1970 and, in 2006, won promotion to the Football League 44 years after the original club resigned from it.

Fairs Cup madness at Elland Road

In February 1966, fighting broke out between Leeds and Valencia players during an Inter-Cities Fairs Cup match at Elland Road which led to the police having to come onto the pitch to separate them, before the referee took both teams off for ten minutes to cool down. When they eventually came back out again, both Jack Charlton and Valencia's Francisco Vidagany were not amongst them as they were informed they had both been sent-off for the incident that sparked the brawl. There were only ten minutes left when play resumed and only five of those minutes had passed when Valencia's Jose Sanchez Lage poleaxed Jim Storrie and was also dismissed. Afterwards Leeds manager Don Revie said "If you have to go into Europe and that's the way they play, we are better off out of it."

Everton's strange Cup Final reshuffle

Fred Pickering was Everton's top scorer in the 1965-66 season with 22 goals but had no involvement in his side's 1966 FA Cup Final victory over Sheffield Wednesday as the club's manager, Harry Catterick, had dropped him for the match and he couldn't be named as substitute as there were still no subs allowed in the FA Cup in '66. Catterick's decision to leave out Pickering was simply that he felt the centre-forward had failed to regain his confidence after recovering from a knee injury, although he had led the line in each of Everton's three League matches leading up to the final. His number nine shirt on the day was taken by Alex Young who usually played inside-right and had only scored nine times that season, with Young's place at inside-right going to Mike Trebilcock who had only made seven League appearances for the club since being signed from Plymouth in December.

Everton won the match 3-2 (after being 2-0 down), with Trebilcock being the unlikely two-goal hero, although his Wembley heroics would earn him only four further first-team outings for Everton before they sold him to Portsmouth 20 months later.

When Wembley was exclusive

For 17 years between 1949 and 1966 (inclusive), the only domestic football matches played at Wembley were the FA Cup Final and the FA Amateur Cup Final, plus the unpublicised Inter-Varsity match between Oxford and Cambridge's university teams which was staged at the venue from 1953.

White City Stadium

The Uruguay v France match at the 1966 World Cup was the only World Cup finals match ever played at London's White City Stadium. The only reason it was played there and not at Wembley was because it was on a Friday and, in those days, Friday night was one of Wembley's greyhound racing nights, and greyhound racing was still a very popular spectator sport in the 1960s that attracted large crowds and was televised by the BBC.

White City stadium was also a greyhound racecourse, but, unlike Wembley, was rarely used for anything else after Queens Park Rangers ceased playing their home games there in 1963. It had originally been built for the 1908 London Olympics before being converted into a dog track in 1927. As well as being the only World Cup match ever played at the stadium, Uruguay v France was also the last ever professional football match played there before it was closed and then demolished in the mid-1980s. The last competitive match of any kind played at the stadium was an Olympic Games qualifier between Great Britain and Spain on 10 April 1968. It finished 0-0 and 1-0 to Spain on aggregate meaning the Great Britain football team failed to qualify for that year's Mexico City Olympics. Only 2,300 spectators were present to witness their failure. The stadium's capacity was 93,000.

England – the pioneering world champions

No international team or club side outside of the USSR had ever played without wingers until Alf Ramsey's England did so for the first time against Spain in December 1965. In the World Cup the following summer, they also played without wingers from the quarter-finals onwards, operating a formation that was, ostensibly, 4-3-3, but in reality, was more of a 4-4-2. Brazil had played a kind of 4-3-3 at the 1962 World Cup, but only because they had one of their wingers play deep. No international side had played a proper 4-3-3 with no wide players until Ramsey's England did so, and certainly no team at any level had ever played 4-4-2 before. Once England did it, however, so the whole world soon followed, with the 4-3-3 becoming the standard formation throughout football by the 1970s, before the 4-4-2 superseded it later that decade.

Was the '66 World Cup really that big?

England's quarter-final match against Argentina in the 1966 World Cup was played in front of a Wembley crowd that was 10,000 below the stadium's capacity, and even the crowd for the final against West Germany was 7,000 below capacity. There had been more at the England v Scotland game the previous year.

George Cohen

The World Cup winners' medal England's George Cohen won in 1966 was the only major medal of his footballing career.

The World Cup that was a pre-season tournament

The 1966 World Cup Final was played just three weeks before the start of the 1966-67 English League season and just two weeks before Liverpool and Everton contested the Charity Shield.

It wasn't all about Wembley

Although the 1966 World Cup is most associated with Wembley, there were actually only nine matches in the tournament that were played there, compared with 19 in the north of England.

Geoff Hurst

While the fact that Geoff Hurst scored a hat-trick for England in the 1966 World Cup Final is known by practically everyone, what is not so well known is that Hurst only had seven caps and two international goals going into the match, and that the match would be the only one of his international career in which he scored more than once without converting a penalty. He scored another hat-trick against France in March 1969, but it included two penalties and scored twice against Scotland two months later but one was a penalty. In each of his other 46 internationals he scored just once or not at all.

George Raikes

George Raikes was the only England international of the 19th century who lived to see England win the World Cup in 1966. Raikes was an amateur player who never played in the Football League, but he kept goal for England four times during the 1894-95 and '95-96 seasons. His death, at the age of 93, came five months after England became World champions.

Stoppage time

There was no stoppage time played at the end of the 1966 World Cup Final. Geoff Hurst scored England's fourth goal just before the half-hour mark in extra-time and the referee blew the final whistle during the celebrations, meaning West Germany didn't kick off again. While it was unusual for a team not to kick-off after conceding a goal, a match with no stoppage time wasn't especially rare in those days as stoppage time, when it was played, tended to only be a matter of seconds anyway. The 1968 European Cup Final (Man United v Benfica) was another high profile game of the period that didn't appear to have any time added on at the end and the 1969 FA Cup Final (Man City v Leicester) only went about 20 seconds over the top. And this wasn't really something that changed much during the '70s and '80s either. When referee George Courtney blew the final whistle at the end of the 1980 FA Cup Final (West Ham v Arsenal) without adding any time on, no one thought it strange.

Nor did anyone think it particularly unfair when Fulham were denied promotion on the last day of the 1982-83 season after the referee ended their game at Derby after 88 minutes and 42 seconds because hundreds of Derby fans on the touchline were encroaching onto the pitch. Fulham were losing 1-0 and needed to win to go up and they complained about not being able to complete the match, but most people agreed with Gordon Milne, the manager of Leicester who went up instead. Milne suggested that ending the match 78 seconds early didn't make any difference as 78 seconds wasn't long enough for Fulham to score the two goals they needed. Today, to suggest that there are only 78 seconds left when a match is in the 89th minute would be ludicrous, but back then Milne was pretty close to being scientifically correct.

Six years later Arsenal won the League title at Liverpool in the last game of the season, which was shown live on TV. "We're now well into time added on," said ITV commentator Brian Moore when the clock was only 32 seconds past the 90 minutes. He then went on to say, "Arsenal will come streaming forward now in what will surely be their last attack," when just 73 seconds of stoppage time had passed. Arsenal scored from that attack, and, at the time, it was probably the latest goal ever seen in a live televised game. Today, it's time would have been recorded as 90+2 but because goals in stoppage time were so rare then, there was no method for recording when they were scored so the minute of the goal was just given as '90' as was the case with all stoppage time goals at that time and for many more years to come.

Even in the late-90s, stoppage time was still only about one or two minutes long in most games. Stoppage time of five minutes or more is very much a 21st century phenomenon, a by-product of multiple substitutions, players playing for free-kicks, players staying down after a challenge and elongated goal celebrations by the corner flag.

Back to the grass roots

Two of England's 1966 World Cup winning side – Geoff Hurst and Gordon Banks – went on to manage Telford United in the 1970s. Hurst became Telford's player-manager in 1976 and, upon taking over, organised a friendly between Telford and the '66 World Cup Final team which all of that team took part in. Banks took over at Telford in 1979 and, as well as being their manager, was also the club's raffle ticket seller.

Bobby Tambling

Bobby Tambling was the first player ever to score five goals in a match that was televised in England, doing so for Chelsea in their 6-2 First Division win at Aston Villa on 1 October 1966. Typical of the days when English footballers showed good, old-fashioned English restraint, Tambling didn't celebrate any of his goals.

Swindon Town – world champions

Six months after England won the World Cup, a West Ham side featuring the World Cup winners Bobby Moore, Geoff Hurst and Martin Peters were beaten 3-1 in an FA Cup replay by Third Division Swindon.

The fist-swinging '60s

Reports of fighting between rival groups of football fans in England date back to the 1920s, but it was in 1963 that they first started to generate a lot of media coverage. In December of that year, Everton played Glasgow Rangers at Goodison Park in a glorified friendly to decide the 'British champions' and the fighting between rival fans outside the ground was the first incident of its kind to make national headlines. The same month, an article in *Charles Buchan's Football Monthly* lamented, "Here a few bottles [thrown], there a maniac with a dart. Lunatics who vent their spleen with brawls on the terraces of grounds other than their own, idiots who throw toilet rolls onto the pitch, yobbos who wreck excursion trains. Put together, it makes a savage, sad story".

And it was one that only got worse. As the 1966 World Cup approached there were genuine fears it would be marred by hooliganism, and although it wasn't in the end, the season that followed saw a big escalation in supporter fighting. It was early in this season that 'hooligan gangs' were first mentioned in the British press, and it was during the same season that fans first came to see one end of their ground as a 'home end' that had to be defended from infiltration by away fans who in turn saw the same end as a territory that had to be 'taken'. The 1966-67 season, therefore, was probably the first season of ritualized (rather than spontaneous) violence at English football matches and it culminated on the season's penultimate Saturday, which was, according to the *News of the World*, "Soccer's Day Of Shame", as a match between West Ham and Manchester United saw 20 fans hospitalized following fighting both inside and outside the ground.

Consequently, the following season the first attempts were made by clubs to segregate home and away fans at matches and eventually, in 1970, the FA advised all Football League clubs to erect fencing on their terraces to prevent fans moving from one part of the ground to another.

It's strange but true, that before the arrival of the hooligan gangs (later known as 'firms' or 'crews') in the 1960s, there were no such things as 'home' and 'away' ends – or sections – at English football grounds. There were no doubt ends that the home fans preferred, but they weren't exclusively for home fans and wouldn't be made so by the clubs until the 1970s. In the 60s, fans – both home and away – could stand on whatever terrace they liked and often changed ends at half-time. The 'away' sections at modern grounds, therefore, are the lasting legacy of 1960s hooliganism.

Ron Davies

In the autumn of 1966, Southampton's Ron Davies scored in each of ten consecutive First Division matches for Southampton but was only on the winning side in three of them. Davies finished the season with 43 goals in all competitions despite the fact that Southampton finished just one place above the relegation zone and only won two cup ties. Of Davies's 37 League goals, 20 came in matches that Southampton didn't win.

Tony Allden

Enfield's 23-year-old defender Tony Allden died after being struck by lightning during an FA Amateur Cup tie against Highgate in February 1967. Several other players were hospitalized by the lightning bolt which caused the game to be abandoned after 28 minutes. Although both sides were from Greater London, the rescheduled match took place at Aston Villa's Villa Park and was made a benefit match for Allden's family. It attracted a crowd of 31,632, which was 10,000 above Villa's average home gate of that season.

Norwich City – best team in Europe

When Manchester United won the League title in 1966-67, their only home defeat of the season was to Second Division Norwich in the fourth round of the FA Cup. Norwich went on to finish eleventh in Division Two that season, while seven members of the United team they beat would be in the side that won the European Cup the following season.

When Young England were (much) better than England the world champions

England v Young England was an (almost) annual friendly that was played on the evening before the FA Cup Final eleven times between 1958 and 1969. The Young England side consisted of the younger stars of the First Division, most of whom were England under-23 internationals, and in 1967 they triumphed 5-0 against a senior England side that contained six of the team that had won the World Cup the previous summer. The following year, Young England again embarrassed their senior opponents by winning 4-1. Five of the defeated England players that night would play in the semi-finals of the European Championships three weeks later.

Blackpool's deceptively bad season

Blackpool's First Division campaign of 1966-67 included a 6-0 win at home to Newcastle, a 5-1 win at Southampton, a 3-1 win at Tottenham (who finished third), a 3-1 win at Liverpool (who finished fifth) and a 1-0 win at Everton (who finished sixth). They also beat the eventual League champions Manchester United 5-1 at home in the League Cup. These may sound like scorelines from a successful season but, in fact, Blackpool finished bottom of the First

Division that season with the 6-0 win over Newcastle being their only home victory in the League.

Bobby Blackwood and Les Allen

Colchester United's Bobby Blackwood broke his jaw twice during the 1966-67 season. Both times in collisions with QPR's Les Allen.

The Charlton brothers

At the end of the 1966-67 season, Jack Charlton won the Football Writers' Association Football of The Year award a year after his brother Bobby had won the same award.

Getting nasty in the '60s

During the 1960s, English football became increasingly dirtier and more ill-tempered, as is shown by the rise in the number of sending-offs as the decade progressed. In the 1960-61 season, the Football League's 2,028 matches produced only 18 dismissals, which works out as one every 112.7 games. This was the last time the number of sending-offs in an English League season was below 20. During the mid-60s, it was over 40 per season and in 1966-67 the number hit 50 for the first time even though the rules on what constituted a sending-off offence hadn't changed.

Ron and Peter Springett

In the 1966-67 season, Ron Springett was Sheffield Wednesday's first-choice keeper, while his younger brother, Peter, was the first-choice keeper at Queen's Park Rangers. Then in the summer that followed, the two clubs exchanged them.

Jimmy Hill

Jimmy Hill spent less than six years in football management, but during that time he led Coventry to the Third Division title in 1963-64 and then to the Second Division title three years later. These promotions took the club into the top-flight for the first time in their history, and the news that the man who got them there was resigning broke just two days before their first ever fixture in Division One.

Hill was 39 at the time, and he was not only quitting Coventry, but quitting football management altogether to go and work in television. In fact, he wasn't quite gone, as he did stay on as caretaker manager until the club found his successor in October 1967, which was when he also went into publishing and launched his own magazine in *Jimmy Hill's Football Monthly*, which he also wrote for and co-edited. The following year he became head of sport at London Weekend Television, as well as the country's first regular TV pundit when he began giving weekly analysis of the games televised on *The Big Match*. When the show's regular commentator, Brian Moore, was ill in January 1973, it was the try-anything Hill who stood in for him to provide the commentary for an FA Cup tie between Brighton and Chelsea, the only match he ever provided a TV commentary for. Later that year, Hill moved to the BBC to present *Match of the Day*, and two years later returned to Coventry as managing director, before becoming chairman in 1978, a post he would hold for five years whilst still presenting the BBC's flagship football show.

Prior to going into management, Hill had made over 300 appearances as an inside-forward for Brentford and Fulham, once scoring five times in a match for Fulham at Doncaster in March 1958. It was during his years at Fulham that he was also Chairman of the PFA and, in 1961, successfully campaigned for the abolition of the maximum wage for players. It's unlikely anyone has ever performed so many different and varied roles connected to the game as Hill did. He even acted as a stand-in linesman during an Arsenal v Liverpool First Division match in 1972. It was also Hill who originally put forward the idea of increasing the number of points awarded for a win from two to three at a committee meeting of the Football League in 1980.

Loans

Only 18 players were loaned from one Football League club to another in the 22 years between the end of the Second World War and 1967. This was because the loaning out of players was only allowed in exceptional circumstances in those days, but that all changed from the start of the 1967-68 season when the Football League granted all clubs the freedom to take players on no-fee 'temporary transfers' from other clubs provided they didn't have more than two at the same time.

Coventry's John Docker was the first player to make a loan move under the new rules when he joined Torquay in July 1967, although Docker didn't play on the opening day of the '67-68 season, which makes the Blackburn goalkeeper John Roberts the first player to play as a modern loanee when he appeared for Chesterfield at Crewe on 19 August 1967. Roberts ended up staying at Chesterfield for the entirety of that season, playing in 49 of their 50 League and cup games. Docker, by contrast, only made five appearances during his loan spell at Torquay, which turned out to be the only five appearances he would ever make in the Football League. Aside from Docker and Roberts, only 15 other players went out on loan that season, which would suggest the bringing in of a loanee was still seen as something of a desperate measure taken only by teams blighted by injury.

17 players then went out on loan the following season, but in 1969-70 there was a notable increase when 31 players did, and then as the 70s progressed the number of loans went through the roof. Between the 1974-75 and 1976-77 seasons, more than 400 loan moves were made between Football League clubs, which was probably more than the football authorities ever anticipated and why they changed the rules for the following season. From 1977-78 the rule that a club couldn't have any more than two loan players at the same time was replaced by one that stated a club couldn't have any more than two per season. In fact, very few did take more than two per season anyway, but the new rule still did the trick and the number of loans dropped considerably in '77-78 and then dropped even further over the two seasons that followed. In the 1975-76 season there had been 138 loan moves between Football

League clubs. In 1979-80 there were just 53. Then in '80-81 it was only 26 as the Football League banned all loans unless the loaned player was a goalkeeper. This was probably one of the shortest-lived rule changes ever as it lasted only one season, leading to the number of loans shooting up to 99 in 1981-82, the highest total since '76-77.

Unlike today, players who went out on loan in the late-20th century, didn't usually become important members of the team they were loaned to. With all clubs having reserve teams that played in competitive reserve leagues, clubs did not need to loan out their non-first-team players to give them 'game time', and so those who went out on loan tended to be transfer-listed misfits. 91 of those 138 loans of 1975-76 saw the loanee make fewer than ten appearances for the club he joined, and it was this, plus the fact that almost all the loan activity went on in the lower divisions, that meant the steep rise in the number of loans that occurred in the 1970s happened largely under the radar.

Of the 47 loanees who did make more than ten appearances for the club they joined in 1975-76, 29 had their transfers made permanent, which would suggest many clubs in the '70s were using the loan system to trial potential permanent signings, which certainly wasn't what it was designed for. This probably continued in the '80s and '90s as well, as it was only in the 21st century that clubs began taking players on loan that they couldn't afford to sign in any other capacity.

Tony Lee

In September 1967, Bradford City beat Chesterfield 3-1 in a Fourth Division match with all three goals being scored by 19-year-old Tony Lee who would play his last ever game in the Football League just 18 months later. Aside from those three against Chesterfield, Lee's only other League goal was the winner for Darlington against Port Vale in February 1969, although not all sources credited him with it.

Alan Wilks

In October 1967, Queens Park Rangers beat Oxford 5-1 in the League Cup with Alan Wilks scoring all five of their goals. Wilks only scored three times in the League that season.

Ray Mabbutt

In October 1967, Bristol Rovers' Ray Mabbutt scored a hat-trick in his side's 5-4 Third Division win at Northampton, which was pretty remarkable for a 31-year-old playing the first game of his career as a forward, and who was already beginning to wind down that career by going onto a part-time contract. Mabbutt then kept his place up front for the next game at Tranmere and grabbed another couple in a 3-3 draw. Before this five-goals-in-two-games blast, Mabbutt had never scored more than twice in a season.

Ken Simpkins

Hartlepools goalkeeper Ken Simpkins was played as a forward in a Fourth Division match against Port Vale in November 1967 and scored the winning goal in his side's 3-2 victory.

Punishing Peterborough

On 20 November 1967, Peterborough remained fourth in the Third Division after a John Fairbrother hat-trick had given them a 3-2 win at home to Grimsby. Things, however, weren't looking good for the club as three days earlier they had been found guilty of four counts of paying illegal bonuses to players over the previous two seasons and were facing possible expulsion from the Football League, a punishment that had been recommended by a joint FA and Football League commission. In those days there was no non-League pyramid and so going into non-League football would have meant going into regional football – probably the Midland League – from which they would possibly never return. It certainly seemed a harsh punishment, since Peterborough's claim that they were merely ignorant of the rules was perfectly plausible. "My fellow directors and I have always tried to act properly and in a correct manner without hiding anything. We thought everything we did was above board," said the club's chairman, John Thornley.

The day after the Grimsby game, the FA announced its punishment and it was demotion to Division Four at the end of the season, which, although severe, still probably came as a relief to everyone at the club. This, of course, meant that, although they were fourth in the table at the time, the club had to play their remaining 27 fixtures knowing that they couldn't go up or even stay up. They went on to win eleven of those last 27 games to finish ninth, after which the Football League deducted them 19 points to put them bottom. They would spend six seasons in the Fourth Division before eventually going up as champions in 1974.

Arsenal's post-war first

When Arsenal's Peter Storey and Frank McLintock were both sent-off at Burnley in December 1967, it was the first time since the Second World War that two players from the same side had been dismissed in the same Football League game. The second time wouldn't be until March 1975, and again it would be two Arsenal players – Bob McNab and Alan Ball.

When 12 Goals over two games couldn't separate them

When Chelmsford met Oxford in the first round of the FA Cup in December 1967, the original match finished 3-3 and so did the replay.

The last time top-flight fixtures and an England international were played simultaneously

24 February 1968 was the last ever Saturday that England were in action while there was a top-flight fixture programme going on at the same time. The England match was against Scotland at Hampden Park, and it was also the last time England ever competed in two competitions in the same match, as it was both a Home internationals fixture and a qualifier for the European Championships. While it was taking place, there were seven First Division matches in progress.

Alan Gowling

Alan Gowling scored on his senior debut for Manchester United in March 1968 when he was still an economics student (at a time when few people went to university) and only playing for United on an amateur contract. Many sources claim Gowling was an England Amateur international, but he wasn't officially, although he did play for Great Britain in the qualifiers for the 1968 Olympics, and the Great Britain team was, essentially, the England Amateur team in all but name.

Gowling eventually got a professional contract with United in September 1968, but didn't establish himself in their first-team until the 1971-72 season. Having done so, he was then promptly sold by United to Second Division Huddersfield in the summer that followed. Gowling went on to spend three seasons with Huddersfield, scoring 58 League goals for them, which was pretty impressive considering the club were relegated in two of those seasons. In all three seasons, he scored three times as many as Huddersfield's second-top scorer.

Having gone from being a first-team regular with First Division Manchester United to a Fourth Division player in little over two years, Gowling then returned to the top-flight in the summer of 1975 when Newcastle bought him for £70,000. His first season on Tyneside saw him score 30 goals across all competitions which was six more than Newcastle's star man Malcolm Macdonald got that season, making the 1975-76 season the only full season of Macdonald's career in which he was out-scored by one of his teammates.

Gowling's goalscoring dropped-off after that and he never played for England, but few players' careers have ever rivalled his for peculiar achievements and unexpected twists. And his scoring exploits somehow seemed all the more unlikely considering he always looked less like a professional footballer than he did the economics graduate that he was.

The Golden Vision

The Golden Vision was a Ken Loach-directed edition of BBC1's *The Wednesday Play* that first aired in April 1968, and which probably stands as the only meeting of football and the arts in the 1960s. Focusing on the lives of a group of Everton supporters, it was, like much of Loach's work of the period, a pseudo-documentary, and it enhanced the realism by breaking-up the acted scenes with real documentary footage of Everton training sessions and team talks, match footage of two Everton matches from November 1967 (a 1-1 draw at home to Man City and a 2-2 draw at Arsenal) and interviews with Everton players, directors and coach, Wilf Dixon. The players interviewed were Alex Young, Ray Wilson, Brian Labone and Gordon West, with Labone and West both speaking very negatively about their trade. "I prefer to pit my skill against the opposition," said Labone, "but in some teams they're told to go out and cripple or clog whoever happens to be the star player on the other side... people are going out there, playing under pressure, knowing that the result is all important and football is being sacrificed for results". West, meanwhile, sounded as if he wished he had chosen a different career altogether. "I don't enjoy playing at all on a Saturday," he confessed, "from three o'clock on, until twenty to five, I can't wait for it to finish". And this from a man who played 399 times for Everton, was both a League title and FA Cup-winner and won three England caps.

Attack, attack, attack (with fluidity)

Manchester City's League title success of 1967-68 was down largely to the extreme fitness training and all-out attack approach employed by coach Malcolm Allison who was the man most responsible for coming up with team tactics even though he wasn't team manager (Joe Mercer was). In a period when English football was becoming more defensive, Allison went against the grain to make City more attacking and also had them attack with a fluidity that was unusual for the time. Francis Lee and Mike Summerbee constantly switched between wide and central attacking positions during games, Neil Young had a free role and could pop up anywhere and midfielder Colin Bell frequently moved into goalscoring positions and finished like a striker (he scored 17 in all competitions that season). City also passed quicker than any English team had done before and had their full-backs push forward with pace long before attacking full-backs were common.

With these tactics, City managed to win the League with a squad that contained no internationals until Summerbee was given his England debut in February, and then contained no more until Bell was capped by England after the domestic season was over. The same tactics, however, didn't work quite so well the following season. City finished 13th in 1968-69, having been second from bottom after nine games. They also fell to Turkish champions Fenerbahce in the first round of the European Cup, with their players being unable to perform in the hostile atmosphere of the away leg that saw soldiers with rifles standing around the pitch.

Football in colour (although not for most)

Although matches had been filmed in colour for *Pathe News* cinema screenings before, the first English football match to be televised in colour was the 1968 FA Cup Final between West Bromwich Albion and Everton. This game was shown on BBC2 as, at the time, BBC2 was the only channel with the superior 625-line transmission and so was the only channel capable of broadcasting in colour. Since, however, not all TVs at the time could receive BBC2, the match was also shown on BBC1 in black and white. West Bromwich Albion's Jeff Astle scored the only goal of the game and in doing so became the first player in England to score a televised goal in colour.

In November 1969, BBC1 and most ITV regions also moved to colour transmissions and from here on televised football in colour became the norm, although this didn't make much difference to most people as it wasn't until 1976 that the majority of households in Britain had a colour set. This means that although we know the 1970 and 1974 World Cups through colour clips, they were originally watched in black and white by most people in Britain.

The forgotten first half of a famous match

Manchester United's 4-1 victory over Benfica in the 1968 European Cup Final is perhaps the most famous match played at Wembley in the 1960s after the '66 World Cup Final, although few remember just how niggly the first half was. In all there were 32 fouls committed in the first period, which works out as one every 84.4 seconds. United committed 19 of them and Benfica 13.

Jimmy Rimmer

Manchester United didn't bring on a substitute in the 1968 European Cup Final, but if they had done it would have had to have been goalkeeper Jimmy Rimmer as he was the only player they had on the bench.

A double-landmark TV moment for England

England's friendly against West Germany in Hannover on 1 June 1968 was the first non-tournament England match played in mainland Europe that was shown live on British television, as well as the first England match broadcast in colour. The match was a warm-up for England's European Championship semi-final against Yugoslavia four days later. Germany won 1-0 – as did Yugoslavia.

Not good enough

When England lost to Yugoslavia in the semi-finals of the 1968 European Championships, they only managed one on-target goal attempt in the whole match, and it came from defender Bobby Moore.

Alan Mullery

England's defeat to Yugoslavia in the semi-finals of the 1968 European Championships was the 424th match played by the national side and it was the first in which an England player was sent-off. The player dismissed was Alan Mullery for retaliation in the 88th minute, and it was the only dismissal in a match that Yugoslavia's Dobrivoje Trivic had spent committing fouls left, right and centre. Most sources say Mullery's retaliation was against Trivic, although some reports at the time said it was Miroslav Pavlovic that he floored. Manager Alf Ramsey said of the sending-off, "It would appear that you can kick a player in front of the referee and get away with it, but if you kick in retaliation and the referee doesn't see it, you get sent-off".

The second sending-off of an England player came a year later in Mexico and again it was Mullery, although it doesn't count as it wasn't an official international.

The never-ending Fairs Cup

The Inter-Cities Fairs Cup was once so drawn-out that Leeds beat Ferencvaros in the final of the 1967-68 competition just one week before they played Standard Liege in the first round of the following season's competition.

Action replays

The BBC first began showing slow-motion replays during their match coverage at the start of the 1968-69 season. Initially the replays were just taken from the gantry camera, but in 1970 cameras began being positioned behind the goal in order to show replays of goals being scored from a different angle. It was also in 1970 that ITV began showing action replays and that the World Cup coverage had them for the first time. Slow-motion replays were initially quite controversial as it was felt they undermined the authority of referees by showing up their mistakes and highlighting them to millions of TV viewers. "It is surely wrong," said a 1970 edition of *Football League Review*, "that the men who have to make split-second decisions out there on the pitch, in situations super-charged with tension, should be faced with inquisition from a magic eye".

Until the mid-1980s, TV companies didn't overdo it with the replays, only showing one of each goal or goal attempt deemed worth showing again. Slow-motion replays of such things as goal celebrations and players' reactions to incidents were first seen in the coverage of the 1998 World Cup.

Joe Royle

It's not true that no one in Britain had seen anything like 'the Cruyff turn' until Johan Cruyff produced it against Sweden in the 1974 World Cup. In September 1968, the *Match of the Day* cameras had captured Everton's Joe Royle beating Chelsea's David Webb with an identical trick in a First Division match at Stamford Bridge.

Manchester United getting the Argentinian treatment

Four months after winning the 1968 European Cup, Manchester United played the two-legged World Club Championship decider against the Argentinian side Estudiantes who had won the South American Cup the same year. At the time Estudiantes were a side with a terrible reputation for foul play and, in the first leg in Argentina, they immediately set about living up to it by committing no fewer than eight fouls in the first ten minutes of the match. According to a contemporary article in *Soccer Star*, this was the beginning of a night of "butting, body-checking, dangerous kicking [and] scything" by the Argentinians. After 15 minutes, Nobby Stiles was head-butted by Carlos Bilardo, who wasn't sent-off, either for that or the horror tackle he made on Bobby Charlton later in the game that left Charlton's leg pouring with blood and needing stitches. Stiles, however, was dismissed in the second half for what was apparently little more than a gesture of annoyance.

In the second leg, it was George Best who was sent-off along with Estudiantes' Jose Hugo Medina who was pelted with coins by the angry United fans as he left the field, with at least one of the coins appearing to hit him in the face. This was the only time an English club experienced the World Club Championship during its days of high notoriety when it wasn't much more than an annual exhibition of Argentinian brutality against Europeans. And United got off light. Celtic in 1967 and AC Milan in '69 had it even worse.

Jimmy Greenhoff

When Leeds finished fourth in the First Division in 1967-68 their 21-year-old forward Jimmy Greenhoff scored 18 goals in all competitions, but this wasn't enough to prevent Leeds from offloading him to Second Division Birmingham at the start of the following season. Greenhoff spent just one season at Birmingham, and it was a pretty mixed one in which he scored eleven goals in his first ten games but only one in his next 18. After leaving Birmingham he returned to the First Division with Stoke and would not play outside of the top-flight again until he joined Fourth Division Crewe from Manchester United in December 1980. His debut for Crewe at home to Darlington came just two weeks after his last game for Man United.

Steve Melledew

In the autumn of 1968, Rochdale had five consecutive 1-1 draws with Steve Melledew scoring the Rochdale goal in all five of them.

Geoff Hurst (again)

Geoff Hurst scored a first-half hat-trick and a second-half hat-trick when West Ham beat Sunderland 8-0 in a First Division match in October 1968. This still stands as the last time a player has scored six in a match in any of the top four tiers of English football, and it's unlikely to be repeated seeing as strikers now tend to be substituted once a game is wrapped-up and no more goals are needed.

Billy Best and Gary Moore

Southend were 5-1 up after 71 minutes of an FA Cup second round tie against Brentwood in December 1968 with Gary Moore having scored four of their goals. At that point, Moore's partner up front, Billy Best, hadn't got on the scoresheet, but he ended up bettering Moore that afternoon as he went on to bag five in the last 19 minutes, with four of them coming in the final six minutes. In the previous round, Southend had beaten King's Lynn 9-0 with Moore and Best both getting hat-tricks in that one as well. This meant that the pair scored 15 goals between them in the first two rounds of that season's FA Cup. Best scored again in the third round and fourth round, at which point Southend were eliminated.

Malcolm Allison (again)

After verbally abusing a linesman in a First Division match at Southampton in December 1968, Manchester City coach Malcolm Allison was called before the FA disciplinary committee for the seventh time in five years and issued with a lifetime ban from the touchline. The ban was eventually lifted ten years later after Allison returned from working abroad to manage Plymouth, but while it was in force he could only watch games from up in the stands during the almost-two seasons he was manager of Man City (having graduated to that role in October 1970) and the three-and-a-bit seasons he was manager of Crystal Palace. In December 1970, Allison was also given a two-month ban from working with his players and attending Man City home games after angrily confronting the referee at half-time of a City match at home to Burnley (a match City won 4-0!).

Aldershot's '69 slide

On 4 January 1969, Aldershot beat Newport 4-0 at home to maintain a three-point lead at the top of Division Four, and yet they didn't go on to win promotion that season, nor even finish in the top half of the table. They ended up a lowly 15th after losing all but seven of their final 22 games.

The longest wait for promotion

When Rochdale and Halifax both won promotion from Division Four in 1969, it was the first promotion for either club since they had entered the Football League together 48 years earlier. Both had briefly been members of Division Three (in Rochdale's case only for one season) but were only made so due to the restructuring of the lower divisions that took place in 1958. The two clubs had been moved from Division Three North into the new national Third Division which hardly counts as 'winning promotion'.

Bournemouth were another club that took 48 years to win their first Football League promotion, which came in 1971 and was an immediate bounce-back to Division Three from which they had been relegated the previous season. Prior to that relegation, they had completed 39 consecutive seasons (either side of the War) in the third tier of English football.

Bob Moncur

When Newcastle beat Hungary's Ujpest Dosza 6-2 on aggregate in the final of the 1969 Inter-Cities Fairs Cup, three of their goals were scored by club captain Bob Moncur who had never scored a goal in senior football before. Prior to the first-leg, Moncur had made 114 appearances in his career (all for Newcastle) without scoring.

Don Rogers

Don Rogers scored 32 League and cup goals for Swindon in the 1966-67 season, 28 for them in '67-68 and 30 in '68-69. Scoring 90 goals in three seasons would have been a rare feat even for a striker, but Rogers was a winger.

Going full circle in the 1960s

Northampton Town rose from the Fourth Division to the First Division and then dropped back to the Fourth Division again all in the space of nine seasons between 1960-61 and 1968-69. Winger Barry Lines played for them throughout this circular journey.

Doing it the hard way

Rochdale's Fourth Division promotion of 1968-69 was achieved despite the fact that they only won four of their first 22 matches.

They were 14th in the table going into their Boxing Day fixture, but ended up finishing third.

The 1-0 Cup run

In the 1968-69 FA Cup, Leicester won 1-0 in the fourth round, 1-0 in the fifth round, 1-0 in the sixth round and 1-0 in the semi-final. They then lost 1-0 in the final.

Tony Book

Tony Book was captain and ever-present for Manchester City when they won the League title in the 1967-68 season, and also captained their 1969 FA Cup-winning side, their 1970 European Cup-Winners' Cup-winning side and was the joint winner of the 1969 Football Writers' Association Football of the Year Award. All remarkable achievements for a player who never played international football at any level, never made his debut in the top-flight of English football until one month before his 32nd birthday, and who was still playing for Bath City in the Southern League at the age of 29.

When the English were fake Americans

In May 1969, West Ham, Wolves and Aston Villa all took part in the North American Soccer League's International Cup competition (which was actually a league) but did so under the names of US clubs. West Ham competed as Baltimore Bays, Wolves as Kansas City Spurs and Villa as Atlanta Chiefs. The other clubs in the competition were Dallas Tornado who were represented by the players of Dundee United and St. Louis Stars who were really Kilmarnock.

This was all part of the British football authorities attempts to help promote the game in the US, and if it all sounds pretty bizarre, it's no more so than what happened the following year when Coventry competed under their own name in the North American Soccer League's regular season, but did not figure in the league table as they were only there for the American clubs to pick up extra points against.

England's 4-0 win that doesn't count

In June 1969, England beat Mexico 4-0 in Guadalajara, but it's not recognised as an official international because England were billed as an 'English FA XI', even though the line-up was made up entirely of players from the England squad that were touring South and Central America at the time. Eight players who would play for England at the following year's World Cup took part in the match, including Jeff Astle who scored twice but would never score in an official international. A largely different England line-up billed as 'England' had drawn 0-0 with Mexico in an official international three days earlier.

The football weeklies

As previously mentioned, Britain's first proper football magazine was *Charles Buchan's Football Monthly* which was launched in 1951, but it was *Soccer Star* that would become the country's first successful football weekly. Arriving for the start of the 1952-53 season, and originally called *Raich Carter's Soccer Star* (Carter's name would be dropped from the title in 1955), *Soccer Star*, like Buchan's magazine, covered football from all four divisions of the Football League, as well as non-League football and Scottish football and was even known to carry articles on schoolboy level football. It would remain Britain's only weekly football magazine for 15 years up to 1967, and in the 1957-58 season became the first publication to print every team line-up from every Football League match and major cup game, something it would continue doing until it ceased publication in 1970.

It was in October 1967 that *Jimmy Hill's Football Weekly* became the first weekly rival to *Soccer Star*, with the second one, *Goal*, arriving in August '68, and the third, *Shoot!*, a year later. Of these, *Goal* was similar to *Charles Buchan's Football Monthly* and *Soccer Star* in that it featured critical journalism and was clearly aimed mainly at adult readers as evidenced by its two-page football pools guide and body-building advertisements. *Jimmy Hill's Football Weekly* probably was as well, although it was a fairly slim and bland magazine, while *Shoot!* was totally devoid of critical journalism, presented only a positive image of the game and appeared to be aimed largely at children of secondary school age. Needless to say, there was no pools guide in *Shoot!* but there were plenty of advertisements for children's games.

The editors of *Shoot!* clearly felt that the more a magazine catered for the kids, the better it would sell, and it wasn't long before this philosophy became the dominant one within the industry. Of the four new football weeklies that arrived in 1970, two – *Striker* and *Score 'n' Roar* – contained comic strips amongst their photos and articles, and a third – *Scorcher* – was a full-blown football comic. The same year, *Soccer Star* and *Jimmy Hill's Football Monthly* both disappeared, suggesting the day of the football weekly for adult readers was nearing its end. Four years later, *Goal* got taken over by *Shoot!*, effectively meaning that *Goal* was gone as well, even if, for a while, *Shoot!* carried the words "incorporating Goal" on its front cover and referred to itself as 'Shoot/Goal' in its pages. Several other football weeklies would come and go over the following years and decades, but none would be as essential to adult football enthusiasts as *Soccer Star* had been in the 1950s and '60s nor to the footie-mad kids as *Shoot!* was in the '70s.

The FA Trophy

For 76 years the only national English Cup competition exclusively for non-League clubs was the FA Amateur Cup, but it wasn't open to the best non-League sides as these paid their players and so were ineligible for it. This situation was finally addressed in 1969 when the FA created the FA Trophy, a competition for non-League clubs whose players were, what we now call, semi-professionals. Originally referred to simply as 'the Non-League Cup' by much of the press, the Trophy is notable for being the first ever competition to have a Wembley final from its inception. The first one in 1970 was played three weeks after that year's FA Cup Final, and saw Macclesfield beat Telford 2-0 in front of 28,000 spectators.

George Best

George Best scored six times in Manchester United's 8-2 win at Northampton in the third round of the FA Cup in February 1970, which was his first game back following a 28-day suspension that covered five matches. Best's feat that day is famous largely due to the fact that it was the first time a player had scored six in a televised match. In fact, it was a doubly-televised match as two different ITV companies covered it with each sending their own commentator. Granada covered it for viewers in the Lancashire and Merseyside areas with commentary from Gerald Sinstadt, while ATV did so for Midlands' viewers with Hugh Johns providing the commentary. After scoring six that day, Best then managed only four from his next 25 appearances in all competitions.

A penalty in an instant

In February 1970, Sheffield United conceded a penalty after just 32 seconds of a Second Division match at Blackburn. There have been faster penalties, but what makes this one so bizarre is that Blackburn were awarded it having only had two kicks of the ball in the match. United had kicked-off but quickly gave away possession allowing Blackburn to punt it forward to the galloping Eamon Rogers with their first kick. Their second kick was then made by Rogers to take the ball past the last defender at which point he was brought down by Alan Hodgkinson in the United goal. Don Martin then had Blackburn's third kick of the game (and his first) when he dispatched the penalty, although this was as good as it got for the home side as United came back to win 2-1.

Banning the TV cameras

On 14 February 1970, Everton sat second in Division One, two points behind the leaders, Leeds, but their match against Arsenal that day was not televised because Everton had banned the cameras from the ground. Their reason for doing so was simply that they felt they had been on TV too many times already that season. They had previously banned the TV cameras from their ground in the 1965-66 season as well, as had Burnley, with the Burnley chairman, Bob Lord, ejecting a BBC TV crew from Turf Moor when it turned up to televise the club's FA Cup third round replay against Bournemouth.

The most recent example of a club banning TV cameras from their ground was when Chelsea did so throughout the 1989-90 season. This was really more of a big deal than the previous occasions since by then it was routine to have TV cameras present at all top-flight matches and yet Chelsea (or more specifically, their chairman, Ken Bates) didn't allow action from any of the club's home games to be shown on TV that season. They did, however, videotape all the games themselves and sold VHS cassettes of them in their club shop.

Name changes

There have only ever been two instances of a Football League club changing its name during the course of a season, which was when Woolwich Arsenal became The Arsenal in April 1914 and Swansea Town became Swansea City in February 1970. Less abrupt changes of name occurred in 1902 when Newton Heath became Manchester United, in 1905 when Small Heath became Birmingham City and in 1919 when Leicester Fosse became Leicester City. In 1972, Bournemouth and Boscombe Athletic gave up their status as the League club with the longest name when they changed it to 'AFC Bournemouth', and in 1983, Chester became 'Chester City'. Hartlepools United were so called because they represented both Hartlepool's old town and West Hartlepool, so logically dropped the

'S' and the 'United' from their name when the two Hartlepools merged to become a single borough in 1968 (although they would restore the 'United' in 1977). The most subtle change to a name was undoubtedly made by Queen's Park Rangers in 1967 when they simply removed the apostrophe, while Clapton Orient had the most delayed name change when, in 1946, they finally became 'Leyton Orient' nine years after relocating to Clapton's neighbouring district. They eventually dropped the 'Leyton' from their name in 1966 but restored it in 1987 to become the club that's gone through the most changes of name whilst in the Football League.

Walsall were originally in the Football League as 'Walsall Town Swifts' and Port Vale as 'Burslem Port Vale', but both clubs changed their names during spells out of the League.

The most defensive semi-final?

The 1970 FA Cup semi-final between Leeds and Manchester United produced only one goal in five and a half hours of football. Leeds won the second replay 1-0 following two 0-0-after-extra-time draws.

Villa's unwanted first

Aston Villa won five League titles in seven years between 1894 and 1900, and then 70 years later became the first ever former League champions to be relegated to the third tier of English football.

Not wearing the badge

Although England had worn the three lions on their shirt since the 19th century, the sight of club shirts with badges on them didn't become common until the 1960s. Before then, the stitching of the club badge onto players' shirts was something mainly only done for FA Cup Finals, as it was the football clubs' way of dressing the players for the big occasion. For other Cup games and League games, the wearing of the badge was generally seen as unnecessary.

Even in the 1969-70 season, there were still seven top-flight sides that played with no badges on their shirts, including eventual champions Everton who became the last team to win the League title without displaying their badge. In fact, Everton were a club that seemed especially opposed to badge-wearing, having previously broken with tradition by displaying no badge on their shirt in both the 1966 and '68 FA Cup Finals. The letters 'EFC' would eventually be put on their shirt in 1972, but there would be no badge displayed until the 1978-79 season.

Like Everton, Sunderland also went for initials rather than a badge, and in 1973, their captain, Bobby Kerr, became the last man to lift the FA Cup with no badge on his shirt. Sunderland's shirt would eventually display the badge for the first time in 1977. Other clubs that – Cup Finals aside – waited until the 1970s before putting their badge on their shirt include Manchester United, who first wore a badge on their regular shirt in 1971, Manchester City, whose regular shirt first displayed one in '72, and West Ham, whose regular shirt only featured the club badge once it got seriously jazzed-up in 1976. 1976 was also the year Queens Park Rangers removed the badge from their shirt a year after they put it on for the first time. After this, their shirt would remain badge-free until the start of the 1978-79 season.

The 3-3 draw between Everton and Queens Park Rangers at Goodison Park on 4 March 1978 was the last in the top-flight between two teams not displaying their club badges.

Bottom of the pile

Bradford Park Avenue finished bottom of the Fourth Division in the 1967-68, 1968-69 and 1969-70 seasons, and remain the only club ever to have finished as the worst in the Football League in each of three consecutive seasons. During those three seasons they won only 15 of their 138 League matches, losing 90 of them, with their 3-0 win over Hartlepool in March 1970 being the only one of the 138 in which they scored more than twice. Their only cup win of these three seasons was something of an anomaly in the circumstances as it was against Third Division Grimsby in the first round of the FA Cup (in December 1967) and was by a resounding 4-1 scoreline.

The end for Bradford Park Avenue

In the autumn of 1969, Herbert Metcalfe, a Manchester businessman, took control of ailing Bradford Park Avenue and ploughed much of his own money into the club in an attempt to turn around its fortunes. Metcalfe's interference in team selection and the appointment of a new manager, however, did not go down well with the players and 19 handed in transfer requests simultaneously, including Bernard Rafferty who had only signed for the club the previous day.

At the end of that season, Park Avenue achieved the unique distinction of finishing bottom of Division Four for the third season running, after which they were voted out of the Football League. Metcalfe then died on a scouting trip to Scotland three months later. Four seasons in the Northern Premier League followed their demotion, during which time they lost their ground and were forced to share Bradford City's Valley Parade. They eventually folded at the end of the 1973-74 season, with their final game being at home to Great Harwood in front of just 698 spectators. Less than 30 years earlier, the club had been in the second tier of English football and averaging home gates of more than 17,000.

Curtain-closing Aldershot

Exeter, Bradford Park Avenue, Brentford and Chester all played their final game of the 1969-70 season against Aldershot. Exeter did so on 15 April, Bradford on 20 April, Brentford on 29 April and Chester on 30 April.

Playing in the sand

The 1970 FA Cup Final was a strange spectacle in which the ball couldn't bounce and could only roll slowly owing to the hundred ton of sand that had been used to patch up the poor state of the Wembley pitch. The pitch's condition prior to the sand covering would later be put down to The Horse of the Year Show having been staged on it the week before, but this isn't true. The 1970 Horse of the Year Show was later in the year and at a different venue and there had been no equestrian event at the stadium since The Royal International Horse Show in the summer of '69.

The under-the-radar European final

When Manchester City played Gornik Zabrze in the final of the 1970 European Cup-Winners' Cup, the 80,000-capacity ground in which it was staged – Vienna's Praterstadion – was 90 per cent empty. The 8,000 people who did turn up included roughly 3,000 City fans who would have been the only Englishmen who saw the game live as it was played on the same night as the Chelsea v Leeds FA Cup Final replay and so never got a look-in on British television (see below).

When An FA Cup Final replay was one of the biggest national events we've ever had

The highest TV viewing figure for a domestic English football match is 28.5 million for the 1970 FA Cup Final replay between Chelsea and Leeds. This match was watched by more people than watched England's World Cup quarter-final against West Germany the same year, more people than watched the England v West Germany semi-final at the 1990 World Cup, more people than watched the Euro 96 semi-final between England and Germany, more people than have ever watched a European Cup or Champions League Final, or an athletics final at the Olympics or any tennis match at Wimbledon. It was even watched by more people than watched the first Moon landing the previous year. It's peculiarly high rating, however, may have had something to do with the fact that it was the first ever domestic English football match to be aired during prime time, it was broadcast live on both BBC1 and ITV when BBC2 was the only other channel, and the BBC2 programmes that clashed with it included a *Man Alive* documentary on modern issues facing the Catholic church, a *Canvas* documentary about the 19th century artist Charles Conder and another documentary about news reporting in continental Europe.

John Faulkner

The only two games John Faulkner ever played for Leeds came a week either side of the 1970 FA Cup Final, and he scored an own goal in the first and suffered a broken kneecap in the second. As Leeds had signed Faulkner from amateur side Sutton, these were also his first two games in professional football.

Banned from Europe

Derby qualified for Europe for the first time in their history at the end of the 1969-70 season but were banned from it by the FA over 'administrative gross negligence'. This 'negligence' included paying captain Dave Mackay £2,000 to write articles in the club programme.

The Anglo-Italian Cup

In its inaugural year of 1970, the Anglo-Italian Cup was a post-season competition played over four weeks in May and contested between six English clubs and six clubs from Italy. The Italian clubs included four that finished in the top six of the Italian league in the

1969-70 season, but England's representatives were somewhat less impressive, being Wolves and West Bromwich Albion who had both just finished in the bottom half of Division One, Sunderland and Sheffield Wednesday who had both just been relegated from Division One and Middlesbrough and Swindon who were both in Division Two.

In many ways, the Anglo-Italian Cup was an innovative competition that veered away from the norms of previous ones. The 12 teams were split into three groups containing two English clubs and two Italian clubs each, with the two English clubs playing the two Italian clubs home and away but no matches being played between teams from the same country. The standard two points for a win and one for a draw were awarded, but there was also an extra point awarded for every goal scored, which led to the peculiar situation of Napoli earning just as many points from losing 4-3 to Sheffield Wednesday as Swindon did by beating Juventus 1-0. Equally peculiar was Swindon reaching the final despite only finishing second in their group while West Brom topped their group and went out. This was because the final had to be contested between the best performing English club in the group stages and the best performing Italian club and Swindon got more points than West Brom even though they finished lower in their group. The final was played on the home ground of the Italian finalists and always would be, presumably because the Italians created the competition and, therefore, thought the trophy should always be lifted in Italy. One other innovation, that was scrapped after the first year, was that a player could only be given as offside if he was in, or level with, the opposition penalty area.

Ultimately, the 1970 Anglo-Italian Cup wasn't a success, with poor crowds and two of the matches in Italy being abandoned due to rioting by Italian fans. The first of these was Lanerossi Vicenza v West Bromwich Albion where the riot was sparked by a brawl between the players, while the second was the final itself between Napoli and Swindon, which was abandoned after 79 minutes but awarded to Swindon who were 3-0 up at the time. The Swindon players lifted the trophy while the rioting went on in the stands and then fled down the tunnel just before it spilled over onto the pitch. Swindon's Don Rogers later said he moved from the wing to a more central attacking role during the game simply to put more distance between himself and the Napoli fans who had been pelting him with missiles.

The following year, the final was contested between Bologna and Blackpool and televised live on BBC1, although probably only because it coincided with that week's edition of their regular Saturday afternoon sports show, *Grandstand*. Unfortunately, when *Grandstand* finished, so too did the live coverage of the game and so the viewers never got to see Blackpool win it in extra-time. After returning home, the Blackpool players paraded the trophy through the town before 50,000 applauding locals. Briefly the Anglo-Italian Cup seemed like a big deal, and it did again a year later when a crowd of 75,000 watched Roma take on Blackpool in the '72 final, but these two events were very much anomalies. Attendances in the group games remained stubbornly low and, in 1973, the competition lost its identity as a post-season competition by having the matches played intermittently between February and May. The 1973 competition proved to be the last of the original Anglo-Italian Cup, although it was revived in 1976 as a competition for semi-professional sides. It ran for a decade in this incarnation but only once was it won by an English side, which was Sutton United in 1979.

The Esso 1970 World Cup Coin Collection

At the beginning of 1970, English motorists began getting a free silver coin with a portrait of an England player on it every time they paid for four gallons of petrol at an Esso garage. These coins were part of 'The Esso World Cup Coin Collection' that was launched to mark that summer's World Cup, although as the coins were minted before even England's provisional squad was announced, they could only feature players seen as being in contention for a squad place. There were 30 coins to collect in all, and ten were of players who ended up not making the squad, while Nobby Stiles and Alex Stepney did make the squad but didn't feature on the coins. Several of the players who appeared in the collection were still yet to win an England cap, including Peter Simpson, Henry Newton and Alan Oakes who all went on to end their careers as uncapped players.

For 2/6 (two shillings and sixpence) a mounting board could be bought from Esso garages upon which the coins could be mounted to form an inner circle of eleven coins and an outer one of 19. The confusing words on the guide read, "the inner circle is intended to hold the England World Cup team as it is selected", which seems to suggest the creators either believed England would play the same eleven in every game, or the inner circle was for the eleven who played in the final that England never reached.

Two years later, Esso launched another coin collection to mark the centenary of the FA Cup that featured the badges of all the past winners still in existence.

Peter Thompson

Preston and Liverpool winger Peter Thompson was named in the provisional squads for the 1962, 1966 and 1970 World Cups but didn't make the final squad for any of them.

In the Charts

Colin Grainger was a winger who made 325 Football League appearances for various clubs in the 1950s and '60s, whilst also working as a professional singer. In June 1963, he shared a bill with The Beatles, but he never had a hit single. Nor did Lonnie Donegan with his 1966 World Cup song 'World Cup Willie', probably because it wasn't the sort of thing that would have got played on Radio Caroline and it was released in December 1965.

It wasn't until the spring of 1970 that the very different worlds of football and the pop charts first collided when Don Fardon's tribute to George Best, 'Belfast Boy', and the England World Cup squad's 'Back Home' were both in the charts at the same time. Fardon's single was only a minor hit, but 'Back Home', (written by the same writers that had penned Cliff Richard's 1968 chart-topper and Eurovision Song Contest entry 'Congratulations') reached number one and remained there throughout the three weeks leading up to the start of that summer's World Cup. It was eventually knocked off the top by Christie's 'Yellow River' on the day England beat Romania in their first match of the tournament (the new chart came out on a Tuesday in those days), although it was still in the top ten when England arrived home after losing in the quarter-finals and still at number 15 the following week.

As well as the single, England's 1970 World Cup squad also recorded an album called *The World Beaters Sing the World Beaters* which included cover versions of the late-60s number one hits 'Puppet On A String', 'Ob-La-Di-Ob-LA-Da', 'Sugar Sugar' and 'Lily The Pink'. It reached number four in the album charts in the same month that The Doors' *Morrison Hotel* only got to number 12.

12 years later, another England World Cup squad album appeared for the 1982 tournament in the shape of *This Time*, which was an altogether stranger affair than the 1970 record had been. As well as renditions of the National Anthem, 'Land of Hope and Glory' and 'Abide with Me', it also included spoken-word tracks, versions of theme tunes to TV sports programmes played by the Leyland Vehicles Brass Band, Kevin Keegan's ill-judged 1979 single 'Head Over Heels In Love' and a cover of Queen's 'We Are The Champions' sung solo by Glenn Hoddle. The 1970 World Cup squad were also on it, as 'Back Home' was dug out and included as well. It only reached number 37, but the single taken from it, 'This Time (We'll Get It Right)', sold well and was only kept from number one by Paul McCartney and Stevie's Wonder's 'Ebony and Ivory'.

England's song for the 1986 World Cup, 'We've Got the Whole World At Our Feet' was released with little publicity at the end of a season when football crowds had been at a post-war low and it got no higher than number 66 (which proved not be an omen). The England players also recorded a single for the 1988 European Championships called 'All The Way', which went 'all the way' to number 64 before England went on to lose all of their matches at the tournament.

Then, two years later, came 'World In Motion' and suddenly football was cool. England's song for the 1990 World Cup was really a New Order record with minimal involvement from the England players (aside from the John Barnes rap) and it sounded way beyond the cheap cash-ins that all previous football-related singles had been. As well as spending two weeks at number one, it was also listed as one of the best ten singles of the year by the NME.

The first club squad to record a single was Arsenal's whose 'Good Old Arsenal' – a crude, boisterous sing-along to the tune of 'Rule Britannia' – was released at the end of the 1970-71 season in which they won the double. It reached number 16 in the charts, but not until ten days after their season had finished. The following season Chelsea jumped on the recording bandwagon and did 'Blue Is The Colour' to mark their appearance in the 1972 League Cup Final. The song was much more like 'Back Home' than the Arsenal song was and was a bigger hit than the Arsenal song, reaching number five on the singles chart and number one on the album chart when it was included on the various artists budget LP *Fantastic Hits*. It was a triumphant-sounding song made for a match that Chelsea lost. Leeds also released a single that year for the FA Cup Final, and it too made the top ten. It was imaginatively entitled 'Leeds United'.

Several more football-themed singles were released around FA Cup Final time over the next few years, but no FA Cup Final song would make the top ten again until Tottenham's 'Ossie's Dream' in 1981. Two Scotland World Cup songs did reach the top ten in 1978, however, with Andy Cameron's 'Ally's Tartan Army' doing so in March, meaning it was no longer in the charts by the time the World Cup started. With changed lyrics, it would be adapted into an English terrace song that would be sung for many years by fans when their club was on a good FA Cup run.

Like Kevin Keegan's 'Head Over Heels In Love', Glenn Hoddle and Chris Waddle's 'Diamond Lights' was not about football, but it was in the charts when the pair played together in the 1987 FA Cup Final. The same year the Wedding Present released an album called *George Best* that featured a photo of Best on the front cover but contained no songs about him or his sport.

England fans go abroad (providing they're prepared to blow seven weeks wages on it)

The 1970 World Cup was the first that England fans could travel to easily although they could only do so through an official travel package that cost between £230 and £250 per person at a time when the average weekly wage was £32 per week. The previous time England had played in a World Cup overseas was in 1962 and according to Jimmy Greaves (who played in it) there had been no England fans there at all.

The first overseas tournament that was a TV spectacle in Britain (if you liked late nights and didn't mind missing most of the games)

The 1970 World Cup in Mexico was the first World Cup played outside of Europe that people in Britain could watch live on TV. Not that they could watch much of it as only 14 of the tournament's 32 matches were actually shown live on British television, largely due to the fact that when one match was being played there were usually three others taking place at the same time. Even the four quarter-finals kicked-off simultaneously, which meant England versus West Germany was the only one shown live in Britain, being broadcast on BBC1, while ITV, reasoning that it was pointless to put one of the other matches up against it, showed a movie instead.

Those quarter-finals all kicked-off at seven o'clock in the evening UK time, but many of the other matches in the tournament were on ridiculously late for UK viewers owing to the time difference. Those wanting to watch all of England's four matches live would have needed to stay up until nearly one o'clock in the morning to see the completion of two of them, while the BBC provided a serious endurance test for football fans on the night of the semi-finals, when they showed one live and then the other in its entirety afterwards. Seeing as both games kicked off at eleven o' clock at night UK time and the Italy v West Germany game went to extra-time, then anyone wanting to watch both games wouldn't have been going to bed until gone 3.30 on a Thursday morning. Even the fact that this was the first World Cup televised in colour made little difference in a Britain where 92 per cent of homes that had a TV set still only had a black and white one.

Bobby Moore

Bobby Moore played for England against Romania in the 1970 World Cup just four days after being released from house arrest in Colombia. A bracelet had apparently been stolen from a jeweller's in the foyer of the hotel where the players were staying and Moore was the thief according to the shop assistant and another witness who came forward later. Both claimed to have seen Moore put the bracelet into his tracksuit-top pocket even though the tracksuit-top had no pockets. Moore's hand was also found to have been too big to fit through the gap in the display cabinet.

When talking about the allegations shortly before his death in 1993, Moore suggested he had been a victim of a prank gone wrong by one of the other players, which was something of a surprise to the people in Britain who had spent more than two decades believing this to have been a case of an 'honest' Englishman being framed by 'dodgy' South Americans.

The save (in context)

Gordon Banks' save from Pele in the England – Brazil game at the 1970 World Cup is widely regarded as the greatest save in World Cup history, and it's certainly the most acclaimed save ever made. The fact that it came in only the tenth minute of the match has occasionally been mentioned, but it's never mentioned that it was from an attack that was against the run of play following a strong start by England, or that it was the only save Banks had to make in the first 50 minutes against a team that would finish the tournament with 19 goals from six games.

Jeff Astle

West Bromwich Albion's Jeff Astle scored 35 goals in the 1967-68 season, 26 in 1968-69 and 30 in 1969-70. No top-flight player scored more over those three seasons, and yet Astle only ever won five caps for England and his international career became almost exclusively remembered for one bad miss.

That miss came against Brazil in the 1970 World Cup when Astle was thrown on as a sub with just under half-an-hour left and England trailing 1-0. Within a minute of his arrival, the West Brom man won a header in the Brazilian box to set up a chance for Alan Ball, and it was shortly after this that he had his own big opportunity in the Mexican heat. Brazil's Everaldo miss-kicked inside his own penalty area and the ball ran perfectly to an unmarked Astle who had only Felix in the Brazilian goal to beat. It may not have been an 'open goal' as Michael Archer claimed in his 1978 book *History of the World Cup*, but it was there on a plate and, seeing as Astle was the most prolific marksman in England at the time, the chance couldn't have fallen to a better player. "Astle now!" bellowed an excited ITV commentator, Hugh Johns, firmly expecting Astle's next kick to be the one that transformed him from West Midlands hero to national one. "He misses!" bellowed Johns again an instant later, only this time in disbelief.

The miss turned out not to be costly as England still progressed to the quarter-finals, but it did appear to mark a turning point in Astle's career, which went steadily downhill after the tournament was over. The following season he only managed a modest 15 goals from 48 games and the season after scored just twice in 22 appearances. Injury them forced him to miss most of West Brom's 1972-73 and 1973-74 campaigns and it was at the end of the latter that the club released him. Although still only 32 and having played for England in the World Cup just four years earlier, Astle ended up signing for Southern League Dunstable Town in July 1974, having received no offers from any Football League clubs.

Allan Clarke

Allan Clarke's international debut was also his only ever game in the finals of the World Cup – and he scored the winning goal in it. Clarke had been included in the England squad for the 1970 tournament despite never having played at full international level before and was given his debut in the final group game against Czechoslovakia in which he scored the game's only goal from the penalty spot. The 1-0 win saw England comfortably through to a quarter-final tie against West Germany which Clarke was dropped for and the Germans famously won 3-2. Had England qualified for the 1974 World Cup then Clarke would probably have played in it but their next appearance in the finals wouldn't be until 1982, by which time even Clarke's club career was over.

Peter Bonetti (again)

Peter Bonetti's appearance in goal for England in the quarter-finals of the 1970 World Cup was his only international appearance of that year and the only time he ever played in a World Cup match – either finals or qualifiers.

Two reasons England's 1970 World Cup exit was so unexpected

England's 3-2 defeat to West Germany in the quarter-finals of the 1970 World Cup was the only time they conceded three in a match between 1967 and 1978, as well as the first time in 41 years they had lost from two goals up.

Balls

The white 'Telstar' ball with black hexagons on it was the game's first ever patterned football and is still seen as the classic football design today. It was first seen at the 1968 European Championships, and was subsequently used at the 1970 World Cup, the 1972 European Championships, the 1974 World Cup and the 1976 European Championships, as well as in every European Cup Final between 1972 and 1977 and in most domestic leagues across mainland Europe in the 1970s. In Britain, the ball first went on sale in 1968 (one was seen in a 1969 episode of *The Avengers*), but it was never used in the professional game in either England or Scotland where the use of the plain white ball eventually became universal.

The white ball had originally been used mainly for evening matches in England, but it would become the most commonly used ball in all games during the late-1960s, making its first appearance in an FA Cup Final in 1969. The 1967 and '68 finals had both been played with yellow balls, as had the '63 final, while dark orange balls were used for all the other finals between 1962 and '66. The subsequent pervasiveness of the white ball eventually led to the disappearance of the yellow and dark-orange balls, but it took a while. They were still seen occasionally in Football League games as late as the 1973-74 season and a yellow ball had been used for the 1973 FA Cup Final.

All the balls used in the professional game before the 1980s weighed between 14 and 16 ounces when new just as today's balls do, but unlike today's balls they were made of leather and so absorbed moisture. This meant that they often grew heavier during matches.

Wallace Brownlow

Wallace Brownlow was club secretary at Basford United for 63 years between 1907 and 1970.

Two new cup competitions

The 1970-71 season saw the launch of two new national cup competitions in England in the Watney Cup and the Texaco Cup, with these being the first two competitions in England – other than five-a-side ones – to carry their sponsors' names. The Watney Cup was contested between the previous season's two highest scoring clubs in the top-flight that hadn't qualified for Europe and the two highest scoring clubs in each of the other three divisions that hadn't won promotion, while the Texaco Cup was really just contested between the best clubs in England, Scotland and Northern and Southern Ireland that hadn't qualified for Europe and were willing to take part.

Although it's now largely forgotten, the Watney Cup was seen as a big success when it was first staged in 1970. ITV presenter and commentator Brian Moore claimed it had made an "astonishing impact" and, while this may be something of an exaggeration, attendances were pretty healthy in its inaugural year, due largely to Manchester United's involvement and the fact that it was a pre-season tournament with matches played on Saturday afternoons in the summer. Reading's biggest home gate of the 1970-71 season came against United in the Watney Cup and the 34,007 Hull got against United in the competition was considerably higher than any of their League attendances that season even though they spent their campaign challenging for promotion to the First Division. The two semi-finals and the final were all televised by ITV, with the final – between Derby and Manchester United at Derby's Baseball ground – attracting a crowd of 32,000 and being attended by FIFA President Sir Stanley Rous who presented the trophy. This all lent the competition an air of prestige which was purely superficial, since the Watney Cup was only created to promote the Watney brewery and rake in the sponsorship money for doing so. Thus, when Watney withdrew its sponsorship in 1973, the competition was killed overnight.

The Texaco Cup was more low-profile than the Watney Cup and consisted of evening matches spread throughout the season. The Troubles in Northern Ireland led to the competition being closed to

Irish clubs from 1972, and, in '75, Texaco withdrew its sponsorship which led to it being renamed 'the Anglo-Scottish Cup', although by then it was a lot more Anglo than it was Scottish, with 16 English clubs taking part but only four from Scotland. The competition plodded along with practically no media coverage until 1981, by which time top-flight clubs were no longer taking part. The 1973-74 season had been the last in which all of its English entrants came from the First Division. The biggest ever crowd for a Texaco/Anglo-Scottish Cup game was 37,000 for the semi-final second-leg match between Newcastle and Derby in December 1971.

Penalty shoot-outs

On 5 August 1970, Manchester United beat Hull City 4-3 on penalties at the end of the Watney Cup semi-final played at Hull's Boothferry Crescent. This was the first penalty shoot-out in an eleven-a-side competition staged anywhere in the world and it saw United's George Best become the first ever player to score in one, his teammate Denis Law the first to miss in one and Hull goalkeeper Iain McKechnie the first to make a save in one, although McKechnie later cancelled out his heroics by taking one himself and putting it over the bar. The English football authorities had come up with the idea of shoot-outs for the Watney Cup as it was a pre-season competition that had to be completed over eight days and so there was no time for replays, and it was originally intended that shoot-outs would be unique to this competition.

Two years later, Bristol Rovers won the Watney Cup on penalties and, in doing so, became the first club to win a competition in this manner. At this time, however, the penalty shoot-out was still pretty alien to football and not everyone was certain of the rules. When Peterborough beat Blackpool on penalties in an earlier round, one of their scorers was Don Heath who had been substituted during the game. Peterborough believed this was allowed and so too did the referee, but disgruntled Blackpool were certain it shouldn't have been and put in a complaint. A week later, Stoke's Peter Dobing was equally confused about the rules when taking a penalty against Birmingham in the shoot-out at the end of the FA Cup third place play-off. After his kick was saved, Dobing put away the rebound and initially believed it would count. The FA Cup third place play-off was a meaningless match which was why a shoot-out was allowed to decide it. Settling any other FA Cup match in this way would have been unthinkable at the time and it would be almost another two decades before the competition had its next penalty shoot-out.

In the League Cup, the use of penalty shoot-outs spread incredibly slowly. They were first introduced into the competition in 1976 to decide first round replays only, but 15 years later were still not being used beyond the second round, resulting in a League Cup third round second replay taking place between Crystal Palace and Birmingham in December 1991. This stands as the last ever second replay between English professional clubs in any competition.

Although it was the English who originally devised penalty shoot-outs, their immediate adoption by UEFA meant that, for 20 years, they were a far more common spectacle in European competitions than they were in the English domestic game. Somewhat fittingly considering they were an English idea, the first penalty shoot-out in the European Cup was staged at Goodison Park between Everton and Borussia Monchengladbach in November 1970. Everton won it 4-3 and such was the unfamiliarity with this method of deciding matches that it was described as "the strangest victory" in the following season's *News of the World Football Annual*. Almost a decade later, the penalty shoot-out at the end of the 1980 European Cup-Winners' Cup Final between Arsenal and Valencia became the first to be shown live on British television and even then it was still an unfamiliar sight to British football fans. So much so, in fact, that when it went to sudden death, BBC commentator John Motson felt the need to explain the rules to the viewers.

Over the next six years there would be six more penalty shoot-outs shown live on TV (two in European finals and four in World Cups), which would make them a more familiar sight but not necessarily a welcome one, as it would be a long while before they became widely accepted as a suitable way to settle matches. In 1986, *When Saturday Comes* wrote of penalty shoot-outs deciding knock-out games at that year's World Cup, "Is [the World Cup] a mere commercial exercise, a TV extravaganza? Or is it a competition to decide the world champions of football? If it's the latter, then the games should be decided by playing football, not by an almost totally arbitrary device designed simply to settle the tie as quickly as possible". Four years later, the settling of both semi-finals at the 1990 World Cup on penalties prompted the *Rothmans Football Yearbook* editorial to lament, "not only is this farcical in the World Cup, it has no place in the game at all and we must all take responsibility for allowing it to develop".

In 1991, Torquay became the first club to win promotion on penalties, which was even more farcical. Now the result of a penalty shoot-out was being used to override the points gained over 46 League matches in determining the success of a season.

Women's football (slight return)

In January 1970, the FA lifted its almost-half-a-century long ban on FA-affiliated clubs staging women's football on their grounds, which meant that the newly-formed Women's FA was able to launch the Women's FA Cup for the 1970-71 season.

There had been national cup competitions for women's team's during the inter-War years, but the original Women's FA Cup is the first to have a direct lineage to the modern Women's FA Cup, even though the men's FA would have no involvement in it until 1993.

Back in 1970, of course, attitudes were different to today, and women's football had little chance of being taken seriously. English football had always been, supposedly, the hardest and grittiest in the world, and so it was in England where football was also probably seen as 'a man's game' more than it was anywhere else. Most people in 1970 had never seen a woman kick a football, nor would they for at least the next couple of decades. In schools, girls team-sports were hockey, netball and rounders. The Women's FA Cup, therefore, was almost universally ignored and would pretty much remain so until the following century. Throughout the 1980s and '90s, the Women's Cup Final would always draw a much smaller crowd than the finals of both the FA Vase and the FA Youth Cup, suggesting it was still lower in status than both youth football and the lowest level of non-League football during those decades.

The women finally got their own national league for the 1991-92 season, and that same season the *Rothmans Football Yearbook* (which had been published annually since 1970) included a section on women's football for the first time, but it took up less than half a page of a book that ran to 992 pages in total. Then, the following year, the compilers thought better of it and dropped the women's football section altogether. It wouldn't be revived until the 1995-96 edition of the book which devoted three pages to the women's game, two fewer than it devoted to the Isthmian League.

The longest last three and a half minutes

A goalpost was broken three and a half minutes from the end of Lincoln's Fourth Division match at home to Brentford in August 1970. There was then a 45-minute wait before play could be resumed.

A goal with a truly charmed life

Liverpool hit the crossbar four times and the post once during the first half of a League Cup tie at Mansfield in September 1970. The game eventually finished 0-0.

Billy Bonds

West Ham's Billy Bonds was sent-off, fined heavily and suspended for five League matches after spitting at a Hull City player during a League Cup tie in September 1970. These were the only five West Ham League games that Bonds missed in almost five years between November 1967 and October '72.

So what exactly is a hat-trick?

In the early years of football, a player was only said to have scored a hat-trick if he scored three consecutive goals for his team in the same game. If his three goals were punctuated by goals from other players, then it wasn't a hat-trick. This definition of a hat-trick persisted at least into the 1920s if J.A.H. Catton's 1926 book *The Story of Association Football* is anything to go by, and it still hadn't totally disappeared at the beginning of the 1970s. When *The Big Match* commentator, Brian Moore, credited QPR's Rodney Marsh with a hat-trick against Birmingham in October 1970, a number of viewers wrote in to point out that it wasn't a hat-trick because his three goals weren't consecutive ones. This led to the show's pundit, Jimmy Hill, having to define the term 'hat-trick' the following week. "In Cricket, of course, it is three consecutive wickets" said Hill, "but in football, traditionally through the years, it's generally been accepted that if you get three goals in a match then the boys are happy to credit you with a hat-trick". Hill, it should be noted, was born in 1928, so probably wouldn't have been familiar with the definition of a hat-trick in Catton's day, and in Catton's day there was no greater authority on football than Catton himself.

The Hopeless Trio

At the beginning of November 1970, all of the clubs in the Fourth Division were 16 matches into their 1970-71 campaigns, and the bottom three had only managed one win between them. These bottom three were Newport, Hartlepool and Barrow and the one win was by Hartlepool over Barrow and was only achieved with a penalty. Newport wouldn't get their first League win until 15 January, although they won more games than they lost during the remainder of the season to finish above the other two.

Bob Redford

In November 1970, Bob Redford became the first football fan in England known to have watched a game at all 92 Football League grounds. Many would follow in his footsteps over the years, eventually coming to refer to themselves as members of 'the 92 Club'.

Bobby Gough

In November 1970, Port Vale lost at Shrewsbury by a four-goal margin but still had a hat-trick hero. Bobby Gough scored all three Vale goals in a 7-3 defeat, with his first two being equalisers and the third pulling it back to 6-3. None of the Shrewsbury players scored hat-tricks.

West Ham's shamed nightclubbers

West Ham's 4-0 defeat to Blackpool in the third round of the FA Cup in January 1971 was thought to be partly down to four of the West Ham team that day – Bobby Moore, Jimmy Greaves, Clyde Best and Brian Dear – having been out drinking in a Blackpool nightclub until the early hours of the morning of the game. After this came to light, the West Ham manager, Ron Greenwood, wanted to sack all four, and although he was persuaded not to by the board, Dear – the least valuable member of the group – never played for West Ham again. Of the other three, Greaves was suspended for three games by the club and Moore for two, while Best – who was only on soft drinks on the night in question – was let-off but barely played again that season after getting injured in the next game.

Peter Osgood

In January 1971, Chelsea's Peter Osgood was banned for eight weeks by the FA for picking up his third booking of the season. The harshness of this punishment would suggest that a player getting booked three times in the same season was unprecedented at the start of the 1970s.

Jimmy Greaves (yet again)

Jimmy Greaves scored his 100th goal in English league football at the age of 20, his 200th at the age of 23 and became the top-flight's all-time top scorer when he was 28. His final goal in the top tier of English football – which was his 357th – came for West Ham against West Bromwich Albion in April 1971 and since then no one's come within 70 goals of his record and only one player has come within 100 goals of it. Like Arthur Rowley, Greaves achieved his goalscoring feats despite rarely operating as an out-and-out striker. He spent most of his career playing as an inside-forward when, like all inside forwards in WM formations, he frequently dropped deep and drifted wide, something he also did when playing in 4-3-3 formations in his later years. He was even occasionally used as a conventional winger by Tottenham and reduced his chances of scoring from corners by the fact that he took many of them himself.

Brian Dear

Brian Dear was on West Ham's books for ten seasons in all (1960-61 to 1968-69 and 1970-71) but only ever made 83 first-team appearances for the club. This despite the fact that he scored a very respectable 39 goals in those 83 games, which included five in 20 minutes of a First Division match against West Bromwich Albion in 1965, another top-flight hat-trick against Leicester on Boxing Day 1967 and goals in both the quarter-finals and semi-finals of the 1965 European Cup-Winners' Cup.

Dear's only full season for West Ham was 1967-68 when he made 29 appearances and scored 16 goals. He was still only 24 at the time but his career as a full-time professional was already nearing its end. By the time he was 28 he was playing for Woodford Town in the second tier of the Southern League.

Trevor Francis

Trevor Francis scored 16 goals in the first 16 League games of his senior career when he was still a 16-year-old apprentice. He achieved this feat for Birmingham City in the 1970-71 season, although it would be almost another six years before he made his England debut and another two years after that before he eventually left Birmingham for Nottingham Forest in the first transfer in England to cost a million pound. Four months after signing for Forest, Francis scored the winning goal for them in the 1979 European Cup Final, which was his first ever match in a European competition.

Chris Chilton and Ken Wagstaff

Between 1964 and 1971, Chris Chilton and Ken Wagstaff played together up front for Hull 253 times in major competitions and scored 252 goals between them in those matches. In all matches, they scored 50 goals between them in 1964-65, 60 in '65-66, 40 in '66-67, 35 in '67-68, 38 in '69-70 and 39 in '70-71. In '68-69, Wagstaff scored 21 but Chilton missed a large chunk of the season through injury and only got seven. This was the only season out of the seven that they played together in which they didn't finish as the club's two leading scorers. Chilton – who played for Hull before Wagstaff arrived – scored a total of 219 goals in major competitions for the club, while Wagstaff – whose Hull Career continued after Chilton left – got 193. They remain the two highest scorers in Hull's history. Over the seven seasons they played together there were 45 matches in which they both scored.

The great Leeds v Arsenal title race

Leeds United finished runners-up in the League in 1970-71, despite remaining continuously at the top of the table from the beginning of the season until 17 April. Before Arsenal beat Coventry on 6 April, Leeds had a six-point lead at the top which is bigger than it sounds as in those days only two points were awarded for a win (a six-point lead was, therefore, the equivalent of nine points today). It was on 17 April that Arsenal leap-frogged over Leeds on goal average, but nine days later Leeds were back at the top again after beating Arsenal 1-0 at Elland Road. Leeds were still top when they concluded their League campaign with a 2-0 win over Nottingham Forest on the season's final weekend, but it was only a one-point lead and Arsenal still had one game left to play which was away to Tottenham on the Monday. The complicated nature of goal average meant that an Arsenal win or a goalless draw would win the title for Arsenal whereas a Tottenham win or a score draw would hand it to Leeds. White Hart Lane was full when they closed the turnstiles over an hour before kick-off that night, with an estimated 50,000 fans locked out. Those that got in saw Arsenal clinch the title with a 1-0 win that wasn't even televised (although there were news cameras there). Ray Kennedy scored the winner three minutes from time, but again, the complicated nature of goal average meant the goal was irrelevant – It was the clean sheet that sealed it.

For Leeds, it was the second consecutive season they had finished runners-up and they would finish runners-up again the following season. Five days after clinching the title, Arsenal won the FA Cup as well to become the first team in a decade to bag the League and Cup double.

The most unlikely double winners

The Arsenal side of 1970-71 were probably England's most unlikely ever winners of the League and FA Cup double. The previous season they had only managed a 12th place finish and that had been the club's 17th season in a row without winning a major trophy. Indeed, they went into their double-winning season having only finished in the top six once in eleven seasons and having not got beyond the fifth round of the FA Cup for 13 seasons. And it wasn't as if their success in '70-71 was down to squad-strengthening either, since all of the 16 players they used had played in the club's underwhelming campaign of '69-70 as well.

Jeff Astle and Tony Brown

West Bromwich Albion only finished 16th in the First Division in 1969-70 and only 17th 1970-71, and yet in both seasons they provided the division's top scorer – and it was a different player each time. Jeff Astle topped the scoring lists in 1969-70 with 25 goals and Tony Brown did so the following season with 28. Astle had signed for West Brom from Fourth Division Notts County in 1964, while Brown had joined the club as an apprentice a year earlier.

Arsenal riding their luck in the semis

Arsenal wouldn't have won the League and Cup double in 1970-71 had they not got lucky several times over in their FA Cup semi-final against Stoke. Stoke were 2-0 up at half-time and should have made it 3-0 in the second half when John Mahoney raced clear of the last Arsenal defender only to shoot straight at Bob Wilson in the Arsenal goal. Arsenal then pulled it back to 2-1, but Stoke then wasted another gilt-edged opportunity when Jimmy Greenhoff raced clear with only Wilson to beat but shot over. Arsenal eventually equalised with a last-minute penalty that Stoke conceded from a corner that was only given because the referee hadn't spotted a foul on Stoke keeper, Gordon Banks. The penalty was taken by Peter Storey, and again Arsenal got lucky as Banks seemed strangely rooted to the spot as Storey's soft and down-the-middle kick rolled gently passed him. Banks could have stopped it had he simply stuck out his left foot. Arsenal won the replay 2-0.

The great 1971 FA Cup Final mystery

Nobody's ever been sure who scored Arsenal's first goal against Liverpool in the 1971 FA Cup Final. TV commentators Ken Wolstenholme (on the BBC) and Brian Moore (on ITV) both called it as George Graham, but it was subsequently credited to Eddie Kelly and appeared as Kelly in most – but not all – of the record books for many years before eventually being given back to Graham again. Even asking the players themselves shed no light on the mystery. Kelly said he thought it was Graham's goal and Graham said he wasn't sure and was happy for Kelly to be credited with it.

Gordon Banks

In acclaiming Gordon Banks, the 1971-72 *Rothmans Football Yearbook* described him as "a goalkeeper who will be remembered alongside Sam Hardy, Harry Hibbs and Frank Swift". By this time, Banks had been a World Cup-winner with England and made the most celebrated save of all-time, from Pele in the 1970 World Cup. And yet, on this evidence, he was still considered only on a par with three keepers whose names will mean nothing to most people today.

The Football Pools

Before the National Lottery came along in 1994, 'winning the Pools' was the best chance someone with an ordinary job had of winning a life-changing sum of money. The first Football Pools was launched by Littlewoods in 1923, but it was only after the Pools companies switched to 'treble chance' after the Second World War that the Pools really took off in a big way. Under 'treble chance' punters could pick the matches from the coming Saturday's football fixtures that they thought had the best chance of landing them the 24 points needed for the jackpot, rather than having to take pot luck with the matches they were given as had been the case under the old system. With a drawn game being worth three points, successfully predicting eight draws was the dream of millions of people all over the country and meant that even those who didn't like football were still engaged with it when the final scores were read out at Saturday teatime.

In 1950, the first ever £100,000 prize was paid out on treble chance (which was considerably more money in those days than it is now), with the first £200,000 prize coming in '57 and the first £300,000 one in '59. The publicity surrounding these and other big wins encouraged more and more people to have a go, with the growth in participation continuing even after the Pools companies made it harder to hit the jackpot in 1969 by making only score draws worth three points. The peak years for participation were the early-to-mid-70s, when Pools coupons were being filled out in 12 million households each week at a time when there were only 19 million households in the country. Some of these coupons were then posted to the Pools companies, but the vast majority were handed over, along with the stake money, to collectors who provided no receipt. We were clearly a much more trusting people back then.

It's clear to see just how big the Pools was at that time when we look at various publications from the 1971-72 season. That season saw full-page Pools guides appear in tabloid newspapers as well as in *Goal* magazine which had featured a double-page Pools guide in previous seasons. An advertisement for Littlewoods Pools, meanwhile, occupied the entire back cover of that season's *News of the World Football Annual* which also carried full-page advertisements for five other Pools companies inside. As for the *Rothmans Football Yearbook*, that went to the real extremes by devoting no fewer than 34 pages to the Pools in its 1971-72 edition.

Somehow the Pools didn't seem quite so big in the 1980s, possibly because many of those who reached adulthood after the early-70s saw 'doing the Pools' as a bit of a mums-and-dads' thing, but it was in 1987 when we had our first million pound Pools winner.

The Ref's Revolution

Oldham, Crewe and Fulham only collected three bookings each over their respective League campaigns of the 1970-71 season, a statistic which probably says less about the sportsmanship of those clubs than it does about the leniency of English referees at the time, who, unlike those in other countries, usually only booked or sent-off players for dissent or fighting. This all changed, however, when what was known as 'the ref's revolution' came in at the start of the 1971-72 season. It was only from this point that players being booked for fouls and deliberate handballs became common, and it was also only from this point that the tackle from behind (i.e. going through an opponent to get the ball) was outlawed. Controversially, the Football League and the FA had directed referees to take a hard line secretly, without consulting the clubs which meant that players went into the season's opening matches without any prior knowledge of the more severe punishments that awaited them if they broke the rules, or even knowing that tackling from behind was now against the rules. Consequently, although still low by today's standards, the number of bookings went through the roof by the standards of previous seasons, and it was probably no surprise when, in May at Wembley, Arsenal's Bob McNab became the first ever player to be booked for a foul in an FA Cup Final.

The *Rothmans Football Yearbook* subsequently wrote in its editorial on the season "As statistics of players booked and ordered off mounted, the world could have been forgiven for believing that British players had gone suddenly mad, whereas the truth was that British football was belatedly finding its sanity".

From the following season, the FA made it clear that a player would also be sent-off if he committed two bookable offences in the same game, and that season would see 99 players dismissed in the League, FA Cup and League Cup combined. The highest prior to 'the ref's revolution' was 51 in 1968-69. That's 51 dismissals in 2,287 matches in all domestic competitions – and that was the worst season! In the 2014-15 season, the 380 Premier League matches alone produced 71 red cards.

Perhaps we should have fielded the first team after all

In September 1971, Leeds became probably the first English side ever to be knocked out of a cup competition after fielding an under-strength side against weak opposition. It came in the first round of the UEFA Cup when Leeds, who had finished runners-up in the League the previous season, were drawn against Lierse SK who had finished fourth in the Belgian League. Leeds had rested a few players in the first leg in Belgium but still won it comfortably 2-0, which encouraged Don Revie to rest even more for the second leg. The game at Elland Road saw only four first-team regulars in the starting line-up and by half-time Lierse had already turned the tie around with three goals in a six-minute spell. They then added a fourth in the second half to win 4-0 on the night and 4-2 on aggregate.

The biggest European mismatch

In September 1971, probably the biggest mismatch in the history of European club competitions occurred when Chelsea played the Luxembourg second-tier side Jeunesse Hautcharage in the first round of the European Cup-Winners' Cup. The small town of Hautcharage had a population of just a few thousand at the time and their football club was originally going to concede the tie as they were unable to stage the home leg on a ground that had no floodlights and couldn't afford to travel to London for the away leg. In the end, however, donations paid for both new floodlights and the trip to London and so Jeunesse took on Chelsea with their ragbag team of locals that included four brothers, two players in their 40s, one player in spectacles and another with one arm. Chelsea won the first leg 8-0 away and the second 13-0 at home, with Peter Osgood scoring three in the first leg and five in the second. Ironically, they then lost on away goals to the Swedish club Atvidaberg in the next round, after which they wouldn't play in Europe again for another 23 years.

The longest Cup ties

The longest ever FA Cup tie was the fourth qualifying round tie between Alvechurch and Oxford City in November 1971 which took eleven hours over six matches on five different grounds to complete. Alvechurch lead 2-0 at home at one point in the first game but Oxford came back to force a replay which finished 1-1, with another 1-1 following in the second replay at Birmingham City's St. Andrew's. Next came two 0-0 draws at Oxford United's Manor Ground, before Alvechurch finally won 1-0 in the FA Cup's only ever fifth replay which was staged at Villa Park on 22 November 1971. By scoring the winner, Bobby Hope stands as the only player ever to score in an FA Cup fifth replay and his goal put Alvechurch through to a first round tie against Aldershot which was played just two days later and saw Aldershot run out 4-2 winners against their jaded opponents.

As for the competition proper, there have been several ties that have gone to four replays, but the third round one between Stoke and Bury in January 1955 is the only one where all four replays went to extra-time. Although the first replay was abandoned due to snow, the abandonment didn't come until the 112th minute so the tie still lasted for nine hours and 22 minutes in total. It was Stoke who eventually won it, with Neville Coleman's winner in the fourth replay coming with just a minute of extra-time left.

Although the FA Cup was 83 years old by the 1954-55 season, this was the first ever tie in the competition proper to go to four replays. The second was the Aston Villa v Doncaster fourth round one the following month. In that tie, the second, third and fourth replays were played at Maine Road, Hillsborough and the Hawthorns respectively, whilst the second, third and fourth replays in the Stoke v Bury tie had been at Goodison Park, Anfield and Old Trafford respectively.

Up to and including the 1973-74 season, all FA Cup second replays and beyond were played on neutral grounds, but from '74-75 opposing teams needing a second replay to decide a Cup tie would sometimes toss a coin to see which one would host it. This method of determining the venue of a second replay would gradually become more and more common until second replays on neutral grounds eventually disappeared entirely (at least from the competition proper) after Hull played Rochdale at Leeds in November 1981. Second replays in the competition proper were eventually done away with in 1991, when they were replaced with penalty shoot-outs at the end of the first replay. With this change in the rules, more than a century of marathon Cup ties was brought to an end seemingly on a whim. The last one to go to four replays was the third round meeting of Arsenal and Sheffield Wednesday in 1979, when the two teams played each other three times at Leicester City's Filbert Street, with two of the games coming in the space of three days. Wednesday only finished 14th in Division Three that season but, over the course of the tie, scored no fewer than five equalisers against their top-flight opponents who went on to win the Cup that season.

The last ever FA Cup second replay in the competition proper was the fourth round one between Arsenal and Leeds on 13 February 1991, which was followed by a third replay between the two clubs three days later. In the preliminary and qualifying rounds of the competition, second replays weren't replaced by penalty shoot-outs until 1997.

David Webb

In December 1971, Chelsea defender David Webb played in goal for the whole of a First Division match against Ipswich because Chelsea's first and second choice keepers were both injured and the only other keeper they had was too far away when notified to be able to get to the ground on time. Webb kept a clean sheet in a 2-0 Chelsea win.

The semi-final that took seven weeks to complete

The 1971-72 League Cup semi-final between Stoke and West Ham took seven weeks to complete with it eventually finishing in a different year to when it started. West Ham won the first leg 2-1 at

Stoke on 8 December 1971, but then lost 1-0 at home in the second leg a week later on a night when they were denied an aggregate victory by a Gordon Banks penalty save four minutes from time. It wasn't until the new year that the replay took place and when it did it finished 0-0 thanks to another penalty save from Banks. The teams then had to wait another three weeks before the second replay which Stoke finally won 3-2 with their first goal being scored on the follow-up to yet another saved penalty, this time from Bobby Moore who had temporarily taken over in goal while the West Ham keeper, Bobby Ferguson, was receiving treatment for an injury.

Between the first leg on 8 December 1971 and the second replay on 26 January 1972, the two teams played six League matches each and an FA Cup tie.

Jimmy Pearce

In December 1971, Tottenham's Jimmy Pearce came on as a sub in a UEFA Cup tie away to Rapid Bucharest but was only on the field for ten minutes before being sent-off. During those ten minutes he put Tottenham 2-0 up and then had another goal disallowed.

Where did that title challenge go?

Manchester United were five points clear at the top of the First Division in December 1971 (the equivalent of seven points today) but lost seven League games in a row beginning from New Year's Day and only ended up finishing eighth. Their decline in form had much to do with the decline in form of George Best, a decline in form from which he would never recover.

The pull of the Brazilians

Sheffield Wednesday's biggest attendance of the 1971-72 season was 37,000 for a friendly against the Brazilian club Santos. This despite the fact that the match kicked-off at 2.30 on a Wednesday afternoon. It had also been a friendly against Santos that had provided Wednesday's biggest crowd (49,000) of the 1962-63 season, although that one had been an evening kick-off.

Ian Moore

Ian Moore was Nottingham Forest's top scorer in five out of six consecutive seasons between 1966-67 and 1971-72 despite being a winger. Since his retirement from the game, Moore has always been referred to as Ian Storey-Moore, but the first part of his surname was rarely used during his playing days.

Tommy Wright

Everton's Tommy Wright scored an own goal in the first minute on each of two consecutive Saturdays in March 1972. The first came in a 4-0 defeat at Liverpool, and the second in a 2-1 reverse at home to Manchester City. These proved to be the last two goals of Wright's career before it was ended through injury.

Ian Moore (again)

In March 1972, Derby supposedly signed the Nottingham Forest winger Ian Moore (later known as Ian Storey-Moore) and marked the event by introducing him to the fans ahead of their home game against Wolves. It subsequently transpired, however, that the deal hadn't been completed and Moore joined Manchester United two days later.

George Eastham

George Eastham's winning goal for Stoke in the 1972 League Cup Final was his first goal in any competition since November 1969.

Trevor Pearson

When Second Division Sheffield Wednesday found themselves with no fit keeper towards the end of the 1971-72 season, they called upon a Sunday League amateur called Trevor Pearson to keep goal for them for four matches. After he played in the last one away at Norwich, Pearson then disappeared back to the world of parks football and was never seen in the professional game again.

Francis Lee

Manchester City's Francis Lee scored a record 15 penalties in the 1971-72 season, 13 in the League, one in the FA Cup and one in the League Cup. They came in 15 different matches, and from the start of the season until March, he never went more than three games in a row without scoring from the spot. He also scored another 20 goals that season that weren't penalties.

You know you're hopeless when half of your goals are scored by opponents

Huddersfield only scored four goals in their final 16 League games of the 1971-72 season – and two of them were own goals by West Bromwich Albion's Ally Robertson and Ipswich's Allan Hunter.

Bobby Knox (again)

Bobby Knox made 25 starts for Barrow in the 1971-72 season – 23 as a defender and two in goal when the club's regular keeper, Harry Thomson, was ill.

The brilliant Bests

In the 1971-72 season, George Best scored 26 goals for Manchester United, Clyde Best scored 23 goals for West Ham and Billy Best scored 20 goals for Southend.

Alf Wood

Shrewsbury's Alf Wood scored 40 goals in the 1971-72 season, which was his first season playing up front, having spent the previous seven as a central defender.

The massive club in the third tier

When Aston Villa won the Third Division title in 1971-72, their average League attendance of 31,952 was bigger than that of half of the clubs in the First Division and all of the clubs in the Second aside from Birmingham City.

Tony Read

During the seven years he spent at Luton between 1965 and 1972, Tony Read made 191 appearances as a goalkeeper and another 38 as a forward. Most of his appearances up front came in the 1965-66 season when he finished as the club's second-top scorer with 12 goals.

The most complicated and drawn-out title race ever

On the final full weekend of the 1971-72 First Division season (there were three more fixtures played the following weekend), top-of-the-table Derby played away to second-placed Manchester City with only a point separating the two sides. City won the game 2-0 to go above Derby and finish their season top of the League, but they couldn't be champions as Derby and Liverpool still had to play each other in an outstanding fixture and either one of them or both of them would move above City whatever the result. The match wasn't played for another nine days and it saw Derby win 1-0 to finish their season top of the League but still not confirmed as champions as Leeds and Liverpool both still had one game each left to play, with Leeds only needing a point away to Wolves to take the title and Liverpool needing a win at Arsenal to become champions if Leeds lost. The Wolves v Leeds and Arsenal v Liverpool games were both played on the Monday after the 1972 FA Cup Final which Leeds had won and so were on course to win the two biggest trophies in English football in the space of three days. This seemed the most likely outcome, although, in the end, Leeds lost at Wolves and as Liverpool could only draw at Arsenal, Derby became champions a week after they had played their final game and 16 days after the season's final full Saturday. Their players heard the news whilst on holiday in Majorca. Man City, who had been top after completing their fixtures, ended up finishing fourth, although only a point behind the champions.

Steve Powell

The Derby County side that clinched the League title with a 1-0 win against Liverpool in May 1972 included the 16-year-old apprentice Steve Powell at right-back.

The biggest disallowed goal

Perhaps the biggest and most controversial disallowed goal in English football history is not as well-known as it should be because it came in a game that wasn't televised. The match was Arsenal v Liverpool at the end of the 1971-72 season, which was the final match of the season for both clubs. Liverpool's John Toshack had the disallowed effort in the dying minutes, and it would have won Liverpool the title on that night had it counted. Toshack was given offside by the referee after tapping in from close range, although it was claimed the linesman never flagged.

Geoff Hurst (yet again)

Geoff Hurst scored 248 goals for West Ham between 1961 and 1972, although he began his career as a half-back and only scored once in his first 38 appearances for the club. It was during this less well-known period of his career that he also made his only appearance in first-class cricket, representing Essex against Lancashire in 1962.

Terry Neill

England's 1-0 defeat to Northern Ireland at Wembley in May 1972 is the only international they've ever lost to a goal scored by the manager of a Second Division club. The scorer was Terry Neill who was player-manager of both Hull City and the Northern Ireland national side at the time.

Colin Todd and Alan Hudson

Colin Todd made his England debut against Northern Ireland at Wembley in May 1972, but a week later he withdrew from an under-23 tour and, as a result, was banned from representing his country for the next two years. Todd's reason for withdrawing was to take his family on holiday and Alan Hudson also cited domestic reasons when he withdrew from the same tour. Hudson was issued with the same two-year ban and, as he had not yet won a full cap, holds the unique distinction of being banned from senior international football before he had ever played it.

Getting to Wembley the hard way

Arsenal reached both the 1971 and 1972 FA Cup Finals despite not being drawn at home in any round in either season.

The massiveness of the FA Cup

There was a time when the FA Cup Final was regarded as such a major national event that, between 1964 and 1990, BBC1 broadcast a pre-match build-up to it that was nearly always between three and four hours long. It came in the form *Cup Final Grandstand*, an extended version of the BBC's usual Saturday afternoon sports show *Grandstand* that was devoted either entirely or almost entirely to FA Cup-related features. In 1972, *Cup Final Grandstand* was even longer, as this was the FA Cup's centenary year and so the BBC marked it by giving a build up to that year's final that clocked in at a colossal four hours and 15 minutes. Even by today's standards this seems off-the-scale, and yet in those days and for some years after, the BBC were generally brief in their pre-match build-ups. During the 1970s and '80s, they only usually gave a 15-minute build-up to their live coverage of the European Cup Final, even if an English club was involved, while England's opening game at the 1982 World Cup was preceded by a build-up that began just ten minutes before kick-off despite it being England's first match in the finals of the competition for 12 years.

The fact that the BBC gave so much airtime to the FA Cup Final during an era when it skimped on it for other big games illustrates as well as anything the unparalleled prestige of the FA Cup before the 1990s. Today people often talk about the 'magic' of the FA Cup, but before the '90s the FA Cup wasn't 'magic' – it was massive. In the '60s and '70s, whilst only highlights of League games were shown on TV, the FA Cup Final was always on live, and between 1961 and 1988 it was the only annual sporting event broadcast live every year on both BBC1 and ITV, with the BBC also showing highlights as well in the evening, while ITV showed their highlights the following afternoon. In 1968 and '69, when only BBC2 broadcast in colour, the Cup Final was shown live in black and white on BBC1 and ITV and live in colour on BBC2 at a time when there were no other channels.

Players dreamed of playing in an FA Cup Final as no other football match – indeed no other sporting event – had such a great sense of occasion and national importance. And it wasn't only the players who hungered for FA Cup glory. Attendances showed just how much the competition meant to the fans as well. At the start of the 1990-91 season, the record attendance for 29 of the 44 clubs then in the top two tiers of English football had come in the FA Cup. Wolves won back-to-back titles in 1957-58 and '58-59, but their biggest attendance over those two seasons was for an FA Cup tie against Darlington, while Burnley's two biggest gates of 1959-60 also both came in the Cup even though this was the season that saw them win their first League title in nearly 40 years. In 1970, Leeds got a bigger crowd for their fourth round FA Cup tie against Mansfield than they did for the home leg of their European Cup semi-final against Celtic two months later. In the 1972-73 season, 30,000 more attended the Tottenham v Derby FA Cup fourth round replay than the Tottenham v Derby League match. And in 1980-81, Liverpool got a bigger crowd at home to Altrincham in the FA Cup than they did at home to Manchester United in the League.

When the semi-finals arrived they felt like the biggest games that could ever be played on English club grounds (the first one at Wembley wasn't until 1991). Every year they kicked-off simultaneously on a Saturday afternoon along with all of that day's League matches, and so had the look of regular football fixtures, but were anything but. With the teams involved potentially just 90 minutes away from being a part of one of Britain's most prestigious national events, the sense of anticipation and raw excitement was like nothing else in football. On semi-final weekend, both the BBC and ITV ignored the First Division matches and devoted their highlights shows entirely to the two Cup games, with one being shown on BBC1 on Saturday night and the other on ITV on Sunday afternoon. At the time this seemed like a perfectly natural thing to do. Why would anyone want to watch highlights of League games on a weekend when FA Cup semi-finals had been played? 1990 was the first year that both semi-finals were shown live on TV, and this was the first time ever that two domestic English football matches were televised live on the same day.

It wasn't long after this, however, that the FA Cup began losing its significance. The increase in both the number of games being shown live on TV and the number of games being played at Wembley meant FA Cup Final day no longer seemed quite so special. The media's promotion of the Premier League as a progression from everything that had gone before began to make enthusiasm for the FA Cup seem almost archaic, and the creation of the Champions League did even more damage. Once the biggest clubs in England became so focused on a competition that brought them up against the biggest in mainland Europe, a domestic cup competition that involved lower divisions and non-League sides was always going to seem a bit small fry in comparison.

Today the FA Cup is a shadow of its former self – a kind of romantic relic from a more parochial time – and yet, for about 120 years it was the biggest thing in English football and, judging by the crowds it attracted during those years and the level of TV coverage it got in comparison with other competitions, it was probably bigger then than anything we've got now.

Charlie George

In the 1960s and early-1970s, sport and music belonged to two entirely different worlds. Few musicians appeared to know anything about sport and few sportsmen appeared to have much knowledge of music. When rock stars had long hair, footballers still had theirs short and side-parted, and despite his celebrity status, George Best never met The Beatles and despite coming from Liverpool, The Beatles never supported Liverpool or Everton or anyone else.

Arsenal's Charlie George, therefore, seemed to have passed into another dimension when, in 1972, he was written about in the rock music handbook, *Rock File*. In an essay on the skinhead movement entitled 'Skins Rule', Peter Fowler wrote this about George: "When the skins root for Charlie George at Highbury – they are rooting for themselves. For Charlie is simply one of them who's happened to make it out there on the stage. They hate the opposition, and so does

Charlie. They adore him for his V-signs and his tantrums, just as they adore kicking in the teeth of an enemy fan …Watching Charlie George at Highbury is, for the skins, much the same experience as watching The Who at the Railway Hotel in Wealdstone was for the mods. Or, to cross the Atlantic, the same experience as watching Johnny Cash at San Quentin was for the prison inmates". No footballer had ever been written about like this before.

Midfielders officially exist

The word 'midfielder' was first coined in a match report in the *Cheshire County News and Stockport Chronicle* in November 1888, but it never caught on and it wouldn't be until the 1970s that the position of midfielder became properly recognised within the game. Before then, some players were sometimes said to play in midfield, but this was a somewhat loose and general term rather than a recognised playing position. If a player was a defensive midfielder then he was a 'half-back' (aka 'wing-half'), while an attacking midfielder was an 'inside-forward'. This is plain to see in the 1972-73 *Rothmans Football Yearbook* which listed all the players for each League club under their playing position, with those that we would now call 'midfielders' all listed as either 'half-backs' or 'forwards'. These included Leeds' Billy Bremner, Tottenham's Martin Peters and Chelsea's John Hollins who were all 'half-backs' according to the book, and West Ham's Trevor Brooking, Derby's Archie Gemmill and Queens Park Rangers' Gerry Francis who were all apparently 'forwards'. All of these players then became 'midfield' in the 1973-74 *Rothmans Football Yearbook* which was the first to recognise that such a position existed.

Ted MacDougall

Ted MacDougall scored 96 League and cup goals for Bournemouth over the 1970-71 and '71-72 seasons. This is the biggest two-season haul by a Football League player aside from the 99 Middlesbrough's George Camsell got over the 1926-27 and '27-28 seasons when football was much less defensive. Macdougall's 96 was comprised of 49 in the '70-71 season and 47 the following season and included six in an 8-1 win against Oxford City in the first round of the FA Cup in 1970 and nine in an 11-1 victory over Margate in the following season's FA Cup first round, the latter of which remains a record for the proper rounds of the competition.

MacDougall then scored seven in his first ten games of the 1972-73 season, after which First Division Manchester United paid a record fee for a Third Division player when they bought him for £200,000. By Christmas, MacDougall was United's leading scorer for the season with five goals, but his wife wasn't happy living in the north and so just two months later United sold him to West Ham for £50,000 less than what they paid for him. MacDougall had spent just five months at Old Trafford and made just 18 appearances and he wouldn't spend long at West Ham either, staying there for just ten months before being part-exchanged for Norwich's Graham Paddon in December 1973. This last move made Norwich the third top-flight side to sign MacDougall in 15 months.

A little remembered cup upset

In October 1972, a Manchester United side featuring Bobby Charlton and George Best lost 2-1 at home to Third Division Bristol Rovers in a League Cup replay. Rovers' winner came from a corner four minutes from time, which no doubt more than made up for their disappointment at conceding an equaliser three minutes from the end of the first match.

Derek Possee

Derek Possee only ever played 56 minutes for Millwall during the 19 years and three months he spent as their all-time record League goalscorer. Possee broke the record in the 34th minute of a Second Division match at home to Bristol City on 30 December 1972 and then improved upon his record with another goal two minutes after half-time. But the end of the match would mark the end of his Millwall career as he was sold to Crystal Palace five days later.

The relegated win specialists

Rotherham were relegated from Division Three at the end of the 1972-73 season despite getting off to a flying start that saw them win six of their first eight League games and eight of their first ten League and cup. Going into their home game against Halifax on 23 September, they were second in the table, one place behind Port Vale whose only defeat had been against Rotherham and been a 7-0 thumping as well. Rotherham eventually finished the season with 17 League wins which is still a record for a relegated side. Bournemouth won the same amount and finished seventh and, the previous season, Workington only won 16 in Division Four and finished sixth.

Bobby Charlton

A crowd of 60,538 watched Bobby Charlton's testimonial match (Manchester United v Celtic) in September 1972. This was Manchester United's second biggest gate of that season and remains the biggest crowd ever for a testimonial match.

Don Revie and Billy Bremner

In December 1972, Leeds manager Don Revie announced that he would fine any of his players who argued with the referee during matches and that only captain Billy Bremner would be allowed to engage with the ref at all. He also made Bremner wear an armband to signify his captaincy, making Bremner the first club captain in England to do so. The practice of fining their own players for dissent would also be taken up by Arsenal, Chelsea and Manchester City later in the decade.

The Three v The Six

'The Three v The Six' stands as the only football match ever staged in Britain to mark a political event. The event in question was the entry into the EEC by the UK, the Republic of Ireland and Denmark on 1 January 1973, with 'The Three versus The Six' – which was also known as 'the Common Market Match' – taking place at Wembley two evenings later as part of the British Government's 'Fanfare for Europe'. 'The Three' team was made up of players from the EEC's three new member states and, aside from the Danes Henning Jensen and sub John Steen Olsen, was comprised entirely of players from the English First Division, while 'The Six' represented the EEC's six founding members (West Germany, France, Italy, Belgium, the Netherlands and Luxembourg) and featured eight players who would appear in the following year's World Cup Final (the Germans Bertie Vogts, Franz Beckenbauer, Jurgen Grabowski and Gerd Muller and the Dutchmen Ruud Krol, Wim Van Hanegem, Wim Suurbier and Johan Neeskins). 'The Three' won 2-0 (second goal well offside) in front of a crowd of 36,500 which was only marginally higher than the attendance at the Norwich v Chelsea League Cup semi-final that was played on the same night.

(Maybe) the most unlikely FA Cup-winners

In January 1973, Sunderland were fourth from bottom in Division Two having only won five of their 23 League games. No one at that point could have foreseen them winning major silverware that season, and yet that's exactly what happened when they lifted the FA Cup in May. Their triumph in the Cup was all the more impressive for the fact that they beat eventual League runners-up Arsenal in the semi-final and then Don Revie's Leeds, who finished third in the League, in the Final. They were the first team from outside the top-flight to win a televised FA Cup Final, and also the first club to win the Cup in the same season that they sacked a manager (Alan Brown).

Graham Taylor

Graham Taylor became the Lincoln City manager in December 1972 when he was just 28 years old. He then led them to the Fourth Division title in the '75-76 season when they achieved an all-time points record for any division (under two points for a win) and scored 111 goals at a time when no club had scored more than 90 in a season for nearly a decade. Despite this, Taylor was back in the Fourth Division in 1977 when he took the manager's job at Watford. It was with Watford that he won another Fourth Division title in 1978, before going on to lead them to promotion to the Second Division in '79, the First Division in '82 and then to a runners-up spot in their first top-flight season in '83. Taylor eventually left Watford in 1987, and it was for another downwards move, this time to Second Division Aston Villa. Unsurprisingly, Villa won promotion in their first season under Taylor and were still under Taylor when they finished runners-up in the First Division three years later. After this Taylor was deservedly given the England job and is now probably better remembered for his failures in that post than he is for all of his achievements at club level.

When the Brazilians couldn't hack it in the West Country

Three of Brazil's 1970 World Cup winning side – Pele, Carlos Alberto and Cloadoldo – were in the Santos side that lost 3-2 to Third Division Plymouth in March 1973. This prestigious friendly was arranged at a week's notice and attracted a crowd of 40,000 in a season when Plymouth's average home gate was just 9,000.

Bill Shankly

Bill Shankly is the only manager to have won three League titles with a club that were outside of the top-flight when he took over. He led Liverpool to the title in 1964, 1966 and 1973 and also won the FA Cup with them in 1965 and 1974, as well as the UEFA Cup in 1973. His appointment as Liverpool manager had been in December 1959 when they were in the Second Division and hadn't won anything for 12 years.

Jack Charlton

Jack Charlton didn't score in any of his first 137 appearances for Leeds United but ended up with 95 goals for the club by the time he retired in 1973. Nine of these came during a 17-game run at centre-forward in the 1961-62 season, but the other 86 were all scored whilst playing at centre-back. No Football League defender who didn't take penalties has ever scored more.

Pop Robson

In the 1972-73 season, West Ham's Pop Robson finished top scorer in the top-flight of English football with 28 League goals, and yet still went on to finish his career as an uncapped player. This despite the fact he also scored over 20 First Division goals for Newcastle in both the 1968-69 and '69-70 seasons.

The Charity Shield

The Charity Shield (now known as 'the Community Shield') was launched by the FA in 1908 as an annual football match from which all the proceeds would go to charity. It would eventually become known as the showpiece curtain-raiser to the English football season, but for its first 50 years it wasn't a 'curtain-raiser' at all. Between 1923 and 1958, the Charity Shield was always played on a weekday afternoon in the autumn, and prior to that it was usually the closing, rather than the opening, match of the domestic season. As for being a 'showpiece', it was hardly that either, as it was almost always played on the home ground of one of the clubs involved, something that would continue to be the case until it was eventually moved to Wembley in 1974.

The Charity Shield originally began life as a match that pitted the team that had just won the Football League against the newly-crowned Southern League champions, with Brighton's victory over Aston Villa in 1910 making them the only club from a regional league ever to have won it. After 1912, however, Southern League clubs ceased to be invited to take part, and the participants became seemingly selected at random. No reigning League champions figured in Charity Shield matches between the end of the First World War and 1927, and Cardiff were the only FA Cup winners to do so during that period, when their opponents were the amateur club Corinthian. In fact, no clubs at all contested the Charity Shield between 1923 and 1926 as in these years it was amateurs v professionals. That is to say, a select eleven of amateur players against a select eleven of professional ones, which would be no contest today, but was very much a contest back then. In 1925, the amateurs beat the professionals 6-1 and then beat them again 6-3 the following year.

It was in 1928 that the Charity Shield was first contested between the previous season's League champions and its FA Cup winners, and from 1930 that it became exclusively for the winners of English football's two biggest prizes.

There would, however, be a few exceptions to the rule over the years. In 1950, the Shield was contested between a team selected from the England World Cup squad of that year and one from the FA representative squad that had toured Canada. The game was officially billed as 'England World Cup XI v FA Canadian Touring Team' which made it sound like the latter team were Canadian's visiting Britain. Then, in 1961, Tottenham threw a spanner in the works by winning both the League and the FA Cup. As there couldn't be a Tottenham v Tottenham Charity Shield and allowing a team that hadn't met the qualification criteria compete in it was seemingly out of the question, the FA provided an 'FA XI' as Tottenham's opponents on the day. This eleven comprised nine players from the England side that had toured Europe three months earlier, plus Burnley's Jimmy Robson and Crystal Palace's Johnny Byrne who would make his England debut later that season. Tottenham won the match 3-2 and so, by that measure, were not only the best club side in the country, but better than England as well.

The next team to win the League and Cup double were Arsenal in 1971, and this was when the Charity Shield started to become something of a farce. Arsenal refused to play in it at the start of the following season as they had arranged a pre-season friendly away to Feyenoord on the same day, and so the FA were forced to lapse the rules by having it contested between FA Cup runners-up Liverpool and Second Division champions Leicester. It was hardly ideal, and the FA must have been hoping that no club would ever treat the Charity Shield so dismissively again, but if so, it was a vain hope. The following year both League champions Derby and FA Cup winners Leeds decided to give the Charity Shield a miss, as would League champions Liverpool and FA Cup winners Sunderland the year after. In both those seasons Manchester City helpfully stepped in to play the match no one seemed to want to be a part of, with their opponents being Third Division champions Aston Villa in 1972 and Second Division champions Burnley in '73.

The Charity Shield, it seemed, was on its knees and it was, therefore, probably out of desperation that the FA decided to play it at Wembley in 1974, no doubt reasoning that no team would ever pass up the opportunity to play there. And indeed, they wouldn't, although the '74 Charity Shield between Leeds and Liverpool didn't quite go as the FA had hoped. The crowd was more than 30,000 below the stadium's capacity, the terrace chanting of "you're gonna get your fucking heads kicked-in" was loud and clear enough for all to hear on TV, and Liverpool's Kevin Keegan and Leeds' Billy Bremner were both sent-off for fighting just after Leeds' Johnny Giles should have been sent-off for flooring Keegan with a punch. The match eventually finished 1-1 Before being won by Liverpool on penalties.

This was actually the first match ever to be decided on penalties at Wembley and it made the 1974 Charity Shield an anomaly amongst Charity Shield matches prior to 1993. This was because the Charity Shield was unique amongst football trophies in that it was a trophy that didn't need to be won. Aside from 1974, there were eleven other occasions between 1949 and 1991 when the Charity Shield match had ended in a draw and each time the two teams had shared the Shield, with each retaining it for six months. On the five occasions the match ended in a draw at Wembley, the sharing custom meant the two team captains climbing the steps to the royal box together, being presented with the Shield together and then lifting it together as the two sets of fans cheered and applauded together. In hindsight, it was all a bit odd, but it was kind of in-keeping with the original spirit of the Charity Shield. In the programme notes to the 1950 match, FA Chairman Brook Hirst had wrote, "one of the chief attractions of the event is that in every sense of the word it is a friendly", and after the 1977 match finished in a draw, BBC commentator John Motson had said, "when Liverpool played here in '74 with Leeds and drew it was decided on penalties, but that's not a very satisfactory way of settling this sort of match".

It was probably inevitable in the end that the custom of sharing the Charity Shield would never survive the football authorities obsession with the penalty shoot-out, and in 1993 Manchester United won the Shield on penalties two years after Arsenal and Tottenham became, what turned out to be, the last teams to share it.

Brian Hornsby

Brian Hornsby's home debut for Arsenal was as a substitute against Manchester United on the opening day of the 1973-74 season, but he was on the field for only three seconds before the ref blew for full-time. This was Hornsby's only appearance in the first two months of the season.

The night nothing went right For England

England failed to make it to the 1974 World Cup after drawing with Poland at Wembley in their final qualifier when only a win would have seen them through. The game finished 1-1 which was all Poland needed to qualify and so they came to defend and did little else all evening. Domarski's shot that put them 1-0 up in the 55th minute was their first touch of the match inside the England penalty area. Their second came seven minutes from time.

The disparity in the number of attempts on goal was also crazy considering the game was a draw. All available sources claim it was 36-2 in England's favour, although this does a slight disservice to Poland. True, they only had two attempts on target, but they also had another four that sailed harmlessly high or wide, and while England did have over 30, only a pretty liberal interpretation of an attempt on goal would put it as high as 36. Still, there's no questioning the corner count disparity: England won 21, Poland won two. It was certainly a night of rotten luck for England, with even manager Alf Ramsey's decision to make his only substitution with just 90 seconds left being due to him losing track of time because his watch had stopped. Derby striker Kevin Hector was finally rushed on for his England debut without any time for a warm-up or instructions and had a header cleared off the line a minute later – and even this wasn't Poland's last goal line clearance of the match! England should have won, yet also could have lost. When, in the 81st minute, Lato got clean through with only Shilton in the England goal to beat, he looked almost certain to put the Poles 2-1 up until Roy McFarland grabbed him by the shoulders and pulled him back.

The historian Dominic Sandbrook wrote quite a bit about this match in his 2010 book *State of Emergency* and concluded that "even in an autumn of inflation, bombings and strikes, there were few more compelling symbols of national decline than England's failure against Poland". Certainly, it was a failure that no one saw coming. The Poles were good at home but their 2-0 defeat away to Wales (the only other country in the qualifying group) earlier in the year suggested they didn't travel well. After the match, the press and TV pundits all pointed the finger of blame at England's seemingly complacent manager, although Ramsey's eventual sacking didn't come for another six and a half months, and when it did it wasn't widely welcomed considering the players and most of the public (according to a poll) supported him. England's final two matches under Ramsey were a 1-0 defeat at home to Italy and 0-0 draw in

Portugal. Of the 12 England players who played against Poland, only three would play in the qualifiers for the next World Cup.

Danny Hegan

In September 1961, Sunderland signed the Albion Rovers midfielder Danny Hegan, only to release him two years later having never given him a game. Then more than a decade later (in December '73), they signed him again – this time from Wolves – and played him in just eight games (five as a sub) before releasing him again.

The last years of amateur glory in the FA Cup

The FA Cup second round victories by Alvechurch at home to King's Lynn (6-1) and Hendon away to Merthyr Tydfil (3-0) on 15 December 1973 are notable for being the last ever victories by amateur sides over professional clubs in the FA Cup, although their significance would probably be lost on most, owing to the fact that the two losers were both non-League and would now be classified as 'semi-professional'. In the next round, Hendon drew 1-1 away to First Division Newcastle and missed chances near the end to create what probably would have been the biggest giant-killing ever. England amateur international Ron Haider's second-half equaliser for the visitors certainly deserves to be more famous than it is, especially as the game was televised. Newcastle won the replay 4-0, before going on to reach the final.

The last ever FA Cup victory by an amateur side over a Football League club was Tow Law Town's 5-1 first round win at home to Mansfield in December 1967 and the last victory by an amateur side in the third round of the competition was Sutton United's 4-1 home replay win over the professionals of Hillingdon Borough in 1970. The latter match earned Sutton a fourth round tie at home to League champions Leeds United which they lost 6-0.

Alan Warboys

Bristol Rovers' Alan Warboys was the only player to score three hat-tricks in a four-match League run during the defensive days of the 1970s. He scored all three in his side's 3-1 win at home to Southport on 13 November 1973, then got four in the 8-2 win at Brighton on 1 December, before hitting another hat-trick in the 4-0 win at home to Southend on 8 December. Ironically, these were the only three hat-tricks Warboys scored in 162 appearances for Rovers, and he wouldn't score one again for any club until he hit all three for Hull in their 3-2 win at home to Millwall in March 1978.

Alex Stepney

After 22 League and cup games of the 1973-74 season, Manchester United's joint leading goalscorer was goalkeeper Alex Stepney with two penalties. It wasn't until 29 December that Lou Macari scored his third of the season to move ahead of Stepney.

New Year's Day football arrives

January 1st 1974 was the first New Year's Day that was a public holiday in England and, therefore, also the first aside from the ones that had fallen on a Saturday when there was a full programme of Football League fixtures.

Sunday Football

At the beginning of the 1970s, Sunday was a very different sort of day to what it is today. The Sunday trading laws heavily restricted the types of products that could be sold on a Sunday, although even most of the shops that were legally entitled to open chose not to as Sunday was widely regarded as a day of rest. Opening times of pubs were also limited to just two hours at lunchtime and four in the evening, while cinemas, theatres and restaurants remained closed all day and no professional sport had ever been played on a Sunday. Sundays, therefore, were days when few people went out, leading to peace and tranquillity descending upon Britain's usually busy cities.

The desire to play professional football matches on a Sunday first arose at the beginning of 1974 and was a direct response to the fuel crisis then gripping Britain. An overtime ban by the National Union of Mineworkers had led to a coal shortage and the introduction of emergency energy-saving measures by the Government, with the most drastic being the imposing of the three-day working week. So as there would be no days when everyone was at work simultaneously, the three-day week was spread over six days, with some industries being designated Mondays, Tuesdays and Wednesdays as their working days, and others Thursdays, Fridays and Saturdays. This, of course, meant that there were an awful lot of football fans who wouldn't be able to attend matches on Saturday afternoons because they were at work, and accommodating them by moving the matches to an evening kick-off wasn't an option as the energy-saving measures also included a ban on floodlight use. The football authorities, therefore, gave all football clubs the freedom to move their Saturday matches to Sunday if they so wished, a decision that was much more of a big deal then than anyone could appreciate now. For many, it was an unacceptable break with both British and Christian tradition, with even some within the game being against it. "Playing football and making profits on a Sunday is wrong," said indignant Arsenal chairman Bob Wall, "we will not disturb the peace and quiet of the neighbourhood of Highbury on that day". Alf Ramsey and Brian Clough were also opposed to it on the grounds that Sunday should be a day spent with the family, while Swindon goalkeeper Tony Allan simply refused to play for religious reasons when his club's home game against Bolton was moved to a Sunday.

The first Sunday match was an FA Cup third round tie between Cambridge and Oldham on 6 January, which kicked-off at 11.30 in the morning and saw Oldham's Paul Edwards become the first ever professional footballer to score on a Sunday when he put his side 1-0 up at eight minutes to midday. The Sunday trading laws forbade clubs to charge for admission on the Sabbath, but they did allow for the sale of magazines, and so Cambridge had got around the free admission by raising the price of a programme to the equivalent of the admission price and making the purchase of one a condition for entry, which was something all clubs would do whenever they hosted a Sunday fixture this season.

The Cambridge – Oldham game eventually finished 2-2, and was followed by three other FA Cup ties that day. Then, two weeks later, came the first ever Football League matches to be played on a Sunday, although there were only 12 of them, with all but three being in the Third and Fourth Divisions and none being in the top-flight. In fact, the Stoke v Chelsea game on 27 January was the only top-flight game played on a Sunday this season, which indicates that, for all its historic significance, the allowing of professional football to be played on a Sunday in 1973-74 barely registered at the highest level of the game.

The Three-day week eventually ended on 7 March, although Sunday football continued until 24 March, at which point the FA put a stop to it and Sunday returned to its former state of being a tranquil, sport-free day, which is how it would remain for the next seven years.

It was a Fourth Division match between Darlington and Mansfield on 15 February 1981 that saw professional football on a Sunday make its unexpected return following a Football League decision to give it another go, even though the FA, at this time, were still opposed to it. In all there were 23 Sunday matches played during the closing months of the 1980-81 season, although the fact that 15 of them were in the Fourth Division and none in the top-flight suggests playing on a Sunday was seen at the time as something mainly for the lower levels of the game, a way for poorly supported clubs to boost their gates by giving people somewhere to go on a day when there was little else to do. This would remain the case over the next two seasons when 54 Football League matches were played on a Sunday, with 30 of them being in Division Four, 17 in Division Three, six in Division Two and only one in Division One. The First Division one took place on 6 February 1983 between Swansea and Watford and was the first top-flight match to be played on a Sunday for nine years, but it was Tottenham v Nottingham Forest eight months later that was the real game-changer as far as Sunday football was concerned. This match was moved to a Sunday so as it could be shown live on ITV, and it was the first ever Sunday fixture to be televised. From here on Sunday would be the day for live televised football, and for the biggest games, and that season's League Cup Final between Liverpool and Everton saw football fans travelling to Wembley on a Sunday for the first time ever. Initially the big, televised Sunday match would just be an occasional treat for football fans, but from the 1988-89 season there would be one on every week.

The unlikely end to the record start

Leeds remained unbeaten in all of their first 29 First Division matches of the 1973-74 season, which was a record at the time. Their first defeat eventually came at mid-table Stoke on 23 February and was all the more surprising for the fact that it was a match Leeds led 2-0 at one point and then had a goal disallowed that would have made it 3-0. Stoke came back to win 3-2 with two of their goals coming from defenders (Mike Pejic and Dennis Smith).

Rodney Marsh (yet again)

After Manchester City lost to Wolves in the 1974 League Cup Final, City's Rodney Marsh was so annoyed that he refused to take part in the post-match presentations and so never received his runners-up tankard (it was tankards, rather than medals, for the League Cup in those days).

The first hat-trick of dismissals

On 10 March 1974, Plymouth Argyle became the first Football League club ever to have three players sent-off in the same game when Steve Davey, David Provan and Bobby Saxton were all dismissed in the club's 2-1 defeat at Port Vale.

Lou Macari and Mike Doyle

When Manchester City hosted Manchester United in a First Division match in March 1974, United's Lou Macari and City's Mike Doyle both refused to leave the field after being sent-off together. Referee Clive Thomas then took both teams off before calling the police to the dressing rooms to ensure Macari and Doyle stayed there. The game eventually resumed seven minutes later and finished 0-0.

Joe Waters

When Leicester won 2-0 at Queens Park Rangers in the sixth round of the FA Cup in 1974, both of their goals came from Joe Waters who was making his senior debut in professional football. Waters had previously been playing for Leicester Reserves and had only been drafted into the first-team because Alan Birchenall had failed a late fitness test. After scoring in that sixth round tie, he then scored again at Newcastle two weeks later but this would prove to be his last ever goal for Leicester (and the only one he ever scored in the top-flight). By the end of the season he was back in the reserves again and would make only six first-team appearances in all competitions in the '75-76 season, and then none at all in '76-77 before being loaned out to Grimsby in January. Grimsby subsequently made the move permanent with supporters donating towards the transfer fee and Waters went on to become a mainstay in their first-team. So much of a mainstay, in fact, that of the 297 competitive matches Grimsby played between February 1976 and October 1981, Waters started 296 of them.

The thriller that disappeared from the record books

In March 1974, Nottingham Forest were 3-1 up with half an hour left at Newcastle in the sixth round of the FA Cup when a pitch invasion by Newcastle fans caused the game to be stopped for eight minutes. After it resumed, Newcastle, despite being down to ten men, came back to win 4-3, but the dramatic fight-back turned out to be all for nothing as the result was annulled five days later. The FA agreed with the Forest complaint that the eight-minute stoppage had affected their team's performance and a replay at a neutral ground was ordered. Everton's Goodison Park was the venue chosen and it saw the two teams play out a 0-0 draw before Newcastle went on to win the second replay (also at Goodison) 1-0. This made Newcastle the only team ever to reach the semi-finals of the FA Cup twice in the same season.

The end of the England Amateur team

5 April 1974 was the day the England Amateur side played its last ever match. It came against Scotland at Coventry's Highfield Road and was watched by just 1,221 spectators. In 1956, the same fixture had been played at Wembley in front of a crowd of 50,000. The England Amateur side had been launched in 1906 and won Gold at both the 1908 and 1912 Olympics when competing as Great Britain. Their dissolution in 1974 was due to the FA ceasing to separate players into 'amateur' and 'professional' categories.

From the greatest ever to also-rans in the space of a year

"They play the best football I've seen from any English side ever". So said Crystal Palace manager and ITV pundit Malcolm Allison in December 1973 when speaking of the Leeds United side that were then top of the League. Although Leeds did win the title that season, the same team – albeit without manager Don Revie – only finished ninth the following season. This isn't the lowest ever finish by defending champions, but it is probably the lowest by a team hailed as the greatest champions ever.

Another Rochdale side to contend for the title of the worst team ever

Rochdale only won two of their 46 Fourth Division matches in the 1973-74 season – one at home and one away. They also lost 5-3 at home to non-League Grantham in the FA Cup, and such was the uninspiring nature of their performances that their home attendances fell below a thousand five times during the second half of the season. Of their two League victories, one was courtesy of a penalty converted by Alan Taylor who would score twice for West Ham in the following season's FA Cup Final.

Revie's runners-up

Don Revie was manager of Leeds for 13 seasons between 1961-62 and 1973-74, during which time the club won the League title twice, the FA Cup once, the League Cup once and the Inter-Cities Fairs Cup once. This was a decent enough haul considering Leeds had never won anything before Revie took over, but it could have been so much better considering how many times they finished runners-up during the Revie era. They were runners-up in both the League and the FA Cup in 1965, in the League again in '66, in the Inter-Cities Fairs Cup in '67, in both the League and FA Cup again in 1970, in both the League and the Inter-Cities Fairs Cup in '71, in the League again in '72 and in both the FA Cup and the European Cup-Winners' Cup in '73. To sum-up, in the space of nine seasons from the mid-60s to early-70s, Leeds finished runners-up in the League five times (and to five different clubs), runners-up in the FA Cup three times, and runners-up in a European competition three times. To put this into perspective, during those same nine seasons, no other club finished runners-up in the League more than once, nor in the FA Cup more than once and there were only two other instances of an English club finishing runners-up in a major European competition. Leeds also reached the European Cup Final in their first season after Revie's departure (1974-75), and once again they finished runners-up.

Denis Law (again)

Denis Law's last kick in English football was a back-heeled winning goal for Manchester City at Manchester United in April 1974. The goal provoked a pitch invasion by fans that caused play to be suspended and as soon as it resumed, Law was substituted and would never play domestic football again. He did, however, play two games for Scotland after this, the second of which was against Zaire in that summer's World Cup. As well as this being Law's last ever appearance in senior football, it was also his only ever appearance in a major tournament.

The night Gloucestershire Cup fever grabbed Bristol

When Bristol City hosted Bristol Rovers in the Gloucestershire Cup Final on a Monday night in April 1974, a crowd of almost 16,000 turned up to watch it. This was more than City got in most of their League games that season.

Dave Murray

In the 1973-74 season, Workington's Dave Murray scored twice at home to Doncaster, twice at home to Peterborough, twice at home to Torquay and twice at home to Gillingham, but only scored one other goal that season.

The FA Cup third-place play-off

For five seasons between 1969-70 and 1973-74, the losing semi-finalists in the FA Cup were forced to compete in a play-off to decide third place in the competition. The first two third-place play-offs were played on the evening before the final on neutral grounds in London and were a replacement for the England v Young England matches that had traditionally taken place on Cup Final-eve. They proved, however, to be an ill-conceived replacement and so, for the following year, the fixture was moved to the same day as the following season's Charity Shield, which served to make the FA Cup the only cup competition in the world where the final match was played after the final itself – and three months after it at that! After one more year in this slot, the third-place play-off was shunted again, this time being played in the week after the final.

Not surprisingly, these matches failed to capture the public imagination, and it seemed particularly ill-judged staging them in London on a Friday night when, in 1971, the two teams involved were Everton and Stoke. The attendance for that year's one was only 5,031, which was hardly surprising considering the London venue chosen to host it was Crystal Palace's Selhurst Park which, being in a part of the capital with no tube station, wasn't even the easiest of places for curious Londoners to get to. It was probably because of this low attendance that the FA decided to make the third-place play-offs home games for one of the clubs involved from the following season, which worked in boosting the gates in '72 and '73, but didn't in '74 when only 4,432 turned-up to see Leicester host Burnley. Leicester's average League attendance in the '73-74 season was 24,825.

The 1972-73 edition of the *Rothmans Football Yearbook* omitted the play-off games from its 'FA Cup progress charts' which, otherwise, gave the score of every match played in the proper rounds of the competition between 1961 and 1971. These play-off games, therefore, were being written out of history before they had even become history. The 1980-81 edition of the book also printed 'progress charts' from every FA Cup competition between 1955 and 1979 and again there was no mention of the play-off games. By then it was just like they had never happened at all, and it probably would have stayed that way had the scores of them not began appearing on some websites in the 21st century.

For the record, Manchester United, Stoke, Birmingham, Wolves and Burnley are the only five clubs ever to have finished third in the FA Cup.

The end of the Amateur Cup / the birth of the Vase

By 1974, the FA Amateur Cup had been going for 81 years and was England's second-oldest national cup competition, but it could no longer continue. Amateurism had become known as 'shamateurism' owing to the fact that many so-called amateur clubs secretly paid their players, and so the FA decided the only way to put an end to the situation was abolish the 'amateur' classification altogether, something which immediately rendered the FA Amateur Cup obsolete as it meant there were no clubs with official amateur status anymore. In its place came the FA Vase, which was supposedly for the clubs that used to play in the Amateur Cup, but in reality turned out to be no such thing for all but the smallest former Amateur Cup participants. Of the 64 clubs that played in the first round of the FA Amateur Cup in 1973-74, only eight took part in the FA Vase the following season, as all the others entered the FA Trophy instead. Many of the clubs who were eliminated in the qualifiers of the Amateur Cup in '73-74 also entered the Trophy rather than the Vase in '74-75, with this big increase in entries inflating that season's Trophy to such an extent that there were 102 matches played in the preliminary round just to decide who would compete in the first of the three qualifying rounds.

The fact that anyone who was anyone in non-League football now played in the FA Trophy meant that the FA Vase became a competition for the kind of clubs that existed below Isthmian League level or its equivalent, and it said it all that the first ever winners were Hoddesdon Town, a club that had never once progressed beyond the first round of the FA Amateur Cup. Hoddesdon played in the Spartan League and the team they overcame in the final were Epsom & Ewell who had been voted out of the Athenian League two years earlier and were now playing in the Surrey Senior League. The fact that this match was played at Wembley was either ridiculous or wonderful depending on which way you looked at it.

Georgio Chinaglia

The Italy line-ups against Haiti and Poland at the 1974 World Cup both included Georgio Chinaglia who had grown up in Wales and played English Third Division football for Swansea in the mid-60s.

The Wassall brothers

Probably no two brothers gave such an incredible service to one club as Brendan and Peter Wassall did for Kidderminster Harriers between 1962 and 1974. The 686 appearances Brendan made over those years remains a club record, while the 268 goals he scored for them is little short of incredible considering he was a midfielder. Peter, who was a striker, also made over 600 appearances and is Kidderminster's record goalscorer with 433 goals, a tally which made him the most prolific scorer in England during the years he was playing. Between them the brothers made 1,287 appearances for Kidderminster and scored 701 goals. Admittedly, when viewing their goalscoring achievements, it perhaps should be taken into account that they spent most of their careers playing in the West Midlands (Regional) League which, judging by the high number of goals it produced each season, was hardly noted for good defending. That said, however, phrases like "the dreaded Wassall brothers" and "the legendary Wassall brothers" did appear in the local press in the early-1970s, and so the pair were clearly something special within their own league. Plus, they also stunned Third Division Brighton away from home in the first round of the FA Cup in 1968. Brighton were leading 2-0 in the second half when the two brothers scored within a minute of each other to force a replay.

The birth of the flashy football kit

The new Leeds away strip that was unveiled during the 1973-74 season was the first English football kit to have stylish embellishments added to its basic colours. These being a single white and blue stripe that ran down the outside of each arm and each side of the shorts.

This small, but ultimately, seminal alteration to their kit was the result of a chance meeting between Leeds manager Don Revie and the managing director of the Admiral clothing company, John Griffin, in 1973. Griffin and Admiral's owner, Bert Patrick, believed there was a market for flashy football kits and proposed Admiral redesign the Leeds kit to make it more eye-catching. As it had been Revie himself who had changed Leeds' home kit to all-white in 1961, he was unwilling to have it tampered with, but he did give the company free rein to make changes to the away strip.

Revie was then appointed England manager in the summer of '74 and as, in those days, the England manager was much more than just the 'head coach', Revie also got Admiral to design a new England kit for the post-Alf Ramsey era. England's 2-2 draw away to Yugoslavia on 5 June of that year, therefore, proved to be their last ever match playing in a plain white shirt with no trim and no embellishments aside from the 'three lions' badge. The match finished in a 2-2 draw with Kevin Keegan's brave 75th minute header being England's last ever goal in a kit that made no concessions to style. Just over three months later, England took to the field at Wembley to play Czechoslovakia in their new Admiral kit, featuring a red and blue stripe down each sleeve and round the edge of the new winged collar, as well as a red and white stripe down each side of the shorts which were now royal blue rather than navy as they had been before. The design was hardly revolutionary in world football terms as several teams had played with stripes down each sleeve and each side of the shorts at the 1974 World Cup, but it did mark the dawn of a new ethos in football kit design in Britain.

Once England were playing in a new flashy kit, then it was only a matter of time before the clubs followed suit, although the transition from just the basic colours to the colours with embellishments was a gradual one that made the 1975-76 season look, at times, like a contest between teams from different footballing eras. Manchester United, Coventry, Burnley and Crystal Palace, for example, all played in flashy kits of the future, while Tottenham, Liverpool, Queens Park Rangers and West Ham wore kits that were unchanged from the 1960s. West Ham eventually unveiled an ultra-modern new strip for that season's European Cup-Winners' Cup Final, while most clubs at the higher levels of the game that hadn't already embellished or jazzed-up their kits did so that summer, thus making the 1976-77 season probably the first in which most clubs, at least in the top two tiers of the game, wore kits that were designed to look stylish. It was Arsenal that proved to be the club most resistant to change as they continued to wear their 1960s kit right through to the end of the 1981-82 season.

This growth in eye-catching football kits naturally led to a growth in the popularity of replica kits for schoolboys who wanted to look the business in school games lessons or when playing football in the park with their mates. Replica shirts, however, weren't worn by adults in the late-70s as sportswear didn't double as leisure wear in those days and it would have been almost suicidal to wear a replica shirt to a match at a time when hooliganism was so rampant. In fact, it wasn't until 1982 that replica England shirts were even sold in adult sizes.

Pitch invasions and perimeter fencing

When Jimmy Greaves hit a late winner for Tottenham at home to Manchester United in September 1966, it sparked what may have been the biggest pitch invasion ever seen in England at that time. Like most pitch invasions of the 1960s, It was a joyous, celebratory happening, but the same can't be said of the pitch invasion at the end of the Millwall v Aston Villa game just over a year later. On that day, the Millwall fans assaulted the referee, Norman Burtenshaw, knocking him to the ground and giving him injuries that required first aid treatment. Following this incident, journalist Ken Jones wrote in the *Daily Mirror*, "Threats are useless. Action is needed. If a section of Millwall fans have proved so unruly that they cannot be adequately controlled then they must be caged in. Other countries have done this for years, and it is a long time since we were able to sneer at them".

Eventually football fans in England would indeed be 'caged in', but it wouldn't happen for a long time and in the 1970s pitch invasions came to be a highly visible problem within the game, especially as they were often wilfully disruptive rather than celebratory as most in the '60s had been. The one that caused the 1974 Newcastle v Nottingham Forest FA Cup tie to be suspended appeared to be a deliberate attempt by the Newcastle fans to get the game abandoned, and after another pitch invasion caused the abandonment of Manchester United's final home game of that season, United became the first club to act on a Government proposal of putting barriers between the terraces and the pitch. The Government's working party had suggested four-foot walls, but United instead erected eight-foot fences, similar to those seen in Europe and South America.

The new fences at Old Trafford meant that pitch invasions instantly became a thing of the past there, but other clubs were slow to follow United's lead and so they continued to be very much a thing of the present everywhere else. The 1976-77 season was a particularly prolific one for the pitch invaders, with a number of high-profile matches being blighted by them and a friendly between Aston Villa and Rangers being abandoned because of one. Derby and Manchester United fans fought each other on the pitch that season, while mounted police were used to keep Chelsea and Millwall fans from the pitch at Stamford Bridge, and play was also suspended because of pitch invasions at Nottingham Forest v Chelsea, Newcastle v Man City and Chelsea v Hull when Chelsea manager Eddie McCreadie was given a microphone so as he could beg the fans to allow the match to be completed. The following season Leeds fans tried to get their FA Cup tie with Man City abandoned by invading the pitch as did Millwall fans against Ipswich in the same competition, while pitch invasions also caused play to be suspended in the League games between Leicester and Aston Villa and Brighton and Tottenham.

Obviously, the vast majority of matches weren't marred by pitch invasions, but fears that the craze for them was spreading led many clubs to take the Manchester United course of preventative measure, and so from the summer of 1978 the fences began going up everywhere. In the 1977-78 season only four First Division clubs (Man United, Liverpool, Aston Villa and West Bromwich Albion) had perimeter fencing, but the following season around half did, and by 1980-81 they all did apart from Sunderland and Arsenal.

Perimeter fencing had also been erected at Wembley in 1977, which was just after Scotland fans invaded the pitch and broke the crossbars of the goals at the end of that year's England v Scotland match. That incident, however, was not the reason for erecting the fences as the decision to do so had been taken earlier in the season. Southend were probably the last club to erect perimeter fencing, in December 1988.

After the Hillsborough disaster of 1989, the fences began coming down, but it was a slow process. Most top-flight grounds still had them the season after Hillsborough, and some still did when the Premier League was launched in 1992. The FA had the perimeter fences at Wembley removed for the 1989 FA Cup Final but, after fans ran onto the pitch during and after the game, decided to put them back up again immediately afterwards.

Brian Clough (again)

In November 1973, Brian Clough took over as manager of Third Division Brighton just 18 months after leading Derby to the League title, and just seven months after managing them in a European Cup semi-final against Juventus. Brighton finished a lowly 19th in Division Three in their one season under Clough and also lost 4-0 at home to Southern League part-timers Walton & Hersham in an FA Cup replay, but that didn't stop reigning champions Leeds United from appointing Clough as their new manager at the end of the season. Clough never arrived at Elland Road for the first time until nine days after his appointment, barely spoke to the players for the first two days after his arrival, and then, in his first meeting with them, berated them all for what he saw as the dirty and dishonest way they had played under previous manager, Don Revie. Clough was in charge of Leeds for just six League games before they fired him. Such was his celebrity status at the time, that on the evening of his sacking he appeared on a TV chat show to discuss it.

The rarest of all punishments

1973-74 was the Football League's 75th season and at the beginning of it there had still only ever been three instances of a club being punished with a points deduction. These were Sunderland in 1890-91 for fielding an ineligible player, Stockport in 1926-27 for fielding an ineligible player and Peterborough in 1967-68 for paying illegal bonuses to players (although, as previously mentioned, Peterborough's deduction was made after the season was over and not during it).

Mick Channon

In September 1974, Southampton striker Mick Channon scored the first hat-trick of his senior career in his 337th senior appearance (including internationals). His second hat-trick came eight days later.

Charlie George (again)

In September 1974, Arsenal coach Bobby Campbell said that with more discipline, the club's soon-to-depart forward Charlie George "could be the greatest player in England. He could be England's answer to Johan Cruyff" (then considered the best player in the world). Despite this piece of glowing praise, George only ever won one England cap – in a friendly against the Republic of Ireland in 1976 – when he was played out of position and substituted after 65 minutes. George later said that he felt he had been "picked to fail". The press had been calling for George's England call-up, but George believed England manager Don Revie didn't want him and so just picked him to prove to the press that he wasn't good enough. Years later, George claimed in an interview that he said "fuck you" to Revie as Revie attempted to shake his hand as he left the field, a claim which has been repeated in subsequent books as if it were a fact. "Fuck you", however, is an expression of American origin that didn't reach Britain until much later than the 1970s, so it's highly unlikely George said it (although he may have said the very English "fuck off").

Paul Smith

In January 1975, Huddersfield's 20-year-old midfielder Paul Smith was transferred to Cambridge united for a fee of £1.

The greatest FA Cup upset?

Since the Football League was expanded to three divisions in 1920, there has only ever been one instance of a semi-professional club from a regional league winning away to a top-flight side in the FA Cup, and that was when Wimbledon – then in the Southern League – won 1-0 at Burnley in January 1975. Burnley, at the time, were seventh in the First Division and unbeaten at home for over three months, while the match was Wimbledon's first in the north of England since they had played at Crook Town in the FA Amateur Cup 13 years earlier.

Battering the world champions

West Germany won the 1974 World Cup but, eight months later, were unable to cope with a fired-up England side on a muddy Wembley pitch. England won 2-0 but the scoreline doesn't do justice to their superiority in a match where they had 28 attempts on goal to the Germans five and won 12 corners to the Germans two (and one of those was awarded controversially by the referee after the linesman had signalled a goal-kick). As well as the goals, Kevin Keegan also hit the underside of the bar, Dave Watson had a header cleared off the line and Malcolm Macdonald was only denied a clear run at goal by a cynical Franz Beckenbauer handball that caused Beckenbauer to be booed by the England fans for the remainder of the game. It wasn't until the half-hour mark that the Germans managed their first touch of the ball inside the England penalty area.

Eight of the German starting line-up plus one of their subs that night had played in the '74 World Cup, with five of those having played in the Final (the two scorers in the final, Paul Breitner and Gerd Muller, had retired from international football at the end of the tournament, although Breitner would make a comeback in the early-80s), while only Alan Ball of the England players had ever played in a World Cup and none of the others ever would apart from Kevin Keegan who would finish his career with just one World Cup appearance as a substitute. Incredibly, six of the England team that beat the world champions so impressively wouldn't even play in the qualifiers for the next World Cup which began the following year.

Roger Davies

Roger Davies's Football League career consisted of only 174 appearances and 41 goals, and he never scored more than 12 in a season, but he was the only player to score five goals in a top-flight match in the 1970s. The match was Derby's 5-0 win at home to Luton in March 1975, and after scoring his fifth, Davies then went on to have another couple disallowed, as well as an effort cleared off the line.

Malcolm Macdonald

No player scored more top-flight goals in the 1970s than Malcolm Macdonald (137 for Newcastle and Arsenal), and yet Macdonald only ever won 14 caps for England, was only a sub in five of those matches and got taken off in three of the others. Even scoring five times against Cyprus at Wembley in a European Championships qualifier in April 1975 did little for his opportunities at international level. Macdonald was 25 at the time but won his final England cap just seven months later even though he was the First Division's joint-top scorer in the 1976-77 season. He remains the only player to score five goals in a match at Wembley, as well as the only England player to score five in a match in which no one else scored.

Ron Saunders

Ron Saunders' managerial career saw him lead three different clubs to the League Cup Final in successive years in the 1970s. He was the manager of Norwich when they reached the final in 1973, manager of Man City when they were finalists in '74 and manager of Aston Villa when they won the competition as a Second Division club in '75.

The cursed football team

Four of Stoke City's first-team regulars suffered broken legs in matches during the 1974-75 season. Striker John Ritchie's career was ended by the broken leg he suffered at Ipswich in September, while winger Jimmy Robertson, left-back Mike Pejic and centre-back Dennis Smith all suffered season-ending leg-breaks between December and March, with Robertson's coming in the first minute of the club's Boxing Day fixture at Coventry. Were it not for these injuries Stoke could have won the title that season as they only ended up four points behind eventual champions Derby.

Lost 2-1 again

Carlisle suffered ten 2-1 defeats in a 19-game League run during the 1974-75 season.

Title contenders to mid-table finishers in six weeks

Burnley were second in the First Division with six weeks of the 1974-75 season left, but only ended up finishing tenth.

The ultimate wide-open title race

With just three weeks to go until the final Saturday of the 1974-75 season, Liverpool, Derby, Everton and Stoke were all level on 47 points at the top of the First Division, while Ipswich were one point behind on 46. Never has there been a more wide-open League title race than this and yet, somehow, Derby still managed to win it with a game to spare. In all, the top spot in the League changed hands 21 times during the course of the season (and this at a time when all of the weekend's top-flight games were played simultaneously) and Derby never occupied it for the first time until they scored what proved to be their final victory of the season at home to West Ham on 12 April. Incredibly, they had only been seventh three weeks earlier.

Alan Mullery (again)

Alan Mullery was named the Football Writers' Association Footballer of the Year at the end of the 1974-75 season, despite having spent the entire season at Fulham who only finished ninth in Division Two (although they did reach the FA Cup Final).

Ipswich's alternative history title

For its first 94 seasons the Football League was played under two-points-for-a-win, and only once would the champions have been different had three points been awarded for a victory. This was in 1974-75 when Derby won the title but Ipswich would have pipped them on goal average had it been three-points-for-a-win. Ipswich finished third but won two more matches than Derby.

Up, over and down

Chelsea's final Division one finishing positions between 1967 and 1975 followed a steady, unbroken rise and fall. They were as follows:

1966-67: 9th
1967-68: 6th
1968-69: 5th
1969-70: 3rd
1970-71: 6th
1971-72: 7th
1972-73: 12th
1973-74: 17th
1974-75: 21st

Alan Taylor

West Ham's triumphant FA Cup run of 1975 saw them beat Arsenal 2-0 in the quarter-final with both goals coming from Alan Taylor, Ipswich 2-1 in the semi-final with both goals coming from Alan Taylor and Fulham 2-0 in the Final with both goals coming from Alan Taylor. Taylor's goalscoring heroics would have been impressive were he a renowned goal-getter but were positively bizarre considering he wasn't. In 14 League games for West Ham that season he scored just twice, and the previous season he scored only three (one a penalty) in 42 appearances for Fourth Division Rochdale. After getting his second against Fulham in the '75 Final, Taylor wouldn't score again in the FA Cup until he hit a hat-trick for Burnley against Penrith nine and a half years later.

Woeful Wednesday

At the end of the 1974-75 season, Sheffield Wednesday were relegated to the Third Division for the first time in their history after scoring only five times in their final 21 League games, and only twice in their last 17. They scored their last home goal of the season on 14 December and their top scorer for the season was Eric McMordie who played just nine games for the club on loan from Middlesbrough. McMordie scored six from midfield. The club's highest scoring forwards were Dave Sunley and Brian Joicey with two each.

A thoroughly diminished football club

In 1927, Huddersfield Town became the first club to win the League title in each of three consecutive seasons, but they have never won it since and in 1975 they became the first former League champions to be relegated to the fourth tier of English football.

No need to shout (anymore)

Substitutions were first allowed in the Football League in 1965, and for the first ten years that they were used, the only method of informing a player that he was coming off was to shout to him. It wasn't until August 1975 that a placard with the player's number on it was first used, although as there were no fourth officials in those days, it was usually held aloft by either the coach or assistant manager.

Ian Evans

In August 1975, Crystal Palace beat Colchester 3-2 in a Third Division match with all three of their goals being scored by Ian Evans. This is notable for two reasons. Firstly, it was the first hat-trick by a Crystal Palace player for nearly nine years, and secondly, Evans was a central defender who had only scored five goals in his previous 85 senior appearances.

Chris Balderstone

Chris Balderstone was one of the last men to play both professional football and first-class cricket regularly, and on 15 September 1975 he played cricket for Leicestershire in the County Championships in the afternoon before driving 30 miles to play football for Doncaster in a Fourth Division match in the evening.

Graham Tutt

During the 1974-75 season, Charlton's first choice goalkeeper was 18-year-old Graham Tutt whose career would, effectively, be ended through injury the following season. The horrific injury occurred in a game at Sunderland in February 1976, when Tutt was kicked in the head by Sunderland's Tom Finney and suffered a broken nose, a broken cheekbone and permanent damage to his vision caused by bone fragments going into the back of his eye. A few years later, Tutt resumed his playing career in South Africa and then went to America, but he never played in England again.

George Best (again)

In May 1972, George Best – still only 26 and Manchester United's top scorer in each of the past five seasons – announced his retirement from football, claiming that, because of his drinking, he was no longer physically or mentally up to playing it anymore. He subsequently changed his mind, however, and was back in the United side again for the start of the following season and made 26 consecutive appearances up to December when he decided to quit football for the second time. In February '73, he appeared on BBC1's *Parkinson* claiming that this time his decision was final, but eight months later he was back in the United side again for a home game against Birmingham. Although now a slowed-down shadow of his former self, Best soldiered on through all of the club's next eleven games up to and including a 3-0 defeat at Queens Park Rangers on New Year's Day 1974, after which he missed the next training session and, consequently, was dropped for the next game, and never played for United or in the top-flight of English football again.

When he did eventually resurface, it was to make three guest appearances for Southern League Dunstable Town in friendly matches during the summer of 1974, but he wouldn't play in a professional match again until turning out as a non-contract player for bottom-of-the-Fourth-Division Stockport County in November '75. Best made himself available for Stockport home games only, and the first one against Swansea drew a crowd of 9,220 to the club's Edgely Park ground, up from the 2,789 that had watched the club's previous home game. Best scored in a 3-2 win for County which was his first goal in senior football for two years but would make only two further appearances in Stockport colours.

The following month, Best joined Cork Celtic who he was with for all of three matches before parting company with the club. He was then signed by Second Division Fulham early in the 1976-77 season and showed a surprising level of commitment to them as he went on to make 37 League and cup appearances that season, making it his first full campaign since 1971-72. Not that Best's presence brought Fulham much success. They only managed a 17th place finish and won just nine of those 37 matches Best played in. Best's final appearance for Fulham came in November 1977, after which he went to play in the North American Soccer League, although he remained registered as a Fulham player until Hibernian bought him in November 1979. When he eventually returned to English football (following another spell in America) late in the 1982-83 season it was to make five appearances for Bournemouth in the Third Division, the last of which – which was also his last ever in England – being a 2-2 draw at home to Wigan on 7 May 1983 in front of 4,523 spectators.

It's unlikely any player had such a bizarre career path as George Best, and certainly no one-time European Footballer of the Year did. His fast transition from superstar to wayward has-been meant his official fan club went from receiving 10,000 letters through the post every week in 1970 to closing down just five years later.

Bobby Charlton and Alex Bruce

Bobby Charlton's resignation as manager of Preston in August 1975 was due to his disapproval of the club's proposed transfer of John Bird to Newcastle, although it was less about not wanting to lose Bird as it was about the directors' intention of bringing either

Newcastle's Micky Burns or Alex Bruce to Preston in part-exchange. Charlton said in his resignation statement, "I refuse to have players at the club that I don't want". Six days after his departure the deal went through and it was Bruce who came to Preston where he would be a huge success, hitting 148 goals for them over eight seasons. Charlton – who was only 37 at the time of his resignation – would never have a permanent managerial post in England again.

David Collier

Shrewsbury Town full-back David Collier scored four penalties in his first six appearances in senior football when he was still a 17-year-old apprentice. These all came in Third Division matches early in the 1975-76 season, but Collier's uncanny coolness from the spot before he was even old enough to vote did not lead to a successful career in the game. In fact, he barely had any career at all as a professional, with his last ever appearance in the Football League coming as a non-contract player for Crewe in April 1978 when he was still only 20. After those four penalties right at the start of his career, he wouldn't score again for another two years.

Dying from stifling tactics

The 0-0 draw between Tottenham and Arsenal at White Hart Lane in September 1975 was so bad that afterwards, Tottenham manager Terry Neill told reporters, "It made me feel ashamed. I can't apologise enough to the spectators. It was the kind of stuff that will kill football". The same month, Manchester City came to defend for a League Cup tie at Norwich, which prompted the Norwich manager, John Bond, to warn, "football has no future if teams persist in boring the public".

This idea that English football was dying from stifling tactics was particularly prevalent during the 1970s and was largely supported by attendances which were declining gradually, although still big compared with what they would become in the '80s. In 1973, the FA's director of coaching, Alan Wade, wrote in *FIFA*

News, "Unless we take a long, hard and fearlessly critical look at what is happening in the game, we could be pallbearers at the funeral of football". Three years later, the editorial to the *Rothmans Football Yearbook* described football as "our ailing national game", and Ron Greenwood was full of regret at the way the game had gone when speaking at the press conference he gave after being given the England job permanently (having previously been caretaker manager) in December 1977. "A few years ago", said Greenwood, "the public got what it deserved. It didn't matter how you won, by what means, as long as you won. The ball players in the game were destroyed by kicking them up the backside. By denying them space".

Obviously, these men who bemoaned the tactics of the 1970s were all old enough to remember – and feel nostalgia for – the free-scoring days of the 1950s and early-60s, before the attacking WM and 4-2-4 formations went out of fashion. Younger fans, by contrast, probably saw nothing wrong with the tactics of the teams they were watching in the '70s, and looking at old TV coverage of 1970s matches, they certainly don't appear boring by today's standards. In fact, if anything, they were more entertaining as there was no pressing which allowed teams to bring the play upfield more freely, and also no playing for free-kicks which meant fewer stoppages.

It could also be argued that once goals became less frequent, then they became bigger events in matches, inducing more excitement in both players and fans than they had done before.

Loyal servants

When Leeds entertained Leicester in a First Division match on 27 December 1975, they fielded a starting eleven that had made more than 3,000 League appearances for the club between them. Billy Bremner and Norman Hunter had both played over 500 games for Leeds, Paul Reaney close on 500, Paul Madeley well over 300 and Peter Lorimer, Allan Clarke and Eddie Gray all over 200. The only two in the line-up that had made less than 100 appearances in a Leeds shirt were Frank Gray and Duncan McKenzie.

Advertising

In the mid-1960s, most English football grounds were advertisement-free zones. Only a few had advertising hoardings in front of their stands and terraces, matchday programmes usually carried no advertisements within their pages and shirt sponsorship was still more than a decade off. It was in the late-60s that advertising hoardings at grounds started to become a more common sight, with the adverts reflecting something of the more parochial country Britain was back then. Bovril, John Players cigarettes, the Watney brewery, Stones Ginger Wine, Duckhams engine oil and the TV rental company Visionhire were all amongst the brands on display in those days, but you wouldn't have seen any of them at Arsenal, Liverpool or Newcastle, which were the three biggest clubs to hold out when it came to installing advertising hoardings. Arsenal and Newcastle eventually caved in and installed them in 1974, but Liverpool wouldn't have any before the 1978-79 season.

It was Kettering Town who were the first club to have shirt sponsorship when they advertised Kettering Tyres on their shirts in January 1976, but it wasn't welcomed by the football authorities, with Football League secretary Alan Hardaker registering his objection with a statement spiked with the casual sexism of the time. "Those who go to watch soccer want to see a game of football", said Hardaker, "not to be reminded every time they look at a player that they must go home and tell the wife to change her soap powder". The Following month, the FA banned shirt advertising, but at the start of the 1977-78 season they decided to allow it for non-League clubs only, before extending it to League clubs, but only in games that weren't televised. Probably the second club to have shirt sponsorship was Oxford City whose shirts at the start of the 1978-79 season carried the 'Buzby' logo for the telephones branch of the Post Office (later to become British Telecom), then at the start of the following season Liverpool became the first League club to have a shirt sponsor in the form of Japanese electronics company Hitachi, although because of the TV ban on shirt advertising no footage exists of it. The ban was eventually lifted for the start of the 1983-84 season, although in 1980-81 Nottingham Forest, Bolton and Newcastle all displayed shirt advertisements in televised games and were fined for doing so. The same season also saw an ITV news programme decide not to broadcast the footage it had of a midweek game between Aston Villa and Brighton because the Brighton shirts carried advertisements.

Football ground sponsorship was less contentious when it arrived, although it could be argued that it did come at a cultural cost. Once a ground ceased to be named after the spot where it stood, then its geographical and historical identity was bound to be diminished to some degree. It certainly sounded more romantic watching, say, Mansfield at Field Mill than it would at the One Call Stadium. Most fans, however, would continue to refer to their club's ground by its original name regardless of the sponsor, but this wouldn't be an option for the supporters of clubs whose grounds were built during or after the 1990s and were named after their sponsor from the outset. The first Football League club to adopt ground sponsorship was Scarborough when their Athletic Ground became The McCain Stadium in 1991.

Artificial atmosphere

After Tooting & Mitcham lost at Bradford in the fourth round of the FA Cup in January 1976, they accused Bradford of placing microphones up the home end to make the support noisier (presumably to unsettle Tooting who wouldn't have been used to playing in noisy grounds).

John Manning

When Crewe beat Southport 4-0 at home in a Fourth Division match in February 1976, all three of their second-half goals were scored by John Manning who was playing his first game in senior football for 16 months. Manning was 35 years old at the time and his playing career had seemed to have been over when Barnsley cancelled his contract in April 1975 having not played him since October '74. Crewe eventually recruited him as player-coach in November '75 but until the Southport home game had only ever used him as a coach. After scoring the hat-trick against Southport, Manning went on to make six more appearances that season, scoring two more goals, but he never played again after that.

Chris Nicholl

On 20 March 1976, Aston Villa's Chris Nicholl scored all four goals in his side's 2-2 draw at Leicester. He put the home side ahead twice with own goals before cancelling both of them out himself with goals up the right end. Nicholl isn't the only player to score twice for both sides in an English League match, but he's the only one to have done so in a game in which no one else scored. The two own goals were his second and third in two matches as he had also scored an own goal at Tottenham the previous week.

... And another penalty

When Swindon played Walsall in a Third Division match in April 1976, the score was 3-1 to Swindon after 54 minutes with all of the game's four goals having come from penalties. Alan Buckley had initially put Walsall 1-0 up from the spot, before Walsall's Trevor Anderson converted a hat-trick of penalties in the space of 27 minutes either side of half-time. Dave Syrett and David Moss then added further goals to give Walsall a 5-1 win.

The match that finished eight-a-side

In April 1976, a Southern League match between Wimbledon and Wealdstone saw six players sent-off (three from each side), with four of the dismissals coming during a five-minute spell in the second half when Wimbledon were already 4-1 up.

The best FA Cup run by a third-tier side

When Crystal Palace reached the semi-finals of the FA Cup as a Third Division side in 1976, they won away to higher-division opposition in the fourth, fifth and sixth rounds of the competition. Their fourth round victory at Leeds ended a run of six straight home wins for their opponents who would go on to finish fifth in the First Division that season, while the win at Sunderland in the sixth round was remarkable for the fact that Sunderland had won 20 of their previous 21 home games and would finish the season as Second Division champions. In-between Palace knocked-out Chelsea at Stamford Bridge at a time when Chelsea were an average Second Division side.

Ironically, this great FA Cup run came in the same season that Palace suffered a huge capitulation in the League. After 20 matches they were six points clear at top of the Third Division (under two points for a win), but only won six of their final 26 games to finish fifth.

The end of the minimum admission price

Up to and including the 1975-76 season, the Football League imposed a minimum adult admission price for clubs to stop them undercutting each other to attract fans. In the last season it was 65p which was roughly the price of two pints of beer.

Pat Jennings

Tottenham reached the semi-finals of the League Cup in 1975-76 but fell at the first hurdle in the FA Cup, only finished ninth in the League and didn't play in Europe. It, therefore, says a lot about their goalkeeper Pat Jennings that he was voted the PFA Player of the

Year by his fellow professionals at the end of the season. Three years earlier, Jennings had been named the Football Writers' Association Footballer of the Year and remains the only goalkeeper to have won both awards. 13 months after winning the PFA award, Jennings was thought to be past his best by Tottenham and they allowed him to move on the cheap (£45,000) to Arsenal. This proved to be an incredibly bad piece of business on Tottenham's part as Jennings would still be Arsenal's first-choice keeper seven years later.

Peter Taylor

Peter Taylor won four England caps in 1976 whilst a Third Division player with Crystal Palace. He would never win any more despite subsequently becoming a first-team regular for Tottenham in the First Division.

England's oddest opponents

When the USA staged an international football tournament to mark its bicentenary in 1976, the USA national team was not invited to compete in it. Instead, a Team America was put together from North American Soccer League players of various nationalities. Thus, when England played Team America during the tournament only two Americans were in the Team America line-up which contained no fewer than six British players including the former England captain Bobby Moore. Although England fielded a full-strength side for the match, neither the FA nor FIFA recognised it as a proper international and it does not appear in the record books even though England's other two games in the tournament do.

The arrival of goal difference

The use of goal difference to separate teams that are level on points was first introduced into English football for the start of the 1976-77 season. Goal difference had been used in continental

Europe since the 1960s, in the World Cup since 1970 (although it had not been needed in that tournament) and in Scotland since the 1971-72 season, although probably because they devised it, the English had been reluctant to dispense with the goal average system which they had been using since 1888. As already mentioned, the goal average system involved dividing the number of goals scored by the number conceded. The fact that this meant a 7-2 win was worth less than a 4-1 win was something that hadn't seemed to bother anyone for almost a century.

Malcolm Macdonald (again)

In July 1976, Malcolm Macdonald joined Arsenal from Newcastle for a fee of £333,333. The reason for this bizarre fee? It was a third of a million.

Derek Hales

When Charlton played Hull in a Second Division match in October 1976, Charlton striker Derek Hales scored all three goals in his side's 3-1 win and completed his hat-trick whilst holding both his shinpads in his hand. He had removed the pads seconds earlier as Charlton were about to take a free-kick and was still waiting for the chance to throw them to the bench when he scored.

When bookings and dismissals became more visual

Red and yellow cards were not introduced into the game until the 1970 World Cup and not used in English domestic football for the first time until October 1976, this despite the fact that the idea for them had originally come from English referee Ken Aston. Blackburn's David Wagstaffe was the first player to be red-carded in England, receiving the punishment in his side's Second Division match at Orient on day one of their use. George Best, then at Fulham, also got a red the same afternoon for protesting a free-kick decision at Southampton. Red and yellow cards eventually ceased being used in England in January 1981 but were reintroduced at the start of the 1987-88 season, and have been with us ever since, although are now brandished with much more frequency than they once were.

The Latchford brothers

Between 1974 and 1977, Everton's Bob Latchford scored six goals past his brother, Dave, who was the Birmingham City goalkeeper during those years. Before joining Everton, Bob and Dave had been teammates at Birmingham and, it was while playing for Birmingham in 1972, that Bob scored the only goal he ever put past his other brother, Peter, who was the West Bromwich Albion keeper at the time.

Pat Kruse

In January 1977, Torquay's Pat Kruse scored an own goal just six seconds into a Fourth Division match at home to Cambridge. Kruse attempted to head Cambridge's long punt from kick-off back to his keeper, Terry Lee, but Lee was out of position and slipped when he tried to recover. Just before half-time, Cambridge went 2-0 up when Phil Sandercock scored the second headed own goal of the game.

Trevor Francis and Malcolm Macdonald

When Birmingham and Arsenal drew 3-3 in a First Division match in January 1977, Trevor Francis scored all three of Birmingham's goals, while Malcolm Macdonald got all three of Arsenal's. Macdonald said after the game, "I was far from happy with my performance. Apart from the goals, I played badly".

From hopeless to unstoppable

In the 1976-77 season, First Division Sunderland suffered eight defeats in a row without scoring, before subsequently going on to win 4-0, 6-1 and 6-0 in consecutive matches.

(... And so to) Jimmy Adamson

Jimmy Adamson perhaps had the worst ever start to a managerial reign after taking charge of First Division Sunderland in December 1976. Sunderland lost all of their first seven League games under Adamson without scoring and, during the same period, were knocked out of the FA Cup by Third Division Wrexham despite being drawn at home. The club's run of League defeats eventually came to an end with a 0-0 draw at home to Stoke which was followed by another 0-0 draw at Arsenal, two results which meant Adamson completed his first two months in charge without seeing his side score a single League goal. Sunderland were eventually relegated at the end of the season, although just 17 months later, Adamson was back in the top-flight after being appointed manager of Leeds.

Peter Houseman

Oxford United winger Peter Houseman was killed in a car crash in the early hours of the morning after he had played in his side's 1-0 home defeat to Crystal Palace on 19 March 1977. Houseman's wife, Sally, and two of their friends were also killed in the crash, which was caused by the drunken, speeding driver of the other car involved. Houseman spent most of his career at Chelsea, winning both the FA Cup with them in 1970 and the European Cup Winners' Cup in '71.

The two longest finals

The only two national football finals in England to go to a second replay were the 1954 FA Amateur Cup Final and the 1977 League

Cup Final. The former saw Crook Town beat Bishop Auckland 1-0 at Ayresome Park following a pair of 2-2 draws at Wembley and St James' Park, while in the latter, Aston Villa beat Everton 3-2 after extra-time at Old Trafford following a 0-0 draw at Wembley (when no extra-time was played) and a 1-1 draw at Hillsborough. Of the two, the Villa – Everton match was the longest in the length of time it took to complete, since the second replay wasn't played until four weeks after the first one.

Tony Aveyard

Tony Aveyard died just four days after playing for Scarborough in their 1977 FA Trophy Final victory over Dagenham at Wembley. His death was caused by a head injury suffered in the only game he played after the Final, which was a Northern Premier League game at home to Boston. Aveyard went off injured in that match and then died two days later.

The most all-over-the-place relegation battle of them all

The First Division relegation battle that took place at the end of the 1976-77 wasn't quite as tight as the ones of 1927-28 and 1937-38, but it certainly takes some beating in terms of its all-over-the-place nature. No club was mathematically down going into the final weekend, only Tottenham were relegated on the final weekend and no fewer than five clubs had to fight for their place in the top division in outstanding fixtures played during the week that followed.

On the Monday night, West Ham, who were in the relegation zone, beat Manchester United 4-2 at home to move out of it and seal their safety, while second-from-bottom Bristol City beat the newly-crowned champions Liverpool 2-1 to also move clear of the bottom three, although their safety was not confirmed as they still had one game left against Coventry who were one place behind them on goal difference. On the same night Stoke lost 1-0 at Aston Villa and were relegated having been above the relegation zone before that night.

Also in the mix were Sunderland who went into their Thursday night game at Everton only needing a draw to avoid the drop, although even if they lost they would still survive providing there was a winner in the Coventry v Bristol City game that was played on the same night. Therefore, when Coventry took a 2-0 lead in the 52nd minute of that match it was they and Sunderland who were staying up and Bristol City who were going down despite having beaten champions Liverpool three days earlier. By the time the final whistle blew in the Everton v Sunderland game, however, it was all looking very bleak for the Wearsiders. They had lost 2-0 and Bristol City had come back to level at 2-2. That match still had 15 minutes left to play as it had kicked-off late due to crowd congestion, which meant that Sunderland's only hope of survival was for one of the sides to find a winner in the time that remained, but it was never going to happen. Once the Coventry and Bristol City players became aware that a draw would keep both of them up, they simply spent the remainder of the match backwards and sideways passing.

In the end it was Sunderland, Stoke and Tottenham who went down although, of those three, only Tottenham had been in the relegation zone immediately after the final weekend of the season.

Barney Daniels

Barney Daniels only ever scored 22 goals as a Football League player, with 13 of them coming in Stockport County's first 16 games of the 1976-77 season. Although the goals tailed off for him after this, he still finished as Stockport's top scorer that season with 19 but would only make two appearances for the club the following season before having his contract cancelled. He then rejoined one of his former clubs Ashton United and never played in the Football League again.

Mick Vinter

Notts County's Mick Vinter scored 13 goals in his first 30 appearances of the 1976-77 season – and they all came in away games. Vinter had scored twice at Cardiff, twice at Fulham and got a hat-trick at Millwall, but hadn't scored in 14 homes games, despite playing the full 90 minutes in all of them. His first home goal eventually came in a 5-1 win against Burnley on 2 March, and it turned out to be his last goal of that season.

(Almost) pure Chelsea

When Chelsea won promotion from the Second Division in 1976-77, 15 of the 20 players they used during their campaign had graduated from the club's youth team. These included all three of their ever-presents (Ray Wilkins, Gary Locke and Ray Lewington) as well as six of the eight other players who started more than 20 matches. Of the 80 goals they scored across all competitions this season, 62 of them came from home-grown players.

When Liverpool won the title practically on their home form alone

Liverpool won the League title in 1976-77 despite only winning five of their 21 away games and failing to score more than a single goal in all but one of them. Their top scorer, Kevin Keegan, only scored once away from Anfield in the League.

Mick Channon (again)

No forward made more appearances for England over the 1974-75, '75-76 and '76-77 seasons than Mick Channon did, even though he was a Second Division player at the time.

Ken Wallace (junior and senior)

Ken Wallace was in the Workington line-up for the club's last ever Football League match in May 1977. This was almost 26 years after his father, who was also called Ken Wallace, had played for the same club in their very first game in the Football League in August 1951.

Jimmy Greenhoff (again)

Jimmy Greenhoff scored the winning goal in the 1977 FA Cup Final, but few people realised it initially. Neither BBC commentator John Motson nor his ITV counterpart Brian Moore were sure who the scorer was at first, with Motson giving it to Lou Macari with a question mark ("Has it gone in by Macari, is it?") and Moore saying, "I think Macari will claim it". The TV cameras also followed Macari's celebration while Greenhoff celebrated the biggest goal of his career off-screen. Slow motion replays eventually showed that Macari's shot had deflected off Greenhoff's upper arm before looping in.

The late, late Cup Final replay that never happened

Had the 1977 FA Cup Final gone to a replay, it wouldn't have been played until 27 June – which was more than five weeks after the original match. This was because there were no free midweeks until then owing to the European Cup Final, the Home International Championships and England's tour of South America.

Winning the double with a whimper

Liverpool won the League and European Cup double in 1976-77, despite only winning one of their last six matches of the season.

They drew three and lost one of their last four League games, then lost to Manchester United in the FA Cup Final, before beating Borussia Monchengladbach in the European Cup Final four days later.

Kevin Keegan

Kevin Keegan signed for SV Hamburg just nine days after winning the 1977 European Cup with Liverpool.

Trevor Cherry

Trevor Cherry had two teeth knocked out when Daniel Bertoni punched him in the face during an Argentina – England friendly in June 1977. Bertoni was rightly sent-off, but so too was Cherry for the challenge that provoked the punch even though it was a fair tackle according to England manager Don Revie. Bertoni would score Argentina's third goal in the World Cup Final a year later.

Dave Sexton and Tommy Docherty

Dave Sexton replaced Tommy Docherty as Chelsea manager in 1967 and then, ten years later, replaced him as Manchester United manager.

Phil Parkes (both of them)

There were three matches between Queens Park Rangers and Wolves between 1975 and 1977 in which Phil Parkes kept goal for Rangers at one end of the pitch while a different Phil Parkes did so for Wolves at the other end.

Kenny Burns

During his time at Birmingham City, Kenny Burns played both as a defender and a striker, although in the 1976-77 season he played as a striker only and scored 19 goals in Division One, which included four in a 5-1 win over Derby. He was then signed by newly-promoted Nottingham Forest in the summer that followed but would be used only as a defender by Forest in 1977-78. Burns performed so well in the role that he won the Football Writers' Association Footballer of the Year award at the end of the season and would subsequently spend the remainder of his career playing at the back.

The furthest home game

In October 1977, Plymouth's Home Park ground was the venue for a European Cup-Winners' Cup match between Manchester United and Saint Etienne. The first leg of the tie in France had been marred by crowd trouble which initially saw United expelled from the competition by UEFA before being readmitted on the condition they played the second leg at least 300km from Manchester. They eventually settled on the Devon venue after the FA denied them permission to stage the game in London on account of too many United fans living there. United eventually won the match 2-0 in front of 31,634 spectators, with another 30,000 watching on a screen at Old Trafford.

Ian Callaghan

Ian Callaghan only ever won four England caps but was the only player to play in both the 1966 World Cup and the qualifiers for the 1978 World Cup. His third cap, in 1977, came eleven years after his second.

Brian Joicey

Brian Joicey scored 28 goals for Barnsley in the 1976-77 season, but all of his first nine appearances of the following season were only as a substitute. He eventually got his first start in October and went on to finish as the club's top scorer again, with his 14 League goals being twice as many as any other Barnsley player.

Derek Hales (again)

Charlton's Derek Hales scored 16 goals in his first 13 Division Two games of the 1976-77 season, a run of form that earned him a move to First Division Derby for £280,000 which, at the time, was a record fee for a player outside of the top-flight. Derby, however, failed to get the best out of Hales and he spent just nine months with them before being offloaded to West Ham in September 1977. Upon his arrival back in London, Hales said, "I am determined to stay in Division One, and prove a few people wrong". And he did indeed stay in Division One, but only until West Ham were relegated at the end of that season, after which he moved back to Charlton and never played in the top-flight again.

Colin Lee

On 20 October 1977, Tottenham – then in the Second Division – paid Torquay United £60,000 for the services of Colin Lee, a striker who had only scored a modest four goals in 12 Fourth Division appearances that season. It hardly seemed like an exciting signing, and yet, just 48 hours later, Tottenham beat Bristol Rovers 9-0 in front of the *Match of the Day* cameras with Lee scoring four of their goals.

Panorama

In November 1977, BBC1's *Panorama* screened a documentary on the hooligan gangs that followed Millwall which was comprised mainly of interviews with the hooligans themselves and was, therefore, the first TV programme to give a public platform to such people. The film's reporter, David Taylor, spoke of the hooligans uncritically, sometimes glibly and ended up displaying a certain empathy towards them, concluding that "at Millwall, as at most clubs, violence is only one side of the coin. On the other side are good humour, companionship and a sense of belonging which, for these lads, would be hard to replace. Of course, measures must be taken to curb the excesses of soccer violence, but if those measures drive the terrace fans out of football, the cure may prove worse than the disease".

Afterwards, Sports Minister Denis Howell described the documentary as, "the most irresponsible programme seen on TV for some time", while Millwall felt they had been duped, believing the documentary was going to be about the progress the club was making in combating hooliganism through community projects. They also claimed some scenes were set up for the cameras. The team's manager, Gordon Jago – who was interviewed for the programme – was so disheartened by it all that he resigned and went to work in America.

David Kemp

David Kemp scored 16 goals in Portsmouth's first 24 games of the 1977-78 season but was only on the winning side in four of those matches.

The boss obviously knew his best side

Tranmere fielded the same starting eleven in all of their first 32 League and cup matches of the 1977-78 season. Their first line-up change eventually came on 20 January when Bobby Tynan was injured and replaced by John James who had been the substitute in most of those first 32 games.

Malcolm Poskett

Malcolm Poskett's value rose by 2,400 per cent in the space of 15 months during the second half of the 1970s. Hartlepool bought him from Whitby for £25 in November 1976 and then sold him to Brighton for £60,000 in February 1978.

Gordon McQueen

When Tottenham made a bid for Leeds United's Gordon McQueen in February 1978, McQueen responded by telling reporters "Spurs can go to hell".

Glenn Hoddle

The skill of scoring direct with a curled, rather than a driven, free-kick only evolved in the 1970s, and Tottenham's Glenn Hoddle was the first English player to become a specialist at it. Such free-kicks were seen in the World Cup for the first time in 1978 when Brazil's Dirceu and Peru's Cubillas both scored with one, but Hoddle had scored with two in front of the TV cameras before that tournament, and possibly had done so in other games as well since few matches were televised in those days. The first of Hoddle's televised free-kick goals came in a First Division match against Aston Villa in March 1977, with the second coming at Mansfield in Division Two a year later. He was 19 when he scored the first and 20 when he scored the second. Hoddle was also the first player to score with a curled free-kick in an FA Cup semi-final when he did so against Wolves in 1981, and only a good save denied him a goal from another curled free-kick in the 1986 World Cup quarter-final against Argentina.

The non-League club that were a minute away from going where none had gone before

In 1978, Northern League Blyth Spartans came within one minute of reaching the quarter-final stage of the FA Cup and were then only denied a place in it controversially. They had taken an early lead in their fifth round tie away to Second Division Wrexham and were still 1-0 up when the referee awarded Wrexham a late corner that should have been a goal-kick. The corner was then put out for another corner which was gathered by the Blyth keeper, only for the ref to order it to be taken again as the corner flag had fallen over. Wrexham then scored from the retaken one to force a replay which Blyth would go on to lose 2-1. Blyth aren't the only team of part-timers since the creation of a three-tier Football League to reach the fifth round of the FA Cup, but they remain the only one to do so and force a replay and thus appear in the sixth round draw.

Chris Woods

Goalkeeper Chris Woods never played a League game for Nottingham Forest, but he did win a League Cup Winner's medal with them in 1978. Woods played in seven of Forest's eight League Cup matches that season owing to the club's first-choice keeper, Peter Shilton, being cup-tied. In the final, against Liverpool, he made eleven saves in a 0-0 draw and kept a clean sheet again in the replay which Forest won 1-0. After this, Woods would not make another appearance in senior football until he played the first League game of his career for Queens Park Rangers against Bristol City 17 months later.

The dirty England – Brazil match

In April 1978, England played Brazil in a friendly at Wembley in what was Brazil's first visit to England for 15 years and, therefore, also their first since winning the World Cup for the third time in 1970. Everyone was expecting something of a footballing feast, but what they got instead was possibly the dirtiest friendly ever seen at Wembley. 46 free-kicks were given for fouls (about one every two minutes) and there would have been more had the referee not let a lot go and frequently played the advantage, plus England should have had a penalty. Of the 46 fouls that were given, 27 were committed by Brazil who had five players booked. After the match, England manager Ron Greenwood described the Brazilians as "thuggish". The final score was 1-1 with England's goal, unsurprisingly, coming from a free-kick. Brazil finished third in the World Cup two months later.

Scoring three penalties and still losing

In April 1978, Peterborough scored three penalties at Chester but still ended up losing 4-3. Alan Slough converted all of Peterborough's spot-kicks having also converted one at Oxford three days earlier.

Ted MacDougall and Phil Boyer

Ted MacDougall and Phil Boyer played up front together at four different clubs and in all four divisions of the Football League. They were the two leading scorers in Bournemouth's Fourth Division promotion-winning campaign of 1970-71, and in the Second Division promotion-winning campaigns of both Norwich in 1974-75 and Southampton in '77-78. They had also been the two leading scorers for York City in 1968-69.

What went wrong?

Tranmere were top of the Third Division at the beginning of February 1978 but only ended up finishing 12th that season. They only won two of their final 17 matches and lost all of their last seven away games. The following season they only won six times home and away and were relegated.

The fastest free-fall

Blackpool were relegated from Division Two at the end of the 1977-78 season despite having been eighth in the table (12 places above the relegation zone) with just four Saturdays of the season remaining. By the following weekend (15 April) they had dropped down to ninth and were playing Millwall who were 21st, and yet, incredibly, Millwall would finish four places above Blackpool that season. Blackpool's relegation also came despite their top scorer, Bob Hatton, scoring four hat-tricks in the League.

The great escape

Millwall avoided relegation from Division Two at the end of the 1977-78 season by winning all of their last six matches. They were second from bottom when the late winning streak began and had they failed to win just one of those last six games they would have gone down.

Brian Clough (yet again)

Tom Watson, Herbert Chapman, Brian Clough and Kenny Dalglish are the only four managers ever to have won English League titles with two different clubs. Of these Clough won the fewest titles – only two – but he is the only one of the four who won his titles with two clubs (Derby and Nottingham Forest) that were both in the Second Division when he took over.

The Clarke brothers

Frank Clarke and Wayne Clarke were footballing brothers who were so far apart in age that when Frank made his League debut for

Shrewsbury in February 1962, Wayne was less than a year old. Frank made the last of his 447 League appearances for Carlisle at Chesterfield on 28 March 1978, which was six weeks before Wayne made his senior debut for Wolves away to Ipswich. Wayne went on to be a League title-winner with Everton in 1987 – 13 years after one of his other brothers, Allan, won the title with Leeds.

Whatever happened to the two-goal heroes

There was a period in the 1970s when a Leicester City player getting more than one goal in a match was a super-rare occurrence. It only happened once in the 1976-77 season, not at all in '77-78 and only once again in '78-79, and only then because Billy Hughes was able to complete a brace at home to Brighton by converting penalty. Leicester's top scorer in that 1978-79 season was Trevor Christie whose eight goals came in eight different games and this was the fourth season running that Leicester's top scorer was a player who hadn't scored more than once in any match. Even Frank Worthington's 14 goals in 1976-77 had come in 14 different games.

When Alan Young scored both of Leicester's goals in a 2-0 win at home to Watford on the opening day of the 1979-80 season, it was the first time a Leicester player had scored more than once in a match without the aid of a penalty in almost three years. Then a week later something even rarer occurred when Andy Peake bagged a couple in Leicester's 4-1 win at QPR. This being the first time in four years and eight months that a Leicester player had scored twice in an away game.

John Wark

Ipswich's John Wark hit the post twice in 20 minutes during the second half of the 1978 FA Cup Final against Arsenal. Both efforts were near identical shots from the edge of the box, and both appeared to strike the exact same spot on the same upright

Roger Osborne

Roger Osborne's winning goal for Ipswich against Arsenal in the 1978 FA Cup Final was the only FA Cup goal of his career.

Roger Osborne (again)

Roger Osborne's winning goal for Ipswich in the 1978 FA Cup Final was scored with, what turned out to be, his last kick in senior football for 16 months. He suddenly felt unwell during the goal celebrations and had to be taken off before the game re-started. He then missed all of the 1978-79 season through injury and didn't return until early the following season.

When the FA Cup wasn't dominated by the few

When Ipswich Town won the FA Cup in 1978, they were the 13th different club in 13 seasons to do so. The 12 previous winners had been Everton in 1966, Tottenham in '67, West Bromwich Albion in '68, Manchester City in '69, Chelsea in '70, Arsenal in '71, Leeds in '72, Sunderland in '73, Liverpool in '74, West Ham in '75, Southampton in '76 and Manchester United in '77.

When it was more expensive to read about football than it was to go to the biggest matches

At £2.50, a terrace ticket for the 1978 European Cup Final at Wembley was cheaper than a copy of that season's *Rothmans Football Yearbook*. It was also cheaper than Michael Archer's

History of the World Cup, which was published the same year and was only 93 pages long.

Foreign players in England

In the 1951-52 season, Sweden's star striker at the 1950 World Cup, Hans Jeppson, made eleven appearances (and scored nine goals) for Charlton whilst staying in London for a business course. He was only able to do so because he was an amateur, since at that time an FA rule was in force that stated no professional player born outside of Britain or its Commonwealth could join an English club unless they had been resident in the UK for at least two years. This rule had been introduced in 1931 to prevent Arsenal from looking abroad to sign a new goalkeeper, and it would remain in place until 1978.

Following its rescindment, eleven foreign players were signed by English clubs at the start of, or during, the 1978-79 season, which included two of Argentina's 1978 World Cup-winning side in Osvaldo Ardiles (who went to Tottenham) and Alberto Tarantini (who went to Birmingham), another member of Argentina's World Cup squad in Ricardo Villa (who also went to Tottenham) and the Polish star of two World Cups, Kazimierz Deyna (who went to Man City). While these signings excited the media and supporters, PFA Chairman, Gordon Taylor, was less enthusiastic, warning in July 1979 that "If the trickle of foreign players turns into a flow, it would be detrimental to our members." Taylor then added, "there is also the wider issue of the possible effect on the future of English football", by which he certainly wasn't talking about a positive effect.

Taylor, however, needn't have worried, at least not at first. For one thing, only two foreign players per club were allowed anyway, and also English managers at this time had little knowledge of foreign players and didn't really have the means to scout them, nor did English clubs have the money to compete with Spanish, Italian and German sides for Europe's top players. Also, managers probably saw no reason to doubt the long-held belief that foreign players wouldn't be able to cope with the grit of the English game, a belief that would have been reinforced by the fact that a lot of the early foreign signings didn't make particularly big impacts and the way

English teams filled with British players dominated the European Cup prior to the Heysel ban. Consequently, a decade on from the lifting of the ban on foreign players, there were still very few of them in the English game. Of the 452 players who figured in top-flight matches during the 1988-89 season, only nine were foreign-born and had previously played in mainland Europe or South America. The no-more-than-two-foreign-players-per-club rule was still in place at this time but it was hardly necessary as most clubs didn't even have one.

Black players

In the 1963-64 season, 501 players appeared at English football's highest level and they were all white apart from Stan Horne who made just six appearances for Aston Villa. The following season, Leeds arrived in the First Division and fielded their black South African winger Albert Johanneson in 30 matches, and the season after West Ham gave 25 outings to their mixed-race left-back John Charles. But at a time when Britain's black population was still relatively tiny (it was still under a million at the time of the 1991 census), these two breakthroughs were never likely to be followed by many others. Roll on another decade to the 1975-76 season and ethnic diversity still barely existed in the Football League. An 86th minute strike by West Ham's Clyde Best at home to Sheffield United was the only top-flight goal scored by a black player that season, and when Third Division Millwall signed two black players (Trevor Lee and Phil Walker) at the same time from Epsom & Ewell, it was such an out of the ordinary event that there were TV cameras there to capture one of them (Lee) putting pen-to-paper.

It wasn't until the '76-77 season that the steady rise in the number of black players in England really began, and it was this season that saw Joe Cooke of Fourth Division Bradford become the first black striker to lead the line and finish top scorer for a Football League promotion-winning side. The following season, Nottingham Forest's Viv Anderson became the first black player to play regularly for a League title-winning side, before going on to become a European Cup-winner and England international in 1978-79. The same season that Vince Hilaire (Crystal Palace), Luther Blissett (Watford) and Garth Crooks (Stoke) all played starring roles in promotion-winning campaigns, while Cyrille Regis and Laurie Cunningham were providing much of the excitement in a West Bromwich Albion side that finished third in Division One (Regis would be named the PFA Young Player of the Year at the end of the season). In that 1978-79 season there were five black players who made 20 or more appearances in the First Division. In 1983-84, there were 22 who did, and when Luton visited Southampton on 25 February they became the first English club ever to field a predominantly black line-up. Luton fielded six black players that day, the same amount that the 22 First Division clubs had fielded between them on the last Saturday of February 1979.

The 1983-84 season also saw four black players play for England in Luther Blissett, John Barnes, Mark Chamberlain and Brian Stein. This may not seem like a lot today, but it marked a significant increase at the time considering only two black players had ever played for England before 1982 and none at all had before 1978. Somewhat surprisingly, however, it wouldn't be until 1988-89 that as many as four would play for England in the same season again. In fact, between June 1984 and September 1988, England never fielded any black players aside from John Barnes and Viv Anderson who had both made their international debuts before this period. The reason for this was simply that, although their numbers had increased considerably since the 1970s, black players still remained a fairly small minority amongst Football League players as a whole throughout the 1980s. We can clearly see this when we look at the squad photos of the 92 Football League clubs that appear in the 1988-89 *Rothmans Football Yearbook*. Almost a third of these show squads made up entirely of white players.

Brian Joicey (again)

Brian Joicey's hat-trick for Barnsley against Halifax on the opening day of the 1978-79 season proved to be the last three goals of his career. An injury resulted in Joicey only starting one more match in the next two months, and when he did eventually get back into the starting line-up, he only managed four appearances before suffering a stroke that initially robbed him of the use of one arm and one leg and consequently forced his retirement from the game.

When getting Manchester United at Old Trafford wasn't such a tough draw for lower divisions sides

In August 1978, Manchester United came within five minutes of losing 2-1 at home to Fourth Division Stockport in the League Cup. They eventually came back to win 3-2, but in the next round lost at home to Watford who were in Division Three.

The world stars at Chelsea

In September 1978, Chelsea – then struggling near the foot of Division One – played a friendly against a New York Cosmos side that contained both Johan Cruyff and Franz Beckenbauer in front of a crowd of 40,000. In the days after the game, Chelsea attempted but failed to sign Cruyff who, at the time, had not committed himself to Cosmos.

The dullest start ever?

Reigning champions Nottingham Forest kicked-off their 1978-79 season with a 1-1 draw followed by four straight 0-0 draws (League and cup).

The most unexpected comeback

Chelsea lost all of their first four home games of the 1978-79 season and were 3-0 down with 18 minutes left in the fifth. This was against Bolton, who weren't doing too well themselves, but they were better than Chelsea who were second-from-bottom in the First Division at the time and in such bad form that their manager, Ken Shellito, had threatened to put the entire team up for sale. Their chances of turning around the three-goal deficit in the little time of this match that remained, therefore, seemed almost non-existent, and yet turn it around was exactly what they did. 4-3 to Chelsea was the final score with speedy substitute Clive Walker being the star of the comeback, setting up his side's first for Tommy Langley, before scoring a brilliant equaliser himself and then whipping in the cross that forced Sam Allardyce to concede an own goal for the winner. The second, third and fourth goals all came in the space of five minutes. The fact that Chelsea would remain in the bottom three for the rest of the season and eventually finish bottom makes the events of this afternoon probably the greatest anomaly of the 1978-79 season.

Willie Bell

In October 1978, Willie Bell resigned as manager of Lincoln and went to America to become a member of the religious organisation, Campus Crusade for Christ.

Barrie Vassallo

Maybe the strangest loan move ever was the one that took Barrie Vassallo from Fourth Division Torquay to First Division Norwich in November 1978. At the time of the loan, Vassallo had only played six times for Torquay in almost a year, and he wouldn't get a game at Norwich either. Once his three pointless months in Norfolk were up Torquay cancelled his contract and he dropped into non-League football.

Tommy Docherty

Tommy Docherty sold 17 players and bought 16 during his first 15 months as Derby County manager (September 1977 to December '78). Out of the eleven who played for Derby on the opening day of the 1977-78 season, only three were still with the club by the end of the following season, and this at a time when players didn't move around as much as they do today.

Snowed-off

Of the 46 League games scheduled for New Year's Day 1979, 43 were postponed due to snow.

Derek Hales and Mike Flanagan

In January 1979, Charlton forwards Derek Hales and Mike Flanagan were both sent-off in an FA Cup tie against Maidstone for fighting with each other. Hales was sacked by the club three days later but then reinstated, after which the pair played one more game together before Flanagan – who was Charlton's leading scorer at the time – walked out on the club.

The winter of discontent – and a disrupted FA Cup

The disruption caused to the FA Cup by severe weather conditions wasn't quite as bad in 1979 as it had been in 1963, but it was still bad enough. Only four of the 32 FA Cup third round ties went ahead on the scheduled third round day, with one of those being abandoned at half-time, while all of the ties scheduled for the fifth round day – some of which were rescheduled fourth round ties – also got called off. It all eventually led to a messy week at the end of the winter that saw five original fifth round ties and one fifth round replay, plus two original fourth round ties and two fourth round replays all played over a period of four evenings between Monday 26 February and Thursday 1 March.

Tommy Langley

Tommy Langley scored 16 goals for Chelsea in the 1978-79 season and all but three of them came in games that Chelsea lost.

Trevor Francis (again)

On 9 February 1979, Trevor Francis became England's first million-pound footballer when he moved from Birmingham to Nottingham Forest. Then the following day he played for Forest's third team in front of just 40 spectators.

David Mills

Prior to Trevor Francis becoming the first million-pound footballer, the most expensive player in England was David Mills who had commanded a fee of £482,000 when he moved from Middlesbrough to West Bromwich Albion five weeks before the Francis transfer. Mills was 27 and had never been capped at full international level, which would suggest his fee said more about inflation in the transfer market at the time than it did about Mills as a player. Indeed, once at West Brom, he seemed largely unwanted and in three years at the club was never able to establish himself in their first-team. Following brief spells with Sheffield Wednesday and Newcastle, he eventually returned to Middlesbrough on a free transfer in 1984 and, somewhat surprisingly, finished as their top scorer in the 1984-85 season with 14 League goals, which was more than he had scored in any previous season apart from 1976-77.

The shortest-lived record?

When Carlisle drew 1-1 at Tranmere in a Third Division match on 16 April 1979, they broke the Football League record for most draws in a season with 22. This record was then broken just 19 days later when Norwich recorded their second straight 1-1 in the First Division to move them up to 23 draws.

Steve Brignall

When fifth-in-the-League Arsenal travelled to top-of-the-League Liverpool in April 1979, they had 18-year-old Steve Brignall on the subs bench and brought him on for his senior debut that night. This would prove to be Brignall's only ever appearance in full-time professional football in Britain. The following season he went to play in Norway and was unable to get a professional contract upon his return to England, leading him to spend the remainder of his career as a semi-professional in non-League football.

Clive Allen

Queens Park Rangers' Clive Allen scored a hat-trick in his first ever start in senior football. It came in Rangers' 5-1 win at home to Coventry in April 1979 and would have been a big enough achievement even if QPR had been a good side, but they were second from bottom of the First Division at the time with only one win in their previous 19 games. Allen was 17 years old, and his hat-trick was the first by a QPR player in three and a half years.

Peter Bonetti and Ron Harris

Peter Bonetti and Ron Harris appeared together in the same Chelsea line-up on 542 occasions between 1962 and 1979.

All you need is draws

Norwich only won seven of their 42 First Division matches in the 1978-79 but still finished 12 points above the relegation zone.

As previously mentioned, they had 23 draws, which included no fewer than eight which finished 2-2.

The big drop

Chester finished 16th in Division Three in 1978-79, having been ninth with one weekend of the season left.

They shall not pass

In the 1978-79 season, Liverpool conceded only four goals in their 25 League and cup home games.

Steve Death

The Reading goalkeeper Steve Death kept a clean sheet during all of his side's final eleven matches of the 1978-79 season. The 1,103 minutes he went without conceding a League goal was a record at the time, and was especially remarkable for a keeper who was only five foot, seven and a half inches tall.

Tottenham's friendliest season

Before the 1990s, it wasn't unusual for clubs to play friendly matches during the course of a League season, with many of them being testimonials for players who had completed ten years at the same club. Few, however, could have punctuated their League campaign with as many friendlies as Tottenham did in 1978-79. That season saw them play testimonial matches for Aldershot's John Anderson, Queens Park Rangers' Ian Gillard, Wolves' John McAlle, Gillingham's Graham Knight, West Ham's Billy Bonds and their own Steve Perryman which was also played against West Ham. As well as these, they also travelled to Sweden for a friendly against

IFK Gothenburg and twice to Saudi Arabia for matches against El Nassr and a Saudia Arabian XI. This makes nine friendlies played in under eight months between September 1978 and May 1979, and they fielded full-strength sides in all of them.

The North American Soccer League

The North American Soccer League was founded in 1968, and between 1975 and 1979 was something of a magnet for British players due to the high wages its clubs offered. Indeed, such was its attraction for the British professional that for a while it was seen as a growing threat to the game in England. Most of those who went to play in America full-time were older players whose best days were behind them, but there were many others who were loaned to American clubs from English clubs for the summer (which was when the North American Soccer League season was played) and were sometimes forced to miss the beginning or the end of the English season because of their American commitments. "What if a hundred first-team players decided to do this", said a concerned Football League Secretary Alan Hardaker at the time, "it would embarrass and devalue the League". Meanwhile, the editorial to the 1978-79 *Rothmans Football Yearbook* envisaged a day when a player's American club would always have priority over his English one. "How long before we are having to ask the USA for the 'loan' of our players?" it wondered.

Among the diverse mixture of players who went to America from Britain during this period were England's 1966 World Cup winners, Bobby Moore, Gordon Banks, Geoff Hurst and Alan Ball; the Chelsea legends Peter Bonetti, Peter Osgood, Alan Hudson and Charlie Cooke; Derby County's 1972 title-winners Kevin Hector, Alan Hinton and John O'Hare; Liverpool's stalwart defender Tommy Smith; Arsenal's 1971 double-winners George Graham and Charlie George; Manchester United's 1977 FA Cup winning goalkeeper Alex Stepney; the QPR legend Rodney Marsh; the Middlesbrough legend John Hickton; Millwall's record appearances holder Barry Kitchener; Millwall's record goalscorer at that time

Derek Possee; the first million-pound footballer Trevor Francis; Clyde Best who was one of England's first black stars; Fred Binney who was a prolific goalscorer with Exeter, Brighton and Plymouth; Ted MacDougall who had scored nine goals in an FA Cup tie in 1971; Bobby Stokes who scored the winner in the 1976 FA Cup Final; Peter Withe who would go on to score the winner in the 1982 European Cup Final and, of course, George Best. Also playing in the NASL during this period were Pele, Johan Cruyff, Franz Beckenbauer, Eusebio and Gerd Muller, and the 1977 season provided the surreal sight of the then little-known Aston Villa reject Steve Hunt playing in the same New York Cosmos side as both Pele and Beckenbauer.

Because of its English connections, and the big world stars who played in it, the NASL attracted more media attention in Britain in the late-70s than any other foreign league, with action from matches being shown on ITV's *On the Ball*. Not that it was ever really seen as 'proper' football. For British viewers it was almost a kind of freakshow, what with its smooth, synthetic pitches, all-seater stadiums, female cheerleaders, the players having their names on the backs of their shirts, the 35-yard offside line and extra-time and/or 'shoot-outs' (which weren't the same as penalties) being used to decide every single game that was level after 90 minutes. The NASL also awarded six points for a win and extra points for goals scored and credited players with 'assists' as well as goals at a time when the word 'assist' wasn't a noun in any other country. It's ironic, therefore, that many of the NASL features we sneered at in the 1970s, would become part of the English game in later decades. Synthetic pitches appeared in the Football League in the '80s, and although they were all eventually removed, top level football in England is still played on smooth pitches all season, just as it was in the NASL. All seater stadiums, meanwhile, have been mandatory at the top two levels of English football since 1994, English players have been wearing their names on their shirts since '93 and assists started being recorded in England from 2006, which was almost 40 years after the NASL began recording them.

Interest in the NASL waned in the early-80s and it eventually folded in 1984.

Let your opponents do it for you

Four of Luton's last six goals of the 1978-79 season were own goals scored for them by their opponents.

Crystal Palace low scoring their way to the title

Crystal Palace won the Second Division title in 1978-79 despite failing to score more than a single goal in 18 of their final 22 matches and not scoring more than twice in any of them. Between Christmas and the end of the season, they were the division's joint-lowest scorers with 18 goals.

Receiving the winners' medals wearing the losers' shirts

Because of the exchanging of shirts that went on at the end of the 1979 FA Cup Final, Arsenal's Frank Stapleton, Liam Brady and Graham Rix were all wearing inside-out Manchester United shirts when they were presented with their winners' medals.

The only way to relive the great games

In the days before video recorders became common, it was possible to buy 8mm cine films of big matches to project onto a pull-down screen, as well as LPs of BBC radio commentary of the same matches. "A sound souvenir to stir the memory", went the advertisement in the programme for the 1979 FA Cup Final, "official long playing record album of today's FA Cup Final between Arsenal and Manchester United. The thrills, drama and goals to recapture for years to come on your own record player or radiogram". The advertisement also showed that you could buy an 8mm film of the 1978 World Cup Final for £33, which was more than a third of the average weekly wage of a British manual worker at the time. The idea of watching a classic match for free on a computer screen simply by typing it in would have been the stuff of science fiction to the football fans of 1979.

From second tier also-rans to European champions in four years

Nottingham Forest became champions of Europe just four years after finishing 16th in Division Two. That 16th place Second Division finish came in 1974-75, and four of the players who played for them that season (Viv Anderson, Ian Bowyer, Tony Woodcock and John Robertson) also played for them in the European Cup Final of 1979.

Frank Clark

The last ever game of Frank Clark's career was for Nottingham Forest in their 1-0 win over Malmo in the 1979 European Cup Final. Clark was 35 at the time and, after being released by Newcastle at the end of the 1974-75 season, had been on the point of joining Fourth Division Doncaster when Forest decided to give him a contract. Forest manager Brian Clough had allegedly told Clark "I want you because no one else wants to play left-back at the club, and because you're cheap".

The non-League pyramid arrives (although the Football League's still a closed shop)

The 1979-80 season was the first in which there was a top national tier of non-League football – then called the Alliance Premier League – although for its first seven seasons it provided no direct promotion into the Football League. Instead, its champions had to apply for election as all non-League clubs seeking League status in the past had had to do. Getting into the League this way, however, had always been notoriously difficult and finishing as the undisputed top team in non-League football wouldn't make it any easier. In the 50 years prior to the creation of the Alliance Premier, only five applications to join the Football League from non-League clubs had been successful and over those seven seasons when the champions of the top non-League tier had to apply for election, none would have their applications accepted.

Of these, Altrincham were especially hard done by as they won back-to-back Alliance Premier League titles in 1979-80 and '80-81 and over those two seasons beat three League sides in the FA Cup, including Third Division Rotherham away from home, and took Second Division Orient to a replay. They also held First Division Tottenham to a 1-1 draw at White Hart Lane in the Cup in 1979.

Enfield too seemed to be unfairly rejected when they won the Alliance Premier in 1982-83, since one of the clubs who were favoured over them were Crewe who had just finished in the bottom two of the Football League's basement division for the fourth time in five seasons. Enfield won the title again three years later and again had their application to join the Football League rejected, as did Wealdstone in 1985, despite having just become the first ever non-League side to win a national league and a national cup competition in the same season by completing the Alliance Premier League and FA Trophy double.

Scarborough would eventually be the first non-League club promoted into the League in 1987.

Asa Hartford

In the summer of 1979, Asa Hartford moved from Manchester City to Nottingham Forest for, what was then, a fairly hefty fee of £450,000. Hartford then went on to play in all of Forest's first three games of the 1979-80 season, all of which were victories, but after the third one – a 4-1 win at home to Coventry – he received an extreme public slating from Forest manager Brian Clough who said of Hartford, "he is running all over the place without discipline. He had never played disciplined football in his life. If he is no good, he will go". And sure enough, Hartford did go, and went swiftly. Transferred to Everton five days later for less than Forest paid for him. His move to Everton came just eleven days after his Forest debut.

Tom Ritchie

Tom Ritchie scored from a penalty in all of Bristol City's first four League and cup games of the 1979-80 season.

Alan Shoulder

Alan Shoulder scored six penalties in Newcastle's first seven League games of the 1979-80 season.

Steve Daley

In September 1979, Steve Daley became Britain's most expensive footballer when he moved from Wolves to Manchester City for 1.4 million, which seemed an absurdly inflated price for a 26-year-old midfielder who had never played at full international level and never would. Daley spent just 17 months at City before going to America and when he eventually returned to England in November 1983, it was to join Burnley who were then in the Third Division.

The unbeatable newcomers

Nottingham Forest went 49 First Division home games unbeaten between August 1977 and November 1979. This is not a top-flight record, but it is a record for a club that were newly promoted to the top-flight when the run began. They also went 42 League games unbeaten home and away during the same period which was a record for all four divisions at the time.

Steve Murcott

Coventry's City's only clean sheet in their first nine games of the 1979-80 season was achieved with the 18-year-old Steve Murcott in goal. Murcott had played for Coventry's youth team earlier in the day but had never played at senior level before and never would again. His big moment had come when Coventry played Norwich at home on 1 September. The club's first-choice keeper, Jim Blyth, had injured himself in the warm-up so Murcott was drafted in simply because Coventry didn't have another keeper at the ground. Blyth's freak injury kept him out for over four months, but he was replaced in the other games he missed by Les Sealey. Murcott was eventually sacked by Coventry for disciplinary reasons in August 1981.

Phil Boyer

Phil Boyer scored 18 goals in Southampton's first 12 home games of the 1979-80 season, but didn't score in any of their first 14 away games despite playing the full 90 minutes in all of them. Boyer went on to finish as the top-flight's top scorer that season with 23 League goals, which was an unlikely achievement for a 31-year-old who had won his only England cap four seasons earlier, had only scored seven in 42 League games the previous season and would only get three in 33 the following season.

Paul Cooper

Ipswich Town goalkeeper Paul Cooper saved eight of the ten penalties he faced during the 1979-80 season.

Garry Birtles

Garry Birtles was a European Cup winner in each of his first two full seasons of first-team professional football. Birtles was a 22-year-old carpet fitter playing part-time for Long Eaton United when Nottingham Forest signed him in 1976, and although he only made one appearance in his first season and a half at the club, he eventually became a first-team regular in 1978-79 and was in the line-up when Forest won the European Cup at the end of that season, and then again when they retained it the following season. Indeed, Birtles first ever goal in professional football was in the European Cup – being the first of the two Forest goals that ultimately knocked Liverpool out in 1978. As well as his European achievements, Birtles was also a League Cup winner in 1979, and scored twice in the Final.

John McGovern

Two caps for Scotland under-23s was the full extent of John McGovern's international career, yet because Brian Clough rated him, he remains one of the few players to have won League Championship-winners medals with two different clubs – Derby in 1971-72 and Nottingham Forest in '77-78 – and twice captained a European Cup-winning side – Nottingham Forest in 1979 and 1980. McGovern played under Clough at four different clubs in all – Hartlepool, Derby, Leeds and Nottingham Forest – and was actually signed by Clough twice during the 1974-75 season, firstly for Leeds and then for Nottingham Forest six months later. Clough also tried to sign McGovern when manager of Brighton during the 1973-74 season but McGovern turned the move down.

Paul Johnson (both of them)

There were three matches in the 1979-80 season when Stoke City fielded Paul Johnson in the number three shirt and a different Paul Johnson at number four.

Andy Ritchie

Andy Ritchie only ever scored 13 goals for Manchester United, but they included two hat-tricks. The three he scored against Tottenham in April 1980 were his only goals of that season, a season in which he started only three matches in the League.

Coming from nowhere

Blackburn finished runners-up in the Third Division in 1979-80 despite only being 14th in mid-January. They won 17 of their last 21 games.

The longest FA Cup semi-final

The 1980 FA Cup semi-final between Liverpool and Arsenal was the only one ever to go to three replays. A 0-0 draw at Hillsborough was followed by two 1-1 draws at Villa Park before Arsenal eventually won 1-0 at Coventry's Highfield Road to reach the final which was played just nine days later.

The mother of all disappointing finishes

Arsenal lost the 1980 European Cup-Winners' Cup Final without scoring four days after they had lost the FA Cup Final without scoring.

Emlyn Hughes (and Dave Watson)

No one made more appearances for England in the 1970s than Emlyn Hughes, but because England failed to qualify for the 1974 and 1978 World Cups, he finished his career without ever having played in a major international tournament. Hughes made his international debut in November 1969 and was in the squad for the 1970 World Cup but didn't get a game. After this, England wouldn't reach a major tournament again until they qualified for the 1980 European championships, which began the month after Hughes made his final international appearance (against Scotland in the Home Internationals).

Hughes is the most capped England player to have never played in a major tournament, although he's not the most capped never to have played in a World Cup. That record goes to Dave Watson who played for England between 1974 and 1981 and won one more cap than Hughes did. Unlike Hughes, however, Watson did play in the 1980 European Championships.

Brian Talbot

Brian Talbot started all of Arsenal's 69 League and cup games in the 1979-80 season and was only substituted in two of them. He also played the full 90 minutes in the Charity Shield, started all four matches in Arsenal's pre-season European tour, and played from the start in Ted Drake's Testimonial match at Fulham. Despite being apparently indispensable for Arsenal, however, Talbot was not selected for England's 1980 European Championships squad.

Trevor Brooking

In May 1980, West Ham's Trevor Brooking played in the FA Cup Final, in a Second Division match at Sunderland and for England against Argentina, all in the space of four days.

Glenn Hoddle (again)

Tottenham's Glenn Hoddle scored 19 top-flight goals from midfield in the 1979-80 season, with two of them being amongst the best six of that season according to the people who selected the 'Golden Goals' for ITV's *The Big Match*. Despite this, Hoddle only played in four of England's 13 matches that season and didn't get a game in that year's European Championships until there was already no chance of England making the final. In the earlier games in the tournament, he had been kept out of the central midfield positions by Ray Wilkins and Trevor Brooking who, although both fine players, weren't noted for scoring goals. Indeed, they had only got five between them in the League in 1979-80, with Brooking's three coming in the Second Division.

English hooligans at the Euros

The 1980 European Championships in Italy was the first overseas tournament that England fans travelled to in significant numbers and was, therefore, also the first to experience English hooliganism. Fighting broke out on the terraces half-an-hour into England's opening match against Belgium and ultimately led to play being suspended after the tear gas the police used on the supporters began affecting the players. This was England's first match in a major tournament for a decade and at the end of it no one was thinking much about the football. Prime Minister Margaret Thatcher described it as a "dark day" and England Manager Ron Greenwood said of the offending England fans, "I wish they would all be put in a boat and dropped into the ocean".

Clive Allen (again)

In June 1980, Arsenal broke the British transfer fee record to sign Queens Park Rangers' Clive Allen who had scored 30 goals as an

18-year-old the previous season. Allen, however, would not play a single competitive game for Arsenal, who part-exchanged him for Crystal Palace's Kenny Sansom just 62 days after signing him. To this day, no one knows why Arsenal decided to get rid of a young player they rated so highly without giving him a chance. The Arsenal manager at the time, Terry Neill, would later claim that Allen had looked a bad fit for the side in the pre-season friendlies, but it seems strange they would consider him a waste of money on that evidence alone. The common consensus at the time was that, as much as Arsenal rated Allen, they rated Sansom even higher and so when he became available, they decided to make Sansom their big summer signing rather than Allen, thus resulting in the exchange. This would seem plausible considering Allen was their most valuable player but was not an established member of the side and could even have been surplus to requirements as Arsenal already had two good strikers in Frank Stapleton and Alan Sunderland (who had scored over 50 goals between them the previous season) and there was no such thing as squad rotation in those days. Allen himself was given no explanation as to why Arsenal didn't want him, and after just one season at Palace he returned to QPR.

Liverpool's midfield goal machines

When Liverpool beat the Finnish club OPS Oulu 10-1 at home in the first round of the European Cup in October 1980, eight of their goals came from midfielders. Graeme Souness and Terry McDermott each scored a hat-trick, while Ray Kennedy and Sammy Lee got one apiece. Liverpool had only managed a 1-1 draw in the first leg and it had been McDermott who had scored their goal in that one as well. Souness would go on to score another hat-trick against CFKA Sofia in the quarter-finals, a match Liverpool won 5-1, with all of the goals again coming from midfielders.

Garry Birtles (again)

In October 1980, Manchester United equalled the British transfer fee record to sign Garry Birtles who had scored 51 goals since breaking into the Nottingham Forest first team two years earlier. United saw Birtles as the prolific goalscorer they needed but, incredibly, he failed to score in all of his first 29 League appearances for the club even though he played the full 90 minutes in all but one of them. He was eventually sold back to Forest in the summer of '82 for just a fifth of the price United had paid for him.

Coventry–Talbot

In August 1981, Coventry City announced that they had struck a sponsorship deal with the Talbot car manufacturer and from the start of the 1981-82 season would be calling themselves 'Coventry–Talbot'. Thankfully, the FA refused to allow the name-change.

Ernie Moss

Ernie Moss scored three hat-tricks for Chesterfield in his career, with the third – in March 1981– coming ten and a half years after the second.

Steve Heighway

Steve Heighway made 467 appearances for Liverpool between 1970 and 1981 and during those years was a League title-winner five times, a European Cup-winner twice and played in three FA Cup Finals, scoring in two of them. And yet, Heighway was still playing at amateur level for Skelmersdale United at the age of 22 and claimed never to have even seen a game of football before his family moved to England from Ireland when he was ten.

The back-stanchion controversies

On 26 September 1970, Chelsea beat Ipswich 2-1 at Stamford Bridge with goals from Alan Hudson and Peter Osgood, only Hudson's goal wasn't really a goal. His shot flew wide of the post then bounced back off the outside of the stanchion and the referee appeared to be the only person on the pitch who thought it had gone in even though he was perfectly placed to see that it hadn't. This was probably out on its own as the worst refereeing decision in English football history, until another came along to rival it ten years to the month later, and again it involved the back stanchion. On this occasion, Crystal Palace's Clive Allen hit a thunderbolt free-kick into the top corner at Coventry only to have it disallowed because the referee thought it had hit the crossbar. In fact, the ball struck the stanchion inside the goal before bouncing down at a right-angle and then out in the same way it would have done had it hit the underside of the bar, and the speed with which it happened, not only fooled the ref, but also *Match of the Day* commentator, John Motson. It probably remains the only instance of a referee disallowing a goal because he believed the ball hadn't crossed the line when it had actually gone as far into the top corner as it was possible for it to go.

As previously mentioned, in the late-90s the design of goals in England changed with the back-stanchion being replaced by cords and poles to hold the top corners of the nets in place, meaning a shot into the top corner could never again come down with the force that Clive Allen's did at Coventry.

The promotion chasers who simply stopped scoring

Chelsea were second in Division Two in November 1980 but subsequently had their promotion hopes derailed by an almost unbelievable goal drought that saw them fail to score in 19 of their final 22 League matches. Top scorer Colin Lee hit his 14th League goal of the season in his 16th appearance, but only managed one from 19 after that – and that was a penalty. Despite this chronic lack of goals, Chelsea still somehow managed to remain in the top three until late February.

Malcolm Allison (yet again)

Malcolm Allison managed Plymouth, Manchester City and Crystal Palace – in that order – between 1964 and 1976, and then, following a brief spell abroad, returned to England to manage the same three clubs in the same order between 1978 and 1981.

John Toshack

There have been few more surprising managerial appointments than the appointment of John Toshack as player-manager of Fourth Division Swansea in March 1978. At the time, Toshack was still only 29 years old and had been a League title-winner the previous season with Liverpool, for whom he had finished second-top scorer. Swansea won promotion to the Third Division just eight and a half weeks after Toshack took over, and were then promoted again the following season, a season in which Toshack played himself 28 times in the League and contributed 13 goals. By the 1980-81 season, he was rarely playing but his achievements as a manager continued to mount as Swansea won promotion to the First Division for the first time in their history and in doing so completed the fastest ever rise from the League's basement division to its top-flight (although Wimbledon would equal it later in the decade).

In their first season in Division One (1981-82), Toshack's Swansea continued to look unstoppable, spending much of it as title contenders and being top of the table as late as March, before running out of steam to finish sixth, which was still impressive enough for a club that had been in the Fourth Division just four years earlier. At this point Toshack looked on course to become one of the greats of football management, and yet just two years later he had taken Swansea back to the Third Division and was subsequently sacked (some sources say he resigned) on 5 March 1984. He was still only 34 but would never manage in the Football League again.

Ron Noades

Ron Noades is the only person ever to have held a majority stake in two Football League clubs at the same time. Noades was the majority shareholder at Fourth Division Wimbledon, when, in January 1981, he purchased a 75 per cent stake in Second Division Crystal Palace. He remained the majority shareholder at both clubs until selling his Wimbledon shares to one of the club's directors, Sam Hammam, later that year.

A very full weekend

In the 1980-81 season, Bradford played Fourth Division matches on Saturday 7 March and Sunday 8 March.

Bob Latchford

Bob Latchford only scored six League goals for Everton in both the 1979-80 and 1980-81 seasons, although in each of those seasons his six goals included a hat-trick.

1980-81: the season of the 0-0s

For a team to have four 0-0 draws in a row is an ultra-rare occurrence, yet Tottenham, Bristol City, Brentford and Gillingham all managed it in the 1980-81 season, with Bristol City chalking-up five 0-0s in a six-game run in the League, which included two in 24 hours over the Christmas period. There were also six other occasions this season when teams had three consecutive goalless draws.

The most 0-0s in the League in '80-81 was achieved jointly by Blackburn, Newcastle and Aldershot who all had eleven, although Aldershot played 46 games to Blackburn and Newcastle's 42. Blackburn also had a couple in the League Cup and so had 13 overall, which included three in six days in April. Bristol City had eleven in all competitions and Burnley had ten just in the League. Swindon only had eight, but it could have been a lot worse as over half of their 46 League matches were 0-0 at half-time, with eight of those being consecutive. Chester also went in goalless at half-time in eight matches in a row.

In all, 10.21 per cent of League matches in '80-81 finished goalless, which is the joint highest since the offside law was changed in the 1920s to make scoring easier. Although even before then there was no season that produced as many mind-numbing 0-0 sequences as 1980-81 did. From the start of the following season, the Football League began awarding three points for a win to dissuade teams from playing for draws.

The most settled side ever?

When Aston Villa won the League title in 1980-81, they only used 14 different players during the whole campaign. Of these, seven played in every match, with five of those playing every minute of every match. In fact, in 34 of their 42 matches they didn't even bring on a substitute. Liverpool also used only 14 players when they won the League in 1965-66, although they didn't have as many ever-presents.

Peter Withe

Peter Withe is the only player ever to have finished top scorer for the League title-winning sides of two different clubs, and it was a feat he achieved in only his third full season of top-flight football. Withe's first full season in the top-flight was with Birmingham in 1975-76 when he partnered Trevor Francis up front and scored nine goals. He was then sold to Second Division Nottingham Forest early in '76-77 and went on to finish as their top scorer as they won promotion that season, then joint top scorer when they won the League title in '77-78. Despite this he was sold to Second Division Newcastle at the start of the '78-79 season and spent two seasons in the second tier before First Division Aston Villa signed him at the end of '79-80. He was then Villa's top scorer when they won the

League title in '80-81, before going on to score Villa's winning goal in the European Cup Final the following season.

Withe did all this between the age of 24 and 31. Before he was 24, he had only made 19 appearances in the Football League.

Ipswich blowing the title

Ipswich lost nine League games in the 1980-81 season and seven of them came in their last ten. In late-March they had a one-point lead at the top of the First Division, with a game in hand over eventual champions Aston Villa, but ended up missing out on the title by a four-point margin, even though Villa had a fairly stuttery run-in themselves, suffering three defeats in their last nine games, one of which was at home to Ipswich.

Graham Roberts

No player in the 1980s saw their footballing status rise so much in such a short space of time as Graham Roberts did. Roberts spent the 1979-80 season working as a shipyard fitter's mate while playing football part-time for Weymouth in the Alliance Premier League. He was then bought by First Division Tottenham at the end of that season and by the end of December had firmly established himself in the Tottenham first-team, and went on to become a member of their 1981 FA Cup-winning side just seven months after making his professional debut at the age of 21.

England behind the Iron Curtain

England won nine times behind the Iron Curtain during the Cold War, beating Czechoslovakia and East Germany away in 1963, Poland away in 1966, the USSR away in 1973 and 1986, Bulgaria away in 1979, Hungary away in 1981 and 1983 and Yugoslavia away in 1987. Of these victories, it was probably the one against

Hungary in 1981 that stands as the greatest since it was a World Cup qualifier that England needed to win but seemed to have little chance of doing so.

Hungary away was always going to be England's toughest match in the group and they were going into it in terrible form having lost five of their previous eight matches. Two of these were other World Cup qualifiers against Romania and Switzerland and they had also only drawn with Romania at Wembley, which was why an against-the-odds win in Hungary was so necessary. In the end, two goals from veteran midfielder Trevor Brooking and a Kevin Keegan penalty brought them a well-deserved 3-1 victory which was far more impressive than an important win in eastern Europe would be today, since during the Cold War England fans were unable to travel to places like Hungary in large numbers and so there was no big away support to roar the team on. This, therefore, was an England team playing a crucial match in a place where almost everyone present badly wanted them to lose. To quote the words of match commentator Brian Moore as the players came out, "a night when England need defiance, need their skill, in a stadium where they have been received in the most hostile fashion... it's the sort of atmosphere that would, on this night, make them feel a long way from home." Of the 65,000 spectators in the ground that night, only 400 were England supporters and they were all guarded by Hungarian soldiers. On the TV coverage, the stadium appeared to fall into stunned silence every time England scored. It was all a far cry from the England away games of today and, in the circumstances, the 3-1 win England achieved should rank as one of their greatest ever victories.

The Football League Group Cup (and its successors)

The Group Cup was a cup competition created in 1981 to replace the Anglo-Scottish Cup which had been contested for the final time the previous season. Like the Anglo-Scottish Cup, it was very much an under-the-radar competition that ticked along with no publicity and which even the supporters of the clubs involved showed little interest in (most of the attendances being below 3,000, many were below 2,000). It was contested between 32 clubs from the Second, Third and Fourth Divisions of the Football League, and got its peculiar name from the fact that these clubs were split into eight groups of four in the first round. All of these first round games were played pre-season, with many of them being on Saturday afternoons, but after they were completed there would be no more matches in the competition until December when the winners of each group contested the quarter-finals. The final was eventually played on a Tuesday night in April and saw Second Division Grimsby beat Third Division Wimbledon 3-2 in front of 3,423 spectators at Grimsby's Blundell Park.

The Group Cup ran for just one more season, although it was renamed 'the Football League Trophy' for its second one. The entrants in the second season were mostly the same clubs that had contested the first, although, following their promotions in 1981-82, Norwich and Watford were now in the top-flight. Attendances dropped below 1,000 in six of the matches in this season's competition which Millwall won by beating Lincoln 3-2 in the final at Lincoln's Sincil Bank. After this, the Group Cup/Football League Trophy was put out of its misery and replaced from the start of the 1983-84 season by the Associate Members Cup, a straight knock-out affair exclusively for clubs in the bottom two divisions of the League. This competition also aroused little interest, but that didn't stop the FA from giving it a Wembley final from 1985. Seven years later, it too was renamed 'the Football League Trophy' just as the Group Cup had been, even though it had no real connection to the original competition of that name.

Roger Osborne (yet again)

Roger Osborne's two goals for Colchester in a 4-0 win over Hereford in September 1981 were his first in senior football since scoring the winner for Ipswich in the 1978 FA Cup Final.

Almost the great escape

With eight games remaining of the 1981-82 season, Wimbledon were second from bottom in Division Three and 13 points adrift of safety. They subsequently went on to take 19 points from those last eight games, scoring 18 goals in the process, and in the end only went down on goal difference. Their finish to the season was stronger than that of any of the three teams that won promotion from the same division that season.

The busiest May

Tottenham played ten matches in May 1982 – eight in the space of 18 days in the League, followed by the FA Cup Final (which went to extra-time) and FA Cup Final replay which they won.

Ricky Villa and Ossie Ardiles

Tottenham's Argentinian midfielder Ricky Villa started all three of his side's League matches leading up to the 1982 FA Cup Final but did not play in the Final itself as the match took place just three days after the last-ditch peace talks to solve the Falklands dispute had failed, thus making a military conflict between British and Argentinian forces inevitable. Villa's diplomatic withdrawal from the Tottenham team was partly his own decision and partly the decision of manager Keith Burkinshaw and would seem all the more necessary after Argentinian aircraft attacked the Royal Navy frigate HMS *Ardent* the day before the Final, killing 22 of the crew. Tottenham's other Argentinian star, Ossie Ardiles, hadn't been available for the final as he had left England to join the Argentinian World Cup squad in early-April. His intention to do so had been announced the day before Argentina's invasion of the Falkland Islands and so had nothing to do with the abuse from the crowd he received in the one game he played after the invasion (the FA Cup semi-final against Leicester). Tottenham's decision to loan Ardiles to

Paris Saint-Germain for the first half of the following season, however, was made partly because of Ardiles's reluctance to return to England after the Falklands Conflict.

Coming from the depths to be the best

In 1982, Aston Villa became champions of Europe just eleven years after finishing below Halifax in the Third Division.

Nigel Spink

Nigel Spink's appearance in goal for Aston Villa against Bayern Munich in the 1982 European Cup Final was only his second in senior football, and his first for two and a half years. He came on as substitute after the first-choice keeper, Jimmy Rimmer, hurt his neck in the tenth minute. Spink then went on to keep a clean sheet as Villa became champions of Europe.

Paul Moulden

Paul Moulden scored 289 goals in 40 league games for Bolton Lads Club in the 1981-82 season. He scored eight or more in over half of his matches, got 16 in one of them and 15 in another and only twice failed to finish on a hat-trick. Moulden was probably the best schoolboy goalscorer of all-time, and yet he only went on to play two full seasons as a professional, neither of which were in the top-flight. His best season was 1988-89 when he hit 17 League and cup goals for Manchester City and finished their top scorer as they won promotion from the Second Division. Moulden was still only 21 at the time so still had promise but, in the summer that followed, City part-exchanged him for Bournemouth midfielder Ian Bishop, a deal that kept Moulden in the Second Division. He scored 14 times for Bournemouth in 1989-90 but was sold to Oldham before the season was out. Moulden was never able to establish himself in the first-team at Oldham, and had equally unsuccessful spells at Birmingham, Huddersfield and Rochdale before eventually dropping into semi-professional football.

England in '82

England failed to qualify for the 1974 and 1978 World Cups and wouldn't have qualified in 1982 either had the finals not been expanded to allow places for countries that only finished runners-up in their qualifying groups. In the qualifiers for the 1978 World Cup England had won every game apart from Italy away and yet still failed to make it to the final tournament, whereas their qualification in '82 was achieved following an indifferent qualifying campaign in which they lost to Romania, Switzerland and Norway and were still only third in their group going into the final match. Ironically, they then went on to remain unbeaten in the finals of the '82 tournament, the only time they've ever achieved this in a major tournament played overseas. The '82 World Cup also stands as their best tournament defensively with only one goal conceded in five matches and, until 2006, it was the only tournament they played on foreign soil in which they won over half of their matches. England were the only team that the eventual runners-up West Germany failed to score against and France's 3-1 defeat to England in the opening game was the only defeat the French suffered that wasn't on a penalty shoot-out. France went on to finish third.

England's alphabetically numbered World Cup squad

The shirt numbers of the outfield England players at the 1982 World Cup were allocated in alphabetical order which is why midfielder Trevor Brooking and winger Steve Coppell were both wearing numbers usually worn by defenders (three and five respectively). The only player who was exempt from the alphabetical numbering was Kevin Keegan who was allowed to wear his usual seven shirt. The Argentina squad were also numbered alphabetically at the '82 World Cup with Diego Maradona being their exemption (he wore his usual number ten). In fact, Argentina had also used alphabetical shirt numbering at the 1978 World Cup, as had Holland in '74, so although England's decision to go alphabetical in '82 was strange, it certainly wasn't original.

Norman Whiteside

Norman Whiteside made his senior debut for Manchester United as a 16-year-old apprentice in April 1982 and then played for Northern Ireland in the World Cup just two months later (by which time he was 17). Whiteside started all five of Northern Ireland's matches in the tournament and so, by the time he came home, had made over twice as many appearances in the World Cup (five) as he had at senior club level (two). He was, and still remains, the youngest player to have played in the finals of the World Cup and in the season that followed became the youngest player ever to score in an FA Cup Final two months after becoming the youngest to score in a League Cup Final. Sadly, Whiteside's career was also ended through injury when he was still relatively young. He made his final appearance in senior football for Everton away to Wimbledon in November 1990 when he was still only 25-years-old.

England adopting a future FIFA directive eight years early

It was in a Football League Trophy match between Reading and Oxford on 14 August 1982 that Reading's Lawrie Sanchez became the first ever player to be sent-off for handballing on the goal line to prevent the opposition from scoring. This followed an announcement made the previous month that such handballs, along with professional fouls, should be treated as sending-off offences from the start of the '82-83 season. This directive was peculiar to the

English game and was rescinded anyway the following season, but professional fouls would eventually be made sending-off offences by FIFA from the start of the 1990-91 season, with the same applying to handballs off the line from the beginning of '91-92. Prior to its introduction, a handball off the goal line wouldn't have even warranted a booking, as the awarding of the penalty would have been seen as punishment enough. This had been the case in the 1981 League Cup Final, when the Liverpool midfielder Terry McDermott wasn't booked after finger-tipping a goal-bound West Ham effort onto the crossbar.

Max Thompson

Max Thompson's first two appearances in the top-flight of English football were eight years and nine months apart. He made his senior debut for the then League Champions Liverpool on New Year's Day 1974 which was one day after his 17th birthday but would not play again in the First Division until his debut for Swansea against Tottenham in October 1982 (a game in which he scored). In fact, after making his debut for Liverpool at the age of 17 he would not make another senior appearance at any level of English football until his debut for Blackpool in the Second Division four years later.

Glenn Keeley

Glenn Keeley was sent-off 32 minutes into his only ever appearance for Everton, which was also his first match in the top-flight of English football for more than six and a half years. Everton lost the game 5-0 at home to Liverpool. Keeley was on loan from Second Division Blackburn at the time.

Luther Blissett

Luther Blissett scored a hat-trick in his first start for England – in December 1982 – but never scored for his country again in a further 12 appearances. His first goal was the first ever for England by a black player, but it was hardly befitting of a landmark moment, being a miss-kick in front of an open goal against the whipping boys of Luxembourg when England were already running away with the game. In fact, the night was something of a night of miss-kicks for Blissett as he wasted six other good goalscoring opportunities, four of them being due to him miss-kicking when in scoring positions. It was probably this match that earned him the derogatory nickname 'Luther Miss-it', although even before this he had a reputation at Watford (his club) as a player who scored a lot but missed a lot. His obvious wastefulness in that first England start, and his alleged wastefulness at club level, should not, however, detract from his overall achievements as a goalscorer. Despite all those miss-kicks against Luxembourg, Blissett still went on to finish that season as the top-flight's top scorer (with 27 for Watford), making him the first ever black player to do so. He was also the first black player to score 200 goals in the Football League, a feat he achieved during his third spell at Watford in 1991.

John Lyons

On 5 November 1982, Colchester beat Mansfield 2-0 at home in a Fourth Division match with both of their goals coming from John Lyons who would commit suicide just six days later. At the time of his death, Lyons was Colchester's leading scorer of the '82-83 season with 13 League and Cup goals from 25 games.

Football's greatest fall

Bristol City dropped to the bottom of Division Four when they lost 1-0 to Rochdale on 4 December 1982, which was just over three years after a 2-0 home win over Wolves had lifted them to sixth in Division One. In-between they had suffered three relegations in three seasons.

David Nish

In the 1982-83 season, the player-manager of West Midlands (Regional) League side Gresley Rovers was David Nish, who had been Britain's most expensive footballer when he had moved from Leicester to Derby in 1972, had been a League title winner with Derby in 1975, and had still been playing in the top-flight in late 1978. Whilst playing for and managing Gresley, Nish was also working full-time as a milkman.

Les Bradd

Les Bradd made the last of his 556 League appearances and scored the last of his 182 League goals on New Year's Day 1983, when playing for Bristol Rovers at Cardiff. This was both the only appearance Bradd ever made for Rovers and the only appearance he ever made as a loanee (he was on loan from Wigan).

Chelsea gifting it to Derby

In February 1983, Derby won 3-1 at Chelsea with two own goals and a penalty.

Paul Walsh

Paul Walsh made 41 League appearances for Luton in the 1982-83 season and scored hat-tricks in three of them but only four times (some sources say five) in the other 38. Walsh finished the season on 13 (or maybe 14) League goals which is the lowest amount that a player who scored three hat-tricks has ever finished on.

Kevin Bremner

Kevin Bremner played and scored for five different clubs in the 1982-83 season (Colchester, Birmingham, Wrexham, Plymouth and Millwall).

Ian Wallace

In the summer of 1980, Nottingham Forest paid £1.25 million for Coventry City striker Ian Wallace, then three years later sold him to the French club Brest for the knock-down price of £60,000 because they couldn't afford his wages. Wallace finished as Forest's top scorer in each of the three seasons he was with them.

The Australian tour

In June 1983, England played Australia three times in three different Australian cities in the space of eight days. Australia had no great footballing tradition and no full-time professionals, but they still managed to frustrate England with they're ultra-defensive tactics, with the three deadly dull matches finishing 0-0, 1-1 and 1-0 to England. England manager Bobby Robson said after the first game, "they were so negative, the goalkeeper got more passes than anyone". Australian coach Frank Arok responded by saying, "entertainment was the duty of England, not us". Nigel Spink, Nick Pickering, Mark Barham and Danny Thomas all made their only ever England appearances in these games.

Peter Taylor (again)

Peter Taylor finished top scorer for First Division Tottenham in the 1978-79 season when he was 26 years-old. This proved to be his last full season of top-flight football and just four years later he was playing for Maidstone United in the semi-professional Alliance Premier League.

Ian Allinson

Perhaps Arsenal's strangest signing of the 1980s was the signing of Ian Allinson on a free transfer from Fourth Division Colchester in August 1983. At that time Allinson had never played at any level higher than the third tier of English football and, with his 26th birthday not far away, could hardly be described as 'promising'. Yet, after a first season as a fringe player at Arsenal, Allinson somewhat surprisingly finished as their joint-top scorer in the League the following season.

Tony Caldwell

At the beginning of the 1983-84 season, Tony Caldwell was an electrician who was only playing for Bolton on a part-time contract. But when Bolton beat Walsall 8-1 on September 10th he became the first player to score five goals in a Football League match for eight and a half years.

Tony Woodcock and Ian Rush

Arsenal's Tony Woodcock scored five times in the first 49 minutes of a First Division match at Aston Villa in October 1983, and in doing so became only the second player to score five in a top-flight fixture in 15 years. The third was Ian Rush when he put Liverpool 6-0 up against Luton about 40 minutes later. This remains the last time that two players scored five in a top-flight match on the same day, and it's unlikely to happen again, owing to the weekend's top-flight fixtures now being spread over four days and (as previously mentioned) strikers usually getting substituted once a game's already won.

Blackpool's glut of unlikely hat-tricks

Blackpool had four different players score hat-tricks for them over a 12-game spell during the 1983-84 season, and for each of them it was the first hat-trick of their senior career. The players were Nigel Walker, Paul Stewart, John Deary and Ian Britton, and apart from Stewart – who got 12 – none of them even made double-figures for goals that season.

Kevin Keegan (again)

Kevin Keegan scored more than 20 League goals in each of the last three seasons before his retirement, having not scored more than 13 (in England) prior to that. His best season was his last (1983-84) when he scored 27 for Second Division Newcastle. Before joining Newcastle, he had scored 26 for Southampton in the 1981-82 season which had made him the top-flight's top scorer for the only time in what was his last ever season of playing at that level.

Alan Cork

Alan Cork scored 29 Third Division goals for Wimbledon in the 1983-84 season, having only made 13 League appearances over the previous two seasons due to a broken leg. The season before he broke his leg he had been the Fourth Division's top scorer with 23.

Gary Rowell

Gary Rowell finished as Sunderland's top scorer in six out of seven consecutive seasons from 1977-78 to 1983-84. The only season during this period that he didn't top their scoring lists was 1979-80 when he struggled with injury and didn't score at all.

An unlikely away win in an awful season

At the end of the 1983-84 season, Wolves finished bottom of the First Division by 12 points and adrift of safety by 21 points. They won only six of their 42 League games that season, although one of them was away to League leaders and eventual champions, Liverpool.

Terry Cooper

In the 1983-84 season, Terry Cooper played 27 times for Bristol City when he was, not only also their manager, but a director at the club as well. Cooper only put himself in City's starting line-up twice that season but brought himself on as a sub 25 times.

Busy, Busy Tottenham

When Tottenham played away to Anderlecht in the first leg of the 1984 UEFA Cup Final, they did so just 48 hours after playing a First Division match away to Southampton. Paul Miller was the only player who played in both games, and it was Miller who put Tottenham 1-0 up in the second half against Anderlecht.

The Home Internationals

For 36 years up to 1908, the only matches England, Scotland, Wales and Ireland played were against each other, and from the 1883-84 season, the best performing team over these matches would be declared the champions of Britain. This made the British Championship or, as it was more commonly known, the Home International Championship, the world's first international football competition, and by the time it was contested for the final time in 1984 it was 100 years old. And yet, throughout those 100 years people always seemed to care less about the championship aspect of it than they did about the individual matches. Beating England always meant more to the Scottish, Welsh and Irish than winning the overall competition did, and a victory over Scotland meant more to the English than picking up points against the other nations. Perhaps one of the reasons for this was that each season the six games were usually spread over a period of six months or more which made them seem more like stand-alone friendlies. Also, during the competition's first 51 years there was no trophy for the winners, and even after one was introduced in 1935 it never became customary to present it to the winning team. In fact, Jack Charlton claimed in 1976 that he had never even seen the trophy during his England career despite having been a Home Internationals winner many times.

The spread-out nature of the competition was eventually changed in 1969 when it was given a more tournament-like feel by having all the matches played over an eight-day period beginning the Saturday after the FA Cup Final, although there was still no trophy presented to the winning team at the end of it. It would continue as a condensed end-of-season tournament for the next eleven years, with there being a fair bit of disapproval at the way it now forced fatigued players to play three games in eight days in different parts of the UK straight after finishing a long, hard domestic season. In terms of media and supporter interest, however, these eleven years were, perhaps, the golden period of the Home Internationals, and not only because the tournament-like scheduling gave it an identity that it never had before, but also because so many of the top players in England at this time represented the other home nations at international level. In all there were 18 Scottish internationals, six Welsh internationals and four Northern Ireland internationals who were part of League championship-winning sides between 1969 and 1980, and this doesn't include George Best who played in all nine of Northern Ireland's Home Internationals between 1969 and 1971.

The final game of this golden period was a 2-0 win for England over Scotland at Hampden Park on 24 May 1980. The following year the Home Internationals weren't completed due to England and Wales's refusal to travel to Northern Ireland amidst the Troubles, and from 1982 the fixtures became more spread out again. The final Home Internationals in 1984 saw all four nations finish on three points, with Northern Ireland taking the Championship on goal difference. After this, England and Scotland declared they would not be taking part anymore as they no longer wanted to be obligated to play matches against Wales and Northern Ireland every season.

The European Championships Britain didn't watch

Because none of the home nations qualified for it, the 1984 European Championships generated little interest in Britain and, aside from the final, none of the matches were shown live on British TV.

Mike Barrett

In August 1984, Mike Barrett died of lung cancer just three months after playing his final game for Bristol Rovers and less than four months after scoring twice in his side's 3-1 win over Lincoln City. He was 24 years old, and his death came only two weeks after his cancer was diagnosed.

1984-85: The hooligans' most destructive season

Large scale fighting amongst rival football supporters had been around since the 1960s, but it never seemed quite so ruinous to the game as it did in the 1984-85 season. The following is a list of the major hooligan-related stories of that year.

1 September: The First Division match between Coventry and Leicester sees play suspended for eleven minutes due to fans fighting on the pitch.

20 October: eight people are hurt and 63 are arrested following fighting at the Second Division match between Huddersfield and Leeds.

8 November: In order to protect the country's reputation abroad, FA Secretary Ted Croker warns fans not to travel to Turkey for England's forthcoming World Cup qualifier.

8 January: Play in the FA Cup third round replay between Darlington and Middlesbrough is held up for ten minutes after Middlesbrough fans invade the pitch.

11 January: The FA order the Burton Albion v Leicester third round FA Cup tie to be replayed behind closed doors due to Burton having conceded five goals in the original match after their keeper had been concussed by a missile thrown from the crowd.

13 February: A hundred arrests are made following fighting amongst rival fans during the first leg of the League Cup semi-final between Sunderland and Chelsea.

4 March: The second leg of the League Cup semi-final between Chelsea and Sunderland sees play stopped while mounted police clear the pitch of invading fans. More than 100 arrests are made and 20 police officers injured. The police are still on the pitch when Sunderland score their third goal.

13 March: Play in the Luton v Millwall FA Cup tie is suspended for 25 minutes when Millwall fans invade the pitch and fight with police. 31 police officers and 68 others are injured, and £15,000 worth of damage is done to Luton's ground. FA Chairman Bert Millichip believes it is this night that killed off England's chances of hosting the 1988 European Championships.

28 March: Prime Minister Margaret Thatcher chairs a ministerial meeting to discuss the problem of football hooliganism. Four days later the Government meet with football representatives in an attempt to find solutions.

27 April: Chelsea pen in fans with an electric fence for their home game against Tottenham (although they make a late decision not to turn it on).

6 May: Play in the Second Division match between Notts County and Manchester City is suspended for 30 minutes after Manchester City fans invade the pitch.

16 May: At the Birmingham v Leeds Second Division match, 110 arrests are made as violence leads to 96 police officers being injured and a boy being killed when a wall collapses. The trouble causes the start of the second half to be delayed by 30 minutes.

29 May: 39 people are killed following crowd trouble before the start of the European Cup Final between Liverpool and Juventus at the Heysel Stadium in Belgium. Liverpool fans had entered the neutral section of the ground to fight with the Juventus fans who were occupying it, and the deaths were caused by a wall collapsing as people attempted to clamber over it to escape the violence. The incident causes the kick-off of the game to be delayed by an hour and 25 minutes. 14 Liverpool fans are subsequently convicted of manslaughter and each jailed for six years.

31 May: In the wake of the Heysel disaster, the FA bans all English clubs from competing in Europe next season, although two days later UEFA ban English clubs from Europe indefinitely.

12 June: Another meeting between Prime Minister Margaret Thatcher and football representatives takes place to discuss the problem of football hooliganism. It's at this meeting that the idea of identity cards for football supporters is put forward, although contrary to popular belief it's not an original idea. The Labour Minister of Sport had suggested the same thing in 1974.

Dave Watson

When Dave Watson came on as a substitute for Notts County at Shrewsbury in September 1984, it was his first appearance for the club since Boxing Day 1967. County had sold him to Rotherham in January '68 and the 16 years and eight months that passed before his return is the longest gap any player has ever had between two separate spells with the same club.

The worst ever response to conceding a goal?

Wimbledon went 1-0 up in the 44th minute of a Second Division match against Portsmouth in October 1984, and then went 2-0 up immediately afterwards when Portsmouth's Noel Blake scored an own goal straight from the re-start without a Wimbledon player touching the ball.

Ford Motors packing them in

In October 1984, an FA Vase preliminary round match between Ford Motors and Graham Street Prims was reputedly attended by only four spectators. And this in a competition that culminated in a Wembley final.

Simon Farnworth

Bolton goalkeeper Simon Farnworth saved a penalty in each of three consecutive matches in the autumn of 1984.

Gordon Davies

Gordon Davies scored five goals in his first five games for Chelsea after joining them from Fulham in November 1984, but Chelsea only played him in ten more matches after that and he scored only one more goal for them before being transferred to Manchester City in October '85. After just one full season at City, Davies returned to Fulham where he went on to become their all-time top scorer.

Wayne Harrison

In January 1985, the then reigning League champions Liverpool paid Second Division Oldham £250,000 for their forward Wayne Harrison, which made Harrison the most expensive 17-year-old in the world at the time even though he had only made five appearances for Oldham's first-team. A succession of injuries, however, and one near-fatal accident when he fell through the roof of a greenhouse, meant Harrison would never play for the senior Liverpool side and would only ever make six more senior appearances – three on loan to Oldham and three on loan to Crewe – before retiring from football at the age of 23. The only two senior goals of his career came for Oldham in a 2-1 defeat at Huddersfield in a Second Division match on Boxing Day 1984 and at home to Brentford in a 2-1 win in the third round of the FA Cup in January 1985. Probably no striker who made national headlines scored fewer goals in their career. Harrison died from pancreatic problems on Christmas Day 2013 at the age of 46. His death did not make the same sort of headlines that his transfer to Liverpool had 29 years earlier.

Kerry Dixon

Kerry Dixon was the top scorer at three different levels of football in consecutive seasons in the 1980s. He was the Third Division's top scorer in the 1982-83 season when at Reading, then moved to Chelsea and became the Second Division's top scorer in 1983-84, and then, following Chelsea's promotion, finished as the First Division's top scorer (joint with Gary Lineker) in 1984-85. In the last of these seasons Dixon was still uncapped and stands as the last uncapped player to finish a season as the top-flight's top scorer (although he would make his England debut in the summer that followed).

Ian Botham

As well as being the most high-profile English test cricketer of the 1980s, Ian Botham also had one of the strangest ever football careers, since it spanned six seasons as a non-contract player with Scunthorpe United but consisted of only eleven appearances. Botham made two appearances as a sub for Scunthorpe in the 1979-80 season, then after playing no football in '80-81, came back to make four starts for the club in 1981-82, followed by no appearances again in '82-83, and then three starts in 1983-84, and two more substitute appearances in '84-85. Also pretty strange was the fact that Botham wore the number nine shirt in the games he started even though he was a defender. Scunthorpe were his club of choice because he lived not far from there, in the town of Epworth.

The worst finish by the runaway champions?

Everton lost three of their last four First Division matches of the 1984-85 season but still won the title by a 13-point margin. One of those late-season defeats was 4-1 at Coventry who were in the bottom three going into the game.

The worst back-to-back seasons

Cambridge United finished the 1984-85 season bottom of Division Three a year after finishing bottom of Division Two and it's unlikely any club has had two worse back-to-back seasons. They won just eight of the 88 League matches they played over those two campaigns, going a record-breaking 31 games without a win in 1983-84 and losing 33 of their 46 games of '84-85 when they were relegated with seven games still left to play. Their only win in the second half of the latter season didn't come until they were already down.

Imprisoned at 13th

Wimbledon spent almost all of the last five months of the 1984-85 season stuck in 13th position in Division Two. During this period, they managed to record two back-to-back 5-0 wins without moving up and lost 4-0 and 6-1 in consecutive games without dropping down. A 2-1 win on the last day of the season eventually moved them up to 12th.

Just when you thought you were safe

Norwich were relegated from the First Division at the end of the 1984-85 season despite never having occupied a place in the relegation zone during their campaign and having moved eight points clear of it following a 2-0 win at Chelsea in their final match. Three days after that victory at Chelsea, Coventry won the first of their three outstanding matches 1-0 at Stoke to move within five points of Norwich, then six days later, they beat Luton 1-0 at home to move within two points of Norwich, and then three days after that they stuffed champions Everton 4-1 at home to complete their great escape and send Norwich down. Norwich had been eleventh in the table (out of 22) in mid-April and their relegation came 12 days after they had completed their season.

The last 100,000 crowd

The 1985 FA Cup Final between Manchester United and Everton was the last football match in England to be attended by 100,000 spectators.

The incredible shrinking ground

The enforcement of sports ground safety regulations in 1985 caused the capacity of Halifax's home ground, The Shay, to be cut from 16,500 to just 3,000. Not that it really mattered, since most of their home crowds that season were barely above 1,000 and their biggest was only 2,500.

Ian Wright

Ian Wright made 34 appearances for Second Division Crystal Palace in the 1985-86 season having only ever played Sunday league football at the start of the previous season. Wright was still a Sunday league player at the age of 21 and yet went on to score 165 top-flight goals for Palace, Arsenal and West Ham, as well as winning 33 England caps.

Keith Bowen

Keith Bowen scored 18 goals for Colchester in the 1984-85 season but early the following season he broke both his legs in a car crash and never played professionally again.

The Full Members Cup

The Full Members Cup was a cup competition that no one wanted, and no one could see the point of other than the people who came up with the idea, and yet despite the media ignoring it and the fans staying away, it would limp along for seven seasons. Launched by the Football League at the start of the 1985-86 season, it was a competition exclusively for the clubs in the top two tiers of English Football, although in the first season only five First Division clubs agreed to compete in it, and Manchester United, Liverpool, Tottenham and Arsenal never would. This, plus the fact that it had no TV coverage, left it seriously lacking in prestige and this was reflected in its abysmal attendances. In the first season there were 27 matches played prior to the final, with 19 drawing crowds of less than 5,000 and ten of those being below 3,000. There was just 4,029 at Manchester City v Leeds, 2,274 at Leeds v Sheffield United and a pitiful 1,086 at Coventry v Millwall even though Coventry were a top-flight side at the time. Ironically that year's final saw Chelsea beat Man City 5-4 in what remains the highest scoring Wembley final ever, although it says a lot about the standing of the competition that both teams had played a League match the previous day.

If anything, things got even worse the following season with First Division Charlton attracting just 821 for the visit of Birmingham and 817 when they hosted Bradford. These were the two lowest crowds of the 20th century for a competitive game in which the home side was a top-flight club (although Charlton were ground-sharing with Crystal Palace at the time). As well as these, the all-Second Division tie between Millwall and West Bromwich Albion also drew a crowd of under a thousand and Wembley was over half empty for that year's final between Charlton and Blackburn.

Attendances generally remained low over the years that followed, with even Everton and Chelsea getting gates of below 4,000 on one occasion each, but there would also be a few decent attendances as well from 1989 which was the year the Nottingham Forest v Crystal Palace semi-final became the first game in the competition outside of the final to draw a crowd of over 20,000. Then, in 1990, came a crowd of over 30,000 when Sheffield Wednesday played Sheffield United in the second round.

It now seems strange that, despite the competition's lack of prestige, clubs always fielded full-strength sides in its matches as, at that time, 'resting' players had not yet become common practice in English football.

The Screensport Super Cup

The Screensport Super Cup was launched in the 1985-86 season as a cup competition for the clubs that would have been playing in Europe were it not for the post-Heysel ban. The six participants, therefore, were Everton who would have been in the European Cup, Manchester United who would have been in the Cup-Winners' Cup and Tottenham, Liverpool, Southampton and Norwich who all would have been in the UEFA Cup. The matches were only shown on Cable TV which most of the country didn't have access to at the time and attendances were poor, most notably for Tottenham's semi-final first leg match at home to Everton which drew a crowd of just 7,548. Everton reached the final on 19 March but had to wait seven weeks before finding out who their opponents would be and then nearly another five months after that before eventually playing in the final – and even then it was only the first-leg. Their opponents in the final were Liverpool who won the trophy on 30 September 1986 which was over a year after they played their first match in the competition.

The English brothers

Brothers Tom and Tony English were both sent-off together whilst playing for Colchester in a Fourth Division match at Crewe in April 1986.

Norwich v Sheffield United – the end of an era for televised football

During the 1970s and early-to-mid-80s, the BBC's *Match of the Day* showed highlights of a number of Second Division matches during the course of a season as well as some games from the Third Division as well. The last Division Two match to be televised for the BBC's flagship highlights show was Norwich v Sheffield United on

22 March 1986, which would prove to be the last time the BBC televised a League match from below the top tier until it launched *The Football League Show* 23 years later.

The best ever start by a team that came nowhere

Manchester United won all of their first ten First Division matches of the 1985-86 season and had a ten-point lead at the top of the table in October, but only ended up finishing fourth.

Kenny Dalglish

When Liverpool won the League title in 1986, the goal that clinched it – away to Chelsea on the last Saturday of the season – was scored by player-manager, Kenny Dalglish. Dalglish remains the only player-manager ever to have won the League title, although he only started himself in 17 of their games that season (and also made four appearances as a sub). Dalglish went on to steer Liverpool to two more titles as player-manager in 1987-88 and '89-90, but in these seasons he was barely a player at all, making only three substitute appearances in total over the two campaigns.

Steve Castle

When Orient won 4-1 at Rochdale in their final match of the 1985-86 season, all of their goals were scored by Steve Castle who had gone into the match on no goals from 22 appearances that season. Indeed, that was Castle's record after the season's final weekend, as the Rochdale game was a game in hand played on the Monday night that followed.

Becoming homeless

A few weeks after the end of the 1985-86 season, Bristol Rovers announced they would be leaving their Eastville ground where they had been playing for nearly 90 years and that their last home game of the season just gone (against Chesterfield) would be their last ever on that ground. The fans who attended that game, therefore, didn't know that when they left the ground at the end they would never be going back.

Eight months earlier, Charlton's home ground, The Valley, had also been closed for good, and although the Charlton fans did get some warning, they certainly weren't given long to get used to the idea. When they turned up for their home game against Crystal Palace on 7 September 1985, they were handed leaflets informing them that the next home match against Stoke would be their last ever at the ground that had been their home for 63 years and that after that they would be playing all subsequent 'home' games at Palace's Selhurst Park. The leaflet helpfully provided directions to Palace's ground, even though most Charlton fans had probably already been there. Charlton went on to win promotion that season with many of their fans boycotting the Selhurst games and they remain the only club ever to reach the top-flight of English football whilst playing their 'home' games on another club's ground.

Charlton would eventually return to The Valley in 1992 following a campaign by supporters that included forming their own political party to stand in the local elections (the Valley Party). Bristol Rovers, however, would never return to Eastville. Indeed, it would be another ten years before they even returned to Bristol.

The next Football League club to lose their ground without having any plans in place to get a new one were Wimbledon in 1991, and this remains the only ever instance of a top-flight club becoming homeless. Although there had been rumours all season that Wimbledon would be leaving their Plough Lane ground (where they had played for 79 years), there was no official announcement made until ten days after they played their last ever game there. Wimbledon would go on to ground-share with Crystal Palace for eleven years before their owners got the green light to move them to Milton Keynes. This drove the fans to form the breakaway club AFC

Wimbledon who would spend 19 years playing their home games in Norbiton (ground-sharing with Kingstonian for most of that time) before eventually getting their own ground back on the same street that the original Wimbledon had left 30 years earlier.

The club that couldn't stand still

Wimbledon were either promoted or relegated in seven of their first nine seasons in the Football League. They finished 13th in Division Four in their debut season of 1977-78, before going into the following sequence:

> Promoted to Division Three: 1978-79
> Relegated to Division Four: 1979-80
> Promoted to Division Three: 1980-81
> Relegated to Division Four: 1981-82
> Promoted to Division Three: 1982-83
> Promoted to Division Two: 1983-84
> Finished 12th in Division Two: 1984-85
> Promoted to Division One: 1985-86.

They then went on to win the FA Cup in 1988 having never been beyond the fourth round before '85.

1985-86: Where have all the fans gone?

After peaking in the 1948-49 season, football attendances in England went into gradual decline until the 1960s when they levelled off, before going into decline again from 1972, with the decline becoming more drastic after 1980. Eventually they reached their nadir in the 1985-86 season when the average attendance per game across the four divisions of the Football League was just 8,130, down from 12,142 in the 1979-80 season. This meant the game had lost 23 per cent of its match-attending fans in just six years, compared with a drop of only 1 per cent over the six years prior to that.

The 1985-86 season saw nine of the 22 top-flight clubs getting an average gate of less than 15,000, including Ipswich whose crowds had dropped by nearly 40 per cent in just five years. West Ham finished third in '85-86 with an average home attendance of 21,179, which was 5,000 lower than when they had been in the Second Division in 1980-81. Chelsea also had a good season, spending most of it in the top four, but their average home gate of 21,984 was lower than that of their 1978-79 relegation season, and when Aston Villa visited Stamford Bridge in November the crowd was more than 26,000 below the ground's capacity. Also well below capacity was White Hart Lane when Tottenham played Liverpool in March. Liverpool were third in the table at the time and the likes of Glenn Hoddle, Chris Waddle, Ossie Ardiles and Ian Rush were all on the field, and yet the ground was nearly two-thirds empty. The crowd that night was 16,436 which, although poor, was positively colossal compared with the 5,833 that watched the Birmingham v Southampton game the following month. Birmingham, admittedly, were having a terrible season, but even so, such a low crowd for a top-flight game would have been unthinkable just a few years earlier. In the 1972-73 season, the same fixture had attracted over 30,000.

Second Division matches, meanwhile, were attended by fewer people in 1985-86 than had attended Third Division matches in 1980-81. Five second Division clubs averaged less than 5,000 per home game, including Wimbledon who won promotion and Fulham who had averaged over 20,000 per season until the late-60s. Crystal Palace averaged 6,787, an incredible drop of 71 per cent from when they had played at the same level seven years earlier.

It might have had something to do with England reaching the World Cup quarter-finals in 1986, but in the 1986-87 season attendances rose slightly, and they would continue to rise over the years that followed, until by the end of the 1990s they were back up to where they had been in the 1970s. But, by this time, it was different sorts of people who were going. The days of football grounds being packed out with young working-class men and teenage boys would never return.

Alvin Martin

When West Ham's Alvin Martin scored a hat-trick in his side's 8-1 win at home to Newcastle in April 1986, the goals came against three different keepers. Martin Thomas conceded the first but then went off injured at half-time, resulting in outfield players Chris Hedworth and Peter Beardsley both having stints in goal in the second half and also both letting in efforts from Martin (who was a defender by the way).

An England first that was a long time coming

England's 3-0 win against Poland in the 1986 World Cup was their first ever World Cup finals victory by a margin of more than two goals.

And another one

England's 3-0 win against Paraguay in the 1986 World Cup was their first ever in the post-first round stages of a World Cup held in a foreign country.

Gary Stevens (all of them)

Only three players with the name Gary Stevens played in the Football League in the 20th century and two of them played together for England at the 1986 World Cup. The other one played for Shrewsbury in the season leading up to that World Cup and was never capped.

The arrival of the sporting throw-in

The practice of giving the ball back to the opposition from a throw-in if it had been kicked out so a player could receive treatment was first seen at the 1986 World Cup. It was then adopted by English teams at the start of the 1986-87 season, although there was no national decision to do so. It just caught on.

No away fans allowed

In an attempt to avoid the problems caused by hooliganism, Luton decided to ban all away fans from their ground from the start of the 1986-87 season. Shortly into the season, they back-peddled slightly on the idea by making a small number of tickets available to some clubs, but the ban wouldn't be lifted entirely until the start of the 1991-92 season.

The most boring Saturday ever (at least in Division Two)

There were eleven matches played in the Second Division on Saturday 30 August 1986, and of the 22 teams that played in them, none scored more than a single goal on that day. There were four 1-0 home wins, two 1-0 away wins, three 1-1 draws and two 0-0 draws.

So much for home advantage

On Saturday 6 September 1986, there were eleven matches played in the First Division and not a single home win. Little over a year later, on Boxing Day 1987, there would be no home wins again from eleven matches played in the Second Division.

The top-flight force nobody saw coming

Wimbledon topped the highest division of English football for eleven days in September 1986, which was less than four years after they had lost 4-2 at home to Halifax Town in a Fourth Division match and little over nine years after playing Redditch in their final game as a semi-professional club in the Southern League. They eventually finished sixth in the League at the end of the ('86-87) season, ten points ahead of Manchester United who they beat home and away. They also beat Liverpool (the reigning Champions) away, Tottenham away, Chelsea 4-0 away and knocked Everton (the eventual Champions) out of the FA Cup. Their achievements of this season are all the more impressive for the fact that of the 23 players they used during the campaign, 15 had never played first-team professional football for any club other than Wimbledon, and nor had their manager Dave Bassett

Clive Allen (yet again)

Clive Allen scored eleven of Tottenham's first 12 League goals of the 1986-87 season.

Simon Garner

Blackburn's record goalscorer Simon Garner hit four when Blackburn beat Sunderland 6-1 in a Second Division match in September 1986, after which he then failed to score in all of his next 15 League appearances.

Gary Bannister

Queens Park Rangers' Gary Bannister scored after 16 seconds of a home game against Wimbledon in September 1986 and then after 13 seconds at home to Sheffield Wednesday the following month.

The offside trap working like a dream

Coventry City players were caught offside 22 times when they played Wimbledon in a First Division match in October 1986.

Vince/Vinnie Jones

Wimbledon signed Vince Jones from non-League Wealdstone in November 1986 and put him straight into the starting line-up for their next First Division match against Nottingham Forest a few days later. Incredibly, Jones hadn't even been a first-team regular at Wealdstone and appeared to have only been signed by Wimbledon because he was a friend of their manager, Dave Bassett. Vince Jones subsequently became known as 'Vinnie Jones' and went on to make 332 appearances under six different managers in the top division of English football despite being dismissed throughout his career as a player who had nothing to his game aside from fouls and intimidation.

Francis Joseph

Possibly the strangest loan move of the 1980s was Brentford's loaning of Francis Joseph to Wimbledon in March 1987. At the time Wimbledon were a First Division club while Brentford were two tiers below them in Division Three and Joseph wasn't the player he had once been, with injuries having limited him to just 24 League appearances in nearly three seasons. Joseph started two matches for Wimbledon (one against Arsenal) during his loan spell and made another three appearances as a substitute. These were the only five appearances he ever made in the top-flight of English football and the goal he scored in Wimbledon's 2-2 draw at Southampton was his only goal at that level.

Clive Allen (one more time)

For most of the 1986-87 season, Tottenham manager David Pleat operated, what was then, a unique system of playing five in midfield and only one striker. The striker was Clive Allen (who, oddly, wore the number seven shirt) and he scored 49 League and cup goals that season, which was the most by any top-flight player for 56 years. This achievement earned him both the Football Writers' Association Footballer of the Year award and the PFA Player of the Year award, but it didn't earn him much in the way of international recognition. England manager Bobby Robson did not see Allen as right for the national side and handed him only one cap that season.

1987's dramatic last-day drama at the bottom of the League

The 1986-87 season was the first of direct relegation out of the Football League and it couldn't have come at a worse time for Burnley. The club's 1-0 defeat at Crewe in their penultimate match of that season saw them fall to the bottom of the Fourth Division and they were, therefore, looking highly likely to become the first ever former League champions to drop into non-League football (they had won their last title 27 years earlier). In order to stay up they had to win their final match at home to Orient and hope results went their way in at least one of the games between Crewe and Torquay and Swansea and Lincoln. A crowd of 15,781 packed into Turf Moor that afternoon and saw the home side carve out a narrow 2-1 win which was enough to keep them up as Lincoln lost 2-0 at Swansea (back then it was only the bottom club that went down).

It was, however, Torquay who had the most dramatic escape that afternoon. They drew 2-2 at Crewe to stay up on goal difference, but had been 2-0 down at the break and didn't equalise until stoppage time (which wasn't as long in those days as it is now). And to add a bizarre twist, much of that stoppage time had been added on because Torquay's Jim McNichol had needed treatment after being bitten by a dog that had run onto the pitch. And then just to add an extra bit of trivia, Crewe's second goal in that game had been scored by David Platt who would play for England in the semi-finals of the World Cup three years later.

The nine-point reversal on Merseyside

Everton won the 1986-87 League title by a nine-point margin, although it was Liverpool who had had a nine-point lead at the top in March.

Winning the League without big-scoring forwards

When Everton won the League title in 1986-87, their two leading goalscorers, Trevor Steven and Kevin Sheedy, were both midfielders. Their highest scoring forward, Adrian Heath, only got eleven, while no other forward scored more than five.

The play-offs arrive

The 1986-87 season was the first of promotion play-offs, although for the first two seasons they potentially decided a relegation place as well, as each divisional contest was between three teams bidding for promotion plus one from the division above who were trying to stay up. Should the team from the higher division win their play-off contest then they would avoid the drop and the three teams from the lower division would all be denied promotion.

During the two seasons that this system was in operation, Charlton were the only club to avoid relegation through the play-offs when they retained their top-flight place by beating Second

Division Leeds in the Divisions One & Two Play-Off Final of 1987. At this time the final was played over two legs and then went to a replay if the aggregate scores were level after the second leg, and it was in a replay at Birmingham's St Andrew's that Charlton kept their First Division place by turning a 1-0 deficit into a 2-1 win with two goals in the last seven minutes of extra-time. Remarkably, both goals came from defender Peter Shirtliff who had never scored twice in a match before and never would again.

For the following season it was decided that, rather than being played on neutral grounds, any replays should be played at the home of one of the teams involved with a penalty shoot-out being used to decide which one. That year the Division Two & Three Play-off Final between Walsall and Bristol City was the only one that finished level on aggregate and so stands unique as the only match ever to have contained a penalty shoot-out even though it wasn't decided on penalties. The shoot-out was won by Walsall who then won the replay – and thus promotion – on their own ground two days later.

The Wembley final eventually arrived in 1990, although seeing as the teams taking part in the play-offs were the ones that had missed out on automatic promotion, then this seemed a bit like a Wembley final being awarded to failures. That year, Swindon became the first team to win promotion to the top-flight with a play-off victory at Wembley, but they basked in the achievement for only ten days before being demoted to Division Three after admitting making irregular payments to players (they were subsequently allowed to remain in Division Two on appeal). In their place, Sunderland, who they beat in the final, were promoted instead and so had the unique distinction of coming nowhere near automatic promotion (they missed it by eleven points) and losing in the play-offs, but still going up anyway.

The original idea behind the play-offs was to provide a much-needed shot in the arm to the Football League format which was seen to have grown stale by the mid-80s, as indicated by the declining attendances. There was initially worrying talk of remedying this by having the biggest clubs in the country forming a 'Super League' that no other clubs could be promoted into but, in the end, a much less drastic plan was put in place that involved end-of-season play-offs, the reduction of the top-flight from 22 clubs to 20 and automatic promotion into Division Four from the top tier of non-League football.

While the play-offs are largely accepted now, they were pretty controversial in their early years, since the previous system of awarding promotion places according to League position alone was more straightforward, made more sense and was obviously fairer. As *When Saturday Comes* wrote at the time, "[the Play-Offs] introduce a totally unacceptable element of chance into what is, after all, supposed to be the prime test of consistency".

Welcome to the Football League

Scarborough's first ever match in the Football League, against Wolves on the opening day of the 1987-88 season, was held-up for ten minutes due to crowd trouble which resulted in 18 supporters eventually being jailed.

John Aldridge

John Aldridge scored seven penalties in Liverpool's first nine League matches of the 1987-88 season.

Trevor Senior

1983-84 was Trevor Senior's first full season after becoming a full-time professional and he finished it as the League's top scorer with 36 goals (41 in all competitions) for Reading. He then scored 22 in the League (and in a higher division) in 1984-85, 27 in '85-86 and 17 in '86-87 (all for Reading). No player scored more Football League goals over these four seasons than Senior, but he would prove to be one of the most extreme examples of a 'disappointing signing' after moving to top-flight Watford for £300,000 in the summer of 1987. Senior managed just one goal in 24 League appearances – 22 of them starts – for a struggling Watford side before being sold to Second Division Middlesbrough for £100,000 less than what he had been bought for. He had spent only eight months at Watford and would spend only seven at Middlesbrough before they too sold him at a loss. He left Middlesbrough for a return to Reading, seemingly the only club that could bring out the best in him and went on to finish the 1988-89 season as their top scorer once again with 16 in the League and 23 in all competitions.

Glenn Humphries

In October 1987, Glenn Humphries scored an own goal 35 seconds into his Bristol City debut at Rotherham.

Colin Morris

Sheffield United's Colin Morris missed 12 penalties between January 1983 and October 1987. There were, however, another 48 penalties that he put away whilst at the club.

A trio of hat-trick heroes

In November 1987, Manchester City beat Huddersfield 10-1 in a Second Division match with Paul Stewart, Tony Adcock and David White all scoring hat-tricks. This isn't the only time three players have scored hat-tricks for the same club in the same game in professional football in England, but it is the most recent occasion and it's the only time it's ever occurred in a televised match (highlights of the game were shown on ITV).

Dave Caldwell

Dave Caldwell was sent-off five times in the first five months of the 1987-88 season. He was dismissed twice while playing for Chesterfield and then received three red cards in his first six appearances for Torquay.

Alan Shearer

In April 1988, Southampton beat Arsenal 4-2 in a First Division match at the Dell with 17-year-old Alan Shearer scoring a hat-trick in his first ever start in senior football. This made Shearer the youngest ever player to score a top-flight hat-trick.

Ian Muir

A penalty in a 2-1 win at Stockport was the only goal Tranmere's Ian Muir managed in his first 12 League and cup appearances of the 1987-88 season, and yet he eventually went on to score 29 in all competitions that season.

Mark Lawrenson

Mark Lawrenson played 18 times for Liverpool in their League title-winning season of 1987-88 but finished that season as manager of Oxford who ended up bottom of the First Division.

Luton and Forest bookending the Cup Final

The last two League matches of the 1987-88 season were Luton v Nottingham Forest on the day before the FA Cup Final and Nottingham Forest v Luton on the day after the Final. Both matches finished 1-1.

Dave Beasant

Wimbledon goalkeeper Dave Beasant was an ever-present for the club in all four divisions of the Football League. He never missed a single game in their Fourth Division title-winning season of 1982-83, nor in their Third Division promotion-winning season of 1983-84, nor in the two seasons they spent in the Second Division between 1984 and 1986, nor in their first two seasons in the First Division that followed. Beasant's last game for Wimbledon was the 1988 FA Cup Final when, as club captain, he lifted the Cup after making a decisive penalty save that preserved Wimbledon's 1-0 lead.

Laurie Cunningham

Laurie Cunningham was an FA Cup-winner with Wimbledon in 1988 despite only ever making nine appearances for the club during a three-month spell as a non-contract player. That substitute appearance against Liverpool in the '88 Cup Final would prove to be his last in English football before his death in a car crash in Spain the following year. Probably no player won an FA Cup-winner's medal so close to the end of their life.

Viv Anderson

Viv Anderson was in the England squads for the 1982 World Cup, the 1986 World Cup and the 1988 European Championships – but didn't get a game in any of them. He was also in the squad for the 1980 European Championships but only played in the dead-rubber final group game against Spain, his only ever appearance in a major tournament.

When you couldn't have a beer after the game

Before the 1988-89 season, football fans couldn't get a beer straight after the match on a Saturday as all Saturday matches kicked-off at three o'clock in the afternoon and the UK licensing laws didn't allow pubs and bars to open between the hours of 3.00 pm and 5.30 pm (and it should be noted that in those days 5.30 pm was longer after the end of the match than it is today as matches only had ten-minute half-time breaks and usually no more than a couple of minutes stoppage time at the end).

Paul Crichton

When Nottingham Forest goalkeeper Paul Crichton went on loan to Torquay in August 1988, it was the seventh different club he had been loaned to in under two years.

Penalty madness at Palace

A Second Division match between Crystal Palace and Brighton in March 1989 saw Palace score one penalty and then miss two all in the space of five minutes late in the first half. They then missed another penalty in the second half, a half in which Brighton were also awarded a penalty which they scored. Palace's three penalty misses had all been different – one being saved, one hitting the post and one going over. And it was three different players who took them as well, in Mark Bright, Ian Wright and John Pemberton. Bright and Wright's misses came within 95 seconds of each other. Palace won 2-1.

Paul Miller

The first three goals of Paul Miller's senior career were all scored past England's first-choice goalkeeper – and soon-to-be record appearances holder – Peter Shilton in a First Division match in March 1989 when Miller was playing for Wimbledon and Shilton for Derby. Miller was 19 at the time but would only go on to score another seven goals at the highest level of English football before dropping down to play in the lower divisions.

This Paul Miller is not to be confused with the Tottenham defender of the same name.

Dave Waller

Chesterfield's Dave Waller scored in each of seven consecutive games in the spring of 1989 and was the only Chesterfield scorer in all of them.

The Wallace brothers

Southampton fielded brothers Danny, Rod and Ray Wallace together in 27 of their League and cup games during the 1988-89 season.

A rollercoaster 20 years

Derby were promoted to the First Division in 1969, won the League title in 1972, and then won it again in '75, before being relegated back to the Second Division in 1980. They were then relegated to the Third Division in 1984 but climbed back to the top-flight with back-to-back promotions in '86 and '87. They then finished fifth in the League in '89.

Stuart McCall

Everton's Stuart McCall set two FA Cup records in the space of 18 minutes on the afternoon of the 1989 Final. In the 12th minute of extra-time, he hit his second goal of the game to become the first ever substitute to score twice in an FA Cup final. Then, at the end of the match, he became the first player ever to score twice in an FA Cup final and finish on the losing side. McCall hadn't scored at all in 33 League appearances for Everton that season. The only previous occasion he had scored twice in a match was whilst playing for

Bradford away to Plymouth in a Second Division fixture in January 1987 – and he finished on the losing side in that one as well.

When English players not knowing how to waste time cost Liverpool the title

When Poland played the USSR at the 1982 World Cup, Polish winger Wlodzimierz Smolarek took the ball into the corner three times in the game's dying minutes and attempted to hold it there in order to waste time. For English football fans watching on TV, it was the first time they had ever seen this method of time-wasting and they generally viewed it as a strange, unsporting and cynically negative foreign practice. It wouldn't be until the 1990s that English players began doing it as well, which was a bit too late for the Liverpool side of 1988-89.

Liverpool needed only to avoid defeat by a two-goal margin in that season's final game against Arsenal to take the title and their failure to do so had a lot to do with English players not being time-wasters. With the score at Liverpool 0 Arsenal 1 in stoppage time, Liverpool's John Barnes had the opportunity to take the ball into the corner Smolarek-style but chose not to because it wasn't what English players did. Instead, he cut into the box looking to either cross or score himself but only succeeded in giving away possession. Arsenal then immediately counter-attacked and scored a devastating (for Liverpool) second goal with what was their final attack of the game.

That 1988-89 League title climax in detail

After the final Saturday of the 1988-89 season, Arsenal were two points ahead of second-place Liverpool at the top of the First Division, but the season was far from over as Liverpool still had three outstanding fixtures left to play, while Arsenal had two and the final game for both clubs was against each other at Anfield.

On the Tuesday after the season's final Saturday Liverpool beat Queens Park Rangers 2-0 at home to move one point ahead of Arsenal at the top, then, the following night, Arsenal drew 2-2 at home to Wimbledon to put the two clubs level on both points and goal difference. Liverpool then won the FA Cup on the Saturday before beating West Ham 5-1 at home on the Tuesday that followed to move three points clear of Arsenal and improve their goal difference to four better than Arsenal's. Arsenal had led the League from Boxing Day to the final Saturday of the season but now looked to have been pipped at the post. If they beat Liverpool by a two-goal margin in the final game at Anfield on the Friday then they would take the title on goals scored but there seemed little likelihood of it. Liverpool hadn't lost at home for two and a half seasons.

That final game at Anfield was the first ever League title decider to be televised live and it couldn't have been any more dramatic as Arsenal took a surprise 1-0 lead seven minutes into the second half and then landed the title with a second goal from what was their final attack of the season just 100 seconds before the referee blew for full-time. Remarkably, they had achieved what everyone thought was impossible despite manager George Graham deploying a defensive formation on a night when they needed goals. Having already won the FA Cup, it was the second season running that Liverpool had missed out on the League and Cup double by losing their final match unexpectedly. The previous season they had won the League only to then lose to Wimbledon in the FA Cup Final.

The club that gave managers a chance

West Ham had only five different managers in 87 years between 1902 and 1989. These were Syd King (30 years), Charlie Paynter (18 years), Ted Fenton (eleven years), Ron Greenwood (13 years) and John Lyall (15 years). Of the five, only Greenwood had any previous managerial experience, and that was only at Eastbourne United. Paynter, Fenton and Lyall had all been West Ham players, while King had played for the club's earlier incarnation, Thames Ironworks.

John Lyall

John Lyall's 15 years as West Ham manager were a rollercoaster ride to say the least. Under Lyall, West Ham won the FA Cup in 1975 but were relegated from the First Division in 1978. They then went into the 1978-79 season as one of the favourites for promotion but only finished fifth and then finished seventh the following season but surprisingly won the FA Cup. Their side of that season remains the worst FA Cup-winners according to League position. In '80-81, the club won the Second Division title by a huge 13-point margin and were also runners-up in the League Cup, so becoming the first club outside of the top-flight to reach major finals in successive seasons, a feat which has never been equalled. Back in the top-flight, they had reasonable top ten finishes three seasons in a row but only just avoided relegation in '84-85, before finishing third in '85-86, which remains the club's highest ever top-flight finish. Three seasons after that, however, they were relegated back into Division Two and Lyall became the first ever West Ham manager to lose his job over performances on the pitch (rather than disagreements with the board).

Sharing the goals around

Eight different players scored for Liverpool when they beat Crystal Palace 9-0 in a First Division match in September 1989. The only outfield players who didn't score were David Burrows, Ronnie Whelan and substitute Jan Molby. 20 years earlier (almost to the day) Liverpool had had seven different scorers in a 10-0 victory against Dundalk in the European Fairs Cup. In this match they didn't use any substitutes so again had only three non-scoring outfield players – Geoff Strong, Ron Yeats and Emlyn Hughes.

Trevor Francis (yet again)

In September 1989, Queens Park Rangers 35-year-old player-manager Trevor Francis made his first start for the club in nine months and scored all three goals in his side's 3-1 First Division win at Aston Villa. Despite this Rangers sacked him just over two months later.

Frankie Bunn

In October 1989, Oldham beat Scarborough 7-0 in the third round of the League Cup, with Frankie Bunn scoring six of the goals. This was one more than Bunn scored in 29 League games that season.

Not making the corners count

In October 1989, Sheffield United lost 2-0 at home to West Ham in a Second Division match despite winning 28 corners and conceding only one.

Ray Stewart

Ray Stewart scored 84 goals for West Ham between 1979 and 1989, with 76 of them being penalties. No player has scored more penalties in English football, and Stewart's prowess from the spot meant that he went into double-figures for goals in four different seasons despite being a full-back.

When you couldn't follow the scores on a Saturday

Before the 1990s, there was no TV programme or national radio station that provided continuous live updates of latest scores during the course of a Saturday afternoon of League or FA Cup football. BBC1's Saturday afternoon sports show *Grandstand* provided no football coverage between its 10–15-minute lunchtime show, *Football Focus* (originally *Football Preview*), and *Final Score* which didn't usually begin until five minutes before the day's matches were due to end. BBC radio also had its own all-afternoon sports show from 1964 (going under various titles on Radio Three and then Radio Two), and although it featured second-half commentary of a match each week, like *Grandstand*, it too provided no constantly updating latest scores.

From 1960, the highlight of *Grandstand's Final Score* was undoubtedly seeing the full-time scores being printed out on the teleprinter as they came in, an exciting spectacle when the latest scores of most of those games had previously been unknown. In the early-80s, the teleprinter was replaced with a digital text equivalent that was dubbed 'the vidiprinter', although by then many TV sets had teletext, and the BBC's version, Ceefax, did become the first national provider of constantly updating latest football scores.

Before Ceefax, the only way people who weren't at home on a Saturday afternoon could get all the day's final scores before the Sunday morning newspapers arrived was to buy one of the many local sports papers that were rushed out early on Saturday evening. As well containing all the scores, these papers also featured hastily put-together match reports from local games that had been phoned-in – often from public phone boxes – by the papers' reporters. Around the country, these papers were commonly referred to as 'the pink'un' or 'the green 'un' because of the colour of the paper they were printed on, but in London the more conventional-looking *Evening News* and *Evening Standard* performed the same role. Looking at the edition of Sheffield's *Star Green 'un* from 19 October 1968, it's easy to see the flaw in these papers. The front page was clearly put-together while the second half of the matches were in progress, and so while it does give the final scores of all the matches, the mini-reports it provides on them mostly only mention the first-half goals. And so, for example, we're told that Jimmy Greaves scored in the first half against Liverpool, but not that he also scored the winner in the second, while the report of the Manchester United v Southampton match tells us about the goals that made it 1-1 at half-time, but doesn't mention that Southampton won it 2-1 in the second half. This was also the day that Geoff Hurst scored six against Sunderland, although the paper didn't have time to wait and see whether he completed his double-hat-trick and so reported that he only scored five.

The fans find their voice

Today football fans are shown little respect by the clubs and the footballing authorities. They're charged exorbitant prices for season and matchday tickets, as well as for merchandise and food and drink at grounds, and are also forced to travel hundreds of miles on inconvenient days and/or times as games are scheduled to meet the demands of television.

There was, of course, a time when it wasn't like this. When, even at the biggest clubs, admission prices were cheap and it was very rare for a weekend match not to kick-off at three o'clock on a Saturday afternoon. But this isn't to say supporters were treated with more respect in those days. If anything, things were even worse. Most grounds had large areas of uncovered terracing that caused fans to often watch matches whilst being rained upon, and on a packed terrace it was not usually possible to see the whole pitch nor to go and get refreshments or use the toilet at half-time.

As players were not as wealthy, in theory, they were not as remote from the fans as they are today, but it's debatable as to whether they showed them any more respect. Before the 21st century, it was rare for players to applaud their supporters at the end of matches or to acknowledge them after scoring. In October 1970, Wolves' Derek Parkin scored a penalty against Southampton and then, after celebrating with his teammates, contemptuously stuck two-fingers up at his own team's supporters. An act that would be pretty shocking today but was no big deal in an era when the media generally saw football fans as unthinking hordes.

In 1973, FA Secretary Denis Follows had proposed banning all under-18s from football grounds in order to combat hooliganism, and the same season Derby manager Brian Clough described his own club's supporters as "a disgusting lot" for not getting behind the team when they were losing. Nearly 17 years later, Clough, then at Nottingham Forest, punched several of his own club's supporters after they ran onto the pitch to celebrate a victory that put Forest through to the semi-finals of the League Cup. Clough, of course, never behaved like other managers and both of these incidents were controversial at the time, but they were probably just extreme examples of the disrespectful attitude most people within the game had to those who followed it. Even the far more gentlemanly Ipswich manager Bobby Robson seemed dismissive of his own club's supporters when Ipswich reached the FA Cup Final for the first time in 1978. "I am delighted for the club, the directors and the old stagers like Hunter and Mills," said Robson, but failed to express any such delight for the fans.

But then, in those days, supporters were always treated shoddily when it came to the FA Cup Final and had been for decades. Wembley had a capacity of 100,000 before the mid-1980s, and yet, in the 1970s, the clubs that reached the FA Cup Final were only allocated 16,000 tickets each to sell to their supporters. In the early-1960s, it had been just 14,000 each, in the early-50s 12,000 and in the 1920s a paltry 3,500. The clubs, needless to say, had no decent system in place to ensure the most loyal fans got priority when they went on sale, resulting in tens of thousands of the most devoted missing out on their club's big day every year, while the players cashed-in by selling their complimentary tickets to touts, something which was "considered a perk for reaching Wembley," according to West Bromwich Albion's Jeff Astle.

This casual contempt for supporters also led to a total disregard for their safety which played a part in all of English football's three major disasters – the Burnden Park disaster of 1946, the Bradford fire of 1986 and Hillsborough in 1989. The 33 deaths at the Burnden Park game – an FA Cup tie between Bolton and Stoke – wasn't even deemed worth abandoning the match for, with play being resumed as soon as the dead bodies had been cleared from the pitch, while Hillsborough was an horrific consequence of a practice that had been going on for years – i.e. caging in supporters and then not properly controlling the numbers going into the cages. The police's attempt to blame the supporters solely for the disaster was something they probably felt they could get away with at a time when everyone seemed to have such a low opinion of football fans anyway. When one police officer made false claims about the bad behaviour of Liverpool fans inside the ground that day, Britain's biggest-selling newspaper gladly published them under the headline, 'The Truth'.

By the time of Hillsborough, supporters were already starting to speak out against the football authorities and club directors that cared nothing for them. In 1983, plans to merge Oxford and Reading to form 'Thames Valley Royals' had led to Oxford fans invading the pitch before a game against Wigan to stage a sit-down protest and Reading fans taking to the streets for protest marches. Four years later there were more fan protests against proposed mergers between Fulham and Queens Park Rangers (who were to become 'Fulham Park Rangers') and Crystal Palace and Wimbledon. Palace chairman Ron Noades gave out questionnaires to gauge the fans' opinion on the latter merger, but then joked, "I only hope when they fill out the forms they can write".

It was during this period that Bradford City supporters became the first to launch a club fanzine. *The City Gent* arrived in 1984 and was followed two years later by the general football fanzine *When Saturday Comes* which became a cult success despite initially only being sold in a few independent record stores and in the sports bookshop 'Sports Pages' on the Charing Cross Road. The contributors to *When Saturday Comes* wrote about football in the same kind of spikey, punky, irreverent way that *Melody Maker* journalists wrote about music and, in doing so, they kick-started what was little short of a revolution in football writing. At the beginning of the 1987-88 season there were eight club fanzines in circulation in England and Wales. By the start of 1990-91 there were 182. All of these fanzines were printed on photocopiers and sold outside football grounds on matchdays and, as well as their sharp wit, they also offered the kind of insight into teams, players and the supporter experience that could only come from people who had followed the same club through thick and thin for years. The titles of these fanzines were usually smart puns, witty cultural references or cryptic in-jokes and included *Not The 8502* (Bournemouth), *The Ugly Inside* (Southampton), *He's Not Danny Grady* (Crewe), *No, Nay, Never* (Burnley), *Raging Bull* (Oxford United), *A Kick Up The Rs* (QPR), *Friday Night Fever* (Tranmere), *Beyond The Boundary* (Oldham), *4,000 Holes* (Blackburn), *Voice Of The Beehive*

(Brentford), *The Abbey Rabbit* (Cambridge United), *Tales From The Potting Shed* (Preston), *And Smith Must Score!* (Brighton), *Addickted* (Charlton), *Hull, Hell and Happiness* (Hull), *Just A Quick Word, Lads Please* (Leeds), *The Peterborough Effect* (Peterborough), *The Memoirs Of Seth Bottomley* (Port Vale), *When Sunday Comes* (Liverpool), *The Mill On The Maun* (Mansfield) and *Brian Moore's Head Looks Uncannily Like The London Planetarium* (Gillingham). Just looking at these titles alone provides enough evidence that fanzines were a world away from the comparatively stuffy professional sports journalism of the time. The late-80s and early-90s may not have been a golden age for football, but it certainly was for alternative football writing.

And then, in 1992, came *Fever Pitch*. Nick Hornby's memoir of his years as an Arsenal supporter was a unique football book at the time. The first book on football how it was for the ordinary fan who watched regularly from the terraces. It was a book for the fanzine era, and it became a bestseller and, along with the fanzines, did a lot to change the way football supporters were perceived. From here on football fans were no longer seen as unthinking hordes. From here on you could be cool and educated and literate and go to football.

It's also worth noting that, unlike the professional sports journalists of the time, Hornby and the fanzine writers never referred to football as 'soccer', and it was probably because of their influence that this word fell out of favour in Britain.

What an implosion!

In December 1989, Chelsea suffered back-to-back 5-2 home defeats (to Wimbledon and Liverpool) having gone their previous 28 home League matches unbeaten.

Dean Horrix

Dean Horrix was killed in a car crash just eight days after making his debut for Bristol City in March 1990. He was 28 years old and had recently been signed by the club from Millwall. Horrix had scored 20 goals for Reading in the 1984-85 season.

Ian and Gary Bowyer

In the Scunthorpe v Hereford match in April 1990, 18-year-old Gary Bowyer started for Hereford, and his 38-year-old father, Ian, came on as sub. Gary marked the occasion by scoring Hereford's last-minute equaliser with an over-head kick, although he would never be as good a player as his dad who was a League title-winner and twice a European Cup-winner with Nottingham Forest.

Dave Bassett

Dave Bassett won six promotions in the first ten seasons of his managerial career. He led Wimbledon to Fourth Division promotion in 1980-81 and 1982-83, then led them to Third Division promotion in 1983-84 and Second Division promotion in '85-86. After a brief spell at Watford, he then took over at Sheffield United and led them to Third Division promotion in 1988-89 and Second Division promotion in 1989-90.

Lee Martin

Lee Martin only ever scored two goals in English professional football, and one was the winner in the 1990 FA Cup Final replay.

Gary Lineker

Gary Lineker only ever played six full seasons in the top-flight of English football but finished as the top scorer at that level in three of them and remains the only player to have finished a season as the top-flight's top scorer with three different clubs.

He achieved this with 24 goals for Leicester in 1984-85, with 30 for Everton in 1985-86 and with 24 for Tottenham in 1989-90. He would have also have been the top-flight's top scorer for a fourth time in 1991-92 (with 28 for Tottenham) had Arsenal's Ian Wright not scored twice in injury time on the last day of that season.

Brian Moore

Brian Moore commentated on every FA Cup Final for ITV between 1969 and 1988, but he never went to a World Cup until 1990. This was because Moore was also ITV's main football presenter and so had to stay in London in order to present the coverage of the matches and discuss them with the pundits. It wouldn't be until the 1998 World Cup that the presenters and pundits first did their jobs from the country where the tournament was being held.

England's underwhelming 'great tournament'

England reached the semi-finals of the 1990 World Cup despite not scoring more than once from open play in any of their seven matches. Their 1-0 win against Egypt in the group stages was their only normal-time victory of the whole tournament, and their two extra-time victories were both fortunate. In the second round, Belgium hit the post twice before England eventually beat them with a last-minute free-kick, and in the quarter-finals only a penalty seven minutes from the end of normal time saved them from defeat against a Cameroon side missing four first-choice players through suspension.

Steve Bull

Steve Bull only ever made one appearance in the top-flight of English football – as a substitute for West Bromwich Albion in April 1986 – but played in four of England's matches at the 1990 World cup.

Peter Shilton

Peter Shilton kept goal in all of England's matches at the 1982, 1986 and 1990 World Cups. He's by no means the only player to have played in three World Cups, but he is the only one to have done so having not made his World Cup debut until 12 years after his international debut. Shilton had been in England's preliminary squad for the 1970 World Cup and had made his international debut against East Germany in the first match after that tournament. His international career was so long that he was an England teammate of both Geoff Hurst and Paul Gascoigne.

The offside law changes (again)

At the beginning of the 1990-91 season the first change in the offside law for 65 years was made, as from here on an attacking player would now be onside if he was level with the last defender when the ball was played forward. Prior to this season, if you were level then you were offside.

Paul Crichton (again)

In a Fourth Division match between Rochdale and Doncaster in September 1990, Rochdale were awarded a penalty that the Doncaster keeper, Paul Crichton, saved. The referee then ordered it to be retaken, and Crichton saved it again, only for the ref to order another retake which Crichton also saved.

David Longhurst

In September 1990, York City's David Longhurst became the first player for 63 years to die during an English League match that he was playing in. Longhurst – a 25-year-old forward – had a rare heart condition that he was unaware of and suffered heart failure late in the first half of his side's home game against Lincoln. According to some reports, he died in York's medical room after being stretchered off, while others stated that he died on the pitch. York subsequently named a stand after him even though he only ever made eight appearances for them. Longhurst's best season for goals was 1985-86 when he scored 14 for Halifax.

Rising to the occasion

Halifax failed to score in all of their first eight Fourth Division matches of the 1990-91 season, but during that period did score twice (over two legs) against Manchester United in the League Cup.

When the worst team in the League played In Europe

1990-91 was the only season when the team that finished bottom of English football's fourth tier also played in a major European competition. The team was Wrexham, and the competition was the European Cup-Winners' Cup which they had qualified for by winning the Welsh Cup the previous season. In the Cup-Winners' Cup they beat the Danish side Lyngby 1-0 on aggregate in the first round before going down 5-0 on aggregate to Manchester United in the second. This, of course, makes Lyngby the only team ever to lose to the Football's League's worst side in a major European competition and United the only team ever to beat the Football League's worst side en route to winning a major European competition (United won the Cup-Winners' Cup that season).

The bottom tier (almost) mainstays

The 1990-91 season was Hartlepool's 63rd in the Football League and they had spent all but one of them in its bottom tier. In fact, if you include the War years, then the club were constant members of the bottom tier of League football for 47 years after being made inaugural members of Division Three North in 1921. Their only season outside of the bottom tier between 1921 and 1991 was 1968-69 when they finished third from bottom in Division Three.

Fixture congestion? Not a problem

Cambridge United were forced to play five Third Division matches in 12 days in April 1991, and won them all. They beat Bournemouth 1-0 away on the 16th, Shrewsbury 2-1 away on the 18th, Stoke 3-0 at home on the 20th, Bournemouth 4-0 at home on the 24th and Wigan 1-0 away on the 27th. These victories lifted them from seventh to third in the table, before two more wins in May landed them the title.

Peter Shilton (again)

Peter Shilton is the only player ever to have made 100 or more top-flight appearances for each of five different clubs. He played 207 times for Leicester in the top-flight between 1966 and 1974, 107 times for Stoke between 1974 and 1977, 202 times for Nottingham Forest between 1977 and 1982, 188 times for Southampton between 1982 and 1987 and 143 times for Derby between 1987 and 1991.

The strange top-flight season of 1990-91

So Why Was It strange? Here we Go:

Arsenal won the League title despite having two points deducted as punishment for a brawl their players had been involved in at Manchester United, and spending nearly three months without their captain, Tony Adams, due to a prison sentence he had received for drink-driving. Liverpool finished runners-up but may well have won it had their manager, Kenny Dalglish, not resigned suddenly in February when they were top. Crystal Palace finished third having never previously finished higher than 13th in their history, while newly-promoted Leeds finished fourth. Palace had moved up to third spot on 22 December and then remained locked in that position for nearly five months, with Leeds being constantly one place behind them from New Year's Day onwards.

The biggest star and most gifted player in English football at this time was Tottenham's Paul Gascoigne and Tottenham also had England's best goalscorer in Gary Lineker and were managed by future England boss Terry Venables but they only finished tenth, three places behind Wimbledon who were on the brink of becoming homeless. Sheffield United were rock bottom for three months between October and January, before unexpectedly winning seven in a row to lift themselves up to 12th. They eventually finished 13th.

The division's top scorer was Arsenal's Alan Smith with 23, with former Arsenal Players Lee Chapman (Leeds) and Niall Quinn (Man City) close behind on 21 and 20 respectively. The only other top-flight player to get 20 League goals was Wimbledon's John Fashanu, which meant that all four leading scorers in the division were big target men. The two most remarkable First Division scoring feats of this season, however, were both achieved by defenders. Manchester United's joint-top scorer was centre-back Steve Bruce with 13, while full-back Stuart Pearce finished second-top scorer for Nottingham Forest with eleven. Bruce was unusual among central defenders in that he was his club's regular penalty-taker and seven of his League goals this season came from the spot, although none of Pearce's did.

Over all competitions, Bruce scored 19 (including eleven penalties), and Pearce 16 (with no penalties). Incredible figures for defenders of not especially successful sides.

The eventual climax to the title race was also pretty strange by previous standards. On the first Bank Holiday in May, Liverpool's game at Nottingham Forest kicked-off at five so as it could be shown live on TV. Forest won it 2-1 which clinched the title for Arsenal an hour before their game against Man United kicked-off that evening. This was the first time the climax to the title race had been messed-up by the scheduling of matches for TV, but it wouldn't be the last.

Brian Clough and Archie Gemmill

In May 1991, Nottingham Forest manager Brian Clough suspended the club's reserve team coach, Archie Gemmill, after Forest's reserves blew the Central League title by losing three of their last four games.

Des Walker

Des Walker's first goal in senior football came in his 267th appearance and was an own goal in Nottingham's Forest's 1-1 draw at Southampton in January 1991. His second came four months later and it was the own goal that won the 1991 FA Cup Final for Tottenham.

A chaotic beginning

Barnet's first two matches as a Football League club produced 21 goals. They lost 7-4 at home to Crewe on the opening day of the 1991-92 season and then drew 5-5 at home to Brentford in the League Cup three days later.

It can't be that difficult, surely

When Southend's Dean Austin had a penalty saved in the second minute of a Second Division match at home to Wolves in September 1991, it was the seventh penalty in a row that Southend had failed to convert.

An ultra-rare occurrence in a pointless competition

The Full Members Cup had little prestige at the time and is little remembered now, but when Tranmere entertained Newcastle in its first round in October 1991, the game resulted in the first 6-6 draw between two Football League sides in over 30 years. Tranmere's John Aldridge and Newcastle's Mick Quinn both scored hat-tricks before Tranmere went on to win on penalties, although the match itself produced more than twice as many goals as the shoot-out which finished 3-2.

Phil Stant

Phil Stant was the only Falklands War veteran to have become a professional footballer. He was the Fourth Division's top scorer in both the 1988-89 and 1991-92 seasons, when playing for Hereford and Mansfield respectively.

The rule change that changed football

The 1991-92 season was the last before the launch of the Premier League and also, coincidentally, the last when goalkeepers were allowed to pick the ball up from a back pass. The introduction of the back pass rule would remove the opportunity for defenders to bring a match to a standstill by passing back to the keeper, reduce the amount of time a keeper could spend with the ball in his hands and also reduce the number of long drop-kicks a keeper would be able to do during a match. As a result, under pressure defenders would be forced to turn and pass more than they used to, while keepers would, at times, have to pass or clear like defenders. Football in the Premier League, therefore, would immediately be played slightly differently to how football in the First Division had been but it would have nothing at all to do with the Premier League's creation.

Vinnie Jones (again)

In January 1991, Sheffield United's Vinnie Jones earned, what was then, the fastest ever booking in the history of professional football in England when he was shown the yellow card just five seconds into a First Division match against Manchester City. Jones then broke his own record just over a year a later when it took him just three seconds of an FA Cup tie at Chelsea to get booked.

Bob Paisley

Bob Paisley was at Liverpool for 53 years between 1939 and 1992, serving them as a player, a coach, a trainer, an assistant manager, a manager and a director. He came into management relatively late in life at the age of 55 and more out of a sense of duty to Liverpool than any personal ambition, but he still ended up winning the League title six times and the European Cup three times. Paisley's first title as a manager (in 1976) came 29 years after his only title as a player.

Why the European Cup wasn't as big as you'd think

Before the European Cup morphed into the Champions League in 1992, it was a straight knock-out competition with only two rounds preceding the quarter-finals. In 1978, Liverpool received a bye in the first round and then won their second round tie against Dynamo Dresden despite losing the away leg. This meant that they reached the quarter-finals having only won one match in the competition. They then went on to beat Benfica in the quarter-finals and Borussia Moenchengladbach in the semis, before winning 1-0 at Wembley against FC Bruges in the final to become champions of Europe having only beaten four European sides. Real Madrid, Barcelona, Bayern Munich and the two Milan clubs hadn't even been in the competition that year.

Unlike the Champions League, the European Cup wasn't a contest between the giants of European football, but a competition contested between the winners of each national league in Europe (unlike the Champions League, therefore, it was literally for champions only) and, for English sides during this period, it was clearly easier to win once you were in it than it was to qualify for. This is perhaps why, in those days, it never detracted from the prestige of the FA Cup, a competition that had never been easy to win no matter how big a club you were. In fact, Liverpool never won the FA Cup at all during the period (1977-84) when they won the European Cup four times, and when they became champions of Europe for the first time in 1977, they did so without beating any clubs that had ever been champions of Europe themselves. The four teams they beat in reaching that year's final were Crusaders, Trabzonspor, Sainte-Etienne and FC Zurich.

The other main reason that the European Cup didn't detract from the prestige of the FA Cup was that, as with the European Cup-winners' Cup and UEFA Cup, there were no matches at all played in it between early-November, when the second round ties were completed, and early-March, when the quarter-finals began. The first five rounds of the FA Cup were, therefore, played during the four months of the season when there was no European football to take attention away from them. Of course, the European Cup was undeniably big, but during the course of a season it was also something of a sideshow. The Football League and the FA Cup were the main events.

In 1986, English clubs were banned from Europe, and English football just seemed to shrug its shoulders and carry on. Liverpool's stylish title win of 1988 was not diminished by the fact that they would not be playing in the European Cup the following season, and Arsenal's dramatic last-gasp title snatch a year later was no less dramatic by not being rewarded with a place in Europe either. During the European ban every FA Cup Final was eagerly anticipated, and pretty much turned out to be a classic, and no one who enjoyed them was thinking much about the European ban. Arsenal were the first English club to play in the European Cup after the ban was lifted and the two home matches they played in it in the 1991-92 season – which were also their first matches in the competition for 20 years – drew crowds of 24,124 (against FK Austria) and 35,815 (against Benfica). When they had played Cambridge at home in the sixth round of the FA Cup the previous season nearly 43,000 had been in attendance.

Dwight Yorke

Aston Villa's Dwight Yorke missed two penalties against Derby in a fourth round FA Cup tie in February 1992, but still ended up with a hat-trick. Villa won 4-3.

35 seconds behind closed doors

A Third Division match between Birmingham and Stoke in February 1992 was stopped with 35 seconds left to play when supporters invaded the pitch. The fans eventually left the ground assuming the game had ended early, only for the players to come back out again and play the final 35 seconds without spectators.

The demise of Aldershot

Aldershot folded in March 1992 with eight games of their Fourth Division campaign still remaining. They had begun the season well enough, beating Maidstone 3-0 in their first home game, but this would prove to be their last home win before their liquidation seven months later, and also one of only five occasions over those seven months when they scored more than once in a match. Former top-flight players, Keith

Bertschin and Phil Heath were the star names in their attack for most of the season, but they managed just three League goals between them. Former top-flight keeper Peter Hucker (QPR) also made one appearance for Aldershot this season, as did player-manager Brian Talbot, who was a former England international and two-time FA Cup-winner. Talbot resigned in November, and Bertschin, Heath and top-scorer David Puckett had also all gone by the beginning of March, by which time the only players left were giving their services for free as the club could no longer afford their wages. When they played at Barnet on 3 March, the sympathetic home fans organised a collection for them, although the Barnet team were less sympathetic and beat them 5-0. Like all results against Aldershot this season, it would subsequently be expunged from the records.

Aldershot's final match was a 2-0 defeat at Cardiff on 20 March and none of their players who played for them that day would ever play at professional level again.

In the summer following their demise, Aldershot fans formed Aldershot Town who joined the Third Division of the Isthmian League for the start of the 1992-93 season. They would eventually win promotion to the Football League 16 years later.

Kenny Swain

Kenny Swain is the only outfield player ever to have made 100 or more League appearances for each of five different clubs. He made 114 for Chelsea between 1974 and 1978, 148 for Aston Villa between 1978 and 1982, 112 for Nottingham Forest between 1982 and 1985, 113 for Portsmouth between 1985 and 1988 and 123 for Crewe between 1988 and 1991.

The end of the terraces

As previously mentioned, watching matches from a football terrace was never ideal. Being on a packed terrace behind the goal usually meant having your view of the pitch partially blocked by the backs of other people's heads, not being able to see the back of the net or the goal line of the goal in front you, being pushed further down the terrace if there was a 'surge' and having no easy way out to use the toilet or get refreshments at half-time. And yet, for more than a century after the launch of the Football League, this was the experience of the vast majority of fans who attended games at the highest level in England, and also for many who went to matches in the second tier. In the Third and Fourth Divisions the terraces had far fewer numbers on them and were, therefore, more comfortable, but not by much as they were also smaller and could become just as crowded as a First Division terrace if there was a big game on.

At the beginning of the 1970s, the capacity of Birmingham City's St Andrew's ground was 52,800 but it had only 8,000 seats, whilst Newport's Somerton Park had just 672 seats, but capacity for more than 21,000 on the terraces. Wembley in those days had a capacity of 100,000 but only 32,000 seats.

Most of the terracing at League grounds at this time was also uncovered and so provided no shelter from the rain. In fact, Tottenham's White Hart Lane was the only one of the 92 Football League grounds at the start of the '70s that provided cover for spectators in every section. Well over half of Crystal Palace's Selhurst Park was uncovered and almost two-thirds of Portsmouth's Fratton Park was. If Newcastle's St. James' Park was packed to capacity on a rainy afternoon then there would be nearly 40,000 fans watching the match whilst getting wet.

Despite this, however, there is no evidence that bad weather kept the fans away. To stand on the terraces you had to be either naturally hardy and committed or prepared to adopt a hardy and committed mindset on matchdays (as so many did). This led to a special kind of unity on a football terrace, that in turn created a special kind of atmosphere. In his 1968 book, *The Football Man*, Arthur Hopcraft wrote of the football terrace, "In this incomparable entanglement of bodies and emotions lies the heart of the fan's commitment to football. The senses of triumph and dejection experienced here are never quite matched in any seated section of a football ground".

At this time, and for the next 20-odd years, the idea of all-seater stadiums would not have appealed to most fans. The exciting chaos of the packed terrace or the freedom to move around on the half-empty one were essential to the matchday experience for most.

Watching games confined to an allocated seat simply wouldn't have been the same. When, in 1981, Coventry's Highfield Road became the first football ground in England to be converted into an all-seater stadium, objections from supporters forced the club to remove the seating behind one of the goals two years later and replace it with a new terrace.

Following the Hillsborough disaster, the Taylor Report recommended that all football grounds in the top two tiers should become all-seaters by the start of the 1994-95 season, and that all grounds at the lower levels become all-seaters by the start of 1999-2000. The Government acted on the first recommendation but not on the second, and during the first half of the 1990s the terraces in the First and Second Divisions gradually began disappearing. This left those grounds all looking a bit of a mess during this period, with areas of closed-off terracing, or temporary seating or building sites occupying various parts of grounds where supporters had once stood. An odd aspect of this period was that the Taylor Report's recommendations were not big news, nor were the Government's decision to act upon them, and with no internet to spread information in those days, most fans who stood on the terraces in the early-1990s didn't know their days of being able to do so were coming to an end.

Once the conversions to all-seater stadiums were complete, then football ground culture gradually began to change. In the 1970s, '80s and early-90s, the football terraces – especially those of clubs in the top two tiers – were occupied almost exclusively by teenage boys and young men, which was a big factor in their rowdiness and in the violence that sometimes broke-out on them. They simply weren't suitable places for young children, or old people or women. All-seater stadiums, by contrast, were relatively welcoming places for everyone as they brought an orderliness to football grounds that hadn't been there before. The fact that this coincided with the early years of the Premier League was pure coincidence, but it would turn out to be one of the major differences between English football in the Premier League-era and English football in previous periods.

Ian Wright (again)

Ian Wright finished as the top-flight's top scorer at the end of the 1991-92 season with 29 goals for Crystal Palace and Arsenal, but he didn't make the England squad for that summer's European Championships.

The troubled birth of the Premier League

The idea that the FA were planning to create what would become known as the Premier League first became news in April 1991, although then it was being referred to as a 'Super League' and wasn't widely welcomed. Because it involved the top clubs breaking away from the Football League, the Football League were naturally against it, but so too were the PFA, The Football Supporters' Association and, according to a Gallup poll, 68 per cent of fans.

Nevertheless, On 14 June 1991, 16 of the 22 clubs then in the First Division voted in favour of it, with three voting against and the other three abstaining. By 16 August, however, the six rebel clubs had come onboard, and all 22 clubs handed in their resignations to the Football League that day. Initially, the Football League refused to accept the resignations on the grounds that three years notice was required before a club could resign, while there was also talk of the Third and Fourth Division clubs boycotting the FA Cup unless plans for the 'Super League' were withdrawn. All this obstruction then prompted the FA to threaten to stop the 1991-92 League season going ahead altogether. They, of course, never did and the dispute was eventually resolved on 23 September 1991, when the Football League accepted the resignations of the 22 First Division clubs. Then on 12 January 1992, it was announced that the 'Super League' would be called the 'FA Premier League'.

The Premier League was finally launched at the start of the 1992-93 season, although there seemed very little 'super' or 'premier' about it. The only difference anyone could see between it and the old First Division was that the referees didn't wear black.

The 7.45 kick-off

The 1991-92 season was the first in which the majority of midweek matches in England kicked-off at 7.45 pm. Until then, 7.30 had been the standard kick-off time for evening games.

When Sky Sports changed the way we watch football

When Sky Sports took over live coverage of top-flight football from ITV in 1992, it introduced two lasting innovations to it. One was putting a clock and scoreboard in the corner of the screen and the other was amplifying the crowd noise. The latter would make matches in the new Premier League sound like they had more atmosphere than those in the old First Division had had, but it was purely artificial.

Epilogue

And so we end in 1992. But was this really the year that changed English football? Or was it 1996? This being the year that Ruud Gullit and Arsene Wenger became the first two men who were neither British nor Irish to be appointed managers of Premier League clubs. Gullit was made player-manager of Chelsea in the May of that year, with Wenger being given the Arsenal job four months later, and, significantly, both were the first managers of English clubs to see the key to success as buying players mainly from abroad. Gullit, in particular, was little short of a trailblazer in this respect. In only 21 months in charge at Chelsea, he signed eleven players from continental clubs and only two from English ones. In the 1995-96 season, only 14 per cent of players who appeared in the Premier League had come from foreign clubs.

If 1996 wasn't the year that changed football in England, then maybe it was 1998, the year Wenger's Arsenal became the first team loaded with foreign stars to win the title. Or maybe 2003, the year the Russian Oligarch Roman Abramovich bought Chelsea and became the first rich foreign owner to begin bankrolling the success of a Premier League club. Or maybe 2004, the year that Jose Mourinho and Rafa Benitez arrived in England to take charge at Chelsea and Liverpool respectively. Mourinho had previously won the Champions League with Porto, while Benitez had twice won the Spanish title as well as the UEFA Cup with Valencia. The pair's arrival in England, therefore, marked the first time highly successful managers from mainland Europe had taken charge at English clubs.

All of these events were major steps in the globalisation of English football's top-flight, a globalisation which certainly didn't start in 1992, and had still barely got going in 2001 when no Premier League clubs had foreign owners, only three had foreign managers and Alex Ferguson's Manchester United won the title with only four players imported from abroad figuring regularly in their campaign.

Today, of course, the globalisation of the Premier League is very much complete, with England's top-flight now being like a global competition based in England. Foreign club owners are now the norm at the highest level of English football, as are foreign managers and team line-ups that contain few British players. Most of the matches are also screened live across the globe, and the number of fans the biggest English clubs have in foreign countries dwarf the number who come from the cities those clubs represent. Domestic trophies, meanwhile, are now valued less than a place in Europe, a change in priorities that has partly turned England's highest level of football into a qualification competition for the Champions League.

Whether or not all this has made English football any better is a moot point. Certainly, the influx of foreign talent has raised the standard of the football itself considerably. Long gone are the days when we would watch the World Cup and marvel at the skills and cultured football that we never saw in our own country. But also long gone is much of the raw, rugged drive and directness that once set English football apart. In its place we have a tactically sophisticated game littered with cheating. In the old blood-and-thunder days, the best players would try hard not to get brought down. They would stay strong, stay on their feet, ride the tackles and keep going. By contrast, today's players rarely want to 'keep going'. They would rather have the free-kick or the penalty, and if no foul is forthcoming then a well executed dive will usually do the trick in making it look as if there was one. Getting an opponent sent-off has also become an accepted way of winning a match, resulting in the common sight of a not especially bad foul being followed by an absurdly theatrical feigning of injury by the victim.

This is just one of the things that's gone wrong with English football since the birth of the Premier League. Others include the rip-off admission prices; TV companies dictating the scheduling of matches to the great inconvenience of travelling fans; the big clubs stockpiling talented players that they don't need; the inability of smaller clubs to hang on to their best players for any more than two or three seasons; and the way only an elite few clubs have any realistic chance of mounting a title challenge. Between 1960 and 1985, ten of the 26 League champions were clubs that had finished outside of the top six the previous season, and when Aston Villa won the League in 1981 they were the 13th different club in 22 years to do so. Those same 22 years also saw seven clubs relegated less than a decade after becoming champions, as Villa themselves would be in 1987. In 1977, Liverpool had become the first club to retain the title since Wolves in 1959. Such unpredictability is completely unknown in the Premier League era. Since its globalisation, the top-flight of English football offers potential glory only to those clubs that are biggest global brands, and, at the time of writing, Leicester in 2016 remain the Premier League's only surprising champions (there was nothing surprising in Blackburn's bankrolled title of '95).

As the pages of this book illustrate, football has been an ever-changing sport throughout its history, but it's only been during the Premier League era that it's changed in ways that have made it more predictable. Before the Premier League, shrewd managers often built successful teams on small budgets. Today, a club's success level is inextricably linked to its spending level.

Admittedly, football in England is still entertaining. Its huge popularity is proof of that. But it was hugely popular long before we had a Premier League, and back then its popularity was a phenomenon that existed without the hype or the saturation TV coverage or the internet spreading the interest and stoking the passions. Football before the Premier League mattered, and it was frequently astonishing and should certainly not be looked upon as if it doesn't count.

Sources

Michael Archer: *History of the World Cup (Hamlyn, 1978)*

Pete Attaway: *Nottingham Forest: A Complete Record 1865-1991 (Breedon Books, 1991)*

Steve Bailey, Brian Ellis & Alan Shury: *The Definitive Luton Town F.C. (Tony Brown, 1997)*

Simon Basson: *The Definitive Chesterfield F.C. (Tony Brown, 1996)*

David Batters: *York City: A Complete Record 1922-1990*

Tony Brown: *The Football League: Match By Match. Various editions (Soccer Books)*

Tony Brown: *The Ultimate F.A. Trophy and F.A. Vase Statistics Book (the Association of Football Statisticians, 1993)*

Roy Calley: *Blackpool: A Complete Record 1887-1992 (Breedon Books, 1992)*

Rob Cavallini: *The Wanderers: F.C. (Dog N Duck, 2005)*

Rob Cavallini: *Play Up Corinth: A History of the Corinthian Football Club (Stadia, 2007)*

J.A.H. Catton: *The Story of Association Football (Soccer Books, 2006 reprint)*

Gary Chalk & Duncan Holley: *Saints: A Complete Record of Southampton Football Club 1885-1987 (Breedon Books, 1987)*

Scott Cheshire & Roy Hockings: *Chelsea: The Full Statistical Story 1905-1988 (Ron Hockings, 1988)*

Denis Clarebrough & Andrew Kirkham: *A Complete History of Sheffield United 1889-1999 (Sheffield United Football Club, 1999)*

Paul Clayton: *The Essential History of Charlton Athletic (Headline 2001)*

Marvin Close: *1923: Life in Football One Hundred Years Ago (Pitch, 2022)*

Marvin Close: 1953: Life in Football Seventy Years Ago (Pitch, 2023)

Bill Cook: The Official History of Worcester City FC (Worcester City Football Club)

Mark Cooper: The Definitive Portsmouth F.C. (Tony Brown, 1996)

Rob Dean with David Brassington, Jim Brown & Ron Chalk: Coventry City: A Complete Record 1883–1991

Keith Dewhurst: Underdogs: The Unlikely Story of Football's First FA Cup Heroes (Yellow Jersey, 2012)

David Downs & Leigh Edwards: The Definitive Reading F.C. (Tony Brown, 1998)

Eric Dunning, Patrick Murphy & John Williams: The Roots of Football Hooliganism: An historical and Sociological Study (Routledge, 1988)

Gareth Dykes: Oldham Athletic: A Complete Record 1899–1988 (Breedon Books, 1988)

Gareth Dykes: New Brighton: A Complete Record of the Rakers in the Football League (Breedon Books, 1990)

Leigh Edwards: The Definitive Torquay United F.C. (Tony Brown, 1997)

Keith Farnsworth: Sheffield Wednesday: A Complete Record 1867–1987 (Breedon Books, 1987)

Terry Frost: Huddersfield Town: A Complete Record 1910–1990 (Breedon Books, 1990)

Terry Frost: Bradford City: A Complete Record 1903–1988 (Breedon Books, 1988)

Maurice Galsworthy, Garth Dykes & Alex Wilson: Exeter City: A Complete Record 1904–1990 (Breedon Books, 1990)

Paul Gambaccini, Tim Rice & Jonathan Rice: The Guiness Book of British Hit Albums (GRR, seventh edition, 1996)

Paul Gambaccini, Tim Rice & Jonathan Rice: The Guiness Top 40 Charts (Guiness, second edition, 1996)

Harry Glasper: Middlesbrough: A Complete Record 1876–1989 (Breedon Books, 1989)

Roy Goble: *Manchester City: A Complete Record 1887–1987* (Breedon Books, 1987)

Bob Goodwin: *Spurs: A Complete Record 1882–1988* (Breedon Books, 1988)

David Goodyear & Tony Matthews: *Aston Villa: A Complete Record 1874–1988* (Breedon Books, 1988)

Frank Grande: *Northampton Town: The Official Centenary History 1897–1997* (Yore, 1997)

Bill Hern & David Gleave: *Football's Black Pioneers* (Conker, 2020)

Peter Hitchens: *The Phoney War* (I.B. Tauris, 2018)

Andy & Roger Howland: *Oxford United: A Complete Record 1893–1989* (Breedon Books, 1989)

Barry J. Hugman: *The PFA Premier and Football League Players' Records 1946–1998* (Queen Anne Press, 1998)

Simon Inglis: *The Football Grounds of Great Britain* (second edition, Willow Books, 1987)

Mike Jackman: *Blackburn Rovers: A Complete Record 1875–1990* (Breedon Books, 1990)

Mike Jackman: *Accrington Stanley: A Complete Record 1894–1962* (Breedon Books, 1991)

Paul Jannou, Bill Swan & Steve Corke: *Newcastle United: A Complete Record 1882–1990* (Breedon Books, 1990)

Martin Jarred & Malcolm Macdonald: *Leeds United: A Complete Record 1919–1990* (Breedon Books, 1990)

Mike Jay: *Bristol Rovers: A Complete Record 1883–1987* (Breedon Books, 1987)

Mike Jones with Kevin Davies: *Breathe on 'em Salop! Shrewsbury Town Football Club: The Official History* (Yore, 1995

Colin Jose: *NASL: A Complete Record of the North American Soccer League* (Breedon Books, 1989)

Michael Joyce: *Football League Players' Records 1888 to 1939* (SoccerData 2002)

Neil Kauffman & Alan Ravenhill: *Leyton Orient: A Complete Record 1881–1990* (Breedon Books, 1990)

Brian Knight: *Plymouth Argyle: A Complete Record 1903–1989* (Breedon Books, 1988)

David Kynaston: *Modernity Britain 1957 – 62* (Bloomsbury, 2015)

Clive Leatherdale: *Wimbledon: From Southern League to Premiership: A Complete Record* (Desert Island, 1995)

Chris Lee: *Origin Stories: The Pioneers Who Took Football to the World* (Pitch, 2021)

Edward Lee & Ray Simpson: *Burnley: A Complete Record 1882–1991* (Breedon Books, 1991)

Richard Lindsay: *Millwall: A Complete Record 1885–1991* (Breedon Books, 1991)

Gordon Macey: *Queen's Park Rangers: A Complete Record* (Breedon Books, 1993)

Simon Marland: *Bolton Wanderers: A Complete Record 1877–1989* (Breedon Books, 1989)

Gabriel Mantz & Romeo Ionescu: *European National Teams Vol. III* (Printeuro, 2004)

Gabriel Mantz & Romeo Ionescu: *European National Teams Vol. IV* (Printeuro, 2004)

Peter Mason with David Goody: *Southend United: The Official History of the Blues* (Yore, 1994)

Rob Mason with Mike Gibson & Barry Jackson: *Sunderland: The Complete Record* (Breedon Books, 2005)

Tony Matthews: *West Bromwich Albion: A Complete Record* (Breedon Books, 1993)

Tony Matthews: *Birmingham City: A Complete Record* (Breedon Books, 1995)

Tony Matthews with Les Smith: *Wolves: The Complete Record* (Breedon Books, 1994)

Mark Metcalf: *The Origins of the Football League: The First Season* (Amberley, 2013)

Mark Metcalf: *Fred Spiksley: The First Working-Class Football Hero* (Pen & Sword, 2021 reprint)

Ian Morrison & Alan Shury: *Manchester United: A Complete Record 1878–1990* (Breedon Books, 1990)

Gerald Mortimer: *Derby County: A Complete Record 1884–1988* (Breedon Books, 1988)

Ian & Donald Nannestad: *Lincoln City F.C.: The Official History* (Yore)

John Northcutt & Roy Shoesmith: *West Ham United: A Complete Record 1900–1987* (Breedon Books, 1987)

Michael Norton: *The Definitive Scunthorpe United F.C.* (Tony Brown, 1996)

Fred Ollier: *Arsenal: A Complete Record 1886–1988* (Breedon Books, 1988)

Mike Peterson: *The Definitive Hull City F.C.* (Tony Brown, 1999)

Tim Quelch: *An End of Innocence: The Watershed Season of 1959/60* (Pitch, 2021)

Ron Parrott: *Hereford United: The League Era: A Complete Record* (Desert Island, 1988)

Brian Pead: *Liverpool: A Complete Record 1882–1990* (Breedon Books, 1990)

Mike Purkiss with the Rev Nigel Sands: *Crystal Palace: A Complete Record 1905–1989* (Breedon Books, 1989)

Ian Rigby & Mike Payne: *Proud Preston* (Carnegie, 1999)

Jack Rollin: *Rothmans Book Of Football Records* (Headline, 1998)

Ian Ross & Gordon Smailes: *Everton: A Complete Record 1878–1988* (Breedon Books, 1988)

Richard Samuel: *The Complete F.A. Amateur Cup Results Book* (Soccer Books, 2003)

Dominic Sandbrook: *State of Emergency: The Way We Were: Britain 1970–1974* (Allen Lane, 2010)

Dominic Sandbrook: *White Heat: A History of Britain in the Swinging Sixties* (Little, Brown, 2006)

Stan Searl: *Mansfield Town: A Complete Record 1910–1990* (Soccer Books, 1990)

Gordon Small: *The Definitive Hartlepool United F.C.:* (Gordon Brown, 1998)

John Spurling: *Get It On – How the 70s Rocked Football* (Biteback, 2022)

Kevin Palmer: *Cambridge United: The League Era – A Complete Record* (Desert Island, 2000)

Steven Phillips: *The Definitive Rochdale A.F.C.* (Tony Brown, 1995)

David Tossell: *Big Mal: The High Life and Hard Times of Malcolm Allison, Football Legend* (Mainstream, 2008)

David Tossell: *All Crazee Now: English Football and Footballers in the 1970s* (Pitch, 2021)

Les Triggs with David Hepton & Sid Woodhead: *Grimsby Town: A Complete Record 1878–1989* (Breedon Books, 1989)

Dennis Turner & Alex White: *Fulham: A Complete Record 1879–1987* (Breedon Books 1987)

Frank Tweddle: *The Definitive Darlington F.C.* (Tony Brown, 2000)

Dave Twydell: *Rejected F.C. Volume 1* (Yore, 1992)

Dave Twydell: *Rejected F.C. Volume 2* (Yore, 1995)

Keith Warsop & Tony Brown: *The Definitive Notts County F.C.* (Tony Brown, 2007)

Jonathan Wilson: *Inverting the Pyramid: The History of Football Tactics* (Orion, 2008)

David M. Woods: *The Bristol Babe: The First 100 Years of Bristol City FC* (Yore, 1994)

The 1st Eleven: When Saturday Comes issues 1–11: The Half Decent Retrospective (Queen Anne Press, 1992)

Letts Association Football Diary 1985

Non-League Football Club Directory 2017-18 (MW, 2018)

Non-League Football Tables 1889–2004 (Soccer Books, 2004)

The Penguin Book of Rock & Roll Writing (Viking, 1992)

Rothmans Football Yearbook. Various editions (Queen Anne Press/Headline)

Guiness British Hit Singles (Guiness World Records, 13th edition, 2000)

Websites Consulted

bbc.co.uk
bpafc.com
britishnewspaperarchive.co.uk
cambridgerules1848.com
dailymail.co.uk
englishfootballleaguetables.com
footballstadiums.co.uk
fourfourtwo.com
genome.ch.bbcuk
independent.co.uk
lancashiretelegraph.co.uk
lostmediawiki.com
lfchistory.net
manchestereveningnews.com
mirror.co.uk
nme.com
oed.com
rokerreportsbnation.com
royalwebhosting.net
rsssf.org
sheffieldlibraries.blogspot.com
soccerbilia.com
sportsjournalists.co.uk
st.albanscityfc.com
tharsenalhistory.com
thefsa.org
theguardian.com
tvrdb.com

Magazines consulted

Charles Buchan's Football Monthly
Goal
Shoot!
Soccer Star
When Saturday Comes
Various matchday programmes

Sources of quotations where the source isn't mentioned in the text

Frank Arok quote: Liverpool Daily Post, June 13th 1983
Jeff Astle quote: Daily Mirror, May 29th 1971
Steve Bloomer quote: sportsjournalists.co.uk
John Bond quote: Rothmans Football Yearbook 1976-77
Bobby Campbell quote: From David Tossell's All Crazee Now
JAH Catton: All quotes from Catton's The Story of Association Football
Bobby Charlton quote: Rothmans Football Yearbook 1976-77
Brian Clough on Frank Clark: from David Tossell's All Crazee Now
Brian Clough on Asa Hartford: Rothmans Football Yearbook 1980-81
Jack Dunnett quote: Daily Mirror, November 8th 1965
Bob Ferrier quote: Daily Mirror, May 31st 1954
Hughie Gallacher: Attributed quotes taken from the inquest into his death.
Ron Greenwood on England hooligans: theguardian.com
Ron Greenwood on state of English football: Rothmans Football Yearbook 1978-79
Ron Greenwood on Brazil: englandfootballonline.com

Derek Hales quote: *Rothmans Football Yearbook 1977-78*

Alan Hardaker on retain-and-transfer: *Coventry Evening Telegraph*, October 3rd 1963

Alan Hardaker on shirt advertising: *Rothmans Football Yearbook 1976-77*

Alan Hardaker on the North American Soccer League: *Rothmans Football Yearbook 1978-79*

Malcolm Macdonald quote: *Daily Mirror*, January 19th 1977

Gordon McQueen Quote: *Rothmans Football Yearbook 1978-79*

Terry Neil quote: *Rothmans Football Yearbook 1976-77*

Ron Noades quote: *When Saturday Comes No.7*

Otto Olssen quote: *Daily News*, November 11th 1934

Alf Ramsay quote: *Daily Mirror*, June 6th 1968

Don Revie quote: *Torbay Express & South Devon Echo*, February 3rd 1966

Bobby Robson on Ipswich reaching 1978 FA Cup Final: *Rothmans Football Yearbook 1978-79*

Bobby Robson on Australia's tactics: *Daily Mirror*, June 13th 1983

Fred Siksley quote: From Mark Metcalf's *The Remarkable Story of Fred Spiksley*

Gordon Taylor quote: *Rothmans Football Yearbook 1979-80*

Margaret Thatcher quote: theguardian.com

John Thornley quote: *Birmingham Daily Post*, November 18th 1968

Alan Wade quote: *Rothmans Football Yearbook 1974-75*

Walter Winterbottom quote: *Belfast News Letter*, November 17th 1963

www.ingramcontent.com/pod-product-compliance
Lightning Source LLC
Chambersburg PA
CBHW020728160426
43192CB00006B/154